JINI™
IN A NUTSHELL

A Desktop Quick Reference

THE JAVA™ SERIES

Exploring Java™
Java™ Threads
Java™ Network Programming
Java™ Virtual Machine
Java™ AWT Reference
Java™ Language Reference
Java™ Fundamental Classes Reference
Database Programming with JDBC™ and Java™
Java™ Distributed Computing
Developing Java Beans™
Java™ Security
Java™ Cryptography
Java™ Swing
Java™ Servlet Programming
Java™ I/O
Java™ 2D Graphics
Enterprise JavaBeans™

Also from O'Reilly

Java™ in a Nutshell
Java™ in a Nutshell, Deluxe Edition
Java™ Examples in a Nutshell
Java™ Enterprise in a Nutshell
Java™ Foundation Classes in a Nutshell
Java™ Power Reference: A Complete Searchable Resource on CD-ROM
Jini™ in a Nutshell

JINI™
IN A NUTSHELL

A Desktop Quick Reference

Scott Oaks & Henry Wong

O'REILLY®

Beijing • Cambridge • Farnham • Köln • Paris • Sebastopol • Taipei • Tokyo

Jini™ in a Nutshell

by Scott Oaks and Henry Wong

Copyright © 2000 O'Reilly & Associates, Inc. All rights reserved.
Printed in the United States of America.

Published by O'Reilly & Associates, Inc., 101 Morris Street, Sebastopol, CA 95472.

Editor: Mike Loukides

Production Editor: Colleen Gorman

Cover Designer: Edie Freedman

Printing History:

March 2000: First Edition.

ISBN: 1-56592-759-1

[M]

Table of Contents

Preface

This handbook is a desktop quick reference for experienced Java programmers who want to develop services and clients that use Jini. We assume that readers of this book have a good knowledge of how to write programs in Java and some understanding of the complexities of distributed programming.

This book is based on the Jini 1.0 and 1.1 alpha specifications and its implementation by Sun Microsystems. Jini requires the Java 2 platform. It's likely that versions of Jini that postdate Version 1.0 will contain changes that are not discussed in this version of the book.

About the Example Programs

The example programs presented in this book are available online. See *http://www.oreilly.com/catalog/jininut* for how to download them.

Throughout this book, we essentially develop one server and one client; this server and client go through successive revisions as we work through the book. As we make these revisions, we don't rename the classes involved (so that we don't end up with a class called `ServerWithLeasesAndEventsAndActivationAndLogging`).

For each new revision, we present a list of all the classes that are required to run the server and client. In the list, we give the example where the class was last used and also the example where the listing of the class last appeared in the book. If we modify the class in the example, we usually show the modifications in **bold text** (unless they are extensive).

The downloadable examples are organized into a set of example directories that follow this model. Each directory contains the complete code necessary to run the example, even when some of the classes have not changed from a previous example. In general, each example will have two directories: one for the client and one for the server. You'll want to get used to running the client and server from different directories (and ideally from different machines). This will allow you to understand which code is common, which code is application-specific, and which code must be dynamically loaded by the client and server.

The example performs a rather trivial operation, which is certainly not one that you would implement in a Jini environment. We know that this will disappoint some readers, who would prefer to see real-world examples. We feel that misses the point. There is clearly a big difference in the code you write to implement a service that converts integers to strings (as our primary example does) and the code you write to implement a Jini print service that a Jini client can use to print to any Jini printer without any user configuration. But none of the different code is related to Jini; both services require that you use the same set of Jini APIs. Our hope is that you'll gain an understanding of Jini's infrastructure from this book in order to implement your own real-world Jini services.

Organization of This Book

This book is divided into two sections. The first thirteen chapters serve as a Jini tutorial and are designed to teach you how to write Jini clients and services from scratch. These chapters are arranged as follows:

Chapter 1, Introduction to Jini
This chapter introduces the basic concepts of Jini.

Chapter 2, Getting Started with Jini
This chapter discusses how to download Jini, how to set up your environment to work with Jini, and how to start the core Jini services.

Chapter 3, Remote Method Invocation
This chapter discusses how to write an RMI server. We use RMI as the basis of the Jini service we develop in this book, and RMI is a popular choice for implementing Jini services.

Chapter 4, Basic Jini Programming
This chapter discusses how to write a basic Jini service and client. We examine discovery and lookup of Jini services and how to interact with the Jini lookup service.

Chapter 5, Leasing
This chapter discusses Jini's leasing APIs. It shows how to write a service that hands out leases and how clients interact with such a service.

Chapter 6, Remote Events
This chapter discusses Jini's remote event mechanism. It shows how to write a service that delivers events to clients and how clients process those events.

Chapter 7, Service Administration
This chapter discusses the administration interfaces of Jini. It shows how clients can use them to administer a Jini service and how a service must implement those interfaces.

Chapter 8, Miscellaneous Classes
This chapter discusses some miscellaneous APIs that come with Sun's implementation of Jini. Even though these APIs are not part of the Jini specification, they provide some useful features that we incorporate into our basic service.

Chapter 9, Transactions

This chapter discusses the Jini transaction API, which is used to interact with the Jini transaction manager. This is primarily a client-side API, though we discuss the possible ramifications of implementing transactions within a service.

Chapter 10, The JavaSpaces Service

This chapter discusses the JavaSpaces service, one of the core services defined by the Jini specification.

Chapter 11, Helper Services

This chapter discusses the three services that are defined in the 1.1 specification: an event mailbox service, a lease renewal service, and a lookup discovery service.

Chapter 12, Security in Jini

This chapter discusses how Java's underlying security model affects Jini clients and services.

Chapter 13, Service Reference

This chapter provides detailed information on starting the services that come with Sun's implementation of Jini.

The second section, Chapters 14 through 17, is a quick-reference of all classes related to Jini: the classes of the Jini API, Java RMI classes, and miscellaneous classes. This section is arranged by package name. Chapter 18 provides an index to the classes, methods, and fields of Jini API.

Conventions Used in This Book

We use the following formatting conventions in this book:

Italic

Used for emphasis and to signify the first use of a term. Italic is also used for commands in the text, email addresses, web sites, FTP sites, options, file and directory names, and newsgroups.

Bold

If we modify the class in the example, we usually show the modifications in **bold text** (unless they are extensive). Occasionally used to refer to particular keys on a computer keyboard or to portions of a user interface, such as the **Back** button or the **Options** menu.

Letter Gothic

Used in all Java code and generally for anything that you would type literally when programming, including keywords, data types, constants, method names, variables, class names, interface names, and commands when they are part of an example.

Letter Gothic Oblique

Used for the names of function arguments and as a placeholder to indicate an item that should be replaced with an actual value in your program.

Franklin Gothic Book Condensed

Used for the Java class synopses in the quick-reference section. This very narrow font allows us to fit a lot of information on the page without a lot of distracting line breaks. This font is also used for code entities in the descriptions in the quick-reference section.

Franklin Gothic Demi Condensed

Used for highlighting class, method, field, property, and constructor names in the quick-reference section, which makes it easier to scan the class synopses.

Franklin Gothic Book Compressed Italic

Used for method parameter names and comments in the quick-reference section.

By convention, we generally show Unix-style filenames and program command lines. For Windows users, we show the first few examples for both platforms and explain how to convert between them. When we show command lines, they are prefaced by a prompt which is the name of the machine on which the command is running. The prompt is in `fixed-width` font, the command that you type is in **bold type**, and any output from the command is shown in `fixed-width` font. We'd show the command to find out the version of Java used on the machine named piccolo like this:

```
piccolo% java -version
java version "1.2.2"
```

Command lines shown in this book are generally long and will not fit on a single line. However, you must type them in on a single line. Because the command is in bold and the prompt is not, you can tell what a single command is, even when it spans multiple lines.

We'd Like to Hear from You

We invite you to help us improve this book. Please let us know about any errors you find, as well as your suggestions for future editions, by writing to:

O'Reilly & Associates, Inc.
101 Morris Street
Sebastopol, CA 95472
(800) 998-9938 (in the United States or Canada)
(707) 829-0515 (international or local)
(707) 829-0104 (fax)

You can send us messages electronically. To be put on the mailing list or request a catalog, send email to:

info@oreilly.com

To ask technical questions or comment on the book, send email to:

bookquestions@oreilly.com

We have a web site for the book, where we list examples, errata, and any plans for future editions. You can access this page at:

http://www.oreilly.com/catalog/jininut/

For more information about this book and others, see the O'Reilly web site:

http://www.oreilly.com

You can also contact the authors directly at *scott.oaks@sun.com* and *henry.wong@sun.com*.

Acknowledgments

We are enormously grateful to the many people that helped us with this book. Mike Loukides provided us with his usual excellent guidance when necessary and left us alone when we needed it (and tolerated our slight delays with tact).

We were especially fortunate to have an extremely talented set of technical reviewers for this book: David Flanagan, Ron Goldman, Marc Loy, John McClain, and Bill Venners. David set the standard for books of this sort with the incomparable *Java in a Nutshell*; Ron is very active with the Jini Community, including serving as Associated Editor for *www.jini.org*; Marc is the successful owner of Loy Enterprises, Inc. (*www.loyinc.com*); Bill runs the very useful Java and Jini resource *www.artima.com*; and John is an engineer with the Jini group at Sun Microsystems. Despite their busy schedules, these reviewers all provided us with thoughtful recommendations; John even managed to find time to review this book despite his busy schedule and the arrival of the book and a new baby at the same time. This book was greatly improved by the careful comments of all our reviewers, who we cannot thank enough.

We are very lucky to have been supported in the production of this book by an outstanding production staff at O'Reilly. These people are listed in the colophon; without their hard work and talent, this book would be greatly diminished.

Mostly, we must thank our respective families. To James, who has the amazing patience to keep putting up with Scott's long writing-caused absences, and to Nini, whose only requirement to allow Henry to work on this book was to have a wombat on the cover: thank you for everything!

PART I

Introducing Jini

Part I is an introduction to Jini. These chapters provide enough information for you to get started using Jini right away.

CHAPTER 1

Introduction to Jini

When Sun Microsystems released their first Java-enabled browser, the animated image of Duke, Sun's Java mascot, kindled the imagination of countless developers around the world. It wasn't that an animated image on a web page was in itself a really interesting development; there were other ways to animate images on the Web already, and you could argue that the Web suffers from the overuse of pointless animations like that one.

But a large number of people caught on to the idea that it wasn't a dancing Duke that was important: it was what the dancing Duke represented. The technology behind the dancing Duke—a simple programming environment that could take advantage of the network in novel ways—started the excitement behind Java and put it at the forefront of computer software technology.

Which brings us to Jini. Jini is a simple set of Java classes and services that has the potential to create its own revolution because it allows technology to be exploited in new ways. Some people who see a Jini demonstration might look at a camera being added to a network, and devices accessing the camera, and think that nothing really amazing is happening. There are, after all, many ways for systems and network-enabled cameras to interface with each other outside of Jini, and does the world really need another NetCam?

But the technology that drives Jini and the potential impact of Jini on network-based computing is more compelling than it might seem from the surface of a simple demonstration like this. Jini allows co-operating devices, services, and applications (and there's little distinction between these) to access each other seamlessly, to adapt to a continually changing environment, and to share code and configurations transparently. And Jini has the potential to radically alter our use of computer service networks, since it allows and encourages new types of services and new uses of existing networks.

What Is Jini?

In a nutshell, Jini is a set of specifications that enables services to discover each other on a network and that provides a framework that allows those services to participate in certain types of operations. The set of services on a particular network is referred to as the *Jini community*. The Jini specification refers to the community as a *djinn*, but common usage seems to favor the former term (on the other hand, the term Jini community is overloaded, as we'll discuss later).

If you've heard of Jini, chances are that you heard of it terms of hardware devices. Bring your Jini-enabled laptop into a Jini-enabled conference room, and the laptop will automatically be able to find and use the services of the conference room. Want to send output to the conference room printer? Your Jini-enabled laptop will automatically find the printer, seamlessly download any drivers required by the printer, and send it output. You can pull out your Jini-enabled PDA and do the same. And when you take that PDA and go into another office, the PDA will discard knowledge of the conference room printer and automatically find the printer local to the new office.

But Jini is not about hardware and devices: Jini is about services. A Jini-enabled printer provides a print service to the network; that the particular service is provided by a piece of hardware is irrelevant. There may be a software service on the network that also provides the same print service by accepting print requests, rasterizing them, and emailing the rasterized images to a distant recipient.

There are many Jini services that are only software. The core Jini services that we'll examine in this book are examples of such services, and you could think of many others: a service that stores and forwards events would not be hardware-based, nor would a matrix multiplication service (though it could be, if you had a really great vector processor available). Jini blurs the distinction between hardware and software: in a Jini community, everything is a service. This makes Jini appropriate for a number of applications, from integrating devices onto a network to providing enterprise services within your organization.

So the excitement around Jini stems not just from the fact that it allows hardware and applications to interact: it's also that Jini is designed to allow this service interaction to happen in a dynamic, robust way. There are three basic features of this interaction:

- The Jini environment requires no user intervention when services are brought on- or offline (other than starting the service: e.g., by turning on the Jini-enabled device or starting the Jini software service).

- The Jini community is self-healing: it can adapt when services (and consumers of services) come and go.

- Consumers of Jini services do not need prior knowledge of the service's implementation. Instead, the consumer loads the service implementation dynamically, with no configuration or user-intervention required.

These features make Jini ideal for a dynamic environment, where mobile computing devices come and go, where software-based services come and go, or where administration of services must be as simple as possible.

Jini at Work

In order to understand what Jini is, we'll present a high-level description of how a Jini community works. Then we'll look into the technology that enables the behavior that we'll describe.

Our Jini community starts in its simplest possible state: there is a single instance of the Jini lookup service running on this network. Clearly, some piece of hardware must be running this service, but it doesn't matter to us if that hardware is a PC, an IBM mainframe, or a network-enabled Jini lookup service appliance. The Jini lookup service keeps a list of all the Jini services that are available on the network.

Now say we add a Jini-enabled printer to the network. (There's a lot of meaning behind the word "add" here, but we'll address that a little later.) The printer finds the lookup service and then registers itself with the lookup service. It does this registration completely on its own as part of its startup sequence. And this illustrates the first key feature of Jini: it's designed so that user intervention is not required. At this point, there are two Jini services on the network: the lookup service and a print service.

Now let's add a laptop onto the network and start a Jini-aware word processing application on the laptop. The word processor will go out onto the network and find the lookup service (just like the printer did). Because it's not actually providing a service, it may not register with the lookup service; it may just inspect the other services that are registered. When it discovers that a print service is available, it will take appropriate action: it might, for example, enable the Print item in its File menu.

But remember that Jini communities are dynamic: the printer may not yet have been added to the community when we started the word processor. This is not a problem: the word processor can register with the lookup service to be notified when a printer is added to the network. When this notification comes, the word processor can then enable its Print menu item. Or maybe the word-processor will always have its Print menu item enabled, and when the user selects the Print menu item, only then will the word processor attempt to locate a print service. All this flexibility is built into the Jini environment. Similarly, if the printer becomes disconnected from the network, the word processor will be notified and be able to adapt itself to its new environment (e.g., by disabling the Print menu item).

This illustrates the second basic feature of a Jini community: it is self-healing. As services come and go, they register with and unregister from the lookup service. And the key feature that distinguishes this registration from other lookup services is that unregistration happens automatically. When a service registers with the lookup service, the lookup service issues it a lease which the service must periodically renew. If the power supply on the printer fails and it doesn't have a chance to unregister itself explicitly, then after a period of time, the lease will expire and the lookup service will automatically unregister the printer.* This unregistration happens whenever a registered service fails to renew its lease with the lookup service, so it doesn't matter if the device running the service crashed, or if the

---

* Imagine if Internet search engines were able to do that and no longer pointed to dead links.

network failed, or something else: if the service is not accessible, the service is eventually unregistered.

Self-healing works both ways. If the printer became unregistered because a component on the network failed, then when the network is fixed, the printer will automatically reregister its service with the lookup service. The printer doesn't need to know that the network was fixed, nor does a user need to intervene: the Jini code keeps track of the network's state and reregisters the printer automatically when the problem is fixed.

Now let's attempt to print. The first thing that our application must do is ask the user for certain printing parameters—whether to use landscape or portrait paper orientation, whether to print in color, and so on. The list of parameters is specific to the printer, and the dialog box that is presented to the user should reflect only those parameters that are appropriate to the printer.

This means that the application cannot have prior knowledge of the dialog box— it must be able to show a dialog box that is appropriate for printers that have not yet been developed. So rather than attempting to put this sort of knowledge into the application, why not put it into the printer, since the printer is the only thing that actually knows what the dialog box should look like? Then the application can download the class definition for the dialog box from the printer on demand, instantiate the dialog box, and show it to the user.

Similarly, when the parameters are selected and it is time to print, the application must format its data into the correct printer language. The drivers that must normally be loaded by the user can once again be obtained directly from the printer itself. And this is the third major advantage to Jini: the implementation of all these services is loaded dynamically, at runtime, with no configuration.

Eventually, as services come and go, the Jini community may come to resemble Figure 1-1. There may be multiple instances of the lookup service. We might start some of the Jini services that come with Sun's implementation of Jini, including a Jini transaction manager and a persistence service known as the JavaSpaces service. And so on: services will come and go, consumers of those services will come and go, and everything will be tied together by a common network.

Jini Technology

In this section, we'll discuss the technology behind the functionality of the Jini community that we've just examined. Along the way, we'll discuss the terms that are common to a Jini community. These technologies are described more fully in a series of specifications from Sun, but we'll present an overview of those specifications here. The specifications themselves may be downloaded from Sun's web site at *http://www.sun.com/jini/*.

Clients, Servers, and Services

Jini is a distributed computing framework. Hence participants in the Jini network are called clients and servers. But it is a little more complicated than that.

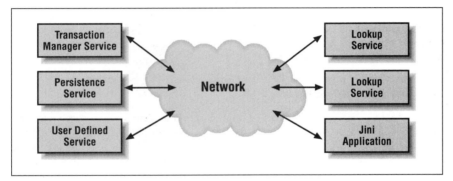

Figure 1–1: A Jini community

First, there's a subtle distinction between a service and a server. A server has an interface, which is the API that it presents to the outside world. This interface is called the *service interface*, or more simply, the service. A server is hence an implementation of a service.

In Jini, the interface is the crucial thing, because the interface is something that both the client and the server know. For example, there is a Jini service called JavaSpaces that defines a persistent store. Sun provides two different servers that implement the JavaSpaces service. A client that wants to use the JavaSpaces service knows about the particular service API, but it doesn't know (or care) about the server's implementation.

The other complicating factor is that many Jini applications are both clients and servers. It is possible to write a Jini application that is only a client—that is, an application that only uses Jini services. But a Jini service may want to use another Jini service; it is a client at that point in time. In fact, all Jini services are Jini clients, because they use at least one other Jini service (the Jini lookup service). So when we speak of a client, the client may in turn itself be a server.

As an illustration, we speak often of a hypothetical Jini print service, which presumably has a service interface that contains, among other things, a print( ) method. This generic service could be represented in a Jini community by any number of servers, including:

- A Jini-enabled printer that runs the print service directly on the printer.

- A software-only service that implements the print( ) method by producing an image on the user's screen.

- A Jini service proxy that runs on an available VM in the community. The proxy can present the print service interface to the community but use a proprietary protocol to talk to the printer: for example, it could send the printer HPGL data via a parallel interface.

Other possible implementations for services such as this one are defined in the *Jini Device Architecture Specification*, which is not a specification per se; it simply discusses some possible implementations of Jini services.

Clients and servers can communicate in a Jini community using any distributed computing protocol, including a home-grown one. The only requirement for communications is that the server must provide a serializable object that implements the service interface. This object will be loaded into the client, and the client will execute methods on that object.

The Jini Lookup Service

The Jini lookup service is the heart of a Jini community. The lookup service is similar in principle to the naming server used in other distributed network paradigms (such as the *COS Naming* server used by CORBA): it holds the registrations of all other services available in the Jini community. An application that wants to use a Jini service finds the desired service by looking for the service's registration within the lookup service. A Jini service must register itself with the Jini lookup service in order for applications to find (and hence be able to use) it.

The Jini lookup service is, as far as the Jini framework is concerned, just another service. So if you write a matrix multiplication server, that server will be a client of the Jini lookup service. At the same time, it is a server of the matrix multiplication service.

The service interface of the lookup service is defined by the *Jini Lookup Service Specification*. Sun's version of Jini comes with an implementation of the lookup service called *reggie*. Jini also comes with core APIs that developers use to interact with the lookup service.

This service interface defines all operations that are possible on the lookup service. In particular, it defines the way in which clients in a Jini community locate services: they do so by requesting services that implement a particular interface. Hence in our example above, in order for the word processor to use the printer, it must know the service interface that defines the print service. It then asks the lookup service for all services that implement the particular service interface. The lookup service returns service objects for all registered services that implement the given interface. At this point, the client has a distributed object that represents the service; the client may invoke methods on that object in order to interact directly with the server.

In our figure above, we showed that there may be multiple instances of the lookup service running in the community. This provides a certain level of redundancy: if one fails, everyone in the community can simply (and automatically) use the other one. A network failure could occur such that the lookup services are unable to communicate with each other, in which case the lookup services will automatically reconfigure themselves so that they contain only the services with which they can still communicate.

Jini lookup services are organized into *groups*. There is a default group (usually called the *public* group), and you can create groups with any name that you want. When you start a lookup service, you specify which group it should hold registrations for. When you search for lookup services, you also specify which group(s) you are interested in. This allows you to segregate services: you could create a lookup service with the group name of "ConferenceRoom01" that registers only the services available within that room. We'll always use the default group.

Lookup Discovery

The Jini lookup service is itself a Jini service; clients use it just as they use any other Jini service. However, there's an obvious bootstrapping problem here. A client that wants to use a print service finds the appropriate server by looking in the Jini lookup service. But how does the client find the Jini lookup service itself?

The answer is one of the fundamental pieces of Jini: a process called *discovery*, which is defined in the *Jini Discovery and Join* specification. This specification defines at the network level the protocol by which clients can find the lookup service; Jini comes with a set of APIs that implement that protocol. A second specification, the *Jini Discovery Utilities Specification*, defines a set of utility classes that are used to work with the protocol.

There are two ways in which a client can discover the Jini lookup service:

Multicast discovery
> In multicast discovery, the client sends out a multicast request of a specified format. All Jini lookup services that see the request will respond to it, and the client is said to have discovered the lookup service(s).

Unicast discovery
> This is somewhat misnamed, since in unicast discovery the client attempts to connect to a lookup server that is known to exist at a particular location (host and port number). In a sense, the client can be said to have discovered whether the lookup service still exists at the expected location.

The discovery protocol of the Jini specification uses a combination of both unicast and multicast discovery in order to find lookup services. For most Jini programming, however, that protocol is hidden by the Jini APIs.

Clients will discover all lookup services that are within the *multicast radius* of the network. The multicast discovery packet will be broadcast on the local network. Routers that join two networks may or may not route the multicast packet between the two networks—it depends on the rules of the router. Many routers will not pass any multicast packets between networks; for those networks, the multicast radius is equal to the local network. Otherwise, the router will forward the multicast packet based on its time to live (TTL) value, which is decremented each time the packet passes through a router. When the TTL value reaches zero, the packet is no longer forwarded onto new networks.

When a Jini service starts, it discovers all the lookup servers on the network by using multicast discovery. It must then register with each discovered lookup server by using Jini's *join* protocol. Remember that there may be more than one instance of the lookup service running on the network; a well-behaved Jini service is required to join each of those services. In addition, the service must continually listen for new lookup services that are started on the network and join each of those services as well. Jini's APIs hide this operation as well.

A pure client that wants only to use services of the Jini community does not participate in the join protocol, since it has nothing to register into the lookup service.

Leasing

One of Jini's prime benefits is that it allows the environment to be robust in the face of service failures. So a service that has joined the Jini community must also actively manage its relationship with the Jini lookup service. When a service registers with the lookup service, it receives a lease from the lookup service. The service must renew that lease before it expires. Otherwise, the lookup service will assume that the service has gone away. The service may intentionally have been stopped or removed, but it may also have crashed, or there may be a network problem that prevents communication between the service and the lookup service. Regardless, when the service fails to renew its lease, the lookup service removes the service from its internal list of registered services.

Hence a well-behaved Jini service must continually renew its lease with every lookup service that it has joined. The *Jini Distributed Leasing Specification* defines a core set of interfaces for leasing, and Sun's implementation of Jini comes with helper classes to manage this renewal as well. The actual leasing protocol, however, is not defined by the Jini specification, though Sun provides a set of utility classes that implements a leasing protocol.

Services are allowed and encouraged to use leasing in their own service definitions where appropriate. For instance, a service that caches data on behalf of a client might use leasing to determine when the client has gone away and when the cached data can therefore be freed.

Leasing is one way in which a Jini community achieves its self-healing robustness. When we bring a new portable Jini-enabled printer into a community, it registers with the community's lookup server(s), and other participants in the community can now find and use the printer. When we remove the printer, the lookup service in essence reconfigures itself: that print service is no longer available.

Entries and Templates

A client locates a server by specifying a particular service interface when using the Jini lookup service. Sometimes, we care only about services with particular *attributes*. For example, an application trying to print to a color printer will need to find a service that has the color printer attribute (and that implements the printer service interface). The *Jini Entry Specification* defines a class that provides for a typed set of objects. The types are considered attributes by the lookup service, which allows clients to specify a template of entries. These templates are then used by the lookup service to determine which registered services match a given request. The APIs to use this template matching are part of the core set of Jini APIs; additional APIs are also defined in the *Jini Entry Utilities Specification*.

Entries are used by other services as well. For example, the JavaSpaces service uses entries to represent the objects that it stores. And you are free to use entries in your own services.

Distributed Events

Jini is designed to work in non-deterministic environments. In our example, we wondered what would happen if the printer were not on the network when the word processing application started.

Clearly, at this point the application cannot print. But it can ask the Jini lookup service to notify it when a printer (or actually, a service that implements the print service interface) enters the Jini community. And the application can use the service at that point. Similarly, the application can be notified if the printer becomes unavailable (i.e., it fails to renew its lease to the lookup service).

This notification occurs through Jini's distributed event mechanism. Jini extends Java's standard event mechanism in the *Jini Distributed Event Specification*, which defines a set of interfaces and conventions for distributed events. Distributed events are necessarily more complex than local events, since they must deal with potential network failures, potential server failures, and so on. Part of this complexity is handled by the core API, and part of it must be handled by Jini applications themselves.

Dynamic Code Definition

In our example, the application that wanted to print automatically downloaded from the printer all classes that it needed to interact with the printer: the dialog box, the drivers, etc. This is a vital requirement for a Jini community, since the user of a service will not know the particular implementation of the server until it actually runs.

Interestingly enough, we accomplished this task using basic facilities of Java: object serialization and dynamic class loading. Jini didn't need to extend Java to be able to provide this functionality, though it did make use of these existing features in a powerful new way.

Jini Transactions

The *Jini Transaction Specification* defines an interface to a transaction service that implements a two-phase commit protocol. Jini specifies the APIs that client and services may use to engage in the transaction, but it does not specify what the actual underlying transaction engine is. Sun's distribution of Jini comes with a transaction engine called *mahalo* that conforms to the Jini transaction specification; other transaction services will eventually be built on top of other products (including, we suspect, commercial-grade transaction managers).

In our example earlier, we made no mention of transactions. That's because transactions are optional in a Jini environment—a Jini service may require transactions, but most services do not. From a client perspective, handling transactions is simple: clients request a transaction object from the transaction manager and pass that object to the server. Handling transactions within a server, however, is a very difficult task.

The JavaSpaces Service

The *JavaSpaces Specification* defines a service that may run within a Jini community. A JavaSpaces server is a simple, tuple-based store that allows other entities to put or take objects from the store based on the state of certain values of attributes in the object. Sun provides two implementations of the JavaSpaces service—one that is persistent between invocations (the *FrontEndSpace*) and one that is not (the *TransientSpace*). Sun's implementation is generically called *outrigger*.

Other Services

The *Jini Technology Helper Utilities and Services Specification* is the first new specification added to the set of Jini specifications; this is the specification on which Jini 1.1 alpha is based. This specification defines three new useful services: a lookup discovery service, an event mailbox service, and a lease renewal services. In addition, this specification defines the new APIs available in Jini 1.1.

Jini and RMI

In addition to introducing Jini in this book, we also provide information on Java's Remote Method Invocation facility (RMI). RMI is a core feature of the Java Standard Edition and Java Enterprise Edition; it is an optional feature of the Java Micro Edition.

At a fundamental level, it's very hard to separate Jini from RMI. You can write Jini services using any distributed programming mechanism. You can write a CORBA service and register the CORBA service with the Jini lookup service. You can write an arbitrary class that uses a proprietary protocol and place an object of that class into the Jini lookup service. Once clients of your service obtain a reference to your service, they will then communicate with your service via CORBA, or your proprietary protocol, or any other protocol.

But in order for your service to participate fully in the Jini community, it must be running on a platform that supports RMI. There are three major reasons for this requirement:

- Distributed events use objects that implement the `Remote` interface, which is an RMI interface.*

- The same is true of some Jini transaction interfaces.

- If you use Sun's implementation of the lookup service, a lookup gives you an object that contains an embedded RMI reference. So in order to receive that object successfully, your underlying VM must support RMI.

This last point will doubtless become more important over time. When there is a standard Jini printing interface, the interface will not contain any direct use of RMI, but we guess that most printer vendors will implement their Jini printing services

---

* In Java 1.3, there will be a change in the way `Remote` objects are handled that will allow them to be implemented without using RMI.

using RMI. When you pull one of those services out of the lookup service, you'll need RMI support in order to use it.

In addition, one of Jini's key features—the ability to download code dynamically to the client—is made possible through RMI (it's possible, but difficult, to do this with your own protocols).

Hence, every Jini service and client will need access to a Java virtual machine that has support for RMI—either the Java standard edition platform or a micro edition platform with RMI support. And given the ubiquity of the RMI infrastructure, RMI is the simplest choice for writing your own services. There is a general requirement for Jini to use the Java 2 Standard Edition platform anyway; the dependence on RMI for key services is an important reason for that requirement.

So what if you have a device with very limited memory and power, such that it can't support the full Java Standard Edition platform? Or what if you have a device that cannot run a Java Virtual Machine at all? There are various strategies for using Jini in an environment that doesn't support RMI (or other features of the Java 2 platform). These strategies all revolve around the availability of a proxy Java Virtual Machine that runs the actual Jini service and then communicates with the device via whatever methods the device has available. There is no specific architecture that devices in a Jini network must follow; they must simply be able, through a combination of native code and proxies on the network, to communicate with the Jini lookup service. The same is true of legacy systems and services—including those legacy CORBA services that you wrote last week: the easiest way to integrate them into a Jini community is often to provide an RMI-based proxy for them.

Proxying is very important in some applications: it's doubtful that your Jini-enabled electric razor will have a standard-edition Java Virtual Machine embedded within it.

However, we must stress that while we believe that RMI is a natural fit for Jini, not all Jini services will be written with RMI. Jini does not define the network protocol that clients and servers use, and there will be many Jini services that use their own protocols to communicate with their clients and that are implemented with other distributed technologies.

Another Distributed Object System

If RMI is so great, then why do we need Jini? To begin, Jini does not replace the RMI infrastructure; it merely adds services that RMI does not support. Furthermore, Jini does not depend on RMI, since the Jini framework can also work with other distributed object frameworks like CORBA or your own protocols. So what does RMI lack?

RMI (like CORBA, servlets, and systems like EJB that use them) is based on a client-server paradigm. The client—an application—has a requirement to accomplish a specific task. In order to help accomplish this task, there are servers on the network that the client can call. These servers are very specific. The client needs to know where the server is, how to reach the server, and what the server can do. If the server becomes unreachable, the client generally will fail.

Jini was designed with a different goal. The goal of Jini is to allow the services on the network to be as robust as possible.

First, a client should not need to know where a particular service is located. A service should be able to be started at any location on the network, and the task of discovering the location of the service by the client should be part of the underlying infrastructure. This eliminates the need to configure the services, allowing the organization of these services to be very dynamic. This also allows for impromptu configurations of services. Temporary configurations can be created simply by starting Jini services on the network. For larger organizations, this can also be a cost saver. Services added to the network can be shared automatically by everyone on the network.

Second, the client should not fail if the service is unavailable or becomes unavailable during execution. Clients should be able either to wait for the desired service or switch to an alternative service on the network. This removes single points of failure on the network. Identical services can be started in different locations to maintain redundancy, and the clients of these services should not fail, even if every copy of the desired service becomes temporarily unavailable. To support this feature, the Jini infrastructure also allows for asynchronous feedback in the form of events. If all services are unavailable, clients can ask to be informed when the services become available. The goal of having redundant services and being able to detect new services as they appear is to make the infrastructure as robust as possible.

Third, clients and services should be proactive in detecting failure conditions. A service that stores data for a client should know that the client no longer exists—and hence no longer needs the data—if the client stops requesting its services. That way, the service won't waste resources holding data the client doesn't need. To support this feature, the Jini infrastructure provides the concept of leasing.

For operations that span more than one method call, services can require that clients maintain a lease. If the clients no longer need the service, it can cancel the lease, which will allow the service to clean up the resources pertaining to the client. In addition, the client is required to renew the lease within an interval that is determined by the service. If the client does not renew the lease in time, the server will assume that the client has failed, and all resources pertaining to the client can be removed.

And finally, there are services that are provided with the Jini system. These services use the Jini infrastructure, and hence are robust enough to support user-defined Jini services. As we've mentioned, primary services in Sun's Jini implementation include the Jini lookup service, the Jini transaction manager, and the JavaSpaces service. With these services, a user-defined Jini service has access to registry services, transactions services, and temporary storage services. In 1.1, Sun's implementation of Jini includes additional services that allow services to delegate lease renewal, delegate lookup service discovery, and use an event mailbox.

Jini Prerequisites

There are certain prerequisites for using Jini, even in a simple case like the one that we've described.

Clearly, Java must exist throughout the network. The lookup service runs on Java, and services must either be run directly on a Java virtual machine or be proxied by a Java virtual machine.

Second, there must be a network. Jini does not specify what the network is; instead, Jini depends upon the Java Virtual Machine to abstract the network away from it. But the protocol that Jini uses to discover the lookup service requires that the underlying network support multicasting, and there aren't really any virtual machines (yet) that support networks other than TCP/IP.

Third, the devices that run the Java Virtual Machines—whether they're computers running services or proxies, or devices like printers that run the service in an embedded virtual machine—must actually be on the network. Jini does not specify how this happens. On a TCP/IP network, the simplest way to accomplish this may be to use DHCP if the device supports it; or it may need to be configured in some other manner. This requirement allows Jini to be protocol-neutral with respect to the underlying network.

Finally, participants in a Jini community must know about each other's interface if they are to use each other. In our example, the application did not need to know the implementation of the print server in order to use it, and it was able to load that service implementation into itself dynamically. But the application did need prior knowledge of the interface of the print service: it needed to know that there was a showPrintDialog( ) method and a print( ) method (or whatever the interface might have been). An application can discover all available services, and it could conceivably use object reflection to learn the interface of each service.* But for the most part, service consumers and service providers must agree upon a common interface for the service to be used effectively.

The Jini Community Process

Earlier, we mentioned that using the term *community* to describe a set of Jini services overloaded that term. There is another Jini community, which is essentially the set of all developers who write Jini services. Some of these developers are more active in the Jini community than others, but all Jini developers—including you, of course—are members of this group.

The Jini community is important because it plays a number of roles in the ongoing development of Jini. Like all Java technology, the specifications for Jini are developed by Sun in tandem with input from developers all over the world. Specifications go through several draft processes, during which Jini community members are encouraged to submit responses to the specifications. Eventually, the final specification is published.

---

* If you're interested in how this might be done, look at the source code for the Jini browser.

But the Jini community extends beyond the traditional Java community role. Jini's success in many markets will depend upon the definition of a set of common and ubiquitous interfaces. As we just described, in order to use a print service, you must know the interface of that service. So members of the Jini community are active in defining exactly what the common print interface should look like. There are similar activities in defining common interfaces in a number of areas, from device-specific things such as printers and cell phones to utility services such as security services.

The Jini community is self-organizing. It's not a company; it's not a standards body—it's a group of developers who are committed to Jini technology and seeing this technology adopted in a variety of places. The Jini community has official meetings; more details about this organization are at *http://www.jini.org/*. This web site also has an active, if unofficial, developer support group.

There are a number of services offered at this site. You can subscribe to the official Jini mailing lists, including the *jini-users* mailing list. This mailing list generates a wealth of information, and the *www.jini.org* site has a searchable archive of this mailing list which is a great place to look for answers when you run into trouble. You can exchange source code with other Jini developers, and see the progress that Jini community groups are making in defining common service interfaces (and even join the groups that are defining those interfaces). In order to make use of this last set of services, you must register and accept the Sun Community Source License (SCSL)—this occurs when you obtain Jini in the first place, as explained in the next section.

The Sun Community Source License

When you download Jini, you agree to be bound by terms of the Sun Community Source License (SCSL). Though similar in broad concept to Open Source licenses (*http://open-source.org/*), the SCSL has some significant differences. These differences stem from the need for Jini services to remain compatible with each other and the evolving Jini specifications: if you make a change to Jini, that's okay under certain terms of the license. You are not required to give those changes back to anyone, but you cannot arbitrarily use the changed code in most environments. You are encouraged to feed changes back through the Jini community process, however, so that others may benefit from your insight and so that the changes may eventually become part of the Jini specification, if appropriate.

If you develop a Jini service, then the interface of that service must be published and free for anyone to use. The implementation of that service, however, is allowed to remain unpublished.

The SCSL has three distinct levels, depending on how you plan to use the Jini code. There's a lot of legal language in the SCSL, and we wouldn't presume to summarize it completely. But at a basic level, the SCSL grants rights at the following levels:

Research use
 This is the most basic level of the SCSL, which covers initial development of Jini services. Under this use, you can tinker with the Jini code and write services for your own research.

Internal deployment use

This level of use is the most obvious departure from other public licenses. Under the SCSL, you essentially agree that you will use the Jini Technology Compatibility Kit (TCK) to test all modifications that you make to Jini as well as all new services that you create. If your code passes the tests in the compatibility kit, you have the free right to use the code internally to your organization.

Note that there is a difference here between the SCSL as it applies to Jini and as it applies to the JDK. There is a general Java Technology Compatibility Kit (TCK) which Java licensees are required to pass in order to ship a Java VM; other developers are not given access to that TCK. But all developers are required to ensure that their Jini code passes the Jini TCK if they are going to distribute their code (even internally).

Commercial use

If you intend to distribute Jini services externally or otherwise profit from the Jini services that you develop, you must execute the commercial use section of the SCSL. This requires negotiating and signing a physical contract with Sun (unlike the previous two cases, to which you can agree on the web). These services must also pass the Jini TCK.

This commercial use clause applies even if you give away the service (although there is no fee involved in that case).

As we said, the SCSL is a legal document, and the summary here is neither fully complete nor a replacement for the actual SCSL. For more details, see the SCSL at *http://www.sun.com/jini/licensing/*.

Summary

We've spent a fair amount of time discussing the technology behind Jini. At its most basic, Jini is both a set of APIs that allow you to develop robust distributed services for a dynamic environment, and a set of services (including an all-important lookup service) that operate in that environment. Jini relies upon a community of developers that works actively to define the interfaces for new services.

After all is said and done, however, it's much easier to understand Jini by actually using it. In the next chapter, we'll show how to install and start Jini's basic services, and then we'll start to develop our own services.

CHAPTER 2

Getting Started with Jini

In this chapter, we'll set up your environment to run the Jini services that come with Sun's implementation of Jini. The first requirement to use Jini is to start with the Java platform. You need a Java platform to run Jini services and applications: specifically, you need the Java 2 Standard Edition platform. Parts of Sun's implementation of Jini use the RMI activation framework, which is not available prior to the Java 2 platform, and parts of the Jini specification require the use of Java 2 classes (such as the `java.util.Map` class). The Java 2 platform can be downloaded from Sun's Java web site at *http://java.sun.com/products/jdk/1.2.**

This web site has the latest information on all aspects of Java—including whitepapers on APIs, information on upcoming technologies related to Java, and links to download the latest version of the JDK. You can directly download VMs for Windows or Solaris from that page, or you can follow the links to find sites that provide Java for other platforms. To start using Jini, you must do the following:

1. Download and unpack Jini.

2. Set up your environment to use Jini.

3. Start the Jini services.

Downloading Jini

Once the Java 2 platform is installed, the process of getting and installing Jini is simple. Jini can be download from Sun's web site at *http://www.sun.com/jini/*. This site illustrates the basic idea of Jini and contains links to download it. At this site, you must register and accept the SCSL before you can actually download Jini. Since Sun's implementation of Jini is written purely in Java, there is no need to choose the platform for the Jini framework.

---

* As we go to print, 1.3 is approaching final release.

There are many important items to download from this site:

The Jini Technology Starter Kit

> The Jini Technology Starter Kit includes the Jini class libraries, Sun's implementation of key Jini services, the Jini specifications, and the javadoc documentation of the class libraries. At the time of this writing, two versions of the starter kit are available: 1.0.1 and 1.1 alpha; archived versions are available as well. We include information on both releases in this book, though the alpha release of Jini is subject to change.

The JavaSpaces Technology Kit

> The JavaSpaces Technology Kit (JSTK) includes Sun's implementations of the JavaSpaces service.

The Jini Technology Core Platform Compatibility Kit

> The Jini Technology Core Platform Compatibility Kit (Jini TCK) contains a set of tests that all Jini services must pass before they can be deployed. Passing this test is a requirement of the SCSL.

You should download and install each of these components.

The Jini Technology Starter Kit

The Jini Starter Kit is itself three components. The first component, the Jini Technology Core Platform (JCP), contains the libraries that provide the core Jini technology. Along with providing the interfaces and classes for lookup, discovery and join, remote events, leasing, and transactions, this component also includes documentation and whitepapers. This component contains the classes that are in the net.jini.core package.

The second component of the Jini Starter Kit is the Jini Technology Extended Platform (JXP) and contains classes that are in the net.jini package (except for those in the net.jini.core package). This component contains the interfaces and classes for the discovery and entry utilities along with their specification. This component also provides the specification for the JavaSpaces technology and the common interface classes for that service. Sun's sample implementation of the JavaSpaces service is provided in another package, the JavaSpaces Technology Kit (JSTK).

The third component of the Jini Starter Kit is the Jini Software Kit (JSK). This component provides Sun's implementation of the services that are specified by the JXP (except for the JavaSpaces service). The JSK also provides many helper classes that add to the simple interfaces provided by the core components. These classes are part of the com.sun package, which means that there is no guarantee that these classes will be available in future distributions.

Together these three components provide the set of class libraries that make up the Jini API. Although the classes in the JSK are not part of the Jini specification, we make frequent use of them in this book. On the other hand, don't make too much of the distinction between the net.jini and net.jini.core packages (that is, the JCP and the JXP). Both are officially part of the Jini specification. The net.jini.core packages contain the minimum set of classes and interfaces that participants in a Jini community must agree upon: if you look up a service you must use the `net.jini.core.lookup.ServiceTemplate` class, and the lookup service must support a known interface (the `net.jini.core.lookup.ServiceRegistrar` interface). The `net.jini` packages contain useful utilities and classes that use the `net.jini.core` classes; your client can choose to use the `net.jini.lookup.ClientLookupManager` class to talk to the lookup service, or it might write its own class to do that. But the `net.jini` packages also contain classes that all participants in the Jini community must agree upon, such as the interface to the JavaSpaces service. So in reality, there is no distinction between the core and extended classes.

The file that is returned from downloading the Jini Technology Starter Kit is named *jini10.zip* (or *jini1_0_1.zip* for Jini 1.0.1, *jini1_1alpha-src.zip* for Jini 1.1 alpha, and so on). This is a simple zip file that can be unpacked by most unzipping tools, or by the *jar* utility that is provided as part of the Java 2 SDK as follows:

```
piccolo% jar -xvf jini10.zip
```

When the file is unzipped, a directory named *jini1_0* (or *jini1_1*) is created. The following files and subdirectories are placed inside this directory:

index.html
> This is the starting page for all the Jini documentation. It contains links to the release notes and specifications for all parts of Jini. The release notes are HTML documents that can be read using a browser. The specifications are in both PostScript and PDF.
>
> A link to the javadoc API documentation of the JCP, JSK, and JSTK classes is also included on this page.
>
> Finally, there is information on how to build the complete package from source, licensing information, and a link that takes you to the Sun web site for more information on Jini.

doc/
> This directory contains the `javadoc` API documentation, documentation for the examples, and release notes for the Jini framework. It is normally accessed through the links mentioned earlier.

example/
> This directory contains the supporting *java.policy* files that are needed by the examples provided with the Jini framework. The Java classes themselves are not in this directory.

lib/ This directory contains the jar files for all of the Jini framework. This includes the jar files that make up the Jini API, the class files used to run Sun's implementation of the Jini services, and the jar files for the examples that are included with the Jini Starter Kit. We will examine this directory in greater detail later in this chapter.

source/
> This directory contains the source code for all components of the Jini framework, including Sun's service implementations (excluding parts of the JavaSpaces service). This directory is needed to build the *lib* directory. The source code is also a great source of documentation.

In the examples in this book, we assume that you have installed Jini into one of these directories:

- *C:\files\jini1_0* for Windows-based platforms

- */files/jini1_0* for Solaris and other Unix-based platforms

Some of the Jini tools use these as their default directory.

The JavaSpaces Technology Kit

The file *jstk1_0.zip* is returned from downloading the JavaSpaces Technology Kit. This file unzips into a directory called *jini1_0*, so it is best to unzip this file in the same location of the Java Starter Kit. The documentation, support files for examples, libraries, and source code will be loaded into their corresponding directories as described previously. This code works with Jini 1.1, even though it does not install into the Jini 1.1 directory.

The Jini Compatibility Test Kit

The TCK comes packaged in a file called *jinitck1_0b.zip*. It unzips into a directory called *jinitck1_0B*. You can install the test kit into a separate directory from the rest of Jini. Passing the TCK is a requirement for services that you develop and put into production (or release to others) under the terms of the SCSL.

Setting Up Your Environment

There are three jar files that correspond to the three components of the Jini Starter Kit. They are *jini-core.jar*, which contains the core Jini technology; *jini-ext.jar*, which contains the extension and utility interfaces; and *sun-util.jar*, which contains the helper classes that are part of the Jini Software Kit. All three of these jar files are in the *lib* directory of the Jini Starter Kit. In order to program with the Jini system, you must place these files into the classpath. There are two ways to accomplish this.

The first method is to use the *-cp* parameter of the *java* application to specify the classpath. When this option is specified, the Java Virtual Machine will use the parameter that follows this option as the path to load the class files from. The classpath should specify the base directories and the jar files that need to be searched for class files. The names for the base directories and the jar files should be separated by a the appropriate platform separator: on Unix systems, a colon (:); on Windows systems, a semi-colon (;).

The second method is to set the CLASSPATH environment variable. If the *-cp* parameter is not used, the environment variable is used to define the location from which to obtain the classfiles. The format of the CLASSPATH environment variable is the same as the format that is used by the *-cp* option.

The other jar files in the *lib* directory are not needed as part of your classpath; they contain implementation code for the lookup service, transaction manager, and so on. When you run these services, you'll specify the jar files that you need, and clients that use these services will obtain the code that they need from an HTTP server that we'll set up later. Do not make the mistake of putting these into your classpath. Even if you have a problem running one of the services we discuss later, and it seems as if putting one of these files into your classpath fixes the problem, that is the wrong thing to do. If these files end up in your classpath, you will have other troubles later on. Similarly, don't copy any Jini jar files to Java's extension directory; that will occasionally cause subtle problems with programs that recover stored information.

When we show command lines in later chapters, we assume that you've put the appropriate jar files in your classpath.

Note that we said you need to set the classpath only to develop with Jini. The services that come with Sun's implementation of Jini and that we show how to run in this chapter are all self-contained: the jar file containing the service contains all of the Jini code required to support the application. Replicating that sort of setup is a good idea for your services when you are ready to deploy them, but it's impractical for testing and developing.

Setting Up a Jini Security Model

We provide more details on the way in which Jini interacts with Java's security model in Chapter 12, *Security in Jini*. For now, we recommend that you create the following file as */files/jini1_0/java.policy.all* (*C:\files\jini1_0\java.policy.all* on Windows):

```
grant {
    permission java.security.AllPermission;
};
```

We'll use this file (via the *-Djava.security.policy* property) in all our examples. For examples based on 1.1, we assume this file exists as */files/jini1_1/java.policy.all*. This is a dangerous file to use in an untrusted environment; make sure to use it in the examples we show only in a trusted environment.

Starting Jini Services

The code that you obtain with Sun's implementation of Jini contains both a set of class libraries that you can use for development and the implementation of a basic set of services that we call the Jini framework. These services include *reggie* (an implementation of the Jini lookup service), *mahalo* (an implementation of the Jini transaction manager), *outrigger* (implementations of the JavaSpaces service), and a simple HTTP server. Sun's implementation of the Jini framework depends on other core services of the Java platform, like *rmid*. Version 1.1 of Jini comes with three additional services: *fiddler* (an implementation of a lookup discovery service), *mercury* (an implementation of an event mailbox service), and *norm* (an implementation of a lease renewal service).

Starting Sun's implementation of the Jini framework involves many steps. There is a GUI tool that can be used to start all of these services, but we are going to start them by hand first in order to understand the services and their requirements.

Users who simply want to start these quickly can skip to the "Using the Start Services GUI Tool" later in this chapter (although that tool does not start the new 1.1 services, and its 1.0 version will not correctly start *reggie* on a Windows platform).

For the bulk of our examples, you must start only the HTTP server, *rmid*, and *reggie*. For our examples in Chapter 10, *The JavaSpaces Service*, you must start *mahalo* and *outrigger*. For our examples in Chapter 11, *Helper Services*, you must also start *fiddler*, *mercury*, and *norm*. If you're interested in getting to code as soon as possible, start the HTTP server, *rmid*, and *reggie*, and continue with the examples in Chapter 3, *Remote Method Invocation* (or Chapter 4, *Basic Jini Programming*, if you already know how to program in RMI); then come back here when you need to learn how to start the additional services.

As presently implemented, these services require a lot of memory, and running them all on a single machine may lead to problems. This is particularly true on a Windows platform, where you should have at least 64 MB of physical memory if you want to run the HTTP server, *rmid*, *reggie*, and one or more examples on the same machine. To run the JavaSpaces service and examples requires at least 96 MB of physical memory. If you have less memory, you'll start to see inconsistent errors, usually related to networking. As a result, you should start only those services you need for a particular example. Even better, of course, is to run pieces of the framework on different machines within the same network.

In this chapter, we show only basic command lines used to start these services. Each contains a number of command-line options and properties; these are listed in Chapter 13, *Service Reference*.

Starting the HTTP Service

Jini does not define the remote mechanism that will be used by clients to contact a service; it merely passes the proxy that represents the service between server and client by using object serialization. In Sun's implementation, these proxies contain RMI stubs that can contact the service in question.

In order for RMI to function correctly, there has to be a mechanism to deliver the class files to the client, which may not have these files in its classpath. In most cases, the class files can be delivered using a standard web server. We simply place the class files that we need to send to the client on the web server, and set the java.rmi.server.codebase property correctly to inform the client where to obtain the class files (see Chapter 3 for more details).

For the core set of services that come with Jini, clients will need to be able to download classes that are in the jar files that were installed into the *lib* directory. So we need an HTTP service to download files from that directory.

In case an HTTP server is not available (or if you want an isolated server that you can control), a simple HTTP server that is written in Java is included with the Jini Starter Kit. To start an HTTP server on the Windows platform on a particular network port (8080) and with a particular root directory, the following command can be used (type the command on one line):

```
C:\> java -jar C:\files\jini1_0\lib\tools.jar -port 8080
         -dir C:\files\jini1_0\lib -verbose
```

On Solaris, the same results can be obtained with the following command (also on a single line):

```
piccolo% java -jar /files/jini1_0/lib/tools.jar -port 8080
              -dir /files/jini1_0/lib -verbose
```

The HTTP server is written in Java so we use the same jar file on all platforms. The differences in the command stem from Windows' use of a different delimiter for directories and an extra specifier to refer to different filesystems.

Also notice that the class files for the HTTP server are self-contained within the *tools.jar* file. There are a few ways to run an application that is in a jar file. The most direct way is to add the jar file to the classpath and specify the class that contains the main( ) method for the application. In this case, we are using the *-jar* option of the java command and directly running the jar file. This works because there is an item in the jar file's manifest that defines the main class for the jar file. This is the class whose main( ) method will run.

The HTTP server will run until it is killed (via a Ctrl-C or other platform-specific method). It is usually easiest to run the server in its own shell window for more control.

Starting the RMI Activation Daemon

The RMI activation daemon is needed by *reggie, mahalo, outrigger, fiddler, mercury*, and *norm*. This is the main reason why the Java 2 platform is necessary for Sun's implementation of Jini. If these Jini services will not be run on a particular host, there is no reason to start the activation daemon on that host (unless you have written your own application that uses activation). To start *rmid*, simply execute it:

```
piccolo% rmid
```

This command should already be in the execution path since it is in the standard JDK 1.2 *bin* directory.

When you run *rmid*, it creates a directory called *log* in its current directory. If *rmid* is restarted, it recreates its state from information in that log. In addition, *rmid* restarts any services (such as *reggie*) that were previously registered with it. For a production environment, that's exactly what you want: you start each service once, and it registers with *rmid*. Then every time *rmid* starts, the services can be restarted; you don't need to restart anything but *rmid*. But in a testing environment, you may not want that behavior; in this case, you should remove the *log* directory before you restart *rmid*.

Services that use *rmid* are called activatable services. Activatable services have a number of interesting properties. The first is that they run under the control of *rmid*. The command that runs an activatable service registers the command with *rmid* and then exits. *rmid* will spawn a new VM that runs the service. So activatable services involve two VMs: the one that registers the command and the one that *rmid* uses to run the service. Command lines for activatable services must specify VM properties for both VMs.

Activatable services are persistent. If an activatable service crashes (or if you use a system utility to kill it), *rmid* will restart it. If the machine crashes, starting *rmid* is sufficient to restart all the activatable services (thanks to the log mentioned above). To stop an activatable service, you must kill *rmid*, kill the activatable services, remove *rmid*'s log (plus the logs of any activatable services, if necessary), restart *rmid*, and then restart only the services that you want.* *rmid* will run until it is killed (via a CTRL-C or other means). It is usually easiest to run this command in its own shell window.

Starting reggie

The Jini lookup service may be started on Solaris with the following (single-line) command:

```
piccolo% java -Djava.security.policy=/files/jini1_0/java.policy.all
          -jar /files/jini1_0/lib/reggie.jar
          http://piccolo:8080/reggie-dl.jar
          /files/jini1_0/example/lookup/policy.all
          /var/tmp/reggie_log
```

To start the Jini lookup service with the Windows platform, use this (single-line) command:

```
C:\> java -Djava.security.policy=/files/jini1_0/java.policy.all
          -jar C:\files\jini1_0\lib\reggie.jar
          http://piccolo:8080/reggie-dl.jar
          C:\files\jini1_0\example\lookup\policy.all
          C:\temp\reggie_log
```

Just like the HTTP server, *reggie* is written in Java and hence uses a similar command line under Windows and Solaris. To convert the command to Windows, simply change the file delimiters and add the filesystem specifiers. There is, however, one parameter that does not change. The format of the URL specifier is not related to the filesystem and is defined by Internet standards; it is the same on all platforms. So in this case, the *http://piccolo:8080/reggie-dl.jar* parameter is the same whether the service is running under Windows or Solaris. In the rest of this chapter, we'll show only the Solaris format for commands.

The first argument on this command line defines the security policy file under which this command will be registered. As with the HTTP server, *reggie* is bundled as part of a jar file and is started with the *-jar* option, which is the next command-line argument.

When clients contact the lookup service, they must obtain class files that provide the implementation of the service. In this case, the client side jar file is placed on the HTTP server that we started earlier and is referenced by the *http://piccolo:8080/reggie-dl.jar* parameter. piccolo is the hostname of the computer on which we ran the HTTP server; this should replaced with the actual hostname of the server machine.

---

* This is not completely accurate. Later, we'll learn about Jini's administratable interface, which allows a client to destroy a service; before an activatable service is destroyed, it unregisters itself from *rmid*. But that requires some programming; prewritten programs to do this don't ship with Sun's present version of Jini.

This URL parameter is used as the `java.rmi.server.codebase` property to tell the client where the class files can be obtained. It should not be a file-based URL, nor should it use `localhost` as the hostname. If we use a file-based URL and the client is on another network host, the file system layout on that other machine must be the same in order for the client to find the jar file. The name `localhost` will resolve to the machine that the client is actually running on, which is probably not the same machine that is running the HTTP daemon. So make sure to use a URL formatted like the one that we've shown.

The next parameter, */files/jini1_0/example/lookup/policy.all*, is the policy file that is passed to the activation group descriptor. This value in the descriptor is used to set the security of the Java Virtual Machine that will run the service. Note that this is different than the policy file specified with the *-D* option: this one specifies the policy file under which the command is run; the *-D* option specifies the policy file under which the program is registered with *rmid*.

The last parameter, */var/tmp/reggie_log* or *C:\tmp\reggie_log*, is the directory that is used by *reggie* to store its log files, which manage the persistence of the lookup server. When *reggie* restarts, it reads the information in the log to recreate its state, including the services that were previously registered with it. In a production environment, that's exactly what you want. When you're testing things and restart *reggie*, however, you don't want this state to be maintained, and you should remove this directory and its contents before you restart *reggie*. Note that the Jini documentation often suggests putting this log file into the */tmp* directory, but since that directory doesn't survive a machine crash, that's not a useful place to put the log in a production environment.

reggie takes a long time to start. It has finished starting when the command line used to start *reggie* completes; it is then registered with *rmid*, which will start the VM for *reggie*. If *reggie* exits, *rmid* automatically restarts it, and *reggie* recreates its state from its log. If you want to restart *reggie* with no state, you must first kill *rmid*, clean up the log directories from *reggie* and *rmid*, restart *rmid*, and then restart *reggie*.

Starting mahalo

The Jini transaction manager service is used by services (like the JavaSpaces service) that need many operations to be treated as a single atomic operation. Like the lookup service, we do not need to start our own transaction service if it is already available on the network. Unlike the lookup service, usage of this service is not very common: most Jini services don't (yet) need a transaction manager. In our case, you must start a transaction manager to run only the examples pertaining to the JavaSpaces service.

An implementation of the Jini transaction manager service, *mahalo*, is provided with the Jini Software Kit and may be started with this single-line command:

```
piccolo% java -Djava.security.policy=/files/jini1_0/java.policy.all
        -jar /files/jini1_0/lib/mahalo.jar
        http://piccolo:8080/mahalo-dl.jar
        /files/jini1_0/example/txn/policy.all /var/tmp/txn_log
```

As with *reggie*, the first argument is the policy file under which mahalo will register with *rmid*, the second (*-jar mahalo.jar*) defines the jar file that contains the application code, the third argument defines the URL from which clients can download the necessary client-side code, the forth file defines the security policy file under which this service will be run, and the fifth argument defines a directory where *mahalo* will maintain its state information.

mahalo is also an activatable service, so all the caveats that apply to *reggie* apply to *mahalo*: it takes a while to start, after which the command line will exit; *rmid* will automatically restart it if it exits; and to restart it without its state you must first kill *rmid*, clean up the *rmid* and *mahalo* log directories, and restart *rmid* (plus the other services you want to run).

Starting outrigger

The JavaSpaces service provides storage for Java objects. Services or clients in the Jini community can use this storage to store short-term data or as a common location to pass data between applications. While the storage can be used for longer term information normally stored into a database, this is not recommended, since the API provided by the JavaSpaces service is not rich enough to support more complicated retrieval needs normally associated with a database.

Unlike the other services mentioned so far, this service is not part of the Jini Starter Kit. In order to start this service, the JavaSpaces Technology Kit (JSTK) must be loaded and installed. The JSTK comes with two versions of *outrigger*. The first version is called the *FrontEndSpace* and is started with the following command (on one line):

```
piccolo% java -Djava.security.policy=/files/jini1_0/java.policy.all
    -jar /files/jini1_0/lib/outrigger.jar
    http://piccolo:8080/outrigger-dl.jar
    /files/jini1_0/example/books/policy.all /var/tmp/JS_log
```

The arguments take the same format as those for *reggie* and *mahalo*. The second version of the JavaSpaces service is called the *TransientSpace* and is started like this:

```
piccolo% java -Djava.security.policy=/files/jini1_0/java.policy.all
    -Djava.rmi.server.codebase=http://piccolo:8080/outrigger-dl.jar
    -jar /files/jini1_0/lib/transient-outrigger.jar
    http://piccolo:8080/outrigger-dl.jar
```

The difference between these two implementations of the JavaSpaces service is that the *FrontEndSpace* is activatable and keeps its data in persistent storage. If it exits, it will be automatically restarted by *rmid*, and it can recover its state from its log directory (*/var/tmp/JS_log* in the previous example). Like the other activatable services we've looked at, to restart it from a clean state requires killing *rmid* and removing the log directories.

If the *TransientSpace* exits, it will lose all its data and *rmid* will not restart it. In fact, *rmid* does not need to be running to run the *TransientSpace*. Because of this difference, there are slight changes to the command line. The URL used for the java.rmi.server.codebase must now be specified as a property; since *rmid* is no longer involved, there is no need to specify a policy file for use under *rmid*

(though you still need a policy file for the command itself); and there is no need
to specify a log directory. The command for the *TransientSpace* does not exit. To
stop it, you must kill it (via CTRL-C or similar mechanism); you can restart it simply by reissuing its command line.

Starting fiddler

In 1.1, Sun's implementation of Jini comes with an implementation of a lookup
discovery service. The lookup discovery service performs discovery on behalf of
its clients; we use it only for the examples in Chapter 11. As with the JavaSpaces
service, there are two implementations of this service: an activatable one and a
transient one. The usual considerations apply: the activatable service will be automatically restarted and will recreate its state from a log, and the transient service
can be killed and restarted from the command line.

To start the activatable implementation of *fiddler*, use this command line:

```
piccolo% java -Djava.security.policy=/files/jini1_1/java.policy.all
        -jar /files/jini1_1/lib/fiddler.jar
        http://piccolo:8080/fiddler-dl.jar
        /files/jini1_1/policy.all /var/tmp/fiddler_log
```

To start the transient implementation of *fiddler*, use this command line:

```
piccolo% java -Djava.security.policy=/files/jini1_1/java.policy.all
        -Djava.rmi.server.codebase=http://piccolo:8080/fiddler-dl.jar
        -cp /files/jini1_1/lib/fiddler.jar
        com.sun.jini.fiddler.TransientFiddler /var/tmp/fiddler_log
```

Note that we've had to specify on the command line the classpath for the jar file
containing the classes that implement *fiddler*. The same jar file is used for both
implementations, but a jar file can contain only one class that is started with the
-jar option. So in the second example, we've had to name the class explicitly.

Starting mercury

In 1.1, Sun's implementation of Jini comes with an implementation of an event
mailbox service called *mercury*. The event mailbox service is used by its clients to
hold events while the client is offline; we use it only for our examples in Chapter
11. This service comes only in an activatable implementation that is controlled via
rmid. It is started as follows:

```
piccolo% java -Djava.security.policy=/files/jini1_1/java.policy.all
        -jar /files/jini1_1/lib/mercury.jar
        http://piccolo:8080/mercury-dl.jar
        /files/jini1_1/policy.all /var/tmp/mercury_log
```

Starting norm

In 1.1, Sun's implementation of Jini comes with an implementation of a lease
renewal service called *norm*. This service will renew leases on behalf of its clients;
we use it only for the examples in Chapter 11. This service comes only in an activatable implementation that is controlled via *rmid*. It is started as follows:

```
piccolo% java -Djava.security.policy=/files/jini1_1/java.policy.all
    -jar /files/jini1_1/lib/norm.jar
    http://piccolo:8080/norm-dl.jar
    /files/jini1_1/policy.all /var/tmp/norm_log
```

Starting Services on Multiple Machines

In a typical Jini community, some of these services run on different machines. Even in a testing environment, this is often the more practical method due to the memory requirements of Sun's present implementation of these services.

You need to start only one instance of the HTTP server; it can serve the jar files for all the services mentioned above. Make sure to specify the correct hostname in the HTTP parameters of the commands that you start. One the other hand, you can start multiple HTTP servers on multiple machines to serve the jar files; in fact, when we write our own Jini services we'll start a new instance of the HTTP server specific to each service. Choosing between these options requires balancing resources against ease of configuration: if you're testing a service, you may not want to copy all of its required files to a centralized HTTP server all the time.

rmid must run on every machine that is running an activatable service. It does not need to run on a machine that runs only the *TransientSpace* version of the Java-Spaces service or the transient version of *fiddler*. So if you run the services on multiple machines, make sure to start *rmid* on each machine as necessary.

Using the Start Services GUI Tool

At this point, we have discussed eight applications: an HTTP server, the RMI activation daemon, and six Jini services. As we mentioned, there is a graphical tool that can start many of these tasks. Using the tool, we simply need to enter information into tabbed panels and click to start the applications. However, the tool has some unfortunate bugs in 1.0; it cannot start any of the 1.1 helper services, and it cannot stop services reliably.

In addition to starting these services, the tool can help us to figure out command lines that we can place into scripts, since it will print out the command line that it uses to start these applications. We can use the tool to configure the application, and then copy the command line that was printed into an editor for incorporation into a script.

Start the tool with this one-line command:

```
piccolo% java -cp /files/jini1_0/lib/jini-examples.jar
    com.sun.jini.example.service.StartService
```

The StartService class will create a panel that contains eight different tabs. The information that each tabbed panel collects is the same information that we have been entering on our command lines.

Since we already know how to start the applications from the command line, let's step through the tool quickly.

Click on the "Jini Jar Files" tabbed panel. This brings up a panel of text fields that allow us to name all of the jar files used in the applications. The first two text fields are used to provide the directory of the jar file for services and the URL root directory for the client jar files. Normally, the jar files for all the services should be in the same directory. If they are not, leave the path to jar files blank and enter the fully qualified name for the corresponding jar files. Similarly, the client jar files are normally provided by the same web server; if they are not, leave the URL blank and enter the full URL for each client jar file. See Figure 2-1 for an example of how this panel would be filled out given our setup. If you installed Jini into the recommended directory, then nothing needs to be changed in this panel.

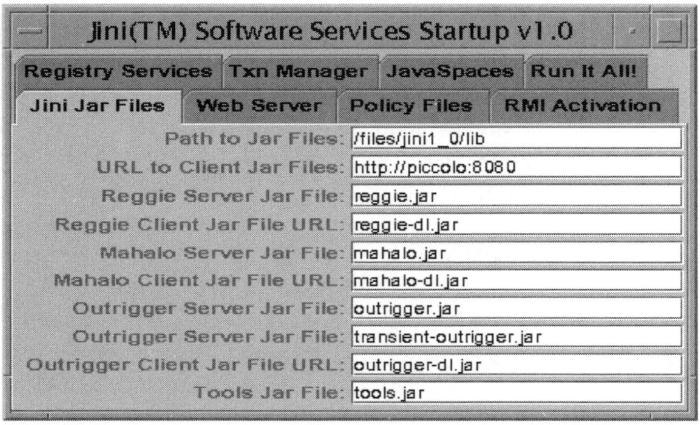

Figure 2-1: Setting the jar files to start services

Next, click on the "Policy Files" tabbed panel. This brings up a panel of text fields that allow us to specify the policy files used by the Jini services. Simply enter the fully qualified name of the three policy files. These correspond to the names that we used in the command-line arguments in starting the services. The txn policy file is used for *mahalo*, the spaces policy file is used for *outrigger*, and the lookup policy file is used for *reggie*. If you installed Jini into the recommended directory, the default values for all these fields will be correct.

At this point, we have entered the common data that applies to the five applications. Let's now configure the individual applications.

Click on the "Web Server" tabbed panel to configure the HTTP server. This tab contains four items. First, we must choose the network port to listen to. The default for this is 8080. The next item specifies the root directory of the web server. This was specified with the *-dir* option on the command line. The third item specifies whether files inside jar files are to be searched. If this item is checked, when the server receives a request for a class file that is not located on the server, it will also check all the jar files in the server's root directory (equivalent to the *-trees* option when starting the HTTP server, an option that we don't usually use). The class file will be extracted from the jar file and delivered to the client. The last parameter is for debugging. If checked, a log of all files served to clients will be printed to the executing shell (the same as specifying the *-verbose* option). You only need to change items in this panel if Jini is not installed in the recommended directory or if you already have a server running on port 8080.

Next, click on the "RMI Activation" tabbed panel to configure *rmid*. This panel contains one text field that allows us to define the parameters to the *rmid* application. Normally, you run *rmid* without any parameters.

Next, click on the "Registry Services" tabbed panel to choose and configure the lookup service. Unlike the other panels, you must enter something in this panel: you must choose the lookup service to use. You should choose the Jini lookup service; the RMI registry choice is here for mostly historical reasons and will not be supported in the future. After choosing a lookup service, you don't normally need to make other changes in this panel.

The choice made in this panel also affects the transaction manager service and the JavaSpaces service, since they must be configured to use the lookup service of choice. If the RMI registry is chosen, the network port that it will listen to can be entered into a text field. If the Jini lookup service is chosen, then two text fields must be configured. The *log* directory is used to specify the location where *reggie* will store its persistent files. The lookup groups text field specifies all the groups that the lookup service will participate in. This text field also specifies the groups that will be used by the transaction manager and JavaSpaces services. Figure 2-2 shows how this pane looks to configure the Jini lookup service.

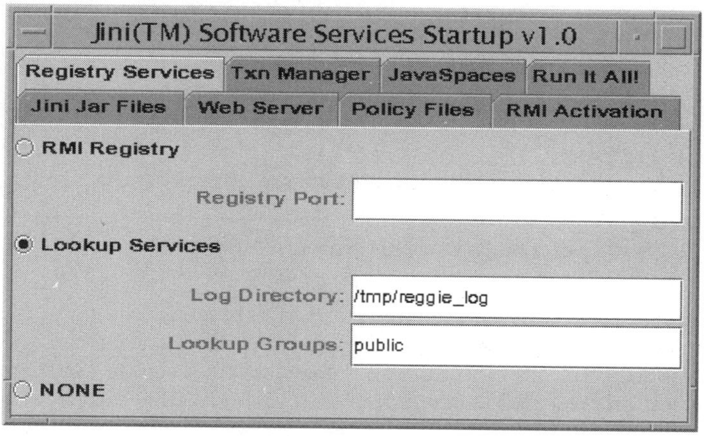

Figure 2-2: Starting the Jini Lookup Service

Next, click on the "Txn Manager" tabbed panel to configure the transaction manager service. There are two fields that must be entered. The *log* directory is used to specify the location where *mahalo* will store its persistent files. On a Windows platform, the default value for this option is *tmp**txn_log*, but that default will not work: you must include the drive specifier (*C:\tmp\txn_log*) for this field. The server options text field is used to specify additional parameters to the command line. The choice of the lookup service, its configuration,. and the lookup service groups to join have already been entered in the "Registry Services" panel.

Next, click on the "JavaSpaces" tabbed panel to configure the JavaSpaces service. In the first text field, you specify the name of the JavaSpace to be used. The second item is a button that chooses the type of JavaSpaces service to start. "Front-End" specifies the persistent version of the JavaSpaces service and "Transient" specifies the non-persistent version. If the "FrontEnd" version of JavaSpaces is chosen, the last text field specifies the location where *outrigger* will store its files (on Windows, the default value for this field is again missing the drive specification).

At this point, all five applications have been configured. Click on the "Run it All" tabbed panel to get to the execution control panel. There will be ten buttons. The left and right sets of buttons start and stop the applications, respectively. This panel is shown in Figure 2-3.

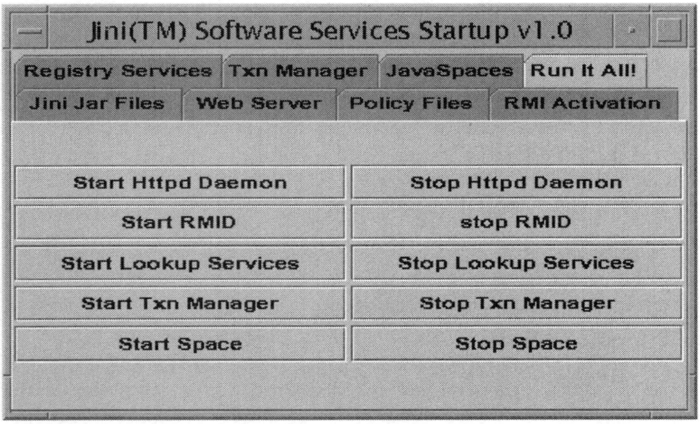

Figure 2–3: Starting and stopping all the services

The buttons are laid out in the preferred order of execution from top to bottom. If some of these services are started in the wrong order, an error can result: the HTTP server and *rmid* must be running before the other service are started. The other services can be started in any order.

Even though there are buttons to stop the services, you cannot expect these buttons to work. As we've discussed, services like *reggie* will be restarted by *rmid* if they exit, so you must shut down *rmid* before you shutdown the services. Even then, using the stop button may not actually stop the service, and you may have to use a platform-specific tool to find the process and stop it.

In the 1.0 version of this tool, a bug on the Windows platform prevents *reggie* from starting correctly from this tool. This is fixed in 1.1.

The Jini Lookup Service Browser

The last application that we will examine in this chapter is a client of the Jini framework. Its purpose is to seek out lookup services and provide information on which services have registered with a particular lookup service. This tool is a good debugging tool to figure out what services are running on your network.

To start the browser, execute this command (on one line):

```
piccolo% java -Djava.security.policy=/files/jini1_0/java.policy.all
   -Djava.rmi.server.codebase=http://piccolo:8080/jini-examples-dl.jar
   -cp /files/jini1_0/lib/jini-examples.jar
   com.sun.jini.example.browser.Browser
```

Running the lookup service browser is similar to running the StartServices tool; it is actually in the same jar file. The only extra requirements are that you must set the properties for the security policy and specify the URL location for the client-side jar files.

If you start this tool before you start the Jini lookup service, you'll see the message "No registrars to select" in the main panel of this tool. A registrar is an instance of the Jini lookup service. Once you start the lookup service (and it has had time to proceed through its startup sequence), this message should change to "1 registrar, not selected." This indicates that the Jini lookup service is running correctly. Figure 2-4 shows how the tool looks when there is one lookup service running on the network.

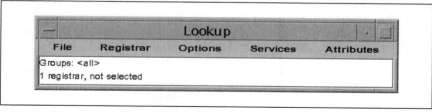

Figure 2–4: The Jini Browser found one lookup service

Much of information displayed in the Jini Lookup Browser will make more sense in later chapters. At this point, we will simply navigate through the browser—do not worry too much about its features.

The File menu is used to specify or restrict which lookup services we're interested in discovering. By default, the tool will find all lookup services on the network. With this menu, the user is able to enter lookup service group names and find only those groups, or the user can select a particular lookup service by hostname (and optionally, by network port). The other choices are administrative to the tool, allowing the user to reset the tool and to exit.

The Registrar menu is used to pick the lookup service to examine. Selecting an item in this menu allows us to examine the services registered with that lookup service. If you select that menu at this time (assuming you've started a lookup service), you should see the name of the machine on which the lookup service is running. If you select that item from the menu, then you'll see the total number of services that are running on the network. If you've only started *reggie*, you'll see the message "Total services registered: 1"; if you've started other services (or start them now), you'll see that number increase. Figure 2-5 shows the how the tool looks when we've selected a registrar that all the 1.0 Jini services (*reggie, mahalo,* and *outrigger*) have registered with.

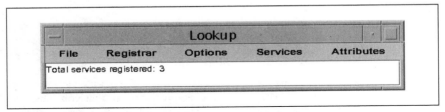

Figure 2–5: The Jini Browser after selecting a registrar

The Services menu and the Attributes menu are used to refine which services within a lookup service we're interested in examining. Picking an item in the service menu means we want to see only services that implement the corresponding interface; picking multiple ones means that the service must implement all the corresponding interfaces. Similarly, selecting one or more attributes narrows our view to services that have the corresponding attributes.

The Options menu is used to specify the display of the Services and Attributes menu. With this menu, we can specify all the types of Java classes that the Services and Attributes menus support. In the default state, services are selected only by their interface; we can also include their class, their superclass, and their attributes superclasses.

Finally, there is also an administration option to this tool. If the *-admin* parameter is provided when we start the tool, the display will be split into two subpanels. Instead of showing the details of the matching services, it will provide the services in a list. The user can click on the list to view or change the details of the service. Once a service is selected, a new window is provided to handle that service.

This window also has many menus. The File menu allows us to reload service information. The Edit menu allows us to add, remove, or change the attributes of the service. And finally, the Admin menu allows us to use the administration interface that is provided by the service. This tool is restricted to three administration interfaces: the joining, lookup, and destroy administration interfaces (see Chapter 7, *Service Administration,* for more information on administration interfaces).

CHAPTER 3

Remote Method Invocation

Remote Method Invocation, or RMI, is a mechanism in which objects that reside in different Java Virtual Machines may invoke methods on each other. It is similar to other distributed programming systems like CORBA or remote procedure calls (RPCs), but it is different from each of these in important ways.

In Chapter 1, *Introduction to Jini*, we discussed the role of RMI in a Jini community: RMI is required for certain features of Jini and is the easiest way for us to show you how to write Jini services. So we're going to start by examining the basics of RMI. If you have a good working knowledge of RMI, you can skip this chapter. If you're interested in getting to Jini code as soon as possible, you should skim this chapter so that you understand the basics of RMI; as we develop more complex systems, we rely more and more on the details presented in this chapter. RMI is also covered in O'Reilly & Associates' *Java Enterprise in a Nutshell* and *Java Examples in a Nutshell*.

RMI is a distributed object system. In RMI, a server will export certain object references; these exported objects are known as *remote objects*. A client can obtain a reference to a remote object in a variety of ways which we'll explore; once the client has the remote object reference, it invokes methods on that object in much the same way as it invokes methods on any other object. The difference is that the invocation of the method happens on the server within the server's VM: the parameters to the method invocation are bundled up by RMI and shipped from the client to the server, which then runs the method. The return value (or exception) of the method is then bundled up by RMI and shipped back to the client.

RMI calls are synchronous: the thread in the client that makes the call is blocked until the return comes back from the server. In programmatic terms, this makes RMI calls look exactly like a regular method invocation. There is some exception handling that is required—all RMI methods throw at least one type of exception— but handling this is the same as handling any other declared exception. So to the client, an RMI call looks the same as any other method call. If we have a remote object ro, a client might invoke an add( ) method on it as follows:

```
int answer = ro.add(2, 2);
```

From the server's perspective, RMI programmatically looks like a series of callback methods. The server will register particular methods with the RMI infrastructure, and these methods will be invoked automatically when a call comes in from a client. The developer does not need to write any code that handles the actual network connections; she must write only code that implements the desired functionality. So apart from some initialization code, a server that corresponds to the client mentioned previously would have a single method called add( ) that looks something like this:

```
public int add(int x, int y) throws RemoteException {
    return x + y;
}
```

Object Serialization

The fundamental difference between RMI and other distributed object systems is that in RMI, all objects may be passed by value or by reference. When a nonremote object is passed between two objects via RMI (whether as a parameter to a method call or as the return value from a method), a copy of the object is made, and both the client and the server will end up with separate copies of that object. Note that this is different not only from other distributed object systems, but from the rest of Java as well: in all other areas of Java, objects are strictly passed by reference. Remote objects, on the other hand, are passed by reference in RMI (at least as far as the developer is aware).

In order to pass an object by value, we must be able to make a copy of the object. This is accomplished by object serialization, which allows us to serialize an object into a byte array; when the byte array is deserialized, we end up with a copy of the original object. Object serialization has several uses, and it is used (transparently to the programmer) to bundle up objects that are passed by value between RMI clients and servers.

Not all objects can be serialized. In order to be serialized, an object must implement either the java.io.Serializable or the java.io.Externalizable interface (which itself extends Serializable). Attempting to serialize an object that does not implement one of these interfaces will result in a java.io.NotSerializableException being thrown. The Serializable interface has no methods, so it's really just an indication the developer of the class has taken the necessary steps to ensure the object will serialize and reconstitute itself correctly. The Externalizable interface has two methods—writeExternal( ) and readExternal( )—that we will discuss later.

In order for an object to work correctly with object serialization, the developer must do the following:

Determine which instance variables need to be marked as transient
> Any variables that are instances of a class that is not serializable must be marked as transient. Serialization is a recursive operation: when an object is

serialized, each of its instance variables is serialized in turn (and when an instance variable is serialized, each of its instance variables is serialized, and so on). If any variable in this chain is not serializable, then it cannot be included in the byte stream. It must be marked transient to prevent the throwing of a NotSerializableException.

There are additional reasons to mark a variable as transient. The byte array that is produced by object serialization contains the value of all the instance variables of the target object, including any private instance variables. If there is sensitive data in those private instance variables, then the developer may prefer to exclude those values from the byte array. This way, if someone gains access to the byte array, that person will not be able to determine the private state of the object represented in the array.

Objects that contain cached data should mark those cached values as transient so that when the object is deserialized, a new value can be retrieved.

Ensure that all superclasses can be reconstituted

Serialization works on all instance variables of a class, including instance variables of its superclasses. This includes not only the public and protected variables that the target class can see, but any private instance variables of the superclass as well.

If the superclass is itself serializable, then all is well: the target class already knows that the superclass can be serialized. If the superclass is not serializable, then object serialization will work only if the superclass has a no-argument constructor. In this case, when the object is reconstituted, all information in the superclass will be lost: the state of the superclass will be initialized by calling the no-argument constructor. The no-argument constructor must be accessible by the target class (i.e., it cannot be private).

Ensure that the object state will be reconstituted correctly

When an object is serialized, the data in any transient instance variable is lost, as is the data in any superclass that is not serializable. When the object is reconstituted, the developer must ensure that the state of the reconstituted object is correct by compensating for this missing data. In addition, static variables have nothing to do with a specific object, so their value is not included with a serialized object.

If nothing is done, the missing data will have its default value: transient instance variables will be assigned their default value, and instance variables in non-serializable superclasses will be assigned a value by calling the no-argument constructor of the superclass. In many cases, this is good enough, and the developer need not take any explicit action. Otherwise, the developer must override certain methods to provide the correct serialization behavior.

For Serializable objects, use the writeObject() method to save any information that will help to reconstitute the object correctly. In typical usage, your writeObject() method should first call the defaultWriteObject() method, which will serialize all nontransient instance variables. You can leave out that call and serialize all those fields explicitly, but that's usually a lot of work. The writeObject() method should then write out any other data desired: you could, for example, write out transient variables in an encrypted format. For nonserializable superclasses, you can sometimes use accessor methods to retrieve enough state to reconstitute the superclass.

When you reconstitute a `Serializable` object, use the `readObject()` method. You must program this method to read data symmetrically to the `writeObject()` method: if you provided the default data, you must use the `defaultReadObject()` method to process that data. If you then wrote an encrypted `transient` variable, you must read in the data, decrypt it, and assign the result to the `transient` variable—and so on, until you've read all the data that the object originally wrote. The `readObject()` method is free to perform any other initialization operations it wants to: if there were `transient` variables that you did not process in the `writeObject()` method, the `readObject()` method could assign some usable value to them.

For `Externalizable` objects, the procedure is similar, except that to write data, you use the `writeExternal()` method. The stream passed to this method has a different interface than the stream passed to the `writeObject()` method, with the result that there is no way to write the default values for an object that is externalizable: you must explicitly write all data that you're interested in reconstituting. Similarly, the `readExternal()` method is used to reconstitute the object, and it must explicitly read all data in the same order in which it was written via the `writeExternal()` method. Unlike a serializable object, an externalizable object never serializes its superclass (even if the superclass is serializable); implementors of the `writeExternal()` and `readExternal()` methods must take care of that detail.

Note that the state of the reconstituted object may be different than the state of the original object. This is neither good nor bad, but it is an important point to consider when you work with serialized objects.

A Serializable Object

Here are two classes that show how you can program an object to save and reconstitute itself correctly. First, a class that is not serializable:

```
public class NotSerializableClass {

    protected int x;

    // If this constructor did not exist, we could not create a
    // serializable subclass
    protected NotSerializableClass() {
    }

    protected NotSerializableClass(int x) {
        this.x = x;
    }

    public int getX() {
        return x;
    }
}
```

This class is a wrapper for `NotSerializableClass` that makes it serializable:

```java
import java.io.*;

public class SerializableClass extends NotSerializableClass
            implements Serializable {

    transient private int nCalls;
    transient private int y;

    // Since this class is serializable, it does not need a no-arg
    // constructor
    public SerializableClass(int x, int y) {
        super(x);
        this.y = y;
    }

    public int getX() {
        nCalls++;
        return super.getX();
    }

    public int getY() {
        nCalls++;
        return y;
    }

    public int getNCalls() {
        return nCalls;
    }

    private void writeObject(ObjectOutputStream oos) throws IOException {
        oos.defaultWriteObject();
        oos.writeObject(new Integer(y + 13));
        oos.writeInt(x);
    }

    private void readObject(ObjectInputStream ois)
                            throws ClassNotFoundException, IOException {
        ois.defaultReadObject();
        y = ((Integer) ois.readObject()).intValue() - 13;
        x = ois.readInt();
        nCalls = 5;
    }
}
```

There are three pieces of data that we must handle explicitly here:

- The instance variable x in the nonserializable superclass, which we read and write as an int.

- The instance variable y, which we "encrypt" by adding and subtracting 13.

- The instance variable nCalls, which we arbitrarily reconstitute with a value of 5 (note that this case is asymmetric between the readObject() and writeObject() methods).

Object serialization is very clever about instance variables and will read or write an object only once to a particular stream. This means that you can successfully serialize objects that refer to each other (like a circularly linked list), despite the infinite loop that might otherwise occur in a naive recursive algorithm. On the other hand, there is a slight performance penalty to this implementation, so object serialization is sometimes slow. In addition, it means that object output streams can become sources of memory leaks, since they hold a reference to every object written to them unless they are periodically reset (which RMI does automatically).

Versioning

The serialized version of a class is dependent upon the interface to that class as well as the instance variables that make up the class. This means that if the class changes, serialized versions of it are not compatible—even if the change doesn't affect the data of the class. For example, adding a definition of the equals( ) method to a class that previously inherited that implementation from its superclass will cause object serialization to think that the class definition has changed.

In general, the class definition that is used to serialize an object must be identical to the class definition that is used when the object is deserialized. This compatibility problem most often creeps up when objects are serialized to some permanent store and retrieved at a later date (when the class definition has changed).

When you change a class definition, you can take steps to ensure that the new definition is compatible with previously serialized objects of that class by defining a special variable in the class as follows:

```
public static final long serialVersionUID = XXXL;
```

The value to substitute for XXX can be obtained by running the *serialver* program on the class before you make any changes to it. If a class does not contain this UID, it is calculated when it is first needed, which is a time-consuming operation. So as soon as your class is stable, you may want to add its UID to save some time when your class is first serialized.

A Simple RMI Example

In this section, we'll present our first RMI example. This example will follow the structure of all examples that we'll present in this book: we must prepare two different directories of source code, one for the client and one for the server. There is always at least one file that is common between the client and server; to make things simple we copy the file between the directories, though you could place the common file(s) in a single directory and set your classpath accordingly. The files used for this example are shown in Example 3-1.

Example 3-1: A Simple RMI Example

```
Common classes
    ConvertService (new)
Server classes
    ConvertServiceImpl (new)
Client classes
    ConvertClient (new)
```

The files in this case are all new, but as we make successive changes to the example by introducing new features, we'll often reuse code from previous examples.

So in these tables, we'll list the example from which we're reusing the code when the code has not changed.

Remote Interfaces

Object serialization is the means by which RMI exchanges non-remote objects between client and server. Now we'll look into exactly what a remote object is. In order for the client and server to be able to operate on the same object, they must agree upon a common interface for that object. That interface is (usually) one that extends the java.rmi.Remote interface. For example, a server that converts integers into strings would have this interface:

```
import java.rmi.*;

public interface ConvertService extends Remote {
    public String convert(int i) throws RemoteException;
}
```

Remote interfaces have the following properties:

- They must extend the java.rmi.Remote interface. The Remote interface is an empty interface; it is used as a type identifier by RMI.

- Every method in the interface must throw java.rmi.RemoteException. They may optionally throw any other exception.

RMI Server Code

A remote object is an object that implements a remote interface. This separation between implementation and interface is very important in RMI and in Jini: the interface specifies the operations that the client may perform on the object, and the interface is the only piece of code that the client must have available at compile time.

There are several strategies for implementing a remote interface, but the simplest one—and by far the most widely used—is to extend the java.rmi.server.UnicastRemoteObject class. A unicast remote object takes care of all of the plumbing necessary to send a reference of the remote object between client and server; it also takes care of the details necessary to invoke method calls between the two. One alternative is to use the static exportObject() method of the UnicastRemoteObject class.

A typical remote object looks like this:

```
import java.rmi.*;
import java.rmi.server.*;

public class ConvertServiceImpl extends UnicastRemoteObject
                                implements ConvertService {

    public ConvertServiceImpl() throws RemoteException {
    }

    // Called by the RMI infrastructure when the client invokes the
```

```
    // remote method
    public String convert(int i) throws RemoteException {
        return new Integer(i).toString();
    }

    public static void main(String[] args) throws Exception {
        // Create an instance of the server and bind it into the
        // naming service. Clients that know the name of the service
        // can then look it up by name.
        ConvertServiceImpl csi = new ConvertServiceImpl();
        Naming.rebind("ConvertService", (Remote) csi);
    }
}
```

There are a few important points about this implementation:

- The constructor of the UnicastRemoteObject class throws RemoteException, so constructors of our object must also throw the exception. A remote exception typically indicates that the underlying network infrastructure to support the remote call could not be created.

- The methods of this class will execute on the server, so any resources that they need must be available to the server.

- Each method may execute concurrently on behalf of several clients. Each client will make a connection in a separate thread, so simultaneous calls from clients will execute concurrently. You must implement any necessary synchronization in the server to account for that.

Starting and stopping the server is a topic that we'll explore more in depth in later chapters. Finding servers is one of the main topics of Jini, and the technique that we use here is one that we'll abandon as soon as we delve into the Jini APIs themselves. But if you want to play with this simple RMI server, you can use the standard *rmiregistry* facility that comes with Java. The code to do that is shown in the main() method of our server.

The java.rmi.Naming class is the class used to interoperate with *rmiregistry* and is the class that we'll replace with Jini-specific code later (when we'll use the Jini lookup service instead of *rmiregistry*).

Stubs and skeletons

A remote object is serialized in a special manner. Rather than making a copy of the object and shipping the object over the wire as we discussed before, remote objects are sent by "reference." In a strict sense, there is no way to send an actual object reference between two virtual machines, so what happens instead is that a special object called a *stub* object is generated for the remote object. The stub object is serialized and sent to the client. The stub object then communicates with a *skeleton* object that remains on the server. This makes the object appear to be passed by reference.

To the developer, this all happens transparently: the client gets an object reference and executes a method on it. Meanwhile, on the server, the appropriate method is invoked automatically; the server developer is unaware that the invocation actually came from the skeleton object. Figure 3-1 shows this in action: the developer writes only the code in the non-shaded portion of the call. All the underlying communication is handled by the stub and skeleton code, which is automatically generated for you.

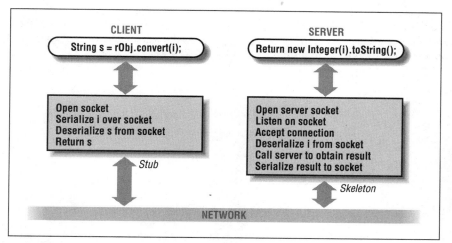

Figure 3–1: Stubs and skeletons are transparent to the developer

In Java 2, this mechanism was changed slightly: rather than a stub on the client that communicates with a skeleton on the server, RMI stubs are now able to communicate directly to the server (without need of a skeleton class). For the most part, this change is transparent to developers, who may still want to generate both stubs and skeletons for compatibility with Java 1.1. But the option now exists to generate these new stub classes if you know that your server will run only in a Java 2 environment. Since Jini requires the Java 2 environment, your Jini code can certainly opt to generate the new style of stubs; when we show an example later, that's the route we'll take.

RMI Naming URLs

RMI (and the Naming class) uses a URL to name its services. Both the client and server must use the same absolute URL to refer to the same object. The protocol of this URL is rmi, the hostname is the host that is running *rmiregistry* (the default for which is localhost), the port number is the port on which *rmiregistry* is running (the default for which is 1099) and the filename is the name of the service. If any piece of the URL is missing, then the Naming class fills it in automatically; hence the string "ConvertService" is equivalent to the URL *rmi://localhost:1099/ConvertService*.

RMI Client Code

Clients of RMI servers need to do two things: they must find the remote object that they wish to work with, and they must invoke methods on that object. Finding the object is something that is easier within the province of Jini, though for now we'll show the appropriate calls (using the Naming class) to find the object in the *rmiregistry*. And invoking methods on the object is the same as invoking a method on any ordinary object. So a simple client looks like this:

```
import java.rmi.*;

public class ConvertClient {
    public static void main(String[] args) throws Exception {
        ConvertService cs =
                (ConvertService) Naming.lookup("ConvertService");
        try {
            System.out.println(cs.convert(5));
        } catch (RemoteException re) {
            System.out.println("Couldn't convert integer " + re);
        }
    }
}
```

The lookup( ) method returns the object reference that we're interested in operating on. We don't know what class this object actually is (it happens to be ConvertServiceImpl_Stub), but we do know its interface, so we can cast it accordingly and invoke the convert( ) method on it.

Running the Example from One Directory

If this is your first exposure to RMI, it is simplest to run the example by placing all the code in the same directory and running everything from that directory. That way, you can deal with the code issues first; later, you can deal with the issues that are required when the client code and server code are in separate directories (and on separate machines). So we'll show first how to run everything from one directory, and then how to run the example in a true distributed fashion.

In order to run our example, here are the necessary steps:

1. Place all the files (*ConvertService.java*, *ConvertServiceImpl.java*, and *Convert-ServiceClient.java*) into a single directory.

2. Compile all the classes:

        piccolo% javac *.java

3. Generate the stub class:

        piccolo% rmic -v1.2 ConvertServiceImpl

    A stub class must be generated for every class that implements a remote interface (just the ConvertServiceImpl class, in our case). This will generate the class ConvertServiceImpl_Stub. Note that the argument to *rmic* is the class name and not the filename (that is, there is no *.class*).

If you use RMI outside of a Jini environment, leave out the *-v1.2* argument to *rmic*. An additional class will be generated (in our case, `ConvertService-Impl_Skel`).

4. Run *rmiregistry*:

```
piccolo% rmiregistry
```

Note that *rmiregistry* must be able to load the server classes (including stub classes). So for now, you must run it from the same directory as the compiled classes. In general, that's not the correct way to set up an RMI environment, but it's easier to get your first example running this way.

This command does not exit. You must run it in a separate window, or in the background if your OS supports it.

5. Run the server:

```
piccolo% java ConvertServiceImpl
```

This command does not exit. You must run it in a separate window, or in the background if your OS supports it.

6. Run the client (and receive its output):

```
piccolo% java ConvertClient
5
```

Transporting Code

In our simple example, we assumed that the client and server were compiled together and ran with the same classpath. This wasn't strictly necessary: the client needed to know the interface of the server at compile time, but it didn't need its implementation. One of the key benefits of RMI—and one that is particularly important in a Jini environment—is that the client could have downloaded the implementation classes as it needed to, on demand from the server.

Code transporting is a fundamental feature of a Jini network. So we'll develop an example here that shows how it works. This example will also show how to set up a client and server that are run from separate directories (that can even be on separate machines). That means that we'll need two sets of files as shown in Example 3-2.

Example 3-2: An RMI Service with Dynamic Code Loading

```
Common classes
    ComplexNumber (new)
    ComplexNumberFactory (new)
Server classes
    ComplexNumberFactoryImpl (new)
Client classes
    ComplexNumberClient (new)
```

In our previous example, the client eventually needed the implementation of the `ConvertServiceImpl_Stub` class (though that was transparent to the developer); the client would have downloaded that code from the server had it not been in the client's classpath. To make things a little clearer, we'll try a slightly different example.

We'll start with two interfaces. Note that the interface files are shared between client and server: this is a common requirement for RMI and Jini services.

Our first interface is for a complex number:

```
public interface ComplexNumber {
    public double getReal();
    public double getImaginary();
    public void setReal(double r);
    public void setImaginary(double i);
}
```

And our second defines a service that can return instances of complex numbers:

```
import java.rmi.*;

public interface ComplexNumberFactory extends Remote {
    public ComplexNumber getInstance(double r, double i)
                                     throws RemoteException;
}
```

Note that the ComplexNumberFactory interface is a remote interface, but the ComplexNumber interface is not, so when the complex number factory returns a complex number, the actual object is serialized and sent to the client.

Here's our complex number factory implementation. Since the ComplexNumberImpl class has package protection, we've put it into the same file as the ComplexNumberFactoryImpl class:

```
import java.rmi.*;
import java.rmi.server.*;
import java.io.*;

// This package class is the class definition of a complex number
// Instances of this class (as well as the class itself) will
// be sent to the client when the client calls the getInstance()
// method
class ComplexNumberImpl implements ComplexNumber, Serializable {
    private double real, imaginary;

    public double getReal() {
        return real;
    }

    public double getImaginary() {
        return imaginary;
    }

    public void setReal(double r) {
        real = r;
    }

    public void setImaginary(double i) {
        imaginary = i;
    }

    public String toString() {
```

```
                return real + " + " + imaginary + "i";
        }
}

public class ComplexNumberFactoryImpl extends UnicastRemoteObject
                                       implements ComplexNumberFactory {

    public ComplexNumberFactoryImpl() throws RemoteException {
    }

    public ComplexNumber getInstance(double r, double i) {
        ComplexNumberImpl cni = new ComplexNumberImpl();
        cni.setReal(r);
        cni.setImaginary(i);
        return cni;
    }

    public static void main(String[] args) throws Exception {
        ComplexNumberFactoryImpl cnfi = new ComplexNumberFactoryImpl();
        Naming.rebind("ComplexNumberFactory", (Remote) cnfi);
    }
}
```

Under typical usage, the client and server will be on completely different machines. Their local classpaths will each have the classes illustrated in Figure 3-2: they must share the interface classes, but everything else is local to either the client or the server.

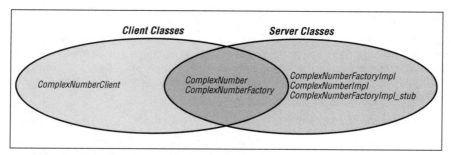

Figure 3-2: Class layout for client and server

When the client receives a complex number from the server, it will receive an instance of the ComplexNumberImpl class. Hence, this class definition must be provided at runtime to the client.

So when the server returns an instance of the ComplexNumberImpl class to the client, it must arrange to deliver the class file for that class as well, and the client must then dynamically load that class file. Java has all the facilities we need to do this (think of an applet loading classes from a web server), and RMI hides most of the details from us: we don't have to worry about annotating the serialized object or loading bytes into a class loader or anything else like that. We merely have to set up our environment to support downloading code in this manner. As we mentioned in Chapter 1, this is another reason why it's preferable to write Jini servers in RMI—simply because those elaborate details are hidden from you.

When the server serializes the ComplexNumberImpl object, it will also send to the client the value of its java.rmi.server.codebase property; that value is a URL. When the client deserializes the object, it will use that URL to load the class file that defines the object. So the simplest thing to do in our case is to put the ComplexNumberImpl class on a web server somewhere. Then when we run the server, we must set the java.rmi.server.codebase property so that it points to that location. Jini comes with a simple web server that we will use for this purpose; you can use that, or a web server that you already have running.

There's one more complication here: the RMI classes that automatically load class definitions with this technique will insist that a security manager be installed into the application that the code is being loaded into (the client, in this case). So we must set a security manager in our client, which now looks like this:

```
import java.rmi.*;

public class ComplexNumberClient {
    public static void main(String[] args) throws Exception {
        System.setSecurityManager(new RMISecurityManager());
        ComplexNumberFactory cnf = (ComplexNumberFactory)
                Naming.lookup("ComplexNumberFactory");
        ComplexNumber cn = cnf.getInstance(5, 8);
        System.out.println(cn);
    }
}
```

Running the Downloadable Code Example

Running this example is much different than our previous example. To begin, we must separate the Java source files onto different machines (or at least different directories) according to the scheme we illustrated previously. For this example, we'll put the client files onto machine client and the server files onto machine server. Then we follow the next steps:

1. Compile the source files:

    ```
    client% javac ComplexNumber.java ComplexNumberFactory.java
                  ComplexNumberClient.java
    server% javac CompexNumber.java ComplexNumberFactory.java
                  ComplexNumberImpl.java ComplexNumberFactoryImpl.java
    ```

2. On the server, create the necessary stub:

    ```
    server% rmic -v1.2 ComplexNumberFactoryImpl
    ```

3. On the server, start *rmiregistry*. A subtle point here is that *rmiregistry* must obtain the stub files from the server in the same way that they will be delivered to the client, so we must make sure that *rmiregistry* does not have any of the server class files on its classpath. We do that by changing to another directory:

    ```
    server% cd /
    server% rmiregistry
    ```

    rmiregistry does not exit. You must start this command in a separate window, or you must start it in the background if your OS supports it.

---

4. Start the HTTP server that we'll use to download code. We'll use the HTTP
    server that comes with Jini and run it on port 8086:

    ```
    server% cd <back to original directory>
    server% java -jar /files/jini1_0/lib/tools.jar -dir . -port 8086
    ```

    Make sure that the server class files are in the current directory (.) or give a
    different *-dir* argument.

    This command does not exit. You must run it in a separate window or in the
    background if your OS supports it.

5. Start the complex number factory server, specifying the correct property from
    which code may be downloaded:

    ```
    server% java -Djava.rmi.server.codebase=http://server:8086/
                 ComplexNumberFactoryImpl
    ```

6. Now we can run the client, giving it the correct RMI URL to find the server,
    and get its output:

    ```
    client% java -Djava.security.policy=/files/jini1_0/java.policy.all
                 ComplexNumberClient
    8.0 + 5.0i
    ```

RMI

A lot of code transfer happens in this step: the client locally loads the Com-
plexNumberClient class, then loads (via HTTP) the ComplexNumberFactory-
Impl_Stub and ComplexNumberImpl classes. Note that the client did not need
to specify anything about where to load the classes from: that information
came from the server, since it is the server that is supplying the classes.

This is the procedure that will be used to run most of the remaining examples in
the book, including the Jini examples.

Activation

In our examples so far, we've started the RMI servers by hand and they've run forever. As an alternative, the RMI Activation daemon (*rmid*) allows us to register
servers; the daemon (which must run forever) then starts servers on an as-needed
basis, and the servers can terminate themselves when they are idle. This reduces
the resources required by a single machine, since it need run only active remote
objects.

To use activation, services are registered with *rmid*. In addition, the service must
make itself available to clients in some way. In this chapter, we use *rmiregistry*,
but in the remainder of the book we'll use the Jini lookup service for that. When a
request comes for the service, *rmid* starts a new VM that runs the service. If the
service VM exits, *rmid* will restart the service in a new VM when the service gets
its next request. There are two major benefits to this approach:

*   It reduces the load on a machine. If our system has thousands of seldom-used
    objects, we can arrange to run only those that are needed at a particular time.

*   It allows services to be persistent across a machine failure or reboot. *rmid* will
    keep track of services that have registered with it and can recreate this state
    when it restarts.

Sun's implementation of Jini makes heavy use of activation; their implementation of the Jini lookup service, for example, is just an activatable RMI service. Services that are activatable look just like regular RMI services with the following exceptions:

- They extend `java.rmi.activation.Activatable` rather than `UnicastRemoteObject`. This is not strictly required, as the object can use the static `exportObject( )` method of the `Activatable` class instead.

- Their constructor must have two arguments: an activation ID and a marshalled data object.
- Their constructor must call a constructor of the `Activatable` class, passing it the activation ID, the port number to listen on (typically 0, meaning a system port is chosen), and other optional arguments. If the `exportObject( )` method is being used, then these arguments are passed to that method rather than a constructor of the `Activatable` class.

In Example 3-3, we'll start with our convert service and change it into an activatable service that uses the following files:

Example 3–3: An Activatable RMI Service

```
Common classes
    ConvertService (listed in Example 3-1)
Server classes
    ConvertServiceImpl (modified from Example 3-1)
Client classes
    ConvertClient (listed in Example 3-1)
```

Note that only the service implementation changes. To change our server into an activatable server, we make the following changes from Example 3-1:

```
import java.rmi.*;
import java.rmi.activation.*;
import java.rmi.server.*;
import java.util.*;

public class ConvertServiceImpl extends Activatable
                        implements ConvertService {

    public ConvertServiceImpl(ActivationID id, MarshalledObject data)
```

Marshalled Objects

Activation uses the `java.rmi.MarshalledObject` class for some of its parameters. A marshalled object is essentially a serialized object: you create a marshalled object by passing a serializable object to its constructor, and the marshalled object stores the serializable object in an internal byte array. You can retrieve the original object by calling the `get( )` method of the marshalled object. Marshalled objects themselves can be serialized; they are often used to save a serialized object to a file.

There is one big difference between a marshalled object and serialized object: the marshalled object contains an annotation that lists the location from which the class was loaded. If the class was loaded from an RMI server, this annotation is the value of the `java.rmi.server.codebase` property.

This difference is important when you reconstitute an object. If you deserialize a regular object, the class definition for that object must be on your classpath. If you call the `get( )` method of a marshalled object, it will load the class definition for the internal object from the original location from which the class definition came.

When *rmid* saves information about an object, it does so in a marshalled data object, so that when *rmid* restarts, it can remember the location that the class definition came from. If your activatable server saves its own state (perhaps using Sun's reliable log class), it must do the same thing.

Marshalled objects also reduce the amount of code an intermediate service needs. The Jini lookup service, for instance, passes objects around as marshalled objects so that the lookup service doesn't need to download all the classes that define the object.

```
                                throws RemoteException {
        super(id, 0);
    }

    public String convert(int i) throws RemoteException {
        return new Integer(i).toString();
    }

    public static void main(String[] args) throws Exception {
        Properties props = new Properties();
        props.put("java.security.policy", args[1]);

        ActivationGroupDesc agd =
                new ActivationGroupDesc(props, null);
        ActivationGroupID agi =
                ActivationGroup.getSystem().registerGroup(agd);
        ActivationGroup.createGroup(agi, agd, 0);

        ActivationDesc ad =
            new ActivationDesc("ConvertServiceImpl", args[0], null);
```

```
        Remote r = (Remote) Activatable.register(ad);

        Naming.rebind("ConvertService", r);
        System.exit(0);
    }
}
```

To start an activatable service, we must do the following:

- Create an activation group. Each group can hold one or more references to activatable objects; the entire group is activated at once in a new VM.

- Create a properties object that contains properties that should be passed to the new VM. Each element in the properties object will be passed to the new VM with a *-D* argument. You should specify at least a Java security policy file for the new VM.

- Create an activation descriptor, which contains the class name of the server, the code base where the implementation of the server can be found, and the marshalled object that will be passed to the server's constructor.

- Register the activation descriptor with *rmid*.

- Register the service with *rmiregistry* (or later with the Jini lookup service).

Note that the server now exits after registration. Once the service is registered, *rmid* will start it in a new VM when the service is actually needed.

Running the Activatable Server

To run this new server, we follow the same steps as in Example 3-2 with these two changes:

1. In addition to running *rmiregistry*, we must also start *rmid*:

    ```
    server% cd /
    server% rmid
    ```

    When it starts, *rmid* will look for a directory called *log* in which it saved its previous state (that is, all the services that it has previously registered). If you restart *rmid* and you want it to start without any saved state, make sure to remove the *log* directory.

    As with *rmiregistry*, make sure that *rmid* does not load any classes from its local classpath, which is why we've started it in the root directory. Also, *rmid* does not exit, so you must start it in a separate window or in the background if your OS supports it.

2. To start the server, we must provide additional arguments: the codebase where we're loading code from, and the policy file to use for the security manager. Note that the codebase and policy file are both an argument to the

program, which tells *rmid* how to run the new service VM, and are also set as properties on the command line, which controls how the initial registration runs:

```
server% cd <back to original directory>
server% java -Djava.rmi.server.codebase=http://server:8086/
        -Djava.security.policy=/files/jini1_0/java.policy.all
        ConvertServiceImpl http://server:8086/
        /files/jini1_0/java.policy.all
```

The remaining steps are the same (including the command line used to start the client).

Terminating Activatable Services

Once *rmid* starts a VM with its services, that VM will continue to run as long as the activatable objects in the server remain active. To mark a service object as inactive, call its inactive( ) method, which returns a boolean value. If the returned value is true, the object has been marked as inactive; if the value returned is false, then the object could not be marked as inactive because there was a client call in progress that needed that object.

The inactive( ) method can return true even if there are clients that still have references to the remote object, as long as a call involving that reference is not pending. This is not a problem, since a subsequent call from the client will just cause *rmid* to start a new VM with the activatable object; the client will be unaware that any of this has happened (except that it takes a certain amount of time to start the new VM, so the call will take longer than might otherwise be expected). If you want to wait until there are no clients that have outstanding references to the server, then your server should implement the java.rmi.activation.Unreferenced interface. Then when its unreferenced( ) method is called, the remote object knows that no clients have an outstanding reference to it; this is often a good time to call the inactive( ) method.*

Once the inactive( ) method has returned true, the object is actually inactive. When the next request comes in for the object, *rmid* will start another VM in which the object will run.

Preserving State

When *rmid* starts a new VM, it instantiates new activatable objects to run in that VM. So an activatable server that runs, marks its objects as inactive, exits, and is restarted will lose any state information that it might have had.

In order to recreate this state, an activatable object must save its state before it is marked inactive and reconstitute that state when it is constructed. It arranges to do that through the marshalled object parameter of its constructor: this data can contain whatever information is necessary for the activatable object to recreate its state. Often, this object is the name of a file that the object can use to store serialized data. The marshalled object is constant between activations of the server: you

---

* There's a race condition here, so that there's no guarantee that the inactive( ) method will return true.

References to Remote Objects

In RMI, two basic objects are involved: the actual remote object that lives on the server and the stub object that is sent to the client. Internally to the RMI code, the server keeps a reference to the remote object, so that the remote object won't be garbage-collected while the client has a reference to it.

The mechanics of this are hidden from the developer, but it uses essentially the same mechanics as the Jini leasing system that we'll discuss in Chapter 5, *Leasing* (although RMI uses a different implementation for its leasing classes). This means that the internal reference will be cleared on the server when either of the following happens:

1. The stub object on the client is garbage-collected and its finalizer is run; the finalizer calls the server and tells it to delete its internal reference.

2. The client fails to renew its lease with the server (which can happen if the client exits, or if there's a network failure between the client and server). By default, the server tells the client to renew its lease every five minutes and grants a lease with an actual duration of ten minutes. Those values can be changed by specifying on the command line of the server the following properties:

```
-Dsun.rmi.dgc.checkInterval=300000
-Djava.rmi.dgc.leaseValue=600000
```

can use a filename to specify where the server should save its data, but you can't use the marshalled object itself to hold the changed state.

Sun's Jini implementation comes with a reliable log class; this class ensures that data written to the file (and restored from the file) is transactionally sound. An object written to the log will either be written fully or not at all, so that a program reading the log will receive coherent data. More details of this facility are given in Chapter 8, *Miscellaneous Classes*. We present a fully activatable Jini service in Chapter 11, *Helper Services*.

Proxying RMI Services

The final point we'll make about RMI is that while we think it is the most convenient mechanism available to implement a remote service, it is not the only one. As a result, RMI interfaces are not generally used to specify the interface of a Jini service. Instead, Jini service interfaces are defined as generically as possible, so that different implementors of the service can use different techniques to implement the service.

For all of our Jini service examples, we'll follow the common technique of defining a generic interface and then implementing it with an RMI proxy. As a result, Example 3-4, our final example of this chapter, requires the following files:

Example 3-4: A Proxied RMI Service

```
Common classes
    ConvertService (modified from Example 3-1)
Server classes
    ConvertServiceImpl (modified from Example 3-1)
    ConvertServiceProxy (new)
Client classes
    ConvertClient (used in Example 3-3; listed in Example 3-1)
```

To change our example interface into a generic one, define it as follows:

```
import java.rmi.*;

public interface ConvertService {
    public String convert(int i) throws RemoteException;
}
```

This interface no longer extends the Remote interface, which frees it from a depen-dence on RMI. Note that even though the method in the interface throws a remote exception, it is not tied to a particular implementation. The RemoteException class is simply a useful exception class that happens to exist in the java.rmi package, but it does not use RMI in any manner. So this interface is still generic: if you implement this service using sockets and your own protocol, you could simply wrap up any socket or I/O exceptions into a remote exception.

You should take time at the beginning of your work to make sure that your ser-vice interface throws remote exceptions appropriately. The alternative is to take the path set out by CORBA: when there's an underlying network or other failure in a CORBA method invocation, a runtime exception is thrown, so that CORBA inter-faces have no explicit exception handling. But Jini is designed for a world in which network failures are common, especially given the dynamic service environ-ment that it wants to support. So Jini services generally require that you explicitly handle communications failure by catching and dealing with remote exceptions.

Implementing an RMI proxy for this interface requires a trivial proxy interface that extends both the remote and service interfaces:

```
import java.rmi.*;

// Combined interface to wrap the generic ConvertService interface into
// an RMI interface
interface ConvertServiceProxy extends Remote, ConvertService {
}
```

And now our service implementation, based on Example 3-1, implements this proxy interface:

```
import java.rmi.*;
import java.rmi.server.*;

public class ConvertServiceImpl extends UnicastRemoteObject
                            implements ConvertServiceProxy {

    public ConvertServiceImpl() throws RemoteException {
    }

    public String convert(int i) throws RemoteException {
```

```
        return new Integer(i).toString();
    }

    public static void main(String[] args) throws Exception {
        ConvertServiceImpl csi = new ConvertServiceImpl();
        Naming.rebind("ConvertService", csi);
    }
}
```

No changes at all are required in the client.

What all this means is that when the client receives the object from *rmiregistry* or the Jini lookup service, it will get an RMI stub that implements the ConvertService interface as well as implementing the ConvertServiceProxy interface (which the client knows nothing about). All of that is transparent to the client, who is happy to get an object that implements the ConvertService interface. The ConvertServiceProxy class file must be placed on the webserver so that the client may retrieve it from the server's java.rmi.server.codebase.

Summary

Though its use is not required, RMI is one of the simplest of Java's distributed object mechanisms with which we can implement Jini services. RMI provides a number of facilities that are well-suited for a dynamic environment: the ability to support distributed method calls easily, the ability for clients to download implementation code transparently, and the ability to be started and stopped on an as-needed basis all make RMI an ideal choice for implementing Jini services. So even though most Jini interfaces will not explicitly require the use of RMI—which is to say that they will not directly extend the Remote interface—we'll use RMI as the basis for almost all our Jini examples.

In the next chapter, we'll start our examination of Jini. In particular, we'll turn this RMI service into a Jini service by learning how to register it with the Jini lookup service and we will modify our client in order to obtain the service from the Jini lookup service.

CHAPTER 4

Basic Jini Programming

In the last chapter, we developed an understanding of RMI and how it behaves as an object-oriented distributed framework. With RMI, we have the capability for applications on any host to invoke methods on objects located on another host. An important feature about this framework is that the underlying infrastructure is well hidden.

That grounding in a distributed object model gives us the necessary background to begin our exploration of Jini programming, which we'll do in this chapter. We'll cover the implementation of a Jini service and a Jini client, and while our initial service will be based on RMI, we'll also show how to write a Jini service that uses other techniques to communicate between the client and server, and one that actually performs all of its work in the client itself. This ability to take advantage of different service implementations is one of the strong benefits of Jini.

The Jini Lookup Service

From now on, we'll be using the Jini lookup service in our examples. In order to understand the Jini lookup service, let's examine some of the more important differences between the RMI registry (and other distributed object registries) and the Jini lookup service:

- The Jini lookup service is found dynamically. A registry usually requires that clients know the registry's location—its hostname and network port.

    While the Jini lookup service provides an equivalent to the location-dependent RMI Naming class (the net.jini.core.discovery.LookupLocator class), it also provides a discovery system on top of the lookup service. With the discovery system, clients of the Jini lookup service do not need the location of the lookup service: they automatically discover the location at runtime.

    As we discussed in Chapter 1, *Introduction to Jini*, you'll typically be able to find Jini lookup services only on your local network. The underlying discovery protocol that is used to find Jini lookup services is based on multicasting, so you'll be able to find lookup services automatically only as far as your network will route multicast packets (which WAN routers often do not). But you can always use a lookup locator to find a lookup service anywhere on your local- or wide-area network (providing you know the service's location).

- The Jini lookup service can store any serializable object; distributed object registries can usually only store specific types of objects (e.g., RMI stubs).

This makes Jini protocol-independent: the Jini lookup service stores arbitrary objects, whether they are from other distributed environments or just objects that will run within the client itself. This is a significant benefit of Jini as compared to other distributed systems.

- Jini finds objects by their type; objects registries usually use an arbitrary name (i.e., a string) to store the remote object.

With RMI, the client and server must use the same fully-qualified URL for the remote object—the server uses that string to store the object in the registry and the client uses it to retrieve the object. The Jini lookup service uses many techniques for the client to find objects that have been stored into the service. The most common of these techniques is by class type. With the Jini lookup service, the client simply specifies a class, superclass, interface, or combination of these. The service will return all objects that match the request.

The Jini lookup service also supports the concept of service IDs and attributes. The service ID is a unique identifier for the service; attributes allow for more specific matching of objects that match the particular class type. For example, a service that supports a particular printer or scanner interface specifies the name or location of the printer or scanner using attributes. With class types and attributes, we can find the specific service that we want; with a service ID, we can always return to that particular service.

- The Jini lookup service is dynamic; object registries are typically static.

Jini services should register themselves with all the lookup services that they discover and Jini clients should use the lookup services interchangeably. This removes the lookup service as a single point of failure. In addition, the Jini lookup service is designed so that service registrations are purged if those services unexpectedly terminate (i.e., the service fails to renew its lease). While something like the RMI registry can be used in the same fashion, this is not the norm and requires a great deal of work by the developer.

- The Jini lookup service is organized into groups.

The Jini lookup services are designed to cooperate; this means that multiple instances of the Jini lookup service will by default support all services on the network. However, the Jini lookup service also supports the concept of groups. Groups allow us to segregate services so that, for example, different departments may have individual services that are not shared between them.

The group(s) that a Jini lookup service supports are significant only during discovery. Once you've discovered a lookup service, you can see all the services that have joined the lookup service. So a lookup service that supports groups A and B will be discovered and joined by a conversion service attempting to locate group A, and a client that discovers the same lookup service by locating group B will see the service registration of the conversion service. In order to segregate lookup services completely, they must listen for distinct groups.

A Simple Service and Client

We'll begin our example by showing a complete service, its implementation, and a client that can use the service. All the features of a well-written Jini service will not be present in our initial implementation; as we work through this book, we'll add those additional features. Following our standard practice, we'll develop source in two directories as shown in Example 4-1.

Example 4-1: An Initial Jini Service and Client

```
Common classes
    ConvertService (listed in Example 3-4)
Service classes
    ConvertServiceImpl (modified from Example 3-4)
    ConvertServiceProxy (listed in Example 3-4)
    ServiceListener (new)
Client classes
    ServiceFinder (new)
    ConvertClient (modified from Example 3-4)
```

The Jini Service

We'll start by converting the RMI server object that we developed in Chapter 3, *Remote Method Invocation*, into a Jini service. To turn our existing code into a Jini service, we'll modify it so that it participates in Jini's discovery and join protocols as we outlined in Chapter 1: the service will use multicast discovery to find all lookup services on the network, and then join (register with) each of those services. So we need to develop two things: a class that handles discovery and a new implementation of the service itself.

Performing discovery and join

The details of the discovery and join protocols are handled for us by the Jini APIs (the LookupDiscovery class that we'll examine a little further on). All we need to do is create a new class (a discovery listener) that will deal with the asynchronous behavior of Jini's discovery system. This class will be alerted when our service discovers a lookup service and when our service needs to discard a lookup service. When we're notified of a new lookup service, we'll join it.

What happens under the covers is this: when our service starts, the Jini classes will send out a special packet that lookup services will respond to; this is how we find the initial set of lookup services. When new lookup services are added to the network, they send out a special packet the Jini classes will see; this is how our program finds out that new lookup services have been added to the network. In both cases, our discovery listener is notified of the presence of the lookup services.

If we encounter an error while talking to a particular lookup service, we must discard that service (it will then be able to be rediscovered if the lookup service recovers). Additionally, if we change the set of groups that we're interested in, lookup services that do not support the new set of groups must be discarded. In both cases, our discovery listener will be informed that the lookup service has been discarded. Here's the implementation of our discovery listener, a new class with this example:

```java
import java.rmi.*;
import java.util.*;
import net.jini.discovery.*;
import net.jini.core.lookup.*;

public class ServerListener implements DiscoveryListener {
    // Hashtable of registration leases keyed by the lookup service
    private Hashtable leases = new Hashtable();
    private ServiceItem item;          // Item to be registered with lookup
    private static final int ltime = 15*60*1000;   // 15 minutes

    public ServerListener(Object object) {
        item = new ServiceItem(null, object, null);
    }

    // Automatically called when new lookup service(s) are discovered
    public synchronized void discovered (DiscoveryEvent dev) {
        ServiceRegistrar[] lookup = dev.getRegistrars();
        // For each discovered service, see if we're already registered.
        // If not, register
        for (int i = 0; i < lookup.length; i++) {
            if (leases.containsKey(lookup[i]) == false) {
                // Not already registered
                try {
                    // Register
                    ServiceRegistration ret =
                                lookup[i].register(item, ltime);
                    // You must assign the serviceID based on what the
                    // lookup service returns
                    if (item.serviceID == null) {
                        item.serviceID = ret.getServiceID();
                    }
                    // Save this registration
                    // Note that we don't actually renew the leases yet
                    leases.put (lookup[i], ret);
                } catch (RemoteException ex) {
                    System.out.println("ServerListener error: " + ex);
                }
            }
            // else we were already registered in this service
        }
    }

    // Automatically called when lookup service(s) are
    // no longer available
    public synchronized void discarded(DiscoveryEvent dev) {
        ServiceRegistrar[] lookup = dev.getRegistrars();
        for (int i = 0; i < lookup.length; i++) {
            if (leases.containsKey(lookup[i]) == true) {
                // Remove the registration. If the lookup service comes
```

```
                    // back later, we'll re-register at that time.
                    leases.remove(lookup[i]);
                }
            }
        }
    }
```

The net.jini.discovery.DiscoveryListener interface supports two methods: discovered( ) and discarded( ). These methods will be called by the Jini lookup and discovery classes when new lookup services are found or a previously discovered lookup service is to be removed. They are passed a single parameter, a net.jini.discovery.DiscoveryEvent object.

When a new lookup service is detected, the discovered( ) method is called. An array of lookup services (net.jini.core.lookup.ServiceRegistrar objects) is returned from the getRegistrars( ) method of the DiscoveryEvent object. The first step is to determine if the lookup service that was found is unknown to us. This is why we have stored all lookup services along with their registrations into a hashtable: we can check the hashtable for the existence of the lookup service.

Once we've determined that we have a new lookup service, we must register our object with that service. To do that, we wrap it into a net.jini.core.lookup.ServiceItem object. To instantiate this service item, we need three things: the object that we will be placing into the lookup service, the unique service ID assigned to the object, and an array of attributes that can be used to further identify the object. In this case, we are passing null for both the service ID and the array of attributes. This means that there will be no attributes stored with this object, and the lookup service will provide the ID assigned to this service object. (We'll discuss the attributes in more detail later in this chapter.)

The service ID is used to distinguish the object when it appears in different lookup services. Our service object will be registered with multiple lookup servers, and other service objects with the same interface may also be registered in those lookup services. Clients need a way to distinguish all of these. If a client retrieves services of the same type from different lookup services, the client can tell whether the objects represent the same instance of the service by comparing the service IDs. In addition, the service ID provides a way for the client to ensure that it uses the same service: a client that wants to select a particular print service as its default printer needs to save only the service ID for that print service. Later, the client knows which print service to use by retrieving the correct service ID.

This means that we must register the same service ID with all lookup services. The actual registration with the lookup service is accomplished with the register( ) method. The two parameters that this method requires are the ServiceItem that we created earlier and an integer which represents the number of milliseconds for which we want the lookup service to grant our lease. We use 15 minutes here, but we'll discuss the notion of leasing a little bit later.

For now, what's important is the register( ) method will return a service registration object that contains, among other things, the service ID assigned to our service. We save that service ID into our service item so future registrations will use the same service ID. When we write a really robust Jini service, we'll actually save this service ID to a file, so if our service crashes, it will come back up with the same service ID (so clients that have saved the service ID of our service will still be able to find us); we'll show that process in Chapter 8, *Miscellaneous Classes*.

When a lookup service is to be discarded, the discarded( ) method of the discovery listener is called. An array of lookup services (ServiceRegistrar objects) is returned from the getRegistrars( ) method of the DiscoveryEvent object. We check the hashtable for the existence of each lookup service in the array and remove it.

The Service Implementation

Here's an implementation of our basic service, modified from Example 3-4:

```
import java.io.*;
import java.rmi.*;
import java.rmi.server.*;
import net.jini.discovery.*;

public class ConvertServiceImpl extends UnicastRemoteObject
                                implements ConvertServiceProxy {

    public ConvertServiceImpl() throws RemoteException {
    }

    public String convert(int i) throws RemoteException {
        return new Integer(i).toString();
    }

    public static void main(String[] args) throws Exception {
        System.setSecurityManager(new RMISecurityManager());

        // Start listening for lookup services
        String[] groups = new String[] { "" };
        LookupDiscovery reg = new LookupDiscovery(groups);
        // Create the instance of the service and register it
        // with all discovered lookup services
        ConvertServiceImpl csi =
                (ConvertServiceImpl) new ConvertServiceImpl();
        ServerListener sl = new ServerListener(csi);
        reg.addDiscoveryListener(sl);

    }
}
```

We have not made any changes to the operational behavior of the ConvertServiceImpl class: it is still using RMI as its transport and is supporting the same ConvertServiceProxy interface. The difference is how it is being registered with the lookup service. We now declare an array of groups, which in this example is a single group specified by a blank string. This is the default group for a Jini lookup service. Note that when Sun's tools like *reggie* specify "public" as the name of a group, they convert that string internally to a blank string so that those tools use the default lookup group.

The registration process starts by instantiating a net.jini.discovery.LookupDiscovery object with an instance of the ServerListener class that we have previously defined. The lookup discovery object is the Jini class that handles the discovery protocol and calls the server listener when it finds new or existing lookup groups.

The Jini Client

Unlike the server, creating the client is a little more complex than just using the Jini lookup service. On the server, the task of registering the object with the lookup service is well defined, and moving from a synchronous registration process to an asynchronous one was handled by a single ServerListener class. On the client, we could conceivably perform a lot more work.

In effect, we must redesign the client to take advantage of the Jini infrastructure. Whether a service is registered with one or many lookup services should have no effect on the server. But the client has many options: should the client use only the first service it finds, or load balance requests across all server objects found? Should the client worry about discarding lookup services that have failed and switch to alternate lookup services?

Those issues are beyond the scope of this quick-reference book. For now, we will write a class that simply returns the first matching service that it finds:

```
import java.io.*;
import java.rmi.*;
import java.util.*;
import net.jini.discovery.*;
import net.jini.core.lookup.*;
import net.jini.core.entry.*;

public class ServiceFinder implements DiscoveryListener {
    private static String[] publicGroup = new String[] { "" };
    private Vector returnObject = new Vector();

    private LookupDiscovery reg;
    private ServiceTemplate template;

    public ServiceFinder(Class serviceInterface) throws IOException {
        this(publicGroup, serviceInterface, (Entry[])null);
    }

    public ServiceFinder(Class serviceInterface, Entry attribute)
                    throws IOException {
        this(publicGroup, serviceInterface, new Entry[] { attribute });
    }

    public ServiceFinder(Class serviceInterface, Entry[] attributes)
                    throws IOException {
        this(publicGroup, serviceInterface, attributes);
    }

    public ServiceFinder(String[] groups, Class serviceInterface,
                    Entry[] attributes) throws IOException {
        // Construct the template here for matching in the lookup service
        // We don't use the template until we actually discover a service
        Class[] name = new Class[] { serviceInterface };
        template = new ServiceTemplate(null, name, attributes);

        // Create the facility to perform multicast discovery for all
```

```java
        // lookup services
        reg = new LookupDiscovery(groups);
        reg.addDiscoveryListener(this);
    }

    // Automatically called when a lookup service is discovered
    // (the listener callback of the addDiscoveryListener method)
    public synchronized void discovered(DiscoveryEvent dev) {
        ServiceRegistrar[] lookup = dev.getRegistrars();
        // We may have discovered one or more lookup services
        for (int i = 0; i < lookup.length; i++) {
            try {
                ServiceMatches items =
                    lookup[i].lookup(template, Integer.MAX_VALUE);
                // Each lookup service may have zero or more registered
                // servers that implement our desired template
                for (int j = 0; j < items.items.length; j++) {
                    if (items.items[j].service != null)
                        // Put each matching service into our vector
                        returnObject.addElement(items.items[j]);
                        // else the service item couldn't be deserialized
                        // so the lookup() method skipped it
                }
                notifyAll();
            } catch (RemoteException ex) {
                System.out.println("ServiceFinder Error: " + ex);
            }
        }
    }

    public synchronized void discarded(DiscoveryEvent dev) {
    }

    // This class is to be used by the client. It will return only
    // the first service object that satisfies the template request.
    public synchronized Object getObject() {
        while (returnObject.size() == 0) {
            try {
                wait();
            } catch (InterruptedException ex) {};
        }
        return ((ServiceItem)returnObject.elementAt(0)).service;
    }

    // If an error is encountered when using a service object, the client
    // should call this method.
    // A new object can then be retrieved from the getObject() method.
    public synchronized void errored(Object obj) {
        if ((obj != null) && (returnObject.size() != 0)) {
            if (obj.equals(
                    ((ServiceItem)returnObject.elementAt(0)).service)) {
                returnObject.removeElementAt(0);
            }
        }
    }
}
```

Just like the ServerListener class, our ServiceFinder class will search for lookup services. However, we don't actually need to keep track of the lookup services: once a lookup service is found, we just ask the lookup service for all services that match the client's interest. This matching is something that we will discuss throughout the remainder of this chapter.

If an object that matches the criteria is found, it is stored into a vector, and we wake up all threads that are waiting for the object. The threads that are waiting for the object will have called the getObject( ) method. So a client uses this class by instantiating it, calling its getObject( ) method to get the matching service, and invoking methods on that service.

The constructor(s) of this class build a net.jini.core.lookup.ServiceTemplate object. This is very similar to the ServiceItem object that we created on the server side. This template is used to search for the particular services. The parameters to the service template are for the three search criteria that we can use:

The service ID
> With this object, we can specify the exact service that we want to find. When we specify null (as we have here), we'll match any service ID.

An array of Class *objects*
> This parameter specifies the classes and interfaces that the service must extend or implement.

An array of attributes
> This parameter allows us to specify more details about the service we are looking for.

When we construct a client lookup object, we can also specify which groups the returned services must belong to; by default, we search in the default public group.

In addition to being a discovery listener, this class will also manage the LookupDiscovery object. This allows the client to instantiate and use a ServiceFinder object without dealing with the particulars of the Jini lookup system.

Once we have the template of the object that we are looking for, we can find the service object by using this template and calling the lookup( ) method of the lookup service (the ServiceRegistrar object). There are two signatures for this method. In the simpler form, only the first service is found—if no matching service is found, a null value will be returned. With the method that we are using (which contains an addition parameter that specifies the maximum number of matches), all the matching objects will be retrieved (up to the maximum number specified). This version returns a ServiceMatches object that contains an array of ServiceItem objects. The Jini API ensures that the lookup( ) method will not return a null array and that the length of that array will not be 0 (unless maxMatches was 0). But the individual elements of the array may contain null values, which indicates that a lookup service was found but that we can't deserialize the instance of the lookup service (which usually means that we forgot to install a security manager in the client, though it could also mean that the lookup service isn't correctly supplying its class definitions). Once we find a valid service objects, we store it in the returnObject vector.

Implementing the client is pretty simple. We provided a getObject( ) method that returns the first service object found. This is the object at the beginning of the vector. There will be no load balancing or testing to see if the object is still valid. Instead, we provide the errored( ) method. If the client catches a remote exception, it should call this method with the offending service object. The method will simply remove the object from the first position of the vector so that the client method can call the getObject( ) method to obtain an alternate service object. The client, based on Example 3-4, now looks like this:

```
import java.rmi.*;
import net.jini.discovery.*;

public class ConvertClient {

    public static void main(String[] args) throws Exception {
        System.setSecurityManager(new RMISecurityManager());

        // Find the service by its interface type
        ServiceFinder sf = new ServiceFinder(ConvertService.class);
        ConvertService cs = (ConvertService) sf.getObject();

        // Now invoke methods on the service object
        System.out.println(cs.convert(5));
    }
}
```

Our only changes here are related to finding the service object. In this simple example, we'll block until the ServiceFinder class discovers and returns a service object, and then either succeed or fail in executing a method on that object. That's good as far as it goes, but a better implementation of the client is for it to handle services that fail. A simple way to achieve that is:

```
ConvertService cs;
boolean done = false;
while (!done) {
    cs = (ConvertService) sf.getObject();
    try {
        System.out.println(cs.convert(5));
        done = true;
    } catch (RemoteException re) {
        cl.errored(s);
    }
}
```

For simplicity, we'll just use the original version in our future examples.

Running the Basic Example

We run this example just as we did all the examples in Chapter 3: we need two separate directories, an HTTP-server to download code from the server to the client, and so on. However, we no longer need to run *rmiregistry*, since that functionality is now handled by the Jini lookup service. We do, however, need to run some of the basic Jini services as we showed in Chapter 2, *Getting Started with Jini*; in particular, we must run the HTTP server, *rmid*, and *reggie*.

To recap, here are the steps to run the example (assuming that the Jini services are already up and running):

1. Compile the source files:

```
client% javac ConvertService.java ConvertClient.java ServiceFinder.java
server% javac ConvertService.java ConvertServiceProxy.java
            ConvertServiceImpl.java ServerListener.java
```

2. On the server, create the necessary stubs and skeletons:

```
server% rmic -v1.2 ConvertServiceImpl
```

3. Start the HTTP server that we'll use to download code. As usual, we'll use the HTTP server that comes with Jini and run it on port 8086:

```
server% java -jar /files/jini1_0/lib/tools.jar -dir . -port 8086
```

   Make sure that the server class files are in the current directory (.)—or alternately give a different *-dir* argument. Remember to start this command in a new window or, if your OS supports it, in the background.

4. Start the service, specifying the correct property from which code may be downloaded and the appropriate security policy file:

```
server% java -Djava.rmi.server.codebase=http://server:8086/
            -Djava.security.policy=/files/jini1_0/java.policy.all
            ConvertServiceImpl
```

5. Now we can run the client and get its output:

```
client% java -Djava.security.policy=/files/jini1_0/java.policy.all
            ConvertService
5
```

In this example, it's very important to run the server before the client. Our client is presently written so that it will find all servers that are running when it starts, but it won't be able to find any servers that are started after it is. That's a problem that we won't be able to fix until we learn about remote events in Chapter 6, *Remote Events*.

Leasing and the Lookup Service

If you ran the last example, you'll notice that the application does not work after a certain amount of time. That's because we haven't yet dealt with a key aspect of the Jini framework: *leasing*.

We discuss leasing more in depth in the next chapter. For now, we'll simply point out that leasing is how Jini services keep track of whether their clients are still alive. When you register a service with the lookup service, that registration is valid for only a short period of time. A lease represents that period of time, and the service is responsible for renewing that lease before it expires. If it fails to renew the lease, the lookup service automatically unregisters the service object. The purpose of this feature is that it makes the system more robust. If our application terminates prematurely, the lookup service deletes our entry after the lease period, and new clients don't waste time attempting to contact our service.

In our previous example, when we registered the service object, we asked for a lease time of 15 minutes. This lease time is only a request. We did not check to see how much time was granted, nor did we handle the renewal of the lease. This means that as soon as the lease has expired, new clients will not be able to find the service.

In this section, we'll develop an example that renews the lease provided by the lookup service. The necessary files to run this example are listed in Example 4-2.

Example 4-2: A Jini Service with Leasing

```
Common classes
    ConvertService (used in Example 4-1; listed in Example 3-4)
Server classes
    ConvertServiceImpl (modified from Example 4-1)
    ConvertServiceProxy (used in Example 4-1; listed in Example 3-4)
    ServiceListener (modified from Example 4-1)
Client classes
    ServiceFinder (used in Example 4-1)
    ConvertClient (used in Example 4-1)
```

Let's add a thread to our service that will renew the lookup service leases. We modify the ServerListener class from Example 4-1 as follows:

```java
import java.rmi.*;
import java.util.*;
import net.jini.discovery.*;
import net.jini.core.lookup.*;
import net.jini.core.lease.*;

public class ServerListener implements DiscoveryListener, Runnable {
    // Hashtable of registration leases keyed by the lookup service
    private Hashtable leases = new Hashtable();
    private ServiceItem item;          // Item to be registered with lookup
    private static final long ltime = Lease.FOREVER;
    private static final int mtime = 30*1000;   // 30 seconds
                                                // (minimum renewal)

    private LookupDiscovery ld;        // The discovery object
                                       // we're listening to

    public ServerListener(LookupDiscovery ld, Object object) {
        item = new ServiceItem(null, object, null);
        this.ld = ld;
        // Start the new thread to renew the leases
        new Thread(this).start();

    }

    // Automatically called when new lookup service(s) are discovered
    public synchronized void discovered(DiscoveryEvent dev) {
        ServiceRegistrar[] lookup = dev.getRegistrars();
        // For each discovered service, see if we're already registered.
        // If not, register
        for (int i = 0; i < lookup.length; i++) {
            if (leases.containsKey(lookup[i]) == false) {
                // Not already registered
                try {
                    // Register
                    ServiceRegistration ret =
                            lookup[i].register(item, ltime);
                    // You must assign the serviceID based on what the
```

```
                          // lookup service returns
                          if (item.serviceID == null) {
                              item.serviceID = ret.getServiceID();
                          }
                          // Save this registration
                          leases.put(lookup[i], ret);
                          // There's a new lease, notify the renewal thread
                          notify();
                      } catch (RemoteException ex) {
                          System.out.println("ServerListener error: " + ex);
                      }
                  }
                  // else we were already registered in this service
              }
          }


          // Automatically called when lookup service(s)
          // are no longer available
          public synchronized void discarded(DiscoveryEvent dev) {
              ServiceRegistrar[] lookup = dev.getRegistrars();
              for (int i = 0; i < lookup.length; i++) {
                  if (leases.containsKey(lookup[i]) == true) {
                      // Remove the registration. If the lookup service comes
                      // back later, we'll re-register at that time.
                      leases.remove(lookup[i]);
                  }
              }
          }


          public synchronized void run() {
              while (true) {
                  long nextRenewal = Long.MAX_VALUE;
                  long now = System.currentTimeMillis();
                  Enumeration e = leases.keys();
                  // Loop to renew all leases that are about to expire
                  // and also to find the time when the next lease will
                  // expire so we know when to run the loop again.
                  while (e.hasMoreElements()) {
                      ServiceRegistrar lookup =
                                  (ServiceRegistrar) e.nextElement();
                      ServiceRegistration sr =
                                  (ServiceRegistration) leases.get(lookup);
                      Lease l = sr.getLease();
                      long expire = l.getExpiration();
                      // See if the current lease has the minimum time.
                      // If we can't renew it, discard that lookup service.
                      // That will generate an event to the discarded()
                      // method, which will actually remove the lease from
                      // our list.
                      try {
                          if (expire <= now + mtime) {
                              l.renew(ltime);
                              expire = l.getExpiration();
                          }
                          if (nextRenewal > expire - mtime) {
                              nextRenewal = expire - mtime;
                          }
                      } catch (LeaseDeniedException lex) {
                      } catch (UnknownLeaseException lex) {
                          ld.discard(lookup);
```

```
            } catch (RemoteException ex) {
                ld.discard(lookup);
            }
        }
        try {
            // Wait until the next renewal time. A new lease
            // will notify us in case the new
            // lease has a smaller time until it must be renewed
            wait(nextRenewal - now);
        } catch (InterruptedException ex) {};
        }
    }

}
```

In this new version, we've added a thread to renew our leases and made some changes to support that thread. The constructor must now save the LookupDiscovery object that is needed by the new thread to handle error conditions. It must also start the new thread. And the discovered( ) method adds a single call to notify the new thread that there is now another lease that it needs to renew.

The implementation of the new thread is straightforward. We iterate through the hashtable and check all the leases, which were found in the ServiceRegistration object that was returned by the register( ) method and saved in the hashtable. If the time remaining on the lease is less than the minimum time, we renew the lease by calling the renew( ) method. Then, we adjust the nextRenewal instance variable to represent the earliest time that a lease will expire. Upon completion of the iteration through the leases, we call the wait( ) method to sleep until this time.

When Will a Lease Expire?

When we registered the service in this example, we specified a lease time of Lease.FOREVER. Then why will we have to renew the lease?

The actual duration of a lease granted by the lookup service is up to the lookup service to determine; the value that we specify is only a request. The lookup service must make a trade-off between the increased network traffic required by frequent lease renewals and the degree to which services will leave a particular community. So our lease renewal thread checks the actual duration of the granted lease and continually renews leases as necessary.

In this example, we also added exception handling code for the renew( ) method. If the lease that we requested is denied, then we simply continue with the old lease. If the lease is an unknown lease, it means that the lease expired and the server object has been removed from the lookup service. In this case we discard the lookup service; we'll reregister with it when the lookup service is rediscovered. If a remote exception occurs, we perform the same operation.

To use this new class with our server, we need change only the way in which the `ServerListener` class from Example 4-1 is constructed:

```
ServerListener sl = new ServerListener(reg, s);
```

The client application does not change in this example.

At this point, we have a complete server. You can convert any RMI service (or RMI client) to a Jini service (or Jini client) using the previous examples. However, to realize fully the advantages of the Jini infrastructure, the services should be modified to use the more advanced features of the Jini framework. Services can use leases to keep track of the existence of their clients. Services can use events to provide a more asynchronous API to their clients. And services and clients can use the provided Jini support services—the Jini transaction manager service and the Jini JavaSpaces service—to take advantage of the self-repairing nature of the Jini infrastructure. We will examine the details of these services in later chapters.

Lookup and Discovery Support Classes

The Jini Starter Kit provides classes that simplify working with the Jini lookup service. In Jini 1.0, there are classes in the `com.sun.jini` package that enable a service to discover and join lookup services very simply. In Jini 1.1, there are classes that enable a client to discovery and search lookup services.

The JoinManager and Other Service Classes

We'll look first at the classes that help a service to discover and join lookup services. In 1.0, most of these classes are part of the `com.sun.jini` package. This means that while they ship with the Jini Starter Kit, they are not official APIs and hence may change at any time. In fact, the most important of these classes—the `JoinManager` class—has moved from the `com.sun.jini` package to the `net.jini` package as part of the Jini 1.1 release; its interface also changed between these releases. Other classes in this category also moved packages between 1.0 and 1.1.

Here are the more useful of these classes that pertain to the lookup service:

net.jini.core.discovery.LookupLocator
> This class is used to locate the lookup service using a unicast protocol. An object of this class type can be obtained by using the `getLocator()` method of the `ServiceRegistrar` object. A `LookupLocator` object can also be created using a URL to define the hostname and network port—much the same way as the `Naming` class in accessing an RMI registry.

> Since an object of this class type uses a unicast protocol to obtain the `ServiceRegistrar` object, it can be used to access lookup services that are beyond the range that can be discovered by the `LookupDiscovery` class.

net.jini.discovery.DiscoveryManagment (1.1 only)
> This interface defines a number of operations related to discovery of the lookup service. Objects that implement this interface are used to perform discovery according to a variety of rules. In Jini 1.1, the `LookupDiscovery` class implements this interface, as do many of the following classes. A given

discovery object may perform unicast, multicast, or a combination of both types of discovery, but since they all implement this interface, they may be operated on in the same way.

com.sun.jini.discovery.LookupLocatorDiscovery (1.0)
net.jini.discovery.LookupLocatorDiscovery (1.1)

This class is very similar to the LookupDiscovery class. However, instead of using a multicast protocol to search for lookup services, an object of this class is provided with an array of LookupLocator objects and hence uses only the unicast discovery protocol. Each locator is used to obtain lookup services. Discovery of lookup services is accomplished by using the LookupLocator objects and notification of found ServiceRegistrars is as before—using DiscoveryListener objects. In 1.1, this class implements the DiscoveryManagement interface.

net.jini.discovery.LookupDiscoveryManager (1.1 only)

This class manages both multicast and unicast discovery. It will perform multicast discovery within your network's multicast radius, and it will also allow you to provide a set of LookupLocator objects and perform unicast discovery to those services. This class implements the DiscoveryManagement interface.

com.sun.jini.lease.LeaseRenewalManager (1.0)
net.jini.lease.LeaseRenewalManager (1.1)

This is a support class that is used in the management of leases. When you register a lease with an object of this class, the lease renewal manager will take the responsibility of renewing leases until you ask it to stop or until a predetermined time has passed.

You can also provide a com.sun.jini.lease.LeaseListener object (net.jini.lease.LeaseListener in 1.1) to this class. The implementation of the lease listener interface requires one method—the notify() method, which is called by the lease renewal manager if it fails to renew a lease.

com.sun.jini.lookup.JoinManager (1.0)
net.jini.lookup.JoinManager (1.1)

The JoinManager class is a "do-it-all" class that accomplishes all of the tasks necessary for a service to interface with the lookup service. It will instantiate a LookupDiscovery object, optionally a LookupLocatorDiscovery object, or a LookupDiscoveryManager object (in 1.1), and install the DiscoveryListener object necessary to handle the discovery objects.

You may also specify a service ID, or—just as with our ServerListener class—the JoinManager can obtain the service ID from the first lookup service. The service ID can be delivered back to the application using a com.sun.jini.lookup.ServiceIDListener object (net.jini.lookup.ServiceIDListener in 1.1) so that you can save it to persistent store. You can specify the groups to join and all the components of the ServiceItem object. The join manager will handle all the lease renewals with the lookup services, even if no LeaseRenewalManger object is explicitly provided.

With the JoinManager class, implementing our example becomes easy. We need only the files listed in Example 4-3, and only the service implementation changes.

Example 4-3: A Jini Service with a 1.0 Join Manager

Common classes
    ConvertService (used in Example 4-2; listed in Example 3-4)
Server classes
    ConvertServiceImpl (modified from Example 4-2)
    ConvertServiceProxy (used in Example 4-2; listed in Example 3-4)
Client classes
    ServiceFinder (used in Example 4-2; listed in Example 4-1)
    ConvertClient (used in Example 4-2; listed in Example 4-1)

The only change for using the JoinManager is in the service implementation:

```java
import java.io.*;
import java.rmi.*;
import java.rmi.server.*;
import net.jini.discovery.*;
import com.sun.jini.lookup.*;

public class ConvertServiceImpl extends UnicastRemoteObject
                            implements ConvertServiceProxy {

    public ConvertServiceImpl() throws RemoteException {
    }

    public String convert(int i) throws RemoteException {
        return new Integer(i).toString();
    }

    public static void main(String[] args) throws Exception {
        System.setSecurityManager(new RMISecurityManager());
        String[] groups = new String[] { "" };

        // Create the instance of the service; the JoinManager will
        // register it and renew its leases with the lookup service
        ConvertServiceImpl csi =
                        (ConvertServiceImpl) new ConvertServiceImpl();
        JoinManager manager = new JoinManager(csi, null, groups,
                                              null, null, null);
    }
}
```

We no longer need to create the ServerListener or LookupDiscovery objects, since everything that we need is handled by the JoinManager object.

The parameters to the constructor of the join manager are:

- The service object that we want to register

- The array of attributes that the server object supports

- The array of groups that we want to register with

- The array of lookup locators that we want to find

- A service ID listener object

- A lease renewal manager

There is also another constructor that allows us to specify a service ID—when we have a saved service ID, we must use that format of the constructor. Otherwise, as in this case, the service ID will be provided by the first lookup service that is discovered. We'll show the former facility later in the book. This example is run with the same command line we've used all along.

In 1.1, the code is slightly different, because the interface to the JoinManager class has changed. To use the net.jini.lookup.JoinManager class, we need to modify the ConvertServiceImpl class from Example 4-3 as shown in Example 4-4.

Example 4–4: A Jini Service with a 1.1 Join Manager

```
Common classes
    ConvertService (used in Example 4-3; listed in Example 3-4)
Server classes
    ConvertServiceImpl (modified from Example 4-3)
    ConvertServiceProxy (used in Example 4-3; listed in Example 3-4)
Client classes
    ServiceFinder (used in Example 4-3; listed in Example 4-1)
    ConvertClient (used in Example 4-3; listed in Example 4-1)
```

Here's the 1.1-based implementation of our service:

```
import java.io.*;
import java.rmi.*;
import java.rmi.server.*;
import net.jini.core.lookup.*;
import net.jini.discovery.*;
import net.jini.lookup.*;

public class ConvertServiceImpl extends UnicastRemoteObject
                implements ConvertServiceProxy, ServiceIDListener {

    public ConvertServiceImpl() throws RemoteException {
    }

    public String convert(int i) throws RemoteException {
        return new Integer(i).toString();
    }

    public void serviceIDNotify(ServiceID id) {
        // For now, this is just a required method
    }

    public static void main(String[] args) throws Exception {
        System.setSecurityManager(new RMISecurityManager());
        String[] groups = new String[] { "" };

        // Create the instance of the service; the JoinManager will
        // register it and renew its leases with the lookup service
        ConvertServiceImpl csi =
                (ConvertServiceImpl) new ConvertServiceImpl();
        LookupDiscoveryManager mgr =
                new LookupDiscoveryManager(groups, null, null);
        JoinManager manager = new JoinManager(csi, null,
                                        csi, mgr, null);

    }
}
```

In this case, the arguments to the constructor of the join manager are:

- The object to be registered.

- An array of attributes associated with the object.

- Either a ServiceIDListener object or the service ID that should be assigned to the service. We'll show an example of this later on; for now, we'll just note that you have to supply one or the other. If you specify null for this argument, the code will not compile, since the compiler can't tell by the argument type which constructor you want to call; this is why we provided an empty serviceIDNotify() method.

- A discovery management object. We use a LookupDiscoveryManager object; you could also use a LookupLocatorDiscovery or a LookupDiscovery object.

- A lease renewal manager object (an instance of the LeaseRenewalManager class will be used if you pass null).

Note that which join manager you use is defined by the import statement in the code: the com.sun.jini.lookup.JoinManager class exists in both 1.0 and 1.1, and its interface in that package is unchanged in 1.1. In the rest of our examples, we'll use the 1.0-based code, because at the time of this writing the 1.1 code is still in alpha and subject to change. Once 1.1 FCS has been released, however, you should migrate your code to the new join manager as soon as practical.

The ClientLookupManager Class

In Jini 1.1, there is a new set of classes that helps clients discover lookup services and find registered services in those lookup services. The most important are:

net.jini.discovery.ClientLookupManager
> This class uses an object that implements the DiscoveryManagement interface and a lease renewal manager to discover all lookup services on the network. It provides a variety of ways for a client to find services in the discovered lookup services through various implementations of the lookup() method, which is used to find a service that matches a particular template. This method can block until a matching service is found, return an array of matching services, and filter the matching services with a ServiceItemFilter object.

The ClientLookupManager class performs the same function as our ServiceFinder class: it allows the client to find a service that implements a particular interface. In Example 4-5, we use the ClientLookupManager to replace the ServiceFinder class.

Example 4–5: A Client with the ClientLookupManager Class

```
Common classes
    ConvertService (used in Example 4-4; listed in Example 3-4)
Server classes
    ConvertServiceImpl (used in Example 4-4)
    ConvertServiceProxy (used in Example 4-4; listed in Example 3-4)
Client classes
    ConvertClient (modified from Example 4-4; listed in Example 4-1)
```

Here's what the new client looks like:

```
import java.rmi.*;
import net.jini.core.lookup.*;
import net.jini.lookup.*;
import net.jini.discovery.*;

public class ConvertClient {

    public static void main(String[] args) throws Exception {
        System.setSecurityManager(new RMISecurityManager());

        // Create the lookup manager to discover lookup services
        ClientLookupManager clm =
                    new ClientLookupManager(null, null);
        Class[] name = new Class[] { ConvertService.class };
        ServiceTemplate st = new ServiceTemplate(null, name, null);

        // Block until a matching service is found
        ServiceItem[] si =
                    clm.lookup(st, 1, 5, null, Long.MAX_VALUE);
        if (si == null || si.length == 0)
            throw new Exception("Can't find service");
        ConvertService cs = (ConvertService) si[0].service;

        // Now invoke methods on the service object
        System.out.println(cs.convert(5));
        clm.terminate();
    }
}
```

When we construct the client lookup manager, we pass null for each parameter.
That means the client lookup manager will use a new instance of the LookupDiscoveryManager class as the discovery manager and a new instance of the LeaseRenewalManager to renew any leases. Then, just as we did in the ServiceFinder
class, we create a ServiceTemplate and use that to look up services. In this case,
the parameters to the lookup( ) method specify:

- The template to look up

- The minimum number of matches to return (the lookup( ) method will block
  until this number of matches are found)

- The maximum number of matches to return

- A ServiceFilter object that can be used to filter the list of returned services
  even further

- The amount of time (in milliseconds) to wait for the minimum number of
  matches before returning an array of size 0

The alpha version of the ClientLookupManager class is fairly buggy (for example,
the code above will hang if there are two matching services running when the
client starts); it is subject to change before FCS. In the remainder of our examples,
we'll continue to use the ServiceFinder class. However, the ClientLookupManager
class does have the advantage that it will discover services that are started after the
client starts, which is something that our ServiceFinder class cannot do until we
learn about remote events in Chapter 6.

Attributes and the Entry Interface

In our examination of the ServiceItem class and the ServiceTemplate class, we briefly touched on the concept of *attributes*. Attributes are used to specify the particulars of the service. For example, while the service may be a printer service, its attributes could be information such as the location of the printer, or configuration information such as whether the printer supports two-sided printing or color, or status information like whether the printer is out of toner or paper. In Jini, attributes are not name/value pairs such as you may be used to working with; they are classes that implement the net.jini.core.entry.Entry interface.

Entry objects are serializable objects that are treated in a special fashion when they are serialized or reconstituted. They are distinguished by the implementation of the Entry interface, which is used purely as a type identifier; it has no methods. Each field of the entry object must be a public object reference. Instance variables of primitive types are not permitted. References to object types that are static, transient, final, or not public are ignored when entry objects are stored or retrieved. Furthermore, these objects must have a default (no argument) constructor. The use of primitive types or the omission of a default constructor will cause an IllegalArgumentException object to be thrown when the object is serialized.

Storing an entry object is accomplished as follows. The fields of an entry object are serialized separately and stored as MarshalledObject objects. This means that if two fields refer to the same object (even indirectly), two copies of the object will be stored in their serialized form. The reason MarshalledObject objects are used is because they can be checked for equality without deserializing the field; this is faster than comparing the deserialized objects, and it means that the lookup service doesn't need to load the class definitions for the object contained within the marshalled object. This allows them to be managed and matched quickly. Fields that are static, transient, final, or not public do not get serialized and are initialized by the default constructor during deserialization.

Matching an entry object requires an additional entry object used as a template, specifying the field values searched for. A template entry object matches an entry object if the type of the template object is the same as or a superclass of the type of the entry object. The fields within the objects must also have the same values. A template with a null value for a field is treated as a wildcard and matches any value for that field. Any fields in the entry object that don't exist in the template object (because of subtyping) match. This may sound complicated, but it's simple. In Example 4-6, we extend our basic example to allow attribute matching (going back to Example 4-3 as the basis for the code so it will run under 1.0).

Example 4–6: A Jini Service with Standard Attributes

```
Common classes
    ConvertService (used in Example 4-3; listed in Example 3-4)
Server classes
    ConvertServiceImpl (modified from Example 4-3)
    ConvertServiceProxy (used in Example 4-3; listed in Example 3-4)
Client classes
    ServiceFinder (used in Example 4-3; listed in Example 4-1)
    ConvertClient (modified from Example 4-3; listed in Example 4-1)
```

Here's our new service implementation:

```
import java.io.*;
import java.rmi.*;
import java.rmi.server.*;
import net.jini.discovery.*;
import net.jini.core.entry.*;
import net.jini.lookup.entry.*;
import com.sun.jini.lookup.*;

public class ConvertServiceImpl extends UnicastRemoteObject
                                implements ConvertServiceProxy {

    public ConvertServiceImpl() throws RemoteException {
    }

    public String convert(int i) throws RemoteException {
        return new Integer(i).toString();
    }

    public static void main(String[] args) throws Exception {
        System.setSecurityManager(new RMISecurityManager());
        String[] groups = new String[] { "" };

        Entry[] attributes = new Entry[2];
        attributes[0] = new Name("Marketing Converter");
        attributes[1] = new Location("4", "4101", "NY/02");

        // Create the instance of the service; the JoinManager will
        // register it and renew its leases with the lookup service
        ConvertServiceImpl csi =
                (ConvertServiceImpl) new ConvertServiceImpl();
        JoinManager manager = new JoinManager(csi, attributes, groups,
                                        null, null, null);
    }
}
```

In our new version of the ConvertServiceImpl class, we are adding two attributes to our service: a name attribute and a location attribute. The name attribute gives our service a name—in this case, the service is an integer converter to support conversion requests in the marketing department. The location attribute is used to inform its users of its location—in this case, the 4th floor, in room #4101, in building NY/02. These attributes are entry objects and are created and provided to the join manager to be published in the lookup service.

While the lookup service will support any attribute that is an Entry object, the following attributes are provided by the Jini framework. Using these attributes will save you from creating a new class type:

net.jini.lookup.entry.Address
    An attribute used to determine the address of the service. Fields include the organization name, the street address, city, state, zip code, and country.

net.jini.lookup.entry.Comment
    An attribute that is used to hold a generic comment. The stored data is a single string object.

net.jini.lookup.entry.Location

An attribute used to determine the location of the service. Unlike the `Address` entry, which can be used to provide contact information of the service provider or owner, this attribute provides the location of the service by specifying the floor, the room number, and the name of the building where the service is running.

net.jini.lookup.entry.Name

An attribute used to provide the name of the service. The stored data is a single string object.

net.jini.lookup.entry.ServiceInfo

An attribute used to provide generic information about the service. Fields include the name of the manufacturer, the name of the vendor, the version of the service, the model number, and the serial number.

net.jini.lookup.entry.ServiceType

An abstract attribute used to provide human readable information. Subclasses of this type should provide a name for the service, a short description, and icons that represent the service.

net.jini.lookup.entry.Status

An abstract attribute used to represent the state of the service. Services should use this base type to represent the status and error conditions of the service.

In order better to understand the use of entry objects, let's examine the client side of the application. Since our `ServiceFinder` class already supports the use of attributes, we just need to use a different constructor in our `ConvertClient` class:

```
import java.rmi.*;
import net.jini.discovery.*;
import net.jini.core.entry.*;
import net.jini.lookup.entry.*;

public class ConvertClient {

    public static void main (String[] args) throws Exception {
        System.setSecurityManager(new RMISecurityManager());

        // Find the service by its interface type
        Entry attribute = new Location("4", null, null);

        ServiceFinder sf =
                new ServiceFinder(ConvertService.class, attribute);
        ConvertService cs = (ConvertService) sf.getObject();

        // Now invoke methods on the service object
        System.out.println(cs.convert(5));
    }
}
```

In our new client example, we specify a single location attribute as part of our search template. The client is still looking for objects that support the `ConvertService` interface, except that there is now an additional requirement that the service must satisfy: the service must be located on the fourth floor. We are not specifying a room number or building name, so we use a `null` value for those fields when we construct a location template; those fields will be treated as a wildcard.

Furthermore, we are not specifying a name attribute, so the name attribute of the service object will not be checked.

Service-Defined Attributes

While the attributes defined by the Jini API suffice for many cases, there will be cases in which we need to write our own attributes. We'll do that in Example 4-7.

Example 4–7: A Jini Service with Service-Defined Attributes

```
Common classes
    ConvertService (used in Example 4-6; listed in Example 3-4)
    Copyright (new)
Server classes
    ConvertServiceImpl (modified from Example 4-6)
    ConvertServiceProxy (used in Example 4-6; listed in Example 3-4)
Client classes
    ServiceFinder (used in Example 4-6; listed in Example 4-1)
    ConvertClient (modified from Example 4-6)
```

Since attributes are simply entry objects (which themselves are simply data objects that follow a design pattern), it is quite easy to implement our own attributes:

```
import net.jini.entry.*;
import net.jini.lookup.entry.*;

public class Copyright extends AbstractEntry
                       implements ServiceControlled {
    // The fields of the Entry --
    // each must be a public, serializable object
    public String owner;
    public String date;
    public String lawfirm;

    public Copyright() {
        this(null, null, null);
    }

    public Copyright (String owner, String date, String lawfirm) {
        this.owner = owner;
        this.date = date;
        this.lawfirm = lawfirm;
    }
}
```

Let's introduce a new attribute—a Copyright attribute. This attribute contains three fields, which represent the owner of the copyright, the date that the copyright was established, and the law firm that will sue whoever violates the copyright. Following the pattern for entry classes, the fields are all public object references, there is a default constructor, and this class implements the Entry interface. It implements the Entry interface by subclassing from the net.jini.entry.AbstractEntry class. While subclassing from the AbstractEntry class is not necessary, it does help, since that class provides a correct implementation of the methods that help in the comparison of entry objects, including the equals() and hashCode() methods.

We have also implemented the net.jini.lookup.entry.ServiceControlled interface. This interface is also used only for type identification. Implementation of this interface marks our entry object as read-only to our clients. The service may change this entry object (attribute) as it likes, but clients may only read this attribute. (It is possible for clients to ask a service to change the value of an attribute; for a discussion of this, see the administration interfaces in Chapter 7, *Service Administration*.)

The server implementation uses this new attribute as follows:

```
import java.io.*;
import java.rmi.*;
import java.rmi.server.*;
import net.jini.discovery.*;
import net.jini.core.entry.*;
import net.jini.lookup.entry.*;
import com.sun.jini.lookup.*;

public class ConvertServiceImpl extends UnicastRemoteObject
                                implements ConvertServiceProxy {

    public ConvertServiceImpl() throws RemoteException {
    }

    public String convert(int i) throws RemoteException {
        return new Integer(i).toString();
    }

    public static void main(String[] args) throws Exception {
        System.setSecurityManager(new RMISecurityManager());
        String[] groups = new String[] { "" };

        Entry[] attributes = new Entry[3];
        attributes[0] = new Name("Marketing Converter");
        attributes[1] = new Location("4", "4101", "NY/02");
        attributes[2] = new Copyright("AJC Marketing", "9/1999",
                                      "Oaks, Wong, Adler, and Mar");

        // Create the instance of the service; JoinManager will
        // register it and renew its leases with the lookup service
        ConvertServiceImpl csi =
                    (ConvertServiceImpl) new ConvertServiceImpl();
        JoinManager manager = new JoinManager(csi, attributes, groups,
                                              null, null, null);
    }
}
```

Once we have our new attribute, using it is almost like using any other attribute. There is only one difference. Since the attribute is not part of the Jini libraries, it must be placed on the web server in order for the client to find it. Furthermore, if the client is actually to use it as part of its template, it will need the class file during the compilation phase also. In our online example code, the client uses the Copyright attribute to lookup its service, which is why we listed the Copyright class as common between client and server.

Other Service Implementations

We started this chapter by taking an RMI service and converting it into a Jini service, and we've used RMI ever since as this basis of our services. However, we don't mean to give the impression that Jini is simply an enhancement to RMI or that RMI is the only way to write a Jini service (even though we do feel it's one of the better ways). So before concluding our initial look at Jini, we'll present two more examples. These examples show that you can use a variety of transports with Jini and that you can architect Jini communities in a variety of ways.

Using Local Execution

Jini allows your service to take advantage of Java's movable code facility so that the service logic can be executed anywhere—and in particular, the service logic can be executed on the client. If you have a device with limited resources, this is an important benefit. In Example 4-8, we develop such a service. Note that since the service interface remains unchanged, so too does the client code. We've also gone back to Example 4-3 as a simpler basis for this example.

Example 4-8: A Jini Service That Executes Locally

```
Common classes
    ConvertService (used in Example 4-3; listed in Example 3-4)
Server classes
    ConvertServiceImpl (modified from Example 4-3)
Client classes
    ServiceFinder (used in Example 4-3; listed in Example 4-1)
    ConvertClient (used in Example 4-3; listed in Example 4-1)
```

Because this is not an RMI service, it no longer needs the ConvertServiceProxy class. Instead, we'll return to our basic implementation with a 1.0 join manager and implement the service as follows:

```
import java.io.*;
import java.rmi.*;
import java.rmi.server.*;
import net.jini.discovery.*;
import com.sun.jini.lookup.*;

public class ConvertServiceImpl implements ConvertService, Serializable {

    public String convert(int i) throws RemoteException {
        return new Integer(i).toString();
    }

    public static void main(String[] args) throws Exception {
        System.setSecurityManager(new SecurityManager());
        String[] groups = new String[] { "" };

        // Create the instance of the service; the JoinManager will
        // register it and renew its leases with the lookup service
        ConvertServiceImpl csi =
                (ConvertServiceImpl) new ConvertServiceImpl();
        JoinManager manager = new JoinManager(csi, null, groups,
                                        null, null, null);
        while (true)
```

```
                        Thread.sleep(1000000);

        }
    }
```

As long as an object is serializable, it can join the Jini lookup service. So this service registers itself (rather than its stub as in previous examples). When a client loads the object from the Jini lookup service, it will get an instance of this class locally, and the convert( ) method will then be executed on the client. The difference comes because the ConvertServiceImpl class is no longer a remote object, so when the object is serialized, a copy of the object itself is transferred to the client.

The server itself must do something to make sure that it keeps running. In the case of an RMI server, the RMI infrastructure starts threads that listen for requests and continue to run after the main thread exits. In this case, while the join manager has started some additional threads, they are all daemon threads, and the server will exit if the main thread exits. So this server simply sleeps forever, which allows its background threads to handle discovery and lease renewals with the lookup service.

Note that while this implementation has nothing to do with RMI, when we run the server we must still specify a java.rmi.server.codebase property. We must place the ConvertServiceImpl class itself in this codebase (rather than generating a stub class and placing that in the codebase) because now the client must load that class definition—and even though the class itself has no connection to RMI, the Jini infrastructure will still use RMI to transfer the object (and class definition) to the client. So this server is run with exactly the same command line as all our other servers (as is the client).

Protocol Wrapping

What if you have an existing service that you want to expose as a Jini service? It's a simple matter of writing a Jini wrapper that calls the existing service, as we show in Example 4-9.

Example 4-9: A Jini Wrapper for an Existing Service

```
Common classes
    ConvertService (used in Example 4-3; listed in Example 3-4)
Server classes
    ConvertServiceImpl (modified from Example 4-3)
Client classes
    ServiceFinder (used in Example 4-3; listed in Example 4-1)
    ConvertClient (used in Example 4-3; listed in Example 4-1)
```

In this example, we'll mimic an existing conversion service that simply uses sockets for its communication. Once again, all the changes are on the server side, which has this implementation (since the changes are extensive, we won't highlight them):

```
import java.io.*;
import java.net.*;
import java.rmi.*;
import java.rmi.server.*;
```

```java
import net.jini.discovery.*;
import com.sun.jini.lookup.*;

public class ConvertServiceImpl implements ConvertService,
                                    Serializable, Runnable {

    // Make this transient, so on all clients it will be false
    // (the default serialization value)
    transient boolean isServer;
    String remoteHost;           // Host where server socket is running
    int remotePort;              // Port of server socket

    ConvertServiceImpl(String host, int port) {
        remoteHost = host;
        remotePort = port;
        isServer = true;
    }

    public String convert(int i) throws RemoteException {
        Socket sock;
        DataOutputStream dos;
        BufferedReader br;
        String s;

        try {
            // Construct the socket to the remote server. Send it the
            // integer and read the returned string. This should only
            // be called by the client.
            if (isServer)
                throw new IllegalArgumentException(
                                "Can't call from server");

            sock = new Socket(remoteHost, remotePort);
            dos = new DataOutputStream(sock.getOutputStream());
            br = new BufferedReader(
                    new InputStreamReader(sock.getInputStream()));
            dos.writeInt(i);
            dos.flush();
            s = br.readLine();
            sock.close();
            return s;
        } catch (Exception e) {
            throw new RemoteException("Convert failed", e);
        }
    }

    public void run() {
        try {
            // On the server, start the server socket and process requests
            if (!isServer)
                throw new IllegalArgumentException(
                                "Should only run on server");
            ServerSocket ss = new ServerSocket(remotePort);
            while (true) {
                Socket s;
                try {
                    s = ss.accept();
                } catch (Exception e) {
                    // Resource error on the server; can't recover
                    return;
```

```
        }
        DataInputStream dis = new DataInputStream(
                                s.getInputStream());
        PrintWriter pw = new PrintWriter(s.getOutputStream());
        Integer I = new Integer(dis.readInt());
        pw.println(I);
        pw.flush();
        s.close();
        }
    } catch (Exception e) {
        // Client disconnected
    }
}

public static void main(String[] args) throws Exception {
    System.setSecurityManager(new SecurityManager());
    String[] groups = new String[] { "" };

    // Create the instance of the service; the JoinManager will
    // register it and renew its leases with the lookup service
    ConvertServiceImpl csi =
        (ConvertServiceImpl) new ConvertServiceImpl(
                        InetAddress.getLocalHost().getHostName(),
                        3333);
    new Thread(csi).start();

    JoinManager manager = new JoinManager(csi, null, groups,
                                null, null, null);
    }
}
```

Once again, a ConvertServiceImpl object will be transferred to clients that use this service. When the client calls the convert( ) method, a socket will be constructed back to the original server and data will be transmitted on that socket. All of this is transparent to the client, which simply calls the same method it always has. And even though the Jini infrastructure uses RMI to transfer the object to the client, once the client has the object, the client and server communicate using their own proprietary protocol.

The commands to run the client and server remain unchanged.

Summary

With the examples in this chapter, we have a fully functional Jini server and Jini client. Both of these programs can find and interact with the Jini lookup service, whether by using standard Jini APIs or additional APIs that are part of Sun's com.sun.jini package. And we've seen examples of how the service can be implemented using RMI, proprietary protocols, and even local execution.

In the next chapter, we'll look into more details about leasing. While leasing is the basis of the contract between the lookup service and Jini services, it is quite useful for services themselves. Understanding leasing is a prerequisite to the techniques needed to complete our basic service.

CHAPTER 5 °

Leasing

In this chapter, we'll discuss Jini's leasing APIs. We've seen how the Jini lookup service uses leasing to keep track of which registered services are still alive. As a client of the lease, our service didn't have to do much with the lease: it had only to renew the lease periodically. In this chapter, we'll look into the details of leasing, including how to program leasing features into your service implementations.

Leasing is probably the most important feature when it comes to the robustness of the Jini infrastructure. With leasing, the lookup service is able to get rid of outdated entries for services that did not or could not clean up after themselves. Without leasing, the lookup service would eventually be bogged down with service objects that are no longer valid. Clients would have to waste time when they received invalid service objects. While leasing does not eliminate the chances of a client obtaining an invalid service object, it restricts the possible set to those services that failed since their last lease renewal.

Similarly, all Jini services that maintain client data should require that the client lease the storage for the data. The leasing time required by the service should be dependent on the requirements of storage. If the service has plenty of space and the request is quite small, the leasing time can be larger than when the service is resource-constrained.

Furthermore, there are a few cases where leasing should be considered even though it is not obvious that client data is stored. The first case involves the storage of session data. This is data that the service maintains between many calls from the client. With session data, the client does not have to keep track of its current state, nor must this state be passed back and forth between the client and the server. Instead, the client obtains a token to represent itself on subsequent requests to the server and a lease to inform the server that it still requires its services. With session data, the service is able to maintain client state, and with leasing, the service is able to clean up after clients.

The second case involves support of remote events. Here, a server must keep a reference to a client listener object. This actually can be considered client data, so leasing for its storage should be apparent. However, what might be overlooked is that the service will actually be the client during the remote event delivery. This means that the service can hang if the client is not available, which in turn can affect all clients of the service. In this case, the lease time should be small, regardless of the resources available on the server. Since clients will probably use the LeaseRenewalManager class to maintain the lease, they will probably not even notice the length of the lease. The only concern is to balance out this need so that the clients will not overwhelm the service, since in most cases, contact with the service is required to renew a lease.

So how do we add leasing to our service? In this chapter, we'll develop an example that requires the client to obtain a lease in order to use the convert service. In turn, the service will use that lease for two purposes: it will deny access if the client does not have a lease, and it will use the lease to track specific session data associated with the client.

This requires a change to our service interface so that the leasing aspect of the service is now visible. On the client side, there are a few changes related to the changes in the service interface. On the server side, however, there are many more changes: the server must create the lease, check to make sure the lease is valid, and keep track of the client data associated with the lease. The files necessary for this example are listed in Example 5-1. Although the code in this example is loosely based on Example 4-3, it has changed so substantially that we will not highlight the changed sections of this code.

Example 5-1: A Service with Leasing

```
Common classes
    ConvertService (modified from Example 4-3; listed in Example 3-4)
    ConvertServiceRegistration (new)
Server classes
    ConvertServiceImpl (modified from Example 4-3)
    ConvertServiceRegistrationImpl (new)
    ConvertServiceProxy (modified from Example 4-3; listed in Example 3-4)
    ServerLandlord (new)
Client classes
    ServiceFinder (used in Example 4-3; listed in Example 4-1)
    ConvertClient (modified from Example 4-3; listed in Example 4-1)
```

Interestingly, the Jini core packages provide little support to help the client or service to create and maintain a lease. This is not surprising: the core supplies clients and services with only those things on which they must agree. So the core provides the net.jini.core.lease.Lease and net.jini.core.lease.LeaseMap interfaces (plus some exceptions) since both sides must agree on those interfaces, but the implementation of the leasing protocol is up to the service. Hence the only API requirement to use leasing is that the lease provided by the service must support the Lease interface and the client must use the Lease interface.

There are a few operational restrictions on a lease that are imposed by the Jini specification. A service that issues a lease must return an actual lease object (rather than a remote reference) to the client, even though the lease object may itself contain references to a remote service. A service is free to grant a lease of any duration up to the amount of time requested by the client, and the service can decide whether the client is permitted to renew the lease. In typical usage, services allow leases to be renewed forever, but that is not a requirement. However, a service

Leases and Lease Maps

The net.jini.core.lease package defines two interfaces: one for a lease and one for a lease map. A lease map is an aggregation of lease objects and is provided as a possible optimization: if your application has to renew several leases with the same landlord, it's more efficient to do so in one call with a lease map rather than in individual calls with single leases.

Every implementation of the Lease class must define the canBatch() method, which determines whether the lease object can be grouped together with a lease passed in via a parameter. In general, this method will return true only if the leases were granted by the same issuer.

For most developers, this is all opaque. The LeaseRenewalManager class will batch leases together if it can. If you implement a landlord, you have to implement the renewAll() and cancelAll() methods, but those are usually implemented by iterating through the lease map.

must respect the lease that it has issued to a client: the service is not allowed to cancel a lease that is held by a client, even if it has received an exception while talking to the client.

The Service Interfaces

In order to use leasing, we must change our service interface. The client must be able to obtain the lease in order to renew it, and the client must now identify itself when it calls the service so that the service knows which session data it should use to satisfy the client's request.

There are several ways to implement this interface; most obviously, the client could retrieve a lease object from the server and pass that object with each request to the server. In Jini, the standard pattern is to hide that sort of token passing and instead use a registration object that embeds the lease (and other information) within it. That's the design pattern used by the lookup service, which returns a ServiceRegistration object that contains the lease. This pattern makes things more complex, since it requires two interfaces, but it's the common way in which Jini services are defined.

The first interface is used to retrieve a registration with the service:

```
import java.rmi.*;

public interface ConvertService {
    public ConvertServiceRegistration getInstance(long duration)
                                    throws RemoteException;
}
```

The second uses the registration object to accomplish its work:

```
import java.rmi.*;
import net.jini.core.lease.*;

public interface ConvertServiceRegistration {
    public String convert(int i) throws RemoteException;
    public Lease getLease();      // note: does not throw RemoteException
}
```

Note that the getLease( ) method does not throw a RemoteException; it is a requirement of the lease specification that the lease be returned as a local object to the client. The lease object will be serialized and passed with the registration object, so the getLease( ) method does not require a call to the service. This enables the client to make the appropriate calls to renew the lease.

The Service Implementation

Now we'll turn to the implementation of the service. The implementation of the service will rely heavily on classes in the com.sun.jini packages that provide a basic implementation of a lease and a renewal protocol called the *landlord proto-col*. The two most useful classes are:

com.sun.jini.lease.LandlordLease

A basic implementation of the Lease interface. An object of this serializable class will maintain an expiration time for the lease and the means to renew the lease. The lease is renewed by using an RMI object stub that supports the Landlord interface and has a unique identifier so that the landlord can distinguish the lease. This unique identifier is called a *cookie*.

Creation of this class is accomplished by using the com.sun.jini.lease.LandlordLease.Factory class. This factory class is actually an inner class of the LandlordLease class.

com.sun.jini.lease.Landlord

The interface that the service must implement in order for the LandlordLease object to be able to communicate with the service. There are four methods—renew( ), cancel( ), renewAll( ), and cancelAll( ). The last two methods are used by the com.sun.jini.lease.landlord.LandlordLeaseMap class which is used to handle a group of leases. For the renewAll( ) method, an object of an inner class of this interface—the com.sun.jini.lease.Landlord.RenewResults class—is returned.

The Service Landlord

The first class that we must develop in the service implementation is a class that implements the Landlord interface. This class will be responsible for handing out, cancelling, and renewing leases (which will be instances of the LandlordLease class). Since clients will make the calls to cancel or renew the lease, those calls must be distributed calls, so we'll implement the landlord as an RMI server:

```java
import java.io.*;
import java.rmi.*;
import java.rmi.server.*;
import java.util.*;
import net.jini.core.lease.*;
import com.sun.jini.lease.landlord.*;

public class ServerLandlord extends UnicastRemoteObject
                            implements Landlord {
    protected Hashtable expiration = new Hashtable();
                            // cookie -> expiration
    protected Hashtable leases = new Hashtable();
                            // cookie -> lease
    protected Hashtable session = new Hashtable();
                            // cookie -> sessiondata
    protected long MAXLEASETIME = 10*60*1000;          // 10 Minutes
    protected LandlordLease.Factory factory =
                            new LandlordLease.Factory();

    public ServerLandlord() throws RemoteException {
    }

    public long renew(Object cookie, long duration)
            throws LeaseDeniedException,
                UnknownLeaseException, RemoteException {

        // Time when the client first attempted renewal
        long now = System.currentTimeMillis();

        // Reset the duration to the maximum that we're willing to give
        if (duration == Lease.ANY ||
            duration == Lease.FOREVER ||
            duration > MAXLEASETIME)
            duration = MAXLEASETIME;

        synchronized (this) {
            Long expire = (Long) expiration.get(cookie);
            if (expire == null)
                throw new UnknownLeaseException();
            // If the lease has already expired, don't renew it
            if (expire.longValue() < now) {
                expiration.remove(cookie);
                leases.remove(cookie);
                session.remove(cookie);
                throw new UnknownLeaseException();
            }
            expiration.remove(cookie);
            expiration.put(cookie, new Long(now + duration));
        }
        return duration;
    }

    public Landlord.RenewResults renewAll(Object[] cookie,
                        long[] duration) throws RemoteException {
        long granted[] = new long[cookie.length];
        Vector denied = new Vector();

        // Try to renew each lease. When one fails, place it in the
        // array of exceptions to be held in the RenewResults object
        for (int i = 0; i < cookie.length; i++) {
```

```
            try {
                granted[i] = renew(cookie[i], duration[i]);
            } catch (LeaseException lex) {
                granted[i] = -1;
                denied.add(lex);
            }
        }
        return new Landlord.RenewResults(granted,
                denied.isEmpty() ? null :
                                (Exception[]) denied.toArray());
    }

    public void cancel(Object cookie)
                    throws UnknownLeaseException, RemoteException {
        synchronized (this) {
            if (expiration.get(cookie) == null)
                throw new UnknownLeaseException();
            expiration.remove(cookie);
            leases.remove(cookie);
            session.remove(cookie);
        }
    }

    public void cancelAll(Object[] cookie)
            throws LeaseMapException, RemoteException {
        Map map = null;
        // Cancel all the leases. If one or more has an exception,
        // then continue but save the exception in a map to be
        // thrown back to the user.
        for (int i = 0; i < cookie.length; i++) {
            try {
                cancel(cookie[i]);
            } catch (LeaseException ex) {
                if (map == null)
                    map = new HashMap();
                map.put(cookie[i], ex);
            }
        }
        if (map != null)
            throw new LeaseMapException("Can't cancel all leases", map);
    }

    // The following methods are not part of the Landlord interface
    // and can be called only by directly using this object.
    static int token = 0;             // Unique ID for cookie
    public Lease newLease(Object sessionData, long duration) {
        long now = System.currentTimeMillis();  // Time when requested
        Integer cookie;                   // Get unique cookie
        synchronized(ServerLandlord.class) {
            cookie = new Integer(token++);
        }

        expireLeases();                    // Make room for new Leases
        if (duration == Lease.ANY ||
            duration == Lease.FOREVER ||
            duration > MAXLEASETIME)
            duration = MAXLEASETIME;

        synchronized(this) {
            Lease l = factory.newLease(cookie, this, duration);
```

```
            expiration.put(cookie, new Long(now + duration));
            leases.put(cookie, 1);
            if (sessionData != null) {
                session.put(cookie, sessionData);
            }
            return 1;
        }
    }

    public void expireLeases() {
        long now = System.currentTimeMillis();
        now = now - 60 * 1000;            // Be conservative by one minute

        synchronized (this) {
            Vector deleteList = new Vector();
            for (Enumeration e = expiration.keys();
                            e.hasMoreElements();) {
                Object cookie = e.nextElement();
                Long expire = (Long) expiration.get(cookie);
                if (expire.longValue() < now) {
                    deleteList.addElement(cookie);
                }
            }
            for (Enumeration e = deleteList.elements();
                            e.hasMoreElements();) {
                Object cookie = e.nextElement();
                expiration.remove(cookie);
                leases.remove(cookie);
                session.remove(cookie);
            }
        }
    }

    // The cookie is an *internal* reference for the LandlordLease.
    // No one outside the lease can access it.
    public Object getSessionData(Lease lease) {
        Object sessiondata = null;
        if (lease instanceof LandlordLease) {
            expireLeases();          // Make sure the lease is still valid
            synchronized (this) {
                for (Enumeration e = leases.keys();
                                e.hasMoreElements();) {
                    Object cookie = e.nextElement();
                    if (lease.equals(leases.get(cookie))) {
                        sessiondata = session.get(cookie);
                        break;
                    }
                }
            }
        }
        return sessiondata;
    }
}
```

This ServerLandlord class is written as a generic class that will provide the storage of session data. In order to store new data, the newLease( ) method is used. The newLease( ) method will store the session data, create a unique ID, and create a lease that will be used to manage the session data. This method will then store the expiration time, a copy of the lease, and the session data into hashtables that are referenced by the unique ID (i.e., the cookie). While creating the lease, it also

---

declares itself as the landlord for the lease, so it must implement the Landlord interface in order to communicate with the lease.

In order to retrieve the session data from the ServerLandlord object, the server uses the getSessionData( ) method, passing it back a copy of the lease. The lease will have probably gone through object serialization between the client and service, which means that it is unlikely that it is the original lease object. In order to check whether the lease is the same, we must use the equals( ) method which, in the case of the LandlordLease object, checks only if the landlord and unique ID are the same. It is unlikely that the expiration time in the two objects is the same, since we are only renewing the lease from the client side. Furthermore, we are not using the cookie to refer to the lease. The cookie (or unique ID) is used by the lease only to communicate with its landlord. This unique ID is not used by the client or by the service directly.

The leases are expired by the expireLeases( ) method. This method goes through the hashtable of leases. If a lease has reached its expiration time, the lease—along with its session data—will be removed from the hashtables. This ServerLandlord class will not automatically expire the leases. This could be accomplished by starting a thread that periodically calls the expireLeases( ) method (which we actually do in Chapter 8, *Miscellaneous Classes*). The only time that we explicitly expire leases is when we create a new lease or when a client request comes in. One reason we may not want the landlord to expire leases automatically is the importance of the session data. This generic class does not know whether the data warrants automatic expiration and leaves this duty to the server implementation.

Finally, the expireLeases( ) method also allows for a one-minute grace period. In the best of circumstances, clients will renew their leases well in advance of their deadline, and the renewals will not be delayed by network traffic in reaching the server. Building in a grace period may help mitigate situations where either of those things goes wrong, although if the renewal arrives 61 seconds late, the client is still out of luck.

In order to work with the LandlordLease object that we obtain in the newLease( ) method, our class must implement the Landlord interface. The renew( ) method is implemented by checking for the existence of the lease and granting the request. This, in turn, is accomplished by updating the expiration hashtable. This implementation does not deny requests, which it could do by throwing a LeaseDeniedException. The only logic that it has restricts the lease time to MAXLEASETIME (ten minutes). This will prevent long leases from being issued, which will increase the robustness of the server. The renewAll( ) method simply calls the renew( ) method to accomplish its task.

The cancel( ) method is also very simple. It checks for the existence of the lease and grants the request. Granting the request is accomplished by removing the lease and the sessiondata from the hashtables. The cancelAll( ) method calls the cancel( ) method to accomplish its task.

Finally, it should be noted that this object is an UnicastRemoteObject object. This means that its stub will be shipped over to the client as part of the Lease object. When the lease is sent to the client, it will contain the cookie, expiration time, and the stub. The session data will not be delivered to the client.

The Service Implementation

Now we must modify the implementation of our server. The server now has two
interfaces that it must support: the `ConvertService` and `ConvertServiceRegistra-
tion` interfaces. We'll start with the latter interface:

```
import java.io.*;
import java.rmi.*;
import net.jini.core.lease.*;

// This class enables the client to hold the lease locally and
// forward the convert request to the service proxy
class ConvertServiceRegistrationImpl
        implements ConvertServiceRegistration, Serializable {

    private Lease lease;
    ConvertServiceProxy server;

    ConvertServiceRegistrationImpl(ConvertServiceProxy server, Lease l) {
        this.server = server;
        this.lease = l;
    }

    public String convert(int i) throws RemoteException {
        try {
            return server.convert(lease, i);
        } catch (LeaseDeniedException lde) {
            // Our interface doesn't throw this exception, so we wrap it
            throw new RemoteException("Lease expired");
        }
    }

    public Lease getLease() {
        return lease;
    }
}
```

This class is returned to the client via the `getInstance()` method of the `Convert-
Service` interface. According to its interface, it must contain the lease object locally
for the `getLease()` method, and it must continue to support the `convert()`
method to perform the actual work of the service.

Because it contains the lease object, this implementation cannot be a `Remote`
object. This is different than our previous implementations, in which we returned
a remote object to the client. In those examples, when the client called the
`convert()` method, it was directly invoking an RMI method call back to the
server. Since we are required to return the lease to the client as an embedded
object, we cannot make this implementation a `Remote` object, so this implementation needs an embedded RMI object so that the `convert()` method can call back
to the server to do the conversion.

We know from previous examples that the service object itself implements the
`ConvertServiceProxy` interface. But now we've introduced a change to that interface: it must now allow a lease to be passed via the `convert()` method. The modified interface looks like this:

```
import java.rmi.*;
import java.rmi.server.*;
import net.jini.core.lease.*;

public interface ConvertServiceProxy extends Remote, ConvertService {
    // We convert the call on the client to this form for the server
    public String convert(Lease l, int i)
                    throws LeaseDeniedException, RemoteException;
}
```

Finally, we can implement the primary logic of the server. With the support of the
ServerLandlord class, implementing the changes is straightforward. The
getInstance( ) method must create the session data, save the session data, and
generate the lease. The last two tasks are accomplished by the server landlord
object. The convert( ) method is also modified to load the session data from the
server landlord; it checks to see if it has previously calculated the current request
and if it has, it returns the cached answer. Otherwise, it calculates and caches the
answer:

```
import java.util.*;
import java.io.*;
import java.rmi.*;
import java.rmi.server.*;
import net.jini.discovery.*;
import net.jini.core.lease.*;
import com.sun.jini.lookup.*;

public class ConvertServiceImpl extends UnicastRemoteObject
                            implements ConvertServiceProxy {

    private ServerLandlord lord;

    public ConvertServiceImpl() throws RemoteException {
        lord = new ServerLandlord();
    }

    public ConvertServiceRegistration getInstance(long duration) {
        Hashtable ht = new Hashtable(13);
        return new ConvertServiceRegistrationImpl(this,
                                    lord.newLease(ht, duration));
    }

    // To convert, first check the cache for previous results. If
    // there's no cache, the landlord has expired the lease. If
    // there's no data in the cache, calculcate the data and put it there
    public String convert(Lease l, int i) throws LeaseDeniedException {
        Hashtable cache = (Hashtable) lord.getSessionData(l);
        if (cache == null)
            throw new LeaseDeniedException("Lease expired");
        Integer I = new Integer(i);
        String s;
        s = (String) cache.get(I);
        if (s != null)
            return s;
        s = I.toString();
        cache.put(I, s);
        return s;
    }
}
```

```
public static void main(String[] args) throws Exception {
    System.setSecurityManager(new RMISecurityManager());
    String[] groups = new String[] { "" };

    // Create the instance of the service; the JoinManager will
    // register it and renew its leases with the lookup service
    ConvertServiceImpl csi =
                    (ConvertServiceImpl) new ConvertServiceImpl();
    JoinManager manager = new JoinManager(csi, null, groups,
                                    null, null, null);
}
}
```

Running the Service

Compiling and running the server requires that we deal with the new classes. The ServerLandlord class must be compiled as usual; since it is a unicast remote object, we must also generate its stub with *rmic*. The stub must be placed on the java.rmi.server.codebase along with the stub from the ConvertServiceImpl class as we've done previously. The other new classes need only to be compiled.

The Client Implementation

Let's now examine our client:

```
import java.rmi.*;
import net.jini.discovery.*;
import net.jini.core.lease.*;
import com.sun.jini.lease.*;

public class ConvertClient {

    public static void main(String[] args) throws Exception {
        System.setSecurityManager(new RMISecurityManager());

        // Find the service by its interface type
        ServiceFinder sf = new ServiceFinder(ConvertService.class);
        ConvertService cs = (ConvertService) sf.getObject();
        ConvertServiceRegistration csr = cs.getInstance(Lease.FOREVER);

        // Because we exit immediately, we don't need to manage the
        // lease in this case, but if we did, here's the simple way to
        // do it.
        LeaseRenewalManager lrm =
            new LeaseRenewalManager(csr.getLease(), Lease.FOREVER, null);

        // Now invoke methods on the service object
        System.out.println(csr.convert(5));
    }
}
```

The client has to obtain a session with the service before calling the convert( ) method; this is accomplished by calling the getInstance( ) method. We are also introducing the use of the LeaseRenewalManager class. This is the class used internally by the JoinManager class in the previous chapter. The purpose of the LeaseRenewalManager class is to renew our lease automatically—eliminating the

---

need for us to create a thread just to keep the leases from expiring. The interface to the LeaseRenewalManager class is similar to the Lease interface. There are methods that renew the lease and cancel the lease. The difference is that with the LeaseRenewManager class, we don't worry if the server grants the full duration of the lease, since the lease renewal manager will automatically renew the lease. There is also the option of using the LeaseListener interface to detect failures of renewing the lease. We are not using that option in this example.

Lease Policies

There are other classes in the com.sun.jini.lease package that can be used to build a leasing service. These classes allow us to abstract certain details when we implement a landlord. Here's a quick overview of these classes:

com.sun.jini.lease.landlord.LeasedResource
This interface should be implemented by classes that contain data to be leased (e.g., session data objects). This interface allows us to encapsulate the lease expiration time, unique cookie, and session data in one object by storing everything together. This class is necessary if either a LeaseManager object or a LeasePolicy object is being used.

com.sun.jini.lease.landlord.LeasePolicy
This interface should be implemented by the class that handles Leased-Resource objects; it handles the details of renewing and cancelling leases associated with those objects. The implementation of this interface must have some mechanism to create new leases and renew leases. The most likely mechanism for managing the leases is a modification of the expiration times of the LeasedResource object that will be passed to it.

By having a lease policy, the landlord can abstract the details of renewing and cancelling individual leases.

com.sun.jini.lease.landlord.LeaseManager
This interface should be implemented by the class that is to handle callbacks from the leasing system. Objects that implement this interface are informed of new registrations and renewals of resources. When a LeaseDurationPolicy object is created, an optional LeaseManager object can be provided, which is called every time a lease is created or renewed by the LeasePolicy object.

com.sun.jini.lease.landlord.LeaseDurationPolicy
This class is an implementation of the LeasePolicy interface. Implementations of the landlord class can defer the creation and renewal of leases to a Lease-DurationPolicy object. The parameters that must be used to construct this class are the factory object that creates leases (which can be the Land-lordLease.Factory object that our ServerLandlord object instantiated), the landlord object, an optional LeaseManager object that will be informed of new registrations or lease renewals, and the default and maximum lease times that will be granted.

Together, these classes all allow us to create a LeasePolicy object that contains the policy of our leases. Then if we want to change policies, we simply substitute a new implementation of the LeasePolicy class. We'll do that in Example 5-2.

Example 5-2: A Service with a Leasing Policy

```
Common classes
    ConvertService (used in Example 5-1)
    ConvertServiceRegistration (used in Example 5-1)
Server classes
    ConvertServiceImpl (used in Example 5-1)
    ConvertServiceRegistrationImpl (used in Example 5-1)
    ConvertServiceProxy (used in Example 5-1)
    ServerLandlord (modified from Example 5-1)
    ServerResource (new)
Client classes
    ServiceFinder (used in Example 5-1; listed in Example 4-1)
    ConvertClient (used in Example 5-1)
```

To convert our server to support these classes, we must first implement a few details. We now need to create a LeasePolicy object that will handle the actual leased resources. We also need to create a LeasedResource object that represents those resources.

We'll start with the leased resource:

```
import net.jini.core.lease.*;
import com.sun.jini.lease.landlord.*;

public class ServerResource implements LeasedResource {
    protected static int token = 0;
    protected Integer cookie;
    protected long expiration;

    public Lease lease;        // Only a copy (not the client's)
    public Object sessionData;

    // Simple resource mapper -- we use a static int to ensure that
    // each lease resource will have a unique cookie
    public ServerResource(Object sessionData) {
        synchronized (ServerResource.class) {
            cookie = new Integer(token++);
        }
        this.sessionData = sessionData;
    }

    public long getExpiration() {
        return expiration;
    }

    public void setExpiration(long expire) {
        expiration = expire;
    }

    public Object getCookie() {
        return cookie;
    }
}
```

The ServerResource object is a data object that supports the LeasedResource interface. In our example, the representation of the data that is to be leased includes the session data and a token that the client will use to find the resource. In this case, the token is a copy of the lease. The other parts of the LeasedResource interface are the cookie that we will use and the expiration time.

For the policy object, we will use the LeaseDurationPolicy class. The five components that need to be passed to the constructor of this class are the maximum lease time, the default lease time, the landlord that controls the leases, an optional lease manager used to track registrations and renewals, and the lease factory object. If the lease factory is not provided, the LandlordLease.Factory will be used by default. In our example, we are willing to accept the default lease factory and don't need to monitor registrations and renewals of leases. Here is our new implementation of the server landlord:

```java
import java.rmi.*;
import java.rmi.server.*;
import java.util.*;
import net.jini.core.lease.*;
import com.sun.jini.lease.landlord.*;

public class ServerLandlord extends UnicastRemoteObject
                            implements Landlord {
        // cookie -> ServerResource
    protected Hashtable resources = new Hashtable();
    protected long MAXLEASETIME = 10*60*1000;       // 10 Minutes
    protected LeasePolicy policy;

    public ServerLandlord() throws RemoteException {
        policy = new LeaseDurationPolicy(MAXLEASETIME, MAXLEASETIME,
                                         this, null, null);
    }

    public long renew(Object cookie, long duration)
            throws LeaseDeniedException,
                   UnknownLeaseException, RemoteException {
        synchronized (this) {
            ServerResource sr =
                           (ServerResource) resources.get(cookie);
            if (sr == null)
                throw new UnknownLeaseException();
            return policy.renew(sr, duration);

        }
    }

    public Landlord.RenewResults renewAll(Object[] cookie,
                          long[] duration) throws RemoteException {
        long[] granted = new long[cookie.length];
        Vector denied = new Vector();

        for (int i = 0; i < cookie.length; i++) {
            try {
                granted[i] = renew(cookie[i], duration[i]);
            } catch (LeaseException lex) {
                granted[i] = -1;
                denied.add(lex);
            }
```

```
        }
        return new Landlord.RenewResults(granted,
                denied.isEmpty() ? null : (Exception[]) denied.toArray());
    }

    public void cancel(Object cookie)
            throws UnknownLeaseException, RemoteException {
        synchronized (this) {
            ServerResource sr =
                    (ServerResource) resources.get(cookie);
            if (sr == null)                    throw new UnknownLeaseException();

            resources.remove(cookie);


        }
    }

    public void cancelAll(Object[] cookie)
            throws LeaseMapException, RemoteException {
        Map map = null;
        for (int i = 0; i < cookie.length; i++) {
            try {
                cancel(cookie[i]);
            } catch (LeaseException ex) {
                if (map == null)
                    map = new HashMap();
                map.put(cookie[i], ex);
            }
        }
        if (map != null)
            throw new LeaseMapException("Can't cancel all leases", map);
    }

    // The following methods are not part of the Landlord interface
    // and can be called only by directly using this object.
    public Lease newLease(Object sessionData, long duration) {
        ServerResource sr = new ServerResource(sessionData);

        expireLeases();                    // Make room for new Leases

        try {
            sr.lease = policy.leaseFor(sr, duration);
            synchronized(this) {
                resources.put(sr.getCookie(), sr);
            }
            return sr.lease;
        } catch (LeaseDeniedException e) {};
        return null;
    }

    public void expireLeases() {
        synchronized (this) {
            Vector deleteList = new Vector();
            for (Enumeration e = resources.elements();
                            e.hasMoreElements();) {
                ServerResource sr = (ServerResource) e.nextElement();
                if (!policy.ensureCurrent(sr)) {
                    deleteList.addElement(sr.getCookie());
                }
```

```
        }
        for (Enumeration e = deleteList.elements();
                       e.hasMoreElements();) {
            Object cookie = e.nextElement();
            resources.remove(cookie);
        }
    }
}

// The cookie is an *internal* reference for the LandlordLease.
// No one outside the lease can access it.
public Object getSessionData(Lease lease) {
    Object sessiondata = null;
    expireLeases();             // Make sure this lease hasn't expired
    synchronized (this) {
        for (Enumeration e = resources.elements();
                       e.hasMoreElements();) {
            ServerResource sr = (ServerResource) e.nextElement();
            if (lease.equals(sr.lease)) {
                sessiondata = sr.sessionData;
                break;
            }
        }
    }
    return sessiondata;
}
}
```

Our new implementation of the ServerLandlord class is simpler. We now maintain a single hashtable instead of three. And handling of the expiration logic—the recalculation of expiration times, and checking whether a lease expired—is provided by the policy class. The interface between the lease and the landlord is unchanged. Using these support classes allows us to abstract the data into a LeasedResource class and allows us to abstract the logic in handling the data into a LeasePolicy class.

In this example, we now have an extra class (the ServerResource class) to compile. Since this class is not distributed to the client, it does not need to be placed on the java.rmi.server.codebase.

Summary

Proper use of leasing is a key benefit of a Jini community, since it allows the participants in the community to manage actively their associations with each other. In particular, this can allow servers to purge any client-specific data that they hold once the associated client is no longer active. While this is a key feature of the Jini lookup service, it's an important benefit in a variety of other services as well.

In the next chapter, we'll learn about Jini's remote event facility. Remote events use leasing as part of their implementation, they play a key part in dealing with the Jini lookup service, and they can be used directly between Jini services and clients.

CHAPTER 6

Remote Events

In this chapter, we'll discuss Jini's remote event APIs. The concept of an event is not new. Basically, it is the ability of one object to notify another object when something has happened. This removes the need for the client to poll the service for information, thus reducing CPU and communication resources. Java's event paradigm was first defined in the JavaBeans specification. In this specification, all events inherit from the java.util.EventObject class and are delivered to listeners that implement listener interfaces that extend the java.util.EventListener interface. With JavaBeans, the receiver must create a listener that it passes to the source of the events. The events are then delivered to the receiver by the source, which calls methods on the stored listener object.

Jini extends this model. The listener is now a Remote interface, which allows events to be passed between different VMs. These extended listeners must implement the net.jini.core.event.RemoteEventListener interface, and the events themselves must inherit from the net.jini.core.event.RemoteEvent class. These new classes are also event listeners and event objects, so they can be used anywhere a generic EventListener or EventObject instance could be used.

Just as in the JavaBeans specification, the remote event model is more of a pattern that should be followed to allow clients and services to communicate rather than an API that handles the details of the infrastructure. In fact, the main requirement for the infrastructure is the use of RMI as its distribution mechanism. A RemoteEventListener object is basically an RMI stub that the source calls to deliver objects to the receiver. As we mentioned in Chapter 1, *Introduction to Jini*, this requirement will change in Java 1.3, when Remote objects will not need to be implemented with RMI.

Leasing is very important when it comes to remote events. The client that registers for events with a service is asking the service to store session data (the event listener) for the client; the service must have a way to track when the client is finished with that data. In addition, when the event is generated, the service makes a callback to the client; this call will block the server if the client is unavailable. For these reasons, it is strongly recommended that a lease be attached to a remote event registration so that the server can eliminate the listeners of failed clients.

A Remote Event Example

In this chapter, we'll develop an example that uses Jini's distributed event mechanism. We'll modify our service so that interested parties can register to be notified whenever a conversion occurs. We'll start with Example 5-2 as a basis, since we'll need to use the leasing code to keep track of the event listeners. The files required for this example are shown in Example 6-1.

Example 6–1: A Service That Delivers Distributed Events

```
Common classes
    ConvertService (modified from Example 5-2; listed in Example 5-1)
    ConvertServiceRegistration (used in Example 5-2; listed in Example 5-1)
    ConvertEvent (new)
Server classes
    ConvertServiceImpl (modified from Example 5-2; listed in Example 5-1)
    ConvertServiceRegistrationImpl (used in Example 5-2; listed in
            Example 5-1)
    ConvertServiceProxy (used in Example 5-2; listed in Example 5-1)
    ServerLandlord (used in Example 5-2)
    ServerResource (used in Example 5-2; listed in Example 5-1)
    ServerDelivery (new)
Client classes
    ServiceFinder (used in Example 5-2; listed in Example 4-1)
    ConvertClient (modified from Example 5-2; listed in Example 5-1)
    ConvertEventHandler (new)
```

There are three classes and interfaces in the net.jini.core.event package that we'll use in this example. They are:

net.jini.core.event.RemoteEvent

This is the superclass for all remote events in Jini. This class contains four pieces of data:

The event ID

Each service is free to pick its own value for the event ID. However, a client that registers for events from a service must receive the same ID in each event delivered as a result of that registration.

The sequence number

Each event has a sequence number, which is used to order the event. The client should use this number to determine whether the event has been delivered out of order or has already been received. The sender of events may skip sequence numbers, but they must always increase by at least one for each new event.

The source of the event

The object that originated the event.

A handback object

This object is supplied by the client during event registration and is sent by the server with each event.

The RemoteEvent class can be used as is, but it is often subclassed to provide more information about the event.

net.jini.core.event.EventRegistration

This class encapsulates the information required for a client to handle an event for which it wants notifications; it includes the lease that the server has issued, the ID of the event(s) that will be sent, the current sequence number for the event, and the object that is generating the event. Use of this class is not required, but it makes implementing event notification much easier.

net.jini.core.event.RemoteEventListener

This interface must be implemented by clients that want to receive remote events. The events are sent to the notify() method of the class that implements this interface.

The Service Interface

To start our example, we must modify our service interface to support registration for event notification. This notification must return a lease so that the server can tell when the client has left the network. As we did in the last chapter, we'll return a registration object that embeds the lease within it, using the EventRegistration class:

```
import java.rmi.*;
import net.jini.core.event.*;

public interface ConvertService {
    public ConvertServiceRegistration getInstance(long duration)
                throws RemoteException;
    public EventRegistration trackConversions(long duration,
                RemoteEventListener rel, MarshalledObject key)
                throws RemoteException;
}
```

This allows the client to specify that conversions be tracked for the given duration and reported to the given listener. Delivered events will contain the key as their handback object.

There is an additional class in this example that is common between the client and server:

```
import java.rmi.*;
import net.jini.core.event.*;

public class ConvertEvent extends RemoteEvent {

    protected int value;
    // Arbitrary ID for our event type
    final static int ID = 1001;

    public ConvertEvent(Object source, int value,
                        long seqno, MarshalledObject key) {
        // The superclass needs our event ID
        super(source, ID, seqno, key);
        this.value = value;
    }

    public int getValue() {
        return value;
    }
}
```

The events in our example are conversion events; they indicate that a client has requested that a particular value be converted. Because we want to include the value as part of the event, we must subclass the RemoteEvent class to store the value. Because we're only tracking one type of event, we're able to hardcode the ID to an arbitrary value; if we were tracking conversions of subsets of numbers or some other schemes, we'd have to come up with a different scheme to assign event IDs. For example, if we provided an interface to register for events when a certain number was converted, we could use that number as the event ID.

The Client Implementation

In this example, many of the changes occur on the client side, because the client must register for and handle the remote event. To register for the event, the client needs to create a remote event listener, which it does by using this new class:

```
import java.rmi.*;
import java.rmi.server.*;
import net.jini.core.event.*;

public class ConvertEventHandler extends UnicastRemoteObject
                                 implements RemoteEventListener {
    public ConvertEventHandler() throws RemoteException {
    }

    public void notify(RemoteEvent rev)
            throws UnknownEventException, RemoteException {
        ConvertEvent cev;
        if (!(rev instanceof ConvertEvent))
            throw new UnknownEventException("Unexpected event type");
        cev = (ConvertEvent) rev;
        long seq = cev.getSequenceNumber();
        int  val = cev.getValue();
        System.out.println("Convert #" + seq + ": " + val);
    }
}
```

Because the RemoteEventListener extends the Remote interface, it must be implemented as a UnicastRemoteObject or exported through the exportObject() method of that class. In this example, we inspect the data contained in the event object (which must be a ConvertEvent object) and print out some of the interesting data.

Here's how the client registers the listener with the service:

```
import java.rmi.*;
import net.jini.discovery.*;
import net.jini.core.lease.*;
import net.jini.core.event.*;
import com.sun.jini.lease.*;

public class ConvertClient {

    public static void main(String[] args) throws Exception {
        System.setSecurityManager(new RMISecurityManager());

        // Find the service by its interface type
        ServiceFinder sf = new ServiceFinder(ConvertService.class);
```

```
ConvertService cs = (ConvertService) sf.getObject();

LeaseRenewalManager lrm = new LeaseRenewalManager();

// Sign up to be notified of all conversions
RemoteEventListener rel = new ConvertEventHandler();
EventRegistration er =
          cs.trackConversions(Lease.FOREVER, rel, null);
lrm.renewUntil(er.getLease(), Lease.FOREVER, null);

// Now do a conversion
ConvertServiceRegistration csr = cs.getInstance(Lease.FOREVER);
lrm.renewUntil(csr.getLease(), Lease.FOREVER, null);

// Now invoke methods on the service object
System.out.println(csr.convert(5));

// We'll sit here, waiting forever for other event notifications
// to happen.
// If you want to exit, you should clean up the leases
// first, e.g.,
// lrm.cancel(er.getLease());
// lrm.cancel(csr.getLease());
// System.exit(0);
    }
}
```

After we have received a reference to the service, we create and register the event listener with the service by calling the trackConversions() method. We do not need a handback object in our example, so we pass null.

The lease that the trackConversions() method returns will be maintained by the same LeaseRenewalManager that we used earlier. Notice also that there is no method in the ConvertService interface to remove the listener from the service. Instead, this is accomplished by cancelling the lease. When the lease is cancelled—or allowed to expire—the service will remove the listener along with any session data that the listener required.

As it's written now, this client will not exit. There are many threads running, including some for the remote event listener object that we did not start explicitly. As long as the lease renewal manager continues to contact the service (and the service stays up), the remote event listener object will stay current on the service and those threads will not terminate. If we explicitly cancel the lease on the remote event listener, then eventually the RMI garbage collection code will clean up the remote reference to the listener object and those threads will terminate and the program will exit. But we've commented that part out; when you run this example, you can run multiple instances of the client and see them each get notifications from requests generated by new clients.

The Service Implementation

On the server side, we must develop a class that delivers the remote events to the client:

```
import java.rmi.*;
import java.rmi.server.*;
```

```java
import java.util.*;
import net.jini.core.lease.*;
import net.jini.core.event.*;
import com.sun.jini.lease.landlord.*;

public class ServerDelivery {
    private Remote source;          // Owner of this delivery object
    private ServerLandlord lord;    // The landlord that manages leases
    private Vector leases;          // Event-specific leases
    private long seqnum = 0;

    // The client-specific session data for the event leases
    // holds the listener and the callback data
    private class SessionData {
        public RemoteEventListener listener;
        public MarshalledObject key;
    }

    public ServerDelivery(Remote source, ServerLandlord ll) {
        this.source = source;
        lord = ll;
        leases = new Vector();
    }

    public synchronized EventRegistration
                addListener(RemoteEventListener l, long duration,
                            MarshalledObject key) {
        SessionData sd = new SessionData();
        sd.listener = l;
        sd.key = key;

        Lease lease = lord.newLease(sd, duration);
        leases.addElement(lease);

        return new EventRegistration(ConvertEvent.ID,
                                     source, lease, seqnum);
    }

    // Deliver an event to all listeners
    public synchronized void deliver(int value) {
        long seq = seqnum++;                 // Deliver request number
        if (leases.isEmpty())
            return;

        lord.expireLeases();                 // Clean up the leases first
        Vector expiredLeases = new Vector();
        // Deliver to each client. Save all the expired leases
        // and remove those leases after the loop
        for (Enumeration e = leases.elements(); e.hasMoreElements();) {
            Lease l = (Lease) e.nextElement();
            SessionData obj = (SessionData) lord.getSessionData(l);
            if (obj == null) {
                expiredLeases.addElement(l);
            } else {
                try {
                    deliverEvent(obj, seq, value);
                } catch (RemoteException rex) {
                    // Can't really do anything here --
                    // cancelling the lease is not allowed;
                    // we'll have to try again next time
```

```
                } catch (UnknownEventException uee) {
                    // The client told us it didn't want these events
                    // anymore, cancel it's registration
                    expiredLeases.addElement(l);
                }
            }
        }

        // Get rid of all the failed clients
        for (Enumeration e = expiredLeases.elements();
                    e.hasMoreElements();) {
            Lease l = (Lease) e.nextElement();
            leases.remove(l);
        }
    }

    // Actually send the event
    private void deliverEvent(SessionData data, long seq, int value)
            throws RemoteException, UnknownEventException {
        ConvertEvent event = new ConvertEvent(source, value,
                                        seq, data.key);

        data.listener.notify(event);
    }
}
```

The creation and delivery of events is managed by the ServerDelivery class. This class contains two public methods: the addListener() method, which adds a new remote event listener; and the deliver() method, which will deliver an event that represents a single integer value to the listeners.

To implement the addListener() method, we build our session data for the listener. This includes the listener and the marshalled object that we hand back. The management of the session data will be handled by our server landlord, which also creates a lease to send back to the client. We also need to save the lease in order to retrieve the session data at a later time. This is done in the leases vector.

In the implementation of the deliver() method, we must first check the lease for expirations. We are about to execute remote requests, and we don't want to block waiting for a failed client. So we reduce our chances of failure as much as possible. The ideal thing to do is to use the com.sun.jini.thread.TaskManager class (or a similar thread pool) to execute these callbacks in another thread, which we do in Chapter 8, *Miscellaneous Classes*.

Unfortunately, expiring the leases does not remove the leases from our private vector. However, since expired leases will no longer have any session data, we can remove any lease in our private vector that does not have session data. If the session data is available, the deliverEvent() method will be called. This method uses the session data—among other objects—to create the remote event and call the notify() method of the event listener. If a remote exception occurs during this attempt, the client has probably failed, but we're not supposed to cancel a lease on behalf of the client, so we can't take any action. If an unknown event exception occurs, on the other hand, then the client has rejected the event and we are free to cancel its lease.

No changes to the `ServerResource` class or the `ServerLandlord` class are required to support these events. So, finally, let's examine the changes to the `ServerImpl` class:

```java
import java.util.*;
import java.io.*;
import java.rmi.*;
import java.rmi.server.*;
import net.jini.discovery.*;
import net.jini.core.lease.*;
import net.jini.core.event.*;
import com.sun.jini.lookup.*;

public class ConvertServiceImpl extends UnicastRemoteObject
                            implements ConvertServiceProxy {

    private ServerLandlord lord;
    private ServerDelivery sender;

    public ConvertServiceImpl() throws RemoteException {
        lord = new ServerLandlord();
        sender = new ServerDelivery(this, lord);

    }

    public ConvertServiceRegistration getInstance(long duration) {
        Hashtable ht = new Hashtable(13);
        return new ConvertServiceRegistrationImpl(this,
                                    lord.newLease(ht, duration));
    }

    // To convert, first check the cache for previous results. If
    // there's no cache, the landlord has expired the lease. If
    // there's no data in the cache, calculcate the data and put it there
    public String convert(Lease l, int i) throws LeaseDeniedException {
        Hashtable cache = (Hashtable) lord.getSessionData(l);
        if (cache == null)
            throw new LeaseDeniedException("Lease expired");
        Integer I = new Integer(i);
        String s;
        s = (String) cache.get(I);
        if (s == null) {
            s = I.toString();
            cache.put(I, s);
        }
        sender.deliver(i);
        return s;
    }

    public EventRegistration trackConversions(long duration,
                    RemoteEventListener rel, MarshalledObject key) {
        return sender.addListener(rel, duration, key);
    }

    public static void main(String[] args) throws Exception {
        System.setSecurityManager(new RMISecurityManager());
        String[] groups = new String[] { "" };

        // Create the instance of the service; the JoinManager will
        // register it and renew its leases with the lookup service
```

```
ConvertServiceImpl csi =
          (ConvertServiceImpl) new ConvertServiceImpl();
JoinManager manager = new JoinManager(csi, null, groups,
                                      null, null, null);
     }
  }
```

We have only a few changes in our ConvertServiceImpl class. First, we must create a ServerDelivery object to handle the delivery of events. The implementation of the trackConversions() method is accomplished by registering the event listener with the delivery object. Then in the convert() method, the delivery object is used to send the events to the registered listeners.

Running the Example

Compiling and running the application introduces a new complexity. For the server, there are only extra classes that need to be compiled; they do not need to be delivered to the client, so they do not need to be in the server's java.rmi.server.codebase.

The client is now very different. The ConvertEventHandler is a remote object. This means that we must compile it, generate its stubs with *rmic*, and place the stubs in a location that can be accessed by the server. This means that we must now run the client with a java.rmi.server.codebase property, and that the client must have a web server available to it as well. This is another good use for the HTTP server that comes with the Jini distribution.

To summarize, here are the steps necessary to compile and run the client (assuming that the Jini lookup service is already up):

1. Compile all the classes:

    ```
    client% javac ConvertClient.java ConvertService.java
            ConvertEvent.java ConvertServiceRegistration.java
            ConvertEventHandler.java ServiceFinder.java
    ```

2. Generate the stubs:

    ```
    client% rmic -v1.2 ConvertEventHandler
    ```

3. Run an HTTP-server on the client to serve the stubs to the server:

    ```
    client% java -jar /files/jini1_0/lib/tools.jar -dir . -port 8087
    ```

    This command does not exit; remember to run it in another window (or run it in the background if your OS supports it). Make sure to supply the correct argument to the *-dir* option. If your client and server are running on the same machine, make sure not to use the same port number for each HTTP server.

4. Run the client and receive its output:

    ```
    client% java -Djava.security.policy=/files/jini1_0/java.policy.all
            -Djava.rmi.server.codebase=http://client:8087/
            ConvertClient
    Convert #6: 5
    5
    ```

The first output line in this case comes from the event notification, which prints the sequence number and the value to be converted (we had already run the client a few times, which is why the sequence number is 6). The second output line is printed by the client's main( ) method. The lines of output for this example may occur in any order: the event delivery is asynchronous to the response to the conversion request.

The commands to run the server are the same as they've been all along.

Remote Events and the Jini Lookup Service

When we examined the Jini lookup service in Chapter 4, *Basic Jini Programming*, we avoided using one of its key features. Now that we have a better understanding of remote events, let's revisit the Jini lookup service. The Jini lookup service provides an asynchronous interface that uses remote events to deliver information about the objects that it maintains. We need this because services can come and go at any time.

For example, what if we started the client before we started the service that it needs? The client will discover the lookup service. It will call the lookup() method on these lookup services, but it won't find the service. At a later time, the service will discover and register itself with all the lookup services. We need a mechanism for the lookup service to notify the client that the service object is now available. Otherwise, the only way that the client will discover the service is if a new lookup service is started and the service discovers and registers with it first.

Hence, the Jini lookup service allows clients to register a remote event listener. The remote events that will be delivered to the clients relate to the changes in the registered services. Clients can be informed if a new service has been added to the lookup service, if a service is being removed from the lookup service, and if the attributes of a service have changed. The Jini lookup service will return to the client a lease that the client must renew. If the lease is cancelled, the remote event listener will stop receiving events.

We'll modify our last example to support receiving events from the lookup service. The files required for this example are listed in Example 6-2.

Example 6-2: A Client That Receives Lookup Service Events

```
Common classes
    ConvertService (used in Example 6-1)
    ConvertServiceRegistration (used in Example 6-1; listed in Example 5-1)
    ConvertEvent (used in Example 6-1)
Server classes
    ConvertServiceImpl (used in Example 6-1)
    ConvertServiceRegistrationImpl (used in Example 6-1;
        listed in Example 5-1)
    ConvertServiceProxy (used in Example 6-1; listed in Example 5-1)
    ServerLandlord (used in Example 6-1; listed in Example 5-2)
    ServerResource (used in Example 6-1; listed in Example 5-1)
    ServerDelivery (used in Example 6-1)
Client classes
    ServiceFinder (modified from Example 6-1; listed in Example 4-1)
    ServiceFinderListener (new)
```

Example 6–2: A Client That Receives Lookup Service Events (continued)

```
ConvertEventHandler (used in Example 6-1)
ConvertClient (used in Example 6-1)
```

All the changes for this example occur in the client code. First, we must write a listener that the client can use to receive the events from the lookup service:

```
import java.rmi.*;
import java.rmi.server.*;
import net.jini.core.lookup.*;
import net.jini.core.event.*;


public class ServiceFinderListener extends UnicastRemoteObject
                               implements RemoteEventListener {
    private ServiceFinder parent;

    public ServiceFinderListener(ServiceFinder parent)
                             throws RemoteException {
        this.parent = parent;
    }

     public void notify(RemoteEvent event)
             throws UnknownEventException, RemoteException {
        if (!(event instanceof ServiceEvent))
           throw new UnknownEventException("ServiceFinderListener");

        ServiceEvent sevent = (ServiceEvent) event;
        ServiceItem item = sevent.getServiceItem();
        if (sevent.getTransition() ==
                    ServiceRegistrar.TRANSITION_NOMATCH_MATCH) {
            parent.addServiceItem(item);
        }
    }
}
```

For our lookup listener, we must implement the single method required of remote event listeners: the notify() method. We first check to make sure that we have received a net.jini.core.lookup.ServiceEvent object—this is the object that will be sent by Jini lookup services. This class contains special data known as the transition, which indicates one of the following three states:

TRANSITION_NOMATCH_MATCH
    A new service that satisfies the lookup template has been registered.

TRANSITION_MATCH_NOMATCH
    A service is being removed from the lookup service, or the attributes of the service have changed such that it no longer matches the lookup template.

TRANSITION_MATCH_MATCH
    A service has changed the attributes it supports, but still matches the template.

In our example, the only transition that we are concerned with is the appearance of new services. Once we get a new service item, we add the item to the list of items in our ServiceFinder object by calling its addServiceItem() method. Here is the new implementation of our ServiceFinder class:

```
import java.io.*;
import java.rmi.*;
```

```java
import java.util.*;
import net.jini.discovery.*;
import net.jini.core.lookup.*;
import net.jini.core.entry.*;
import net.jini.core.event.*;
import net.jini.core.lease.*;
import com.sun.jini.lease.*;

public class ServiceFinder implements DiscoveryListener {
    private static String[] publicGroup = new String[] { "" };
    private ServiceItem returnObject = null;
    private Hashtable items = new Hashtable();

    private Hashtable leases = new Hashtable();
    private LeaseRenewalManager lrm;
    private ServiceFinderListener sfl;

    private LookupDiscovery reg;
    private ServiceTemplate template;

    public ServiceFinder(Class serviceInterface) throws IOException {
        this(publicGroup, serviceInterface, (Entry[])null);
    }

    public ServiceFinder(Class serviceInterface, Entry attribute)
                        throws IOException {
        this(publicGroup, serviceInterface, new Entry[] { attribute });
    }

    public ServiceFinder(Class serviceInterface, Entry[] attributes)
                        throws IOException {
        this(publicGroup, serviceInterface, attributes);
    }

    public ServiceFinder(String[] groups, Class serviceInterface,
                        Entry[] attributes) throws IOException {
        // Construct the template here for matching in the lookup service
        // We don't use the template until we actually discover a service
        Class[] name = new Class[] { serviceInterface };
        template = new ServiceTemplate(null, name, attributes);

        // Initialize for receiving events from the lookup service
        lrm = new LeaseRenewalManager();
        sfl = new ServiceFinderListener(this);

        // Create the facility to perform multicast discovery for all
        // lookup services
        reg = new LookupDiscovery(groups);
        reg.addDiscoveryListener(this);
    }

    // Automatically called when a lookup service is discovered
    // (the listener callback of the addDiscoveryListener method)
    public synchronized void discovered(DiscoveryEvent dev) {
        ServiceRegistrar[] lookup = dev.getRegistrars();
        // We may have discovered one or more lookup services
        for (int i = 0; i < lookup.length; i++) {

            // For each service, register for transition events
            try {
                EventRegistration reg = lookup[i].notify(template,
```

```
                    ServiceRegistrar.TRANSITION_NOMATCH_MATCH,
                        sfl, null, Lease.FOREVER);
            lrm.renewUntil(reg.getLease(), Lease.FOREVER, null);
            leases.put(lookup[i], reg);
        } catch (RemoteException rex) {
            System.out.println("Registration error " + rex);
        }

        // For each service, see what it already has
        try {
            ServiceMatches items = lookup[i].lookup(template,
                                        Integer.MAX_VALUE);
            // Each lookup service may have zero or more registered
            // servers that implement our desired template
            for (int j = 0; j < items.items.length; j++) {
                if (items.items[j].service != null)
                    // Put each matching service into our vector
                    addServiceItem(items.items[j]);
                    // else the service item couldn't be deserialized
                    // so the lookup() method skipped it
            }
        } catch (RemoteException ex) {
            System.out.println("ServiceFinder Error: " + ex);
        }
    }
}

// An error talking to a lookup service caused it to be discarded
// Remove any references to it from our hashtable, and cancel
// our leases to that service
public synchronized void discarded(DiscoveryEvent dev) {
    ServiceRegistrar[] lookup = dev.getRegistrars();
    for (int i = 0; i < lookup.length; i++) {
        try {
            EventRegistration reg =
                (EventRegistration) leases.get(lookup[i]);
            if (reg != null) {
                leases.remove(lookup[i]);
                lrm.remove(reg.getLease());
            }
        } catch (UnknownLeaseException ule) {}
    }
}

public synchronized void addServiceItem(ServiceItem item) {
    items.put(item.serviceID, item);
    notifyAll();
}

// This class is to be used by the client. It will return only
// the first service object that satisfies the template request.
public synchronized Object getObject() {
    if (returnObject == null) {
        while (items.isEmpty()) {
            try {
                wait();
            } catch (InterruptedException ie) {}
        }
        returnObject =
            (ServiceItem) items.elements().nextElement();
    }
```

```
        return returnObject.service;

    }

    // If an error is encountered when using a service object, the client
    // should call this method.
    // A new object can then be retrieved from the getObject() method.
    public synchronized void errored(Object obj) {
        if ((obj != null) && (returnObject != null)) {
            if (obj.equals(returnObject.service)) {
                items.remove(returnObject.serviceID);
                returnObject = null;
            }
        }
    }
}
```

This new implementation of the ServiceFinder class incorporates the use of the service ID to keep track of services. By using the service ID as the key, storing an object with the same service ID automatically replaces a previous entry with the same service ID. Since services generally register themselves with all lookup services, this will reduce the number of objects on our list, since we'll no longer keep a registration from each lookup service. As before, the getObject() method will return the first object in the list. However, since hashtables are unordered, we must also store this object in another instance variable.

To register a remote event listener with the lookup service, we call the notify() method of the ServiceRegistrar object in our discovered() method. This method takes five parameters—the template for the service objects we are looking for, the transitions that we want to be informed of, the remote event listener, the marshalled object that we want handed back to us, and the amount of time that we want to listen for. Once we register the listener, we will pass its lease to a lease renewal manager to maintain. The lease is also stored in a different hashtable for cleanup purposes.

We now must also implement code for the discarded() method. In this example, we search for the lease pertaining to the listener that has been registered with the lookup service and delete the lease from our hashtable. Optionally, we might cancel the lease, but there's a good chance that the lookup service no longer exists (which is why we're discarding it), and if we cancelled the lease here, it might cause this thread to block (if the machine running the lookup service has crashed). If the lookup service is still active, we won't renew our lease to it, and it will soon discard us as a client anyway.

The ConvertClient class does not need to change, since the ServiceFinder class provides the same interface as it always did. The only extra requirement is that we now have to generate the stubs class for our ServiceFinderListener class and place the stub where it can be found by the lookup services—on the client's java.rmi.server.codebase.

Summary

Distributed events serve many purposes in a Jini environment. They are crucial for writing a good Jini client, since they allow the client to be notified when a particular service has joined the Jini community. Additionally, they can be used between any two participants in a Jini community in a service-specific manner. Although event listeners are clients of a particular service, they turn the listening application into a server as well: the remote event listener must implement the `Remote` interface, which means that it must be written as an RMI server (though that requirement changes in Java 1.3).

In the next chapter, we'll look into the topic of how clients can administer a Jini service.

CHAPTER 7

Service Administration

In this chapter, we'll discuss Jini's administration APIs. There must be some means to control or administer any Jini service. Generally, services provide this administration access through the use of exposed APIs. This means that interfaces provided for administration can be handled in the same way as interfaces provided as part of the service. However, Jini provides some support for administration by supplying predefined interfaces and the means to access the service's administration object. Services do not have to use the predefined APIs or follow Jini's admin pattern in exposing its own administration APIs, but doing so makes it easier for administration clients.

Service administration is built around a set of interfaces that a service chooses to implement. The ramification of this is any client that has a service object can call the service's administration APIs. It is up to the service implementor to define and enforce any security requirements the service wants to impose on callers of the administration methods. Those requirements will vary based on the type of service and the environment in which the service is installed.

Administration APIs

Since administration is specific to the service, it is very difficult to define a generic interface that will administer all of the resources or configuration of any service. Hence, Jini provides certain administration APIs that will evolve through the Jini community.

Currently, the administration interfaces are:

net.jini.admin.JoinAdmin
> An administration interface that allows clients of a service to control a service's participation in the join protocol. With this interface, the client can request groups, attributes, and specific lookup services for the service to use. This interface should be implemented to help network administrators configure the services for their network.

net.jini.lookup.DiscoveryAdmin

An administration interface that allows clients to control a lookup service. With this interface, the client can change the groups that the lookup service participates in or the network port number that is used in unicast discovery. Implementations of lookup services should implement this interface.

com.sun.jini.admin.DestroyAdmin

An administration interface that allows clients of a service to control when a service should terminate. With this interface, the client can request that the service cease all operations. Care should be taken with this request since session data and support for other clients will be lost.

com.sun.jini.admin.StorageLocationAdmin

An administration interface that allows clients of a service to control where they should store their persistent data. With this interface, the client can request that the service use a particular directory or network service to store its data. This information is passed as a string, so it is up to the service to interpret the meaning of the string.

Multiple administration interfaces should all be implemented by a single administration object. This administration object is obtained from the service by using the `net.jini.admin.Administrable` interface. Any service can be checked to see whether it implements the `Administrable` interface. If so, the `getAdmin()` method of the interface can be called to get the administration object. With the administration object, we can check to see whether the particular administration interface that is desired is supported.

As our first administration example, we'll modify our service to support the `JoinAdmin` interface. Then we'll modify the client to retrieve attribute information about the service using that interface. Required classes are listed in Example 7-1.

Example 7–1: An Administrable Service

```
Common classes
     ConvertService (used in Example 6-2; listed in Example 6-1)
     ConvertServiceRegistration (used in Example 6-2; listed in Example 5-1)
     ConvertEvent (used in Example 6-2; listed in Example 6-1)
Server classes
     ConvertServiceImpl (modified from Example 6-2; listed in Example 6-1)
     ConvertServiceRegistrationImpl (used in Example 6-2;
          listed in Example 5-1)
     ConvertServiceProxy (modified from Example 6-2; listed in Example 5-1 )
     ServerLandlord (used in Example 6-2; listed in Example 5-2)
     ServerResource (used in Example 6-2; listed in Example 5-1)
     ServerDelivery (used in Example 6-2; listed in Example 6-1)
     ConvertServiceAdminImpl (new)
     ConvertServiceAdminProxy (new)
Client classes
     ServiceFinder (used in Example 6-2)
     ServiceFinderListener (used in Example 6-2)
     ConvertEventHandler (used in Example 6-2; listed in Example 6-1)
     ConvertClient (modified from Example 6-2; listed in Example 6-1)
```

There are no changes to the classes that are shared between the client and server. Implementing an administrable interface doesn't change the basic service contract that exists between participants in a Jini community.

The Service Implementation

The first thing we must provide is an administration object for the ConvertService class. This class will implement the JoinAdmin interface. As always, we have the choice of how to implement that class, and we'll choose to implement it as an RMI server object. So we'll need to write the usual intermediary proxy interface:

```
import java.rmi.*;
import net.jini.admin.*;

public interface ConvertServiceAdminProxy extends JoinAdmin, Remote {
}
```

The JoinAdmin interface—like most of the interfaces defined by the Jini framework—is not a Remote interface. By using the ConvertServiceAdminProxy interface, we can use RMI as our distributed framework, while keeping the JoinAdmin interface as a generic interface that can use any distributed framework.

Now we must write the new class that implements this interface:

```
import java.io.*;
import java.rmi.*;
import java.rmi.server.*;
import net.jini.core.discovery.*;
import net.jini.core.entry.*;
import com.sun.jini.lookup.*;

public class ConvertServiceAdminImpl extends UnicastRemoteObject
                        implements ConvertServiceAdminProxy {
    // The join manager used by our service; this class defers
    // all operations to that manager
    private JoinManager manager;

    public ConvertServiceAdminImpl(JoinManager manager)
                            throws RemoteException {
        this.manager = manager;
    }

    public Entry[] getLookupAttributes() throws RemoteException {
        return manager.getAttributes();
    }

    public void addLookupAttributes(Entry[] attrSets)
                            throws RemoteException {
        manager.addAttributes(attrSets, true);
    }

    public void modifyLookupAttributes(Entry[] attrSetTemplates,
                        Entry[] attrSets) throws RemoteException {
        manager.modifyAttributes(attrSetTemplates, attrSets, true);
    }

    public String[] getLookupGroups() throws RemoteException {
        return manager.getGroups();
    }

    public void addLookupGroups(String[] groups) throws RemoteException {
        try {
            manager.addGroups(groups);
```

```
        } catch (IOException ex) {
            throw new RemoteException("Error in AddGroups", ex);
        }
    }

    public void removeLookupGroups(String[] groups)
                            throws RemoteException {
        try {
            manager.removeGroups(groups);
        } catch (IOException ex) {
            throw new RemoteException("Error in RemoveGroups", ex);
        }
    }

    public void setLookupGroups(String[] groups)
                            throws RemoteException {
        try {
            manager.setGroups(groups);
        } catch (IOException ex) {
            throw new RemoteException("Error in SetGroups", ex);
        }
    }

    public LookupLocator[] getLookupLocators() throws RemoteException {
        return manager.getLocators();
    }

    public void addLookupLocators(LookupLocator[] locators)
                            throws RemoteException {
        manager.addLocators(locators);
    }

    public void removeLookupLocators(LookupLocator[] locators)
                                throws RemoteException {
        manager.removeLocators(locators);
    }

    public void setLookupLocators(LookupLocator[] locators)
                                throws RemoteException {
        manager.setLocators(locators);
    }
}
```

We need to implement all the methods of the JoinAdmin interface. This is simple: since each method of this interface has an equivalent method in the JoinManager class, we can route the admin request to the JoinManager managing the service. For this example, the JoinManager object is passed through the constructor.

We must also perform some special handling for attribute changing. When the client calls the addLookupAttributes() and modifyLookupAttributes() methods, it is changing the attributes of the service. This is why we have to specify an extra parameter when we call the join manager. By informing the join manager that the client is making the request to change attributes, the join manager knows to check the ServiceControlled marker on the attributes. It will deny the request if the client has read-only access to that type of attribute.

In order for the client of the service to obtain the administration object, we must modify the service proxy object and the implementation of the service to implement the Administrable interface:

```
import java.rmi.*;
import java.rmi.server.*;
import net.jini.core.lease.*;
import net.jini.admin.*;

public interface ConvertServiceProxy
                   extends Remote, Administrable, ConvertService {
    // We convert the call on the client to this form for the server
    public String convert(Lease l, int i)
                   throws LeaseDeniedException, RemoteException;
}
```

We don't want to add the Administrable interface to our ConvertService interface, because that interface defines the service methods only. We don't want to
require that all implementors of the ConvertService interface be administrable
(though we strongly suggest it). Neither can we add the Administrable interface
directly to the ConvertServiceImpl class because the methods of the Administrable interface must be part of the object returned to the client.

With this new proxy interface, we can make the appropriate changes to our ConvertServiceImpl class:

```
import java.util.*;
import java.io.*;
import java.rmi.*;
import java.rmi.server.*;
import net.jini.discovery.*;
import net.jini.core.lease.*;
import net.jini.core.event.*;
import net.jini.core.entry.*;
import net.jini.lookup.entry.*;
import com.sun.jini.lookup.*;

public class ConvertServiceImpl extends UnicastRemoteObject
                   implements ConvertServiceProxy {

    private ServerLandlord lord;
    private ServerDelivery sender;
    private JoinManager manager;
    private ConvertServiceAdminImpl admin;

    public ConvertServiceImpl() throws RemoteException {
        lord = new ServerLandlord();
        sender = new ServerDelivery(this, lord);
    }

    public ConvertServiceRegistration getInstance(long duration) {
        Hashtable ht = new Hashtable(13);
        return new ConvertServiceRegistrationImpl(this,
                          lord.newLease(ht, duration));
    }

    // To convert, first check the cache for previous results. If
    // there's no cache, the landlord has expired the lease. If
    // there's no data in the cache, calculcate the data and put it there
    public String convert(Lease l, int i) throws LeaseDeniedException {
        Hashtable cache = (Hashtable) lord.getSessionData(l);
        if (cache == null)
            throw new LeaseDeniedException("Lease expired");
        Integer I = new Integer(i);
```

```
        String s;
        s = (String) cache.get(I);
        if (s == null) {
            s = I.toString();
            cache.put(I, s);
        }
        sender.deliver(i);
        return s;
    }

    public EventRegistration trackConversions(long duration,
                        RemoteEventListener rel, MarshalledObject key) {
        return sender.addListener(rel, duration, key);
    }

    public void setJoinManager(JoinManager jm) {
        this.manager = jm;
    }

    public Object getAdmin() throws RemoteException {
        if (admin == null)
            admin = new ConvertServiceAdminImpl(manager);
        return admin;
    }

    public static void main(String[] args) throws Exception {
        System.setSecurityManager(new RMISecurityManager());
        String[] groups = new String[] { "" };

        Entry[] attributes = new Entry[2];
        attributes[0] = new Name("Marketing Converter");
        attributes[1] = new Location("4", "4101", "NY/02");

        // Create the instance of the service; the JoinManager will
        // register it and renew its leases with the lookup service
        ConvertServiceImpl csi =
                        (ConvertServiceImpl) new ConvertServiceImpl();
        JoinManager manager = new JoinManager(csi, attributes, groups,
                                    null, null, null);
        csi.setJoinManager(manager);
    }
}
```

We must now save the join manager that we are using, so that we can pass it to
the ConvertServiceAdmin object. With the join manager for the service saved, the
implementation of the getAdmin() method is trivial: we instantiate a ConvertServiceAdmin object and return it to the user. We've also reverted to a previous example that supplies attributes for the service; the client will retrieve those attributes.

The Client Implementation

Let's modify our client example to use the administration interface:

```
import java.rmi.*;
import net.jini.discovery.*;
import net.jini.core.lease.*;
import net.jini.core.event.*;
import net.jini.admin.*;
import com.sun.jini.lease.*;
```

```
public class ConvertClient {

    public static void main(String[] args) throws Exception {
        System.setSecurityManager(new RMISecurityManager());

        // Find the service by its interface type
        ServiceFinder sf = new ServiceFinder(ConvertService.class);
        ConvertService cs = (ConvertService) sf.getObject();

        LeaseRenewalManager lrm = new LeaseRenewalManager();

        // Sign up to be notified of all conversions
        RemoteEventListener rel = new ConvertEventHandler();
        EventRegistration er =
                        cs.trackConversions(Lease.FOREVER, rel, null);
        lrm.renewUntil(er.getLease(), Lease.FOREVER, null);

        // Administer the service registration object
        JoinAdmin joinadmin = null;
        // See if it has a join admin object
        if (cs instanceof Administrable) {
            Object admin = ((Administrable) cs).getAdmin();
            if (admin instanceof JoinAdmin)
                joinadmin = (JoinAdmin) admin;
        }
        // If it does, print out its attributes
        if (joinadmin != null) {
            Object[] attrib = joinadmin.getLookupAttributes();
            for (int i = 0; i < attrib.length; i++)
                System.out.println("Attribute: " + attrib[i]);
        }

        // Now do a conversion for ourself
        ConvertServiceRegistration csr = cs.getInstance(Lease.FOREVER);
        lrm.renewUntil(csr.getLease(), Lease.FOREVER, null);

        // Now invoke methods on the service object
        System.out.println(csr.convert(5));

        // We'll sit here, waiting forever for other event notifications
        // to happen.
    }
}
```

In order to get to the join administration methods, we must check whether the service is administrable—that is, whether it implements the Administrable interface. Next, we cast the server object to an Administrable object and call the getAdmin() method in order to obtain the administration object. It is unclear at this point what administration interfaces this object supports, so it must be set to a variable that is an Object class type. Next, we check whether the administration object supports the JoinAdmin interface. If so, we (finally) cast the administration object to a JoinAdmin object and use the methods in the interface. In this example, we ask for the attributes and print them. While we could have also gotten the attributes from the ServiceItem object that is returned from the lookup service, the attributes returned from the administration object come directly from the service and are therefore up to date.

Running the Example

To run the entire example, we must compile the new server files: the `ConvertServiceAdminImpl` class and the `ConvertServiceAdminProxy` interface. We must also generate the stub of the `ConvertServiceAdminImpl` class. The `ConvertServiceAdminImpl_Stub` and `ConvertServiceAdminProxy` classes must both be available to the client, so they must go on the server's `java.rmi.server.codebase`.

Providing a Custom Administration Interface

While the administration interfaces provided by Jini are useful generic cases, most services have to provide either very flexible APIs or a specific administration interface to allow the client better to control the type of resources the service provides. In this section, we'll develop an example that uses such an interface, using the classes listed in Example 7-2.

Example 7-2: A Custom Administration Interface

Common classes
    ConvertService (used in Example 7-1; listed in Example 6-1)
    ConvertServiceRegistration (used in Example 7-1; listed in Example 5-1)
    ConvertEvent (used in Example 7-1; listed in Example 6-1)
    AccessAdmin (new)
Server Classes
    ConvertServiceImpl (used in Example 7-1)
    ConvertServiceRegistrationImpl (used in Example 7-1;
       listed in Example 5-1)
    ConvertServiceProxy (used in Example 7-1)
    ServerLandlord (used in Example 7-1; listed in Example 5-2)
    ServerResource (used in Example 7-1; listed in Example 5-1)
    ServerDelivery (used in Example 7-1; listed in Example 6-1)
    ConvertServiceAdminImpl (modified from Example 7-1)
    ConvertServiceAdminProxy (modified from Example 7-1)
Client Classes
    ServiceFinder (used in Example 7-1; listed in Example 6-2)
    ServiceFinderListener (used in Example 7-1; listed in Example 6-2)
    ConvertEventHandler (used in Example 7-1; listed in Example 6-1)
    ConvertClient (modified from Example 7-1)

We mentioned earlier that, by default, any client can administer a service. The interface we develop in this section addresses part of that problem by providing a mechanism by which administration services can be turned on or off:

```
import java.rmi.*;

public interface AccessAdmin {
    public void denyAdminAccess() throws RemoteException;
    public void allowAdminAccess() throws RemoteException;
}
```

This interface provides two methods. After the `denyAdminAccess()` method is called, all future requests to any method of the administration object will throw an exception. Calling the `allowAdminAccess()` method reactivates those methods. This doesn't completely solve the security issues in using administration, but it does allow us to isolate them: now we need only control who can call the methods of the `AccessAdmin` interface. We could use Java's Authorization and

Authentication Service (JAAS) or other security APIs to implement that control, but that's beyond the scope of this book. From a Jini perspective, that's strictly an implementation detail; no Jini APIs are involved.

Just like the other administration interfaces, this new interface does not require that RMI is used as the distribution framework. So we must modify the Convert-ServiceAdminProxy interface:

```
import java.rmi.*;
import net.jini.admin.*;

public interface ConvertServiceAdminProxy
                extends JoinAdmin, AccessAdmin, Remote {
}
```

Then we must modify our service administration implementation:

```
import java.io.*;
import java.rmi.*;
import java.rmi.server.*;
import net.jini.core.discovery.*;
import net.jini.core.entry.*;
import com.sun.jini.lookup.*;

public class ConvertServiceAdminImpl extends UnicastRemoteObject
                             implements ConvertServiceAdminProxy {
    private JoinManager manager;
    private boolean allowAccess = true;

    public ConvertServiceAdminImpl(JoinManager manager)
                             throws RemoteException {
        this.manager = manager;
    }

    private void checkAccess() {
        if (allowAccess == false)
            throw new SecurityException("Admin access not allowed");
    }

    public Entry[] getLookupAttributes() throws RemoteException {
        checkAccess();
        return manager.getAttributes();
    }

    public void addLookupAttributes(Entry[] attrSets)
                                    throws RemoteException {
        checkAccess();
        manager.addAttributes(attrSets, true);
    }

    public void modifyLookupAttributes(Entry[] attrSetTemplates,
                        Entry[] attrSets) throws RemoteException {
        checkAccess();
        manager.modifyAttributes(attrSetTemplates, attrSets, true);
    }

    public String[] getLookupGroups() throws RemoteException {
        checkAccess();
        return manager.getGroups();
    }
```

```java
public void addLookupGroups(String[] groups) throws RemoteException {
    checkAccess();
    try {
        manager.addGroups(groups);
    } catch (IOException ex) {
        throw new RemoteException("Error in AddGroups", ex);
    }
}

public void removeLookupGroups(String[] groups)
                              throws RemoteException {
    checkAccess();
    try {
        manager.removeGroups(groups);
    } catch (IOException ex) {
        throw new RemoteException("Error in RemoveGroups", ex);
    }
}

public void setLookupGroups(String[] groups)
                            throws RemoteException {
    checkAccess();
    try {
        manager.setGroups(groups);
    } catch (IOException ex) {
        throw new RemoteException("Error in SetGroups", ex);
    }
}

public LookupLocator[] getLookupLocators() throws RemoteException {
    checkAccess();
    return manager.getLocators();
}

public void addLookupLocators(LookupLocator[] locators)
                              throws RemoteException {
    checkAccess();
    manager.addLocators(locators);
}


public void removeLookupLocators(LookupLocator[] locators)
                                 throws RemoteException {
    checkAccess();
    manager.removeLocators(locators);
}

public void setLookupLocators(LookupLocator[] locators)
                              throws RemoteException {
    checkAccess();
    manager.setLocators(locators);
}

public void denyAdminAccess() {
    allowAccess = false;
}

public void allowAdminAccess() {
    allowAccess = true;
}
}
```

All we need to do in the two new methods is set the `allowAccess` flag. All the methods of the other administration interfaces are modified to check the flag prior to execution. If access is denied, a security exception will be thrown, signifying the violation.

There are no modifications to our `ConvertServiceImpl` class or the `ConvertServiceProxy` interface; the `ConvertServiceImpl` class already returns a `ConvertServiceAdminImpl` object for the administration interface. And the `ConvertServiceProxy` object returns an administration object. The compiled `AccessAdmin` interface must be available for clients to download at runtime, and any clients that actually want to use the interface (as we showed earlier with the `JoinAdmin` interface) need the `AccessAdmin` interface at compile time.

Summary

Jini does not define how a service must be administered, but it does provide an administration framework. Services are encouraged to implement the administration interfaces of this framework according to their own needs: some may need to define additional administration interfaces, some may need to add additional security to their implementation, and some may need a completely different administration mechanism.

In the next chapter, we'll look into some miscellaneous APIs that come with Sun's implementation of Jini.

Service
Admin

CHAPTER 8

Miscellaneous Classes

Sun's implementation of Jini comes with a number of useful utility classes. These classes are not part of the Jini specification. They were developed as Sun wrote its implementation of Jini, and they're provided for the same reason all the Jini source code is provided—so that developers can gain a better understanding of Jini.

The classes that we're referring to belong to the com.sun.jini package. We've already used classes from that package, and there's no difference between those that we've used previously and those that we'll examine in this chapter: no classes in the com.sun.jini package are part of the Jini specification, and all such classes are subject to change at any time. Sun makes no claim that these classes will ever become part of the Jini (or any other) specification, that they will continue to be released, and so on. But these classes are too useful to ignore, so we'll present them with the understanding that they might change. On the other hand, remember that the source for these classes comes with Jini; you can use them under the terms of the SCSL. And as time goes by, some of the com.sun.jini classes will move into Jini; we saw in Chapter 4, *Basic Jini Programming*, that many lease classes move from com.sun.jini in Jini 1.0 to net.jini in Jini 1.1. It's unlikely that the classes discussed in this chapter will ever undergo such a move.

These classes allow us to fill in a number of details that we glossed over in previous chapters. In this chapter, we'll show examples of:

- How an event source can deliver events in another thread

- How a landlord can automatically expire leases

- How a service can reliably save its service ID and reuse that ID when it restarts

Collections

The com.sun.jini.collection package contains new classes that are used in Sun's Jini implementation. Unlike classes in the java.util package, these classes do not support the Collection interface, though they do provide general collection functionality.

The com.sun.jini.collection.FastList class provides a doubly linked list. Using this linked list is faster than a typical linked list because some of the synchronization that is required to make a linked list threadsafe has been omitted from the FastList class. Weak synchronization means that multiple threads can traverse the list simultaneously. Hence, the fast list is useful for cases when you have many readers. The developer must ensure that the list is used correctly.

Weak synchronization means that one thread may be accessing a node while another thread is removing it. If you want to ensure that a node is not removed while you are holding a reference to it, you must synchronize the node and then call the removed( ) method on the node. If this method returns true, someone else removed the node. Similarly if you want to remove a node, you must ensure that the node was not removed by a previous thread; the remove( ) method of this class will return true if the node was presently in the list and false if the node had already been removed by another thread.

The list stores objects of type FastList.Node. However, the Node class does not contain any way to store user data, so you should always subclass the Node type to define a class to hold your data. For example, to create a linked list of strings, you could define this class:

```
import com.sun.jini.collection.*;

public class StringNode extends FastList.Node {

    private String value;

    public StringNode(String s) {
        value = s;
    }

    public String getValue() {
        return value;
    }
}
```

Then instances of this class can be inserted into and deleted from a fast list via the add( ), addAfter( ), remove( ), and replace( ) methods. Traversal of the list is accomplished via the next( ) and prev( ) methods of the FastList.Node class.

Internally, the fast list does not remove a node from the list until it traverses the node. In Jini 1.0, you can specify that a thread internal to this class should traverse the list periodically to remove the nodes explicitly; this is controlled by the globalReap( ) method. This feature has been removed in Jini 1.0.1.

Misc. Classes

Thread Utilities

The com.sun.jini.thread package's classes implement various thread operations.

Reader-Writer Locks

The com.sun.jini.thread.ReadersWriter class implements a reader-writer lock. Reader-writer locks allow multiple threads to read a data structure while allowing only a single thread to write a data structure. The data structure is locked for reading via the readLock( ) method (and unlocked via the readUnlock( ) method); the corresponding calls for writing are writeLock( ) and writeUnlock( ). Writers are given precedence over readers: requests for the write lock are honored before requests for the read lock.

Reader-writer locks are useful for data structures that are often searched and seldom updated. If you have a big binary tree of data, there's no reason why multiple threads can't be allowed to access the tree simultaneously as long as they are only reading data, but a thread that needs to update the tree must have exclusive access. This is the ideal situation for a reader-writer lock.

A Thread Pool

The com.sun.jini.thread.TaskManager class implements a thread pool. The thread pool manages a group of threads and an internal queue of tasks; it assigns each task to an idle thread. The task manager starts as many threads as it needs to run all of the activities in its queue, subject to a programmer-defined maximum.

Tasks that are to be run in the task manager are objects that implement the TaskManager.Task interface. This interface allows you to specify the task to be run as well as providing some simple ordering rules (e.g., you can specify that one task must run after another task has completed by implementing the runAfter( ) method to return true if any task in the parameter list must run after the target task).

Thread pools are useful for many operations; in the Jini environment, they are very useful for running operations that might block. For example, sending a remote event is an operation that might block and should therefore be handled in a separate thread; the TaskManager class is a simple way to achieve that without requiring lots of thread setup for each event. Example 8-1 is an enhancement to the ServerDelivery class from Example 6-2 that does just that.

Example 8-1: Event Delivery in a Separate Thread

```
Common classes
    ConvertService (used in Example 6-2; listed in Example 6-1)
    ConvertServiceRegistration (used in Example 6-2; listed in Example 5-1)
    ConvertEvent (used in Example 6-2; listed in Example 6-1)
Server classes
    ConvertServiceImpl (used in Example 6-2; listed in Example 6-1)
    ConvertServiceRegistrationImpl (used in Example 6-2;
        listed in Example 5-1)
    ConvertServiceProxy (used in Example 6-2; listed in Example 5-1)
    ServerLandlord (used in Example 6-2; listed in Example 5-2)
```

Example 8-1: Event Delivery in a Separate Thread (continued)

```
    ServerResource (used in Example 6-2; listed in Example 5-1)
    ServerDelivery (modified from Example 6-2)
Client classes
    ServiceFinder (used in Example 6-2)
    ServiceFinderListener (used in Example 6-2)
    ConvertEventHandler (used in Example 6-2; listed in Example 6-1)
    ConvertClient (used in Example 6-2; listed in Example 6-1)
```

Here's the new implementation of the ServerDelivery class:

```java
import java.rmi.*;
import java.rmi.server.*;
import java.util.*;
import net.jini.core.lease.*;
import net.jini.core.event.*;
import com.sun.jini.lease.landlord.*;
import com.sun.jini.thread.*;

public class ServerDelivery {
    private Remote source;            // Owner of this delivery object
    private ServerLandlord lord;      // The landlord that manages leases
    private Vector leases;            // Event-specific leases
    private long seqnum = 0;
    private TaskManager pool;

    // The client-specific session data for the event leases
    // holds the listener and the callback data
    private class SessionData {
        public RemoteEventListener listener;
        public MarshalledObject key;
    }

    // This class is used to run the delivery of the event in
    // a separate thread, one managed by the TaskManager pool.
    private class CallbackTask implements TaskManager.Task {
        RemoteEventListener listener;
        RemoteEvent re;
        Lease lease;

        CallbackTask(RemoteEventListener rel, RemoteEvent re,
                    Lease l) {
            this.re = re;
            this.listener = rel;
            this.lease = l;
        }

        public void run() {
            try {
                listener.notify(re);
            } catch (Exception e) {
                // We could retry later, but we'll just drop it.
            }
        }

        public boolean runAfter(List tasks, int size) {
            return false;
        }
    }
```

*Misc.
Classes*

```
public ServerDelivery(Remote source, ServerLandlord ll) {
    this.source = source;
    lord = ll;
    leases = new Vector();
    pool = new TaskManager();

}

public synchronized EventRegistration addListener(
        RemoteEventListener l, long duration, MarshalledObject key) {
    SessionData sd = new SessionData();
    sd.listener = l;
    sd.key = key;

    Lease lease = lord.newLease(sd, duration);
    leases.addElement(lease);

    return new EventRegistration(ConvertEvent.ID, source,
                                 lease, seqnum);
}


// Deliver an event to all listeners
public void deliver(int value) {
    long seq;
    synchronized(this) {
        seq = seqnum++;                    // Deliver request number
    }


    if (leases.isEmpty())
        return;
    lord.expireLeases();                    // Clean up the leases first
    Object[] allLeases = leases.toArray();
    for (int i = 0; i < allLeases.length; i++) {

        Lease l = (Lease) allLeases[i];
        SessionData obj = (SessionData) lord.getSessionData(l);
        if (obj == null) {
            leases.remove(l);
        } else {
            deliverEvent(obj, seq, value, l);
        }
    }
}


// Actually send the event
private void deliverEvent(SessionData data, long seq,
                          int value, Lease lease) {
    ConvertEvent event = new ConvertEvent(source, value,
                                          seq, data.key);
    pool.add(new CallbackTask(data.listener, event, lease));

}
}
```

We've changed the deliverEvent( ) method so that instead of sending the event, it now creates the appropriate task and sends the task to the task manager via its add( ) method. In the run( ) method of our task, we deliver the event. Since the event is being delivered on another thread, we no longer need to process delivery exceptions in the deliver( ) method.

We've also changed our synchronization strategy. In earlier examples of this class, we synchronized the deliver( ) method and all other methods that accessed the leases vector so that leases could not be added or removed while the deliver( ) method was running. Now we have removed all synchronization around the leases vector and instead required that the deliver( ) method operate on a copy of the vector (i.e., it uses the toArray( ) method rather than creating an enumeration). This allows us to access the leases array from the task manager queue (although we don't use that feature at present).

A Task Scheduler

The com.sun.jini.thread.WakeupManager class is a general-purpose task scheduler: it manages a list of tasks, each of which is run at a specified time. Each scheduled task can be run in the wakeup manager's thread or in a newly created thread; the latter is preferred if the task will take a long time or if it may potentially block. The wakeup manager is useful any time you need to run a particular task at a particular time; for example, it can be used as the basis of an alternative to the LeaseRenewalManager class if you want to manage your own leases.

When we developed our ServerLandlord class, we were somewhat lazy about expiring its leases. When it was convenient, we checked to see if any leases had expired; otherwise, we didn't worry about it. If instead we wanted to ensure that leases were cancelled as soon as they expired, we would utilize the changes listed in Example 8-2.

Example 8–2: Aggressively Expiring Leases

```
Common classes
    ConvertService (used in Example 8-1; listed in Example 6-1)
    ConvertServiceRegistration (used in Example 8-1; listed in Example 5-1)
    ConvertEvent (used in Example 8-1; listed in Example 6-1)
Server Classes
    ConvertServiceImpl (used in Example 8-1; listed in Example 6-1)
    ConvertServiceRegistrationImpl (used in Example 8-1;
        listed in Example 5-1)
    ConvertServiceProxy (used in Example 8-1; listed in Example 5-1)
    ServerLandlord (modified from Example 8-1; listed in Example 5-2)
    ServerResource (used in Example 8-1; listed in Example 5-1)
    ServerDelivery (used in Example 8-1)
    ConvertServiceImpl (used in Example 8-1; listed in Example 6-1)
    Expirer (new)
Client Classes
    ServiceFinder (used in Example 8-1; listed in Example 6-2)
    ServiceFinderListener (used in Example 8-1; listed in Example 6-2)
    ConvertEventHandler (used in Example 8-1; listed in Example 6-1)
    ConvertClient (used in Example 8-1; listed in Example 6-1)
```

We use the following class to expire the leases:

```
import java.util.*;
import com.sun.jini.thread.*;
import com.sun.jini.lease.landlord.*;
```

```java
public class Expirer implements LeaseManager {
    Landlord landlord;
    WakeupManager manager;
    HashMap tickets;

    // Instances of this class are scheduled to run at a specific
    // time by the wakeup manager -- they will run when the lease
    // has expired, and they will cancel the lease. A lease renewal
    // will remove the task from the wakeup managers queue
    class ExpirerTask implements Runnable {
        LeasedResource resource;

        ExpirerTask(LeasedResource r) {
            resource = r;
        }
        public void run() {
            long now = System.currentTimeMillis();
            long expir = resource.getExpiration();
            if (expir > now) {
                // It was renewed, but we didn't cancel the task in time.
                WakeupManager.Ticket ticket =
                            manager.schedule(expir, this);
                tickets.put(resource, ticket);
            }
            else try {
                landlord.cancel(resource.getCookie());
            } catch (Exception e) {
            }
        }
    }

    public Expirer(Landlord l) {
        landlord = l;
        tickets = new HashMap(13);
        manager = new WakeupManager();
    }

    // The lease has been renewed. A side-effect of registering
    // the new duration will be to cancel the old task from the
    // taskmanager queue.
    public void renewed(LeasedResource resource,
                        long duration, long oldExpiration) {
        register(resource, duration);
    }

    // A lease has been created or renewed. Cancel its old
    // expiration task and create a new expiration task to
    // cancel the lease after it expires.
    public void register(LeasedResource resource, long duration) {
        WakeupManager.Ticket ticket;

        ticket = (WakeupManager.Ticket) tickets.remove(resource);
        if (ticket != null)
            manager.cancel(ticket);
        ExpirerTask task = new ExpirerTask(resource);
        ticket = manager.schedule(resource.getExpiration(), task);
        tickets.put(resource, ticket);
    }
}
```

This class implements the `com.sun.jini.lease.landlord.LeaseManager` interface, which is used in conjunction with the lease duration policy. Every time the policy is asked to renew a lease, it tells the lease manager that a renewal has occurred.

When a new lease is passed to the lease duration policy, it calls the `register()` method of the lease manager, which schedules an expiration task with the wakeup manager (items registered with the wakeup manager must be of type `Runnable`). As leases are renewed, the `renewed()` method is called. The `renewed()` method cancels the previous task in the wakeup manager and schedules a new one at the new expiration time. If the lease is not renewed, the task will eventually be run, cancelling the lease.

You'll notice that the `LeaseManager` interface does not have any methods related to cancelling a lease. If the client cancels the lease with the landlord, our expirer won't find out about it. Eventually, the expirer will attempt to cancel the lease, which will cause an unknown lease exception to be thrown, which the expirer can safely ignore. If your landlord issues leases that are for long periods of time and you want a way to release the lease (so that data associated with the lease can be garbage collected), you'll have to provide your own interface to do that; the `LeaseManager` interface does not provide notice of cancellation.

In order to use this class, we must change our server landlord. We won't show all the code for that class again, since we need to make only minimal changes: when we instantiate the policy, we now pass it a lease manager (i.e., an instance of our `Expirer` class):

```
policy = new LeaseDurationPolicy(MAXLEASETIME, MAXLEASETIME,
                                 this, new Expirer(this), null);
```

We can also remove the `expireLeases()` method from the `ServerDelivery` and `ServerLandlord` classes.

Reliable Logs

The classes in the `com.sun.reliableLog` package implement a reliable logging system. This system allows a program to take a snapshot of a set of data and then periodically provide updates to that set of data. A snapshot must contain the full set of data that the service is interested in preserving. An update may contain any program-defined set of changes, but it often represents a single change to a single piece of data.

The snapshot and updates can be written to disk atomically. Upon restart, the client can recover the state of the data; the logging system reads the snapshot and updates in order to recreate the last saved state. A long-lived client may choose to provide periodic snapshots so that the list of updates does not grow too big; the log keeps only the last snapshot and any updates that follow the snapshot.

Reliable logs are kept in a single directory; it is an error for two services to attempt to use the same directory for their logs. Keep in mind that *rmid* creates a reliable log in the `./log` directory, and that standard Jini services (the lookup service, transaction service, and the persistent JavaSpaces service) also keep logs in the location specified on their command lines.

Reliable logs are instances of the `com.sun.jini.reliableLog.ReliableLog` class. That class takes care of most of the details of the log, such as opening the correct files, ensuring that data is read correctly, and so on. The service operates on instances of this class, calling its `snapshot()` method to create a snapshot and its `update()` method to create an update to a snapshot. Updates are stored sequentially; calling the `snapshot()` method discards all previous update data. The `recover()` method reads in the last snapshot and any updates that have occurred after the snapshot. The reliable log class can detect if the service crashed while creating a snapshot (in which case the previous snapshot and updates are used) or while creating an update (in which case the incomplete update is discarded).

A reliable log is used in conjunction with the abstract `com.sun.jini.reliableLog.LogHandler` class. Implementors of a reliable log must provide a concrete implementation of the `LogHandler` class that defines the following methods:

snapshot(OutputStream os)
> This method is responsible for saving a snapshot of all the data in the class to the given output stream. It typically accomplishes this by wrapping an object output stream around the parameter and writing serialized data to the stream. It is called from the `snapshot()` method of the `ReliableLog` class, which provides the appropriate output stream.

recover(InputStream is)
> This method is responsible for reading in the snapshot, for example, by reading the serialized objects and assigning them to the correct instance variables. It is called from the `recover()` method of the `ReliableLog` class, which provides the appropriate input stream.

applyUpdate(Object o)
> When you are recovering a log, this method is called for each object that was stored to the log in an update operation; the parameter o is the parameter that was passed to the `update()` method. This method is responsible for looking at that object and applying the appropriate update to the saved data. Updates are often handled by creating a new type of object that represents the particular data that was changed and its new value.

Note that there is no `update()` method in the `LogHandler` class: the `ReliableLog` class completely implements the `update()` method by serializing the parameter to the log.

We've discussed three types of data that are appropriate to store in the reliable log:

Join state
> When a service joins the Jini community, it is assigned a service ID from the first lookup service it registers with. The service should save that service ID so that if it restarts, it will come up with the same service ID. In addition, the service should save the groups, lookup locators, and attributes that it uses to configure the join manager.

Session and other state data
> If a service crashes and restarts, clients may want to reconnect to the service, or the service may want to retrieve its last state.

Transaction data

If your service is a participant in a transaction, you'll need to use the reliable log to store prepared data, so that if you crash, you can still commit or abort the data when you restart. This includes the original value of data (in order to abort the transaction), the new value of the data (in order to commit the transaction), and the crash count.

In Example 8-3, we'll extend our basic service to handle data that should be persistent. The full code to run this example is based on Example 8-2 and requires the following files:

Example 8-3: A Service with a Reliable Log

```
Common classes
    ConvertService (used in Example 8-2; listed in Example 6-1)
    ConvertServiceRegistration (used in Example 8-2; listed in Example 5-1)
    ConvertEvent (used in Example 8-2; listed in Example 6-1)
Server Classes
    ConvertServiceImpl (modified from Example 8-2; listed in Example 6-1)
    ConvertServiceRegistrationImpl (used in Example 8-2;
        listed in Example 5-1)
    ConvertServiceProxy (used in Example 8-2; listed in Example 5-1)
    ServerLandlord (used in Example 8-2)
    ServerResource (used in Example 8-2; listed in Example 5-1)
    ServerDelivery (modified from Example 8-2; listed in Example 8-1)
    ConvertServiceImpl (used in Example 8-2; listed in Example 6-1)
    Expirer (used in Example 8-2)
Client Classes
    ServiceFinder (used in Example 8-1; listed in Example 6-2)
    ServiceFinderListener (used in Example 8-1; listed in Example 6-2)
    ConvertEventHandler (used in Example 8-1; listed in Example 6-1)
    ConvertClient (used in Example 8-1; listed in Example 6-1)
```

In previous examples, we sent out events where the sequence number indicated the number of conversions that our service has been asked to perform. If this service is restarted, that number will be reset to 0, and as it is now, the server will be restarted with a new service ID. Instead, we can save those pieces of state in a reliable log using this implementation of the server:

```
import java.util.*;
import java.io.*;
import java.rmi.*;
import java.rmi.server.*;
import net.jini.discovery.*;
import net.jini.core.lookup.*;
import net.jini.core.lease.*;
import net.jini.core.event.*;
import com.sun.jini.lookup.*;
import com.sun.jini.reliableLog.*;

public class ConvertServiceImpl extends UnicastRemoteObject
                implements ConvertServiceProxy, ServiceIDListener {

    private ServerLandlord lord;
    private ServerDelivery sender;
    private ConvertServiceLogHandler handler;
    private ReliableLog log;
    private long seqNo;
```

```
    private ServiceID id;

    // This class holds the information necessary for an update.
    // If we had other data to update at the same time as the
    // sequence number, we'd bundle it into this class. If we had
    // other data to update at another time, we'd create a different
    // class.
    // Make sure the class is static so that when it serializes,
    // it doesn't include a reference to the outer class.
    private static class ConvertServiceUpdateRecord
                        implements Serializable {
        long seqNo;
    }

    // This class reads and writes the reliable log
    class ConvertServiceLogHandler extends LogHandler {
        public void snapshot(OutputStream os) throws Exception {
            ObjectOutputStream oos = new ObjectOutputStream(os);
            Object target;
            if (id == null)
                // write a dummy object
                target = new String();
            else target = id;
            oos.writeObject(target);
            oos.writeLong(seqNo);
            oos.flush();                // Make sure it gets to disk
        }

        public void recover(InputStream is) throws Exception {
            ObjectInputStream ois =
                        new ObjectInputStream(is);
            Object target;
            try {
                target = ois.readObject();
            } catch (Exception e) {
                // No log
                return;
            }
            if (target instanceof ServiceID)
                id = (ServiceID) target;
            // else is was the dummy string
            seqNo = ois.readLong();
        }

        // Called when reading an update; the update was written
        // as a ConvertServiceUpdateRecord
        public void applyUpdate(Object o) {
            if (o instanceof ConvertServiceUpdateRecord)
                seqNo = ((ConvertServiceUpdateRecord) o).seqNo;
            else throw new IllegalArgumentException(
                        "Unexpected update");
        }
    }

    public ConvertServiceImpl(String logDir) throws RemoteException {
        handler = new ConvertServiceLogHandler();
        try {
            log = new ReliableLog(logDir, handler);
            log.recover();
            log.snapshot();     // Clean out all past updates
        } catch (Exception e) {
```

```
                throw new RemoteException("Can't create log", e);
        }

        lord = new ServerLandlord();
        sender = new ServerDelivery(this, lord);
    }

    public ConvertServiceRegistration getInstance(long duration) {
        Hashtable ht = new Hashtable(13);
        return new ConvertServiceRegistrationImpl(this,
                                lord.newLease(ht, duration));
    }

    // To convert, first check the cache for previous results. If
    // there's no cache, the landlord has expired the lease. If
    // there's no data in the cache, calculcate the data and put it there
    public String convert(Lease l, int i) throws LeaseDeniedException {
        Hashtable cache = (Hashtable) lord.getSessionData(l);
        if (cache == null)
            throw new LeaseDeniedException("Lease expired");
        Integer I = new Integer(i);
        String s;
        s = (String) cache.get(I);
        if (s == null) {
            s = I.toString();
            cache.put(I, s);
        }
        sender.deliver(i, getNextSeq());
        return s;
    }

    public synchronized EventRegistration
                    trackConversions(long duration,
                    RemoteEventListener rel, MarshalledObject key) {
        return sender.addListener(rel, duration, key, seqNo);
    }

    private synchronized long getNextSeq() {
        seqNo++;
        try {
            // Update the log with the new seq no; we must wrap
            // this into an object for the update method
            ConvertServiceUpdateRecord csur =
                        new ConvertServiceUpdateRecord();
            csur.seqNo = this.seqNo;
            log.update(csur, true);
        } catch (Exception e) {
            e.printStackTrace();
        }
        return seqNo;
    }

    public void serviceIDNotify(ServiceID id) {
        this.id = id;
        try {
            log.snapshot();
        } catch (Exception e) {
            e.printStackTrace();
        }
    }
}
```

Misc.
Classes

```
public static void main(String[] args) throws Exception {
    System.setSecurityManager(new RMISecurityManager());
    String[] groups = new String[] { "" };

    // Create the instance of the service; the JoinManager will
    // register it and renew its leases with the lookup service
    ConvertServiceImpl csi =
            (ConvertServiceImpl) new ConvertServiceImpl("csiLog");
    JoinManager manager = null;
    if (csi.id != null)
        manager = new JoinManager(csi.id, csi, null,
                                    groups, null, null);
    else manager = new JoinManager(csi, null, groups,
                                    null, csi, null);


}
}
```

When to take a snapshot or an update is up to you. Since we have to save the sequence number for the event ID, we make an update of that data every time that it has changed. You can make as many updates as you like between snapshots, but it helps to take a snapshot periodically just to keep the log at a manageable size; we do that just after we've read the log.

There are many changes in this code, but they boil down to the following:

The log handler

We created the inner ConvertServiceLogHandler class as the actual handler of the log. Note that the snapshot( ) and recover( ) methods are symmetric: we must read the data in exactly the same order that we wrote it.

The update( ) method requires that you pass a single object. Since we're updating a single piece of data, we could have written only the sequence number (wrapped as a Long). If your service needs to update multiple groups of data, the standard procedure is to make new classes that hold the each group of data and write out an instances of those classes. Then in the applyUpdate( ) method you can determine which pieces of data has changed by the type of the parameter object.

Data written with the update( ) method will be flushed to disk if the second parameter to that method is true; the default is not to flush the data to disk. You must explicitly flush data to disk in the snapshot( ) method.

The constructor

The constructor of our service is now responsible for instantiating the log and recovering any state in the log. When we construct the service, we must now pass the directory in which to store the log.

The service ID listener

The first time we use the join manager, we don't pass it a service ID (just as we've done all along). We now also pass it a service ID listener, so it will call us back when the first lookup service assigns us an ID. So our service is now a service ID listener that will get this data and save it to the log.

If we recovered a service ID from the log, we use that ID to register with the join manager.

The event sequence number

Finally, notice that the sequence number is now a property of the `Convert-ServiceImpl` class rather than the `ServerDelivery` class, since we don't want the latter class to know about the reliable log. We won't show the new `ServerDelivery` class since its changes are trivial: the sequence number is now a parameter to its `deliver()` and `addListener()` methods, and it no longer needs its own sequence number instance variable.

Parsing Command Lines

The last set of utility classes that we'll mention allows us to process command-line arguments when we start a program. We've used positional command-line arguments in all our examples, but if you'd like to include option processing, these classes are very useful. There are two such classes:

com.sun.jini.system.MultiCommandLine
This class lets you specify arguments that contain more than one letter (for example, *-port 8080* or *-verbose*).

com.sun.jini.system.POSIXCommandLine
This class lets you specify arguments by combinations of single letters according to POSIX specifications (for example, *-xvf*, which according to POSIX rules is three separate arguments: *-x*, *-v*, and *-f*).

To use either class, follow the same procedure:

1. Create an instance of the appropriate command-line class, passing it the arguments that you want to process (for example, the arguments that were passed to the `main()` method).

2. For each option, call the command-line object to see if the option is set (and, if appropriate, the value that it was set to). For binary options that are either specified or not specified, use the `getBoolean()` method. For other options, use the `getString()` method to return the option value as a string, the `getInt()` to return it as an integer, the `getReader()` to return it as a file reader object, and so on. Each of these methods allows you to specify a default value for the option.

3. Call the `getOperands()` method to return the remaining command-line arguments (those that don't appear with a corresponding hyphen). Even if you don't expect such arguments, you must call the `getOperands()` method, which tests to make sure that there are no remaining options that were (incorrectly) specified on the command line.

Here's how we would use this class to start an HTTP server that accepts up to three optional arguments: *-port port_number, -dir directory,* and *-verbose*:

```
import com.sun.jini.system.*;

public class HttpServer {
```

```
public HttpServer(int port, String dir, boolean verbose) {
    ...
}

public static void main(String[] args) throws Exception {
    MultiCommandLine mcl = new MultiCommandLine(args);
    int port = mcl.getInt("port", 80);
    String dir = mcl.getString("dir", ".");
    boolean verbose = mcl.getBoolean("verbose");
    String[] other = mcl.getOperands();
    if (other.length > 0) {
        System.out.print("usage: java HttpServer ");
        mcl.usage();
        System.exit(0);
    }
    new HttpServer(port, dir, verbose);
}
}
```

If there are addition arguments left after parsing, we call the usage( ) method to print out what the arguments should have been. The parser builds up the string printed by the usage( ) method based on the arguments that it has been asked to parse.

Summary

The Jini specification limits itself to classes that are directly related to the Jini system. However, when those classes were actually implemented, a number of useful subsidiary classes were developed; these classes ship with Sun's Jini implementation. Since we firmly believe in code reuse, we've discussed some of the most useful of those classes. Remember too that more of these type of classes can be found at *http://www.jini.org/*.

In the next chapter, we'll look at Jini's transaction API which can be used to talk to a Jini transaction service. The service itself is quite complicated, but using transactions is easy and is a prerequisite to communicate with some other Jini services.

CHAPTER 9

Transactions

Jini provides a transaction API for clients and services to use, and Sun's implementation of Jini comes with a simple transaction manager called *mahalo*. We showed how to start *mahalo* in Chapter 2, *Getting Started with Jini*, although none of our examples have needed it yet. In this chapter, we'll look at how to use the transaction APIs to interface with *mahalo*, focusing primarily on being a client of a transaction. That's a technique we'll use in Chapter 10, *The JavaSpaces Service*.

We'll then spend some time discussing what it means to be a participant in a transaction in the Jini framework. However, implementing a Jini transaction is very difficult: there are significant data integrity considerations that you must take into account, and the process of keeping track of data modifications in your service becomes quite complex. While we'll present the requirements necessary to be a participant in a transaction, we won't show a full example of how to implement that code, since it is far beyond the scope of a quick-reference book.

Overview of Transactions

By now, we know that the Jini infrastructure is designed to be robust. So far, we've examined that topic in light of services and clients adapting to a dynamic environment by deleting (or creating) references to each other automatically. While this setup solves the issue of maintaining the integrity of the infrastructure, it does not address the problem of what to do when an error occurs. That's where a transaction (or atomic operation) comes in.

An *atomic operation* is an indivisible unit: the operation either succeeds or fails. Changing the value of a byte in memory is typically an atomic operation. If you change the value of a memory location from 0x55 to 0x12, someone who reads the memory location at about the same time will see either 0x55 or 0x12 but not some intermediate value: all the bits of the value change at the same time. Computer hardware defines certain operations as atomic.

A *transaction* is an operation of many steps that is atomic at a logical level. Though a transaction may change many pieces of data, a transaction ensures that either all the data gets changed or none of the data gets changed. For example, to transfer money between your savings and checking accounts, you must subtract an amount from your savings account and add it to your checking account. A transaction ensures that no matter what happens—even if the computer making the transfer crashes in the middle of the operation—the money will either be subtracted from your savings and added to your checking, or nothing will happen. A transaction prevents the case where the money is subtracted from your savings account but never added to your checking account.

Transactions introduce a lot of complexity. For example, if we make a transfer between two bank accounts, we debit the amount from the source account and credit the amount into the target account. If a network error occurs during this operation, is retrying the operation once both parties are back online an acceptable solution? If the debit portion of the operation occurred prior to the error, then money has disappeared from the bank. While the infrastructure was robust enough to recover, the account that the services manage may not be in an acceptable state.

Solving this problem requires the cooperation of all the services involved in the transaction. For example, if the connection to the source bank's service generates an exception during the debit process, has the money actually been debited? Even if we wait for the source bank's service to reestablish contact, how do we know if the operation has succeeded? We can't save the balance of the bank account prior to the operation and compare it to the balance when the service reestablishes contact, because other operations may have modified the balance in the meantime.

This is a complex problem—there can be many operations in a transaction, transactions may have conflicting requirements, and all parties in the transaction must keep track of whether the transaction has failed or succeeded. To address this issue, Jini provides an interface to a transaction manager that knows how to keep track of all the operations and how to manage the parties in the transaction. This allows a series of operations to be grouped into a transaction; the transaction is then either committed or aborted. When a transaction is committed, all data affected by the transaction operations is changed atomically. When a transaction is aborted, all data affected by the transaction operations is rolled back, which means that it is reset to its value before the transaction started.

Parties to a Transaction

In a transaction, there are three parties:

The transaction client
> The transaction client initiates and (usually) terminates the transaction. In Jini, it does this by obtaining a transaction object, providing that object to a series of method calls that the client wants treated as an atomic unit, and then committing the transaction. Only the client can commit the transaction; the client, as well as any other party in the transaction, can abort the transaction. Jini provides a set of APIs that we'll use to be a transaction client.

The transaction manager

The transaction manager oversees the entire transaction. The transaction manager provides the transaction object to the client and keeps track of all participants. When the client commits the transaction, the transaction manager ensures that all participants update their data correctly.

The transaction object is leased by the transaction manager. The client must renew the lease on the object. Failure to renew the lease will cause the transaction manager to abort the transaction.

Jini provides a set of APIs that define the transaction manager interface, and Sun's version of Jini comes with an implementation of the transaction manager called *mahalo*.

The transaction participants

The services to which the client provides the transaction object become transaction participants. Transaction participants have strict requirements with respect to how they must manage data within the transaction.

While the client initiates the transaction, it is the transaction participants that allow (or sometimes require) the use of transactions, because the participants specify in their service interface that the client must provide a transaction object. You'll only need to use transactions when working with such a service; the JavaSpaces service provides such an interface. Most services do not need to be transaction participants.

The Client-Side Transaction APIs

Jini uses a transaction manager to handle transactions. Services indicate that they can participate in a transaction by requiring their clients to pass a transaction object parameter when the client calls a service method. For a client to create a transaction object, it must first find the transaction manager as follows :

```
ServiceFinder sf = new ServiceFinder(TransactionManager.class);
TransactionManager txm = (TransactionManger) sf.getObject();
```

Since the transaction manager is a Jini service, we must find the transaction manager interface in the Jini lookup service. While it would be possible to use this object in conjunction with a unique transaction ID to identify a transaction, Jini provides a transaction object that abstracts those two data elements into a single entity. The transaction objects are created by a transaction factory.

The transaction factory also returns a lease to the client. The client must maintain the lease or the transaction manager will abort the transaction automatically.* Once the transaction is completed, either by committing or aborting the transaction, the lease is cancelled automatically by the transaction manager. Trying to cancel the lease at a later time will generate an UnknownLeaseException.

---

* In the two-phase commit protocol that we discuss later, there is a window of time called the prepare stage that occurs after the client has committed the transaction and before the data is committed. Leases are not allowed to expire during that stage, but the client is generally unaware of that stage anyway.

Here is a summary of the classes and interfaces of the transaction system that the client uses:

net.jini.core.transaction.server.TransactionManager
The interface that is supported by any transaction manager running on the Jini network.

net.jini.core.transaction.TransactionFactory
A class that takes a transaction manager and creates a transaction object that can be used to represent transactions. The methods of this class are `static`; it is not possible to instantiate an instance of this class.

net.jini.core.transaction.Transaction
The interface of the transaction object that is returned from the transaction factory. The purpose of the transaction object is to hide the details of the transaction from the client.

Because transactions are always leased, this interface contains an inner `static` class: the `Transaction.Created` class. This class holds a transaction object and a lease object. Instances of the `Transaction.Created` class are created by the `TransactionFactory` class.

We can obtain a `Transaction.Created` object (an object that contains the `Transaction` object and its lease) as follows:

```
import java.rmi.*;
import net.jini.discovery.*;
import net.jini.core.lease.*;
import net.jini.core.event.*;
import net.jini.core.transaction.*;
import net.jini.core.transaction.server.*;
import net.jini.admin.*;
import com.sun.jini.lease.*;

public class ConvertClient {

    public static void main(String[] args) throws Exception {
        System.setSecurityManager(new RMISecurityManager());

        ServiceFinder sf = new ServiceFinder(TransactionManager.class);
        TransactionManager txm = (TransactionManager)(sf.getObject());

        // Create the transaction object
        // txn.transaction will contain the object that implements
        //      the Transaction interface
        // txn.lease will contain the object that implements
        //      the Lease interface
        Transaction.Created txn =
                    TransactionFactory.create(txm, Lease.FOREVER);

        // Make sure the lease is renewed until we're done
        LeaseRenewalManager lrm = new LeaseRenewalManager();
        lrm.renewUntil(txn.lease, Lease.FOREVER, null);

        boolean commit = true;
        try {
            // Do some transaction-based operations here, passing
            // txn.transaction to services that need it.
```

```
    } catch (Exception e) {
        commit = false;
    }

    if (commit)
        txn.transaction.commit();
    else txn.transaction.abort();

    // The transaction lease was cancelled as a side-effect of
    // the commit or abort.
    lrm.remove(resp.lease);
    }
}
```

This class gives us the basic outline of using transactions: obtain a Transaction.Created object from the transaction manager, renew the lease contained in that object, perform operations that need the transaction contained in that object, and if those operations succeed, commit the transaction.

To use this outline, we need a service that supports transactions. In Chapter 10, we'll use this outline to perform a transaction with the JavaSpaces service, which is the only standard Jini service that supports transactions.

The Jini Transaction Framework

In the next few pages, we'll discuss the technology behind the transaction manager. If you intend to use transactions only as a client, you don't really need to understand all of the details of this technology. On the other hand, if you intend to write a service that is a participant in a transaction, you'll be required to perform certain tasks that we're about to discuss.

The Two-Phase Commit Protocol

The Jini transaction system uses a "two-phase commit" protocol in conjunction with all of the services (known as participants) that are involved in the transaction. Basically, the goal is to treat the transaction as a single atomic unit. Either every operation of the transaction succeeds or fails; partial failures are not allowed. This is accomplished by creating a transaction, performing all of the operations of the transaction, and finishing the transaction using a two-step process known as the two-phase commit protocol.

To create a transaction, we use a transaction object. A transaction object—an object that provides a unique ID to the participants—is used to isolate the transaction's operations. When a service method is called, it must be provided with the transaction object. If the service has not already done so, it must "join" the transaction by registering a callback with the transaction object.

Furthermore, the service must use the transaction object in the management of its internal session data. Any data change that is requested within a transaction cannot be seen outside of the transaction; however, it must be visible inside the transaction. For example, if a variable that is modified inside a transaction is read by a client, the value that the client sees will depend upon the transaction variable that is used by the client. If the client uses the same transaction object, it sees the change; otherwise, it sees the original data. This places a huge burden on the service participating in the transaction.

Simultaneous transactions may place another burden on the service. Since data changes in a transaction are not visible until the transaction completes, an object involved in a transaction may have to be locked during the transaction. This could lead to deadlock for simultaneous transactions. In general, if all data is read-only during the transaction, then simultaneous transactions are easy to implement. Otherwise, an elaborate locking mechanism may be necessary. In most cases, it is probably easiest to have a global lock so that transactions are queued (i.e., the second transaction waits for the completion of the first transaction).

If at any time during the transaction an operation cannot be completed, the client can request that the transaction be aborted. The transaction manager then informs all of the participants in the transaction to rollback (undo) any state changes that are related to the transaction. This effectively restores the services to their state at the beginning of the transaction. The participants are not allowed to fail in this operation, which is a guarantee that the service provides to the transaction system.

Once all of the operations are completed successfully, the client can commit the transaction. The transaction manager will then inform all of the participants in the transaction to commit any state changes that are related to the transaction. However, this process is more complicated; it involves the two-step process known as two-phase commit.

The first phase of this process is the *prepare* phase. The participants are asked to prepare to commit the changes of the transaction. A participant that agrees to prepare its data makes a strict guarantee that the data in question will be committed or aborted even if the participant crashes. This is a stricter guarantee than the service previously provided (by being a participant in the transaction); until this point, if the service had crashed, it could have rolled back the data when it restarted.

Once we've agreed to prepare our data, if we need to restart our service, we must still have all of the information necessary to handle the transaction. We must rejoin the transaction and be prepared to commit or abort. This process requires that we save all of the state changes to persistent storage, but it cannot yet overwrite the actual state of the service (e.g., we might put this information into a log file). If this cannot be accomplished, we can veto the request. Otherwise, we effectively consign the service to be able to commit or abort the transaction at a later time no matter what error conditions occur.

Another option for the participant is to drop out of the transaction. Dropping out is useful when the service was not used in any way that caused its internal state to be changed (perhaps it was used in a read-only fashion). At that point, the participant can clean up any session data, as it will not be asked to commit or abort the transaction.

So the transaction manager will ask all of the participants to prepare themselves. If any of the participants veto the request, the transaction manager must ask all of the participants to abort the transaction. Once all of the participants accept the request, then the transaction manager can commit the transaction. Like the participants, the transaction manager also must guarantee the integrity of the transaction;

it must also survive crashes with the information about the transaction intact. This means that once all the participants are prepared, the transaction manager must log that fact in persistent storage so that it will not abort the transaction once a prepare has succeeded.

During the second phase of the protocol, the transaction manager ensures that the participant actually commits the transaction. The service is not allowed to generate an error condition or abort the transaction once the commit phase of the protocol has started. The client may still get an error condition from the transaction manager (due to a network problems, for example), but the transaction manager will keep trying the request until it has heard from all of the participants—even after it is restarted, if necessary.

Nestable Transactions

A *nested transaction* (or *subtransaction*) is a transaction that has another transaction as its parent. Like other transactions, data changes in a subtransaction can't be seen outside of the transaction (including in its parent transaction) until the subtransaction commits. But the subtransaction does see the uncommitted data changes in its parent transaction.

When a subtransaction is aborted, the parent transaction is unaffected. When the subtransaction is committed, the participants are prepared. However, they are not actually committed; instead, the operations in the subtransaction are promoted to the parent transaction. This allows the data changes in the subtransaction to be visible to the parent transaction while still hiding the data changes from the rest of the world.

The parent transaction can still abort. Since the subtransaction's data changes are part of the parent transaction, the data changes must be rolled back if the parent transaction aborts. For the subtransaction participant, this means that the prepare operation requires an extra task—besides preparing the transaction so that it can commit or abort, the service also must mark in the parent transaction's session data that the subtransaction has been prepared.

When the parent transaction is aborted or committed, all participants—including those in incomplete subtransactions—are aborted or committed. The transaction manager that is managing the subtransaction joins the parent transaction (i.e., the transaction manager of the subtransaction becomes a participant in the parent transaction). If the subtransaction is committed first, the participants are promoted to the parent. If the parent transaction completes first, the subtransaction's transaction manager (as a participant) will route the requests to its participants.

Visibility rules are also more complex with nested transactions. If a service receives a nested transaction, all data changes in the transaction and all data changes of any ancestor transaction are visible to the transaction. Furthermore, data changes in prepared subtransactions may also be visible to the parent transaction. If a subtransaction is prepared and committed, then data changes in the subtransaction are visible. In this case, when the subtransaction is committed, it really means that the subtransaction has or will be promoted to the parent transaction; it becomes fully committed when the parent transaction is committed.

Nested Transactions and the Jini Transaction Service

While the Jini transaction framework is designed to handle nested transactions, Sun's transaction manager (*mahalo*) that is provided with Jini 1.0 and 1.1 does not supported nested transactions.

The Server-Side Transaction APIs

Writing a service that participates in a transaction is difficult. While the transaction participant interface is straightforward, the guarantees that are mandated by the transaction framework are difficult to satisfy. The service must obey the visibility rules of the transaction. The service must have an algorithm to handle simultaneous transactions, or it must synchronize appropriately so that transaction are queued. The service must be able to rollback a transaction at any time. In an unprepared state, the service must survive crashes so that, at a minimum, its state prior to the transaction is reestablished. In a prepared state, the service must survive crashes in a state that can guarantee the resolution of the transaction.

If you must support transactions in your service, then the easiest path may be to defer the transaction semantics to an underlying transaction engine. You can't use the implementation of the JavaSpaces service as a guide, since the source code for that service is not included under terms of the SCSL, and the JavaSpaces service uses an underlying database for much of its semantics anyway.

We'll discuss the server-side APIs here, but due to their complexity, we won't show a complete example that uses them. The key APIs for a server that wants to support transactions are:

net.jini.core.transaction.server.ServerTransaction
> This class implements the Transaction interface, and objects of this class are used by the participant to communicate with the transaction manager. What's interesting is how the service obtains this object:

> * The client obtains a transaction object (and its associated lease) from the transaction factory.

> * The client passes the transaction object to the service when it invokes a service method.

> * The service casts that object into a ServerTransaction object.

> So the object that the client obtained from the transaction manager was a ServerTransaction object all along.

net.jini.core.transaction.server.TransactionParticipant
> When the service receives a transaction, it must join the transaction by calling the join( ) method of the ServerTransaction object. It must pass an object that implements the TransactionParticipant interface to that method, which informs the transaction manager that the service has joined the transaction.

A skeleton implementation of this interface looks like this:

```java
import java.rmi.*;
import java.rmi.server.*;
import net.jini.core.transaction.*;
import net.jini.core.transaction.server.*;

public class ServerParticipant extends UnicastRemoteObject
                                implements TransactionParticipant {

    public int crashcount;

    public ServerParticipant() throws RemoteException {
        // Load log file (if any) and load session data that is needed
        //     to survive crashes.
        // Calculate the crashcount for the log file.
        // If commit or rollback in progress,
        //     get state and finish request
    }

    // Called by the transaction manager to ask the service to
    // enter the prepare state.
    public int prepare(TransactionManager mgr, long id)
            throws UnknownTransactionException, RemoteException {
        // If transaction is unknown, throw UnknownTransactionException.

        // Get information about this transaction from the landlord.
        // If transaction's lease has expired, rollback the transaction,
        //     clean up session data (if landlord hasn't already), and
        //     return ABORTED.
        // If transaction has no changes, clean up session data and
        //     return NOTCHANGED.
        // Prepare the system to survive crashes.
        //    (Store to some log file)
        // Clean up session data and landlord.

        // If error during this process, clean up the mess
        //     and return ABORTED.
        return PREPARED;
    }

    // Called by the transaction manager to tell the service that
    // it must commit (the service will already be in
    // the prepared state).
    public void commit(TransactionManager mgr, long id)
            throws UnknownTransactionException, RemoteException {
        // If transaction is unknown, throw UnknownTransactionException.

        // Update the system to survive crashes.  (Update log file)
        // Commit the transaction, freeing any locked resources.
        // Clean up the system. (Includes information in log file)
    }

    // Called by the transaction manager to tell the service to
    // rollback its changes.
    public void abort(TransactionManager mgr, long id)
            throws UnknownTransactionException, RemoteException {
        // If transaction is unknown, throw UnknownTransactionException.

        // Update the system to survive crashes. (Update log file)
```

```
        // Abort the Transaction. (Includes freeing any locked resources)
        // Clean up the system. (Includes information in log file)
    }

    // The transaction manager will call this only if this service is the
    // only participant in the transaction or is the last unprepared
    // participant (or the transaction manager may call prepare()
    // and commit() separately).
    public int prepareAndCommit(TransactionManager mgr, long id)
            throws UnknownTransactionException, RemoteException {
        int result = prepare(mgr, id);
        if (result == PREPARED) {
            commit(mgr, id);
            result = COMMITTED;
        }
        return result;
    }
}
```

The purpose of the ServerParticipant object is to handle requests from the transaction manager. The service will instantiate a ServerPariticipant object and pass
it to the join() method of the transaction manager. When the client commits or
aborts the transaction, the transaction manager will call the corresponding methods of the ServerParticipant object.

The transaction manager makes four types of requests: a request to prepare the
service for a commit operation, a request to commit the prepared transaction, a
request to abort the transaction, and a method that may be called both to prepare
and commit the request. This last method is used if we are the only participant or
if none of the other participants have any changes to commit. Also notice that the
TransactionParticipant interface is a remote interface, which means that the
ServerParticipant class will use RMI as its transport.

In the prepare() method, we must check to see whether the client session data
specific to the transaction is still available and veto the request if the session data
is no longer available. If the data is available, we must update the log files using
the session data to allow the transaction to be able to commit or abort even if the
service crashes.

In the commit() and abort() methods, we must load the information necessary
from the log file and commit or abort the transaction. Depending on the type of
work necessary, we may have to use a log file during the commit() or abort()
method. This log file allows us to continue the request correctly if we fail during
the commit or abort request. Ideally, it is better to do as much work as possible
during the prepare phase of the two-phase commit process (since we can still veto
the transaction) than in the commit() or abort() methods; you want the commit()
and abort() methods to be as fail-safe as possible.

These methods all receive a transaction manager and an ID as their parameter
rather than a transaction object. The transaction object that abstracts these pieces
of data is used only for communication between the client and service. If the participant needs to find the transaction object, it must search through all its active
transactions for one with the correct ID and transaction manager. The ID is a field
of the ServerTransaction class.

The Jini transaction manager uses the concept of a *crash count*, which should be loaded from a log file by the constructor of the ServerParticipant class. The service provides the crash count to the transaction manager whenever it joins the transaction. A crash count is a long integer that is used to represent the state of the log file; it is used to handle cases where we will be making changes to our unprepared state that cannot survive a crash. To make such a change, we increment the crash count and store it to the log file. We then execute the operations that are desired. Once we reach a saveable state, we save the state of the session, along with any data needed to survive a crash, to the log file and then decrement the crash count and store it back to the log file. If our service crashes at any time after incrementing but before decrementing the crash count, the transaction manager will detect this (because the crash count parameter in the next call to join( ) method will be incorrect) and abort the entire transaction.

Because all the methods of the TransactionParticipant interface receive the transaction ID as a parameter, a service needs only one ServerParticipant object, though it may be more convenient to instantiate a new one for each transaction so that the server participant object can hold transaction-specific data. If there is an instance variable participant that is the one server participant for a service, a service method that supports transactions would follow this skeleton:

```
public String convert(Transaction t, int i) throws TransactionException {
    if (t != null) {
        ServerTransaction st = (ServerTransaction) t;
        st.join(participant, participant.crashcount);
        // st.id will be the parameter passed to the participant
        // when the client commits or aborts the transaction
    }

    // If a transaction is already in progress that will prevent this
    // execution, either wait or return a transaction exception.

    // Calculate conversion, using data that is visible only in this
    // transaction and hiding that data until the participant is told
    // to commit or abort
    String conversion = ...;

    // Before returning, update the log file in case the service crashes

    return conversion;
}
```

Miscellaneous Transaction Issues

There are two minor issues that need further explanation. Throughout our discussion about the two-phase commit process, we kept discussing the concept of a guarantee that the service can commit or abort a prepared transaction. In reality, there is no such thing as a guarantee. It is possible for the service to fail, and for the log file to get corrupted with it. When we discuss the concept of a guarantee, the best that we can infer is a commitment to survive the crash and be able to complete the request. Depending on the importance of the service, the commitment of the service implementor to this endeavor can be to use every available technique to minimize the chances that the service does not fail and is able to survive the crash. Or it can ensure that the critical sections are as small as possible so that there is a pretty good chance that the system will not crash during those critical sections.

The other issue has to do with deadlock. In general, if we're managing data changes, we need to lock that data. This introduces the possibility that two transactions will lock each other's data and deadlock. Since a service does not know what other services are participants in the transaction, there's no simple way to ensure that deadlock is avoided. The solution to this problem is to use timeouts. If the transactions can timeout, sooner or later one of the transaction will abort, thus freeing the resources necessary to complete the other transaction.

Summary

In Jini, transactions are frequently used from the clients of the JavaSpaces service, and the technique to do so is a simple Jini API. While the Jini APIs to be a participant in a transaction are also simple, the semantics that are required to implement those APIs are complex. Fortunately, few services need to support transactions.

CHAPTER 10

The JavaSpaces Service

This chapter covers the JavaSpaces service that comes as part of Sun's Jini implementation. The interface to this service is part of the Jini specification, but Sun's implementation is proprietary. Unlike the rest of Sun's implementation, the source code for the JavaSpaces service does not ship with Jini and is not covered by the SCSL.

At first glance, the JavaSpaces service looks like a very simple persistent store. It is, however, a full-fledged Jini service: it can be located by using the Jini lookup service, it stores Entry objects, and it uses Entry objects as templates to match and retrieve stored objects. This is the second use we've seen of Entry objects; in Chapter 4, *Basic Jini Programming*, we saw that Entry objects are used to specify attributes for matching services within the Jini lookup service.

Objects stored in a JavaSpaces service are leased—the service is free to delete an object once the lease is cancelled or is allowed to expire. A remote event listener can register to be informed when new matching objects are inserted into the space. And finally, a space supports execution of its operations within the Jini transaction framework.

The JavaSpace interface is very simple: it supports only four primitive operations. Entry objects can be written to the JavaSpace, Entry objects can be read from the JavaSpace, Entry objects can be taken from the JavaSpace (i.e., read and removed), and listeners can be registered to be informed when Entry objects are inserted into the space. However, despite the simplicity of the API, JavaSpaces is based on research from the arena of distributed and parallel programming. There are many ideas and techniques involving JavaSpaces that are beyond the scope of this book.

You might be tempted to consider the JavaSpaces service as a database service. That is not a good idea. The space that is provided to the client is leased, which means that objects that are stored there will be deleted unless the client maintains the lease.

The objects in the space are also globally available. This means that the space can be used to pass objects between different applications in an uncoupled manner. It can be used as a shared data structure that many distributed applications can access and process. It can be used to synchronize actions between applications. Even though the primitives of the JavaSpaces service are simple, it can be used as the building block for very complex distributed algorithms.

The JavaSpaces API

Access to the JavaSpaces service is obtained from the Jini lookup service. Hence, to find a JavaSpaces service in the Jini network, we search specifying the net.jini.space.JavaSpace interface:

```
ServiceFinder sf = new ServiceFinder(JavaSpace.class);
JavaSpace space = (JavaSpace) sf.getObject();
```

There are seven methods in this interface. They support the four primitive operations, plus one additional administrative method. We'll look at these methods grouped by operation.

The "write" Operation

There is a single method used to write to a space:

```
public Lease write(Entry entry, Transaction txn, long lease)
    throws TransactionException, RemoteException
```

This method takes three parameters: the Entry object that is to be written, the transaction object for this operation, and a lease time for the Entry object to be stored. This method returns a lease for the object.

If a null object is passed for the transaction parameter, the write operation is considered to be in its own transaction. This means that the Entry object can be read or taken from the space as soon as the write operation has completed. If a transaction object is used, the Entry object cannot be read or taken from the space outside of the transaction until the transaction is committed. If the transaction is aborted, the Entry object will be removed from the space.

The "read" Operation

Two methods are available to read entries from a space:

```
public Entry read(Entry tmpl, Transaction txn, long timeout)
    throws UnusableEntryException, TransactionException,
        InterruptedException, RemoteException

public Entry readIfExists(Entry tmpl, Transaction txn, long timeout)
    throws UnusableEntryException, TransactionException,
        InterruptedException, RemoteException
```

Both of these methods take three parameters: the Entry object that is to be used as a template, the transaction object for this operation, and a timeout interval used to cancel the request if an Entry object that matches the template cannot be found. These methods return a matching Entry object. If none is found within the specified timeout, then a `null` object will be returned. Only one object (an arbitrary one) is returned if there are many objects that match the template.

If a `null` object is passed for the transaction parameter, the read operation is considered to be in its own transaction. This means that it is unable to read any objects that are written during a transaction until that transaction has been committed. If a transaction object is used, the objects that are written during the transaction can be read (in addition to any entry objects written outside of any transaction).

The objects in the space are unordered. If a transaction is used, there is no preference for returning `Entry` objects that are inside the transaction over `Entry` objects outside of the transaction—any entry object that can be seen by the transaction can be returned. Also, if a transaction is used and an object outside of the transaction is returned, it becomes partially locked. It can still be read outside of the transaction since it hasn't changed. However, it cannot be taken from the space until the transactions that have read it are all completed.

A client will only wait for a matching object for the specified time. If the timeout elapses, a `null` object is returned. If you want to block until an object is found, use `Long.MAX_VALUE` as the timeout value. If you don't want to wait for a matching entry object, use `JavaSpace.NO_WAIT` (or a value of zero) as the timeout value.

If a value of `null` is passed as the template, any object can be returned. If multiple reads are executed using the same template, the method calls may return the same object each time. Multiple calls cannot be used to cycle through all of the objects that match the template. Comparison of objects is done with the `equals()` method—objects returned by `read()` are only copies of the original object. This is an important reason to make sure that the `equals()` method is implemented correctly for each type that the `Entry` object contains.

The `readIfExists()` method returns an object only if a matching object exists in the space. If no entries that match the template can be found, it will return `null`. However, this method is not equivalent to `read(...,...,NO_WAIT)`. The `readIfExists()` method will still block if it finds a matching object that is not yet visible (i.e., an object being modified in another transaction). You can specify a timeout value for this method to limit the amount of time to wait for such an object.

The "take" Operation

Two methods exist to remove objects from the space:

```
public Entry take(Entry tmpl, Transaction txn, long timeout)
    throws UnusableEntryException, TransactionException,
        InterruptedException, RemoteException

public Entry takeIfExists(Entry tmpl, Transaction txn, long timeout)
    throws UnusableEntryException, TransactionException,
        InterruptedException, RemoteException
```

The take operation is similar to the read operation, except that the object that is returned is removed from the space. There are minor semantic differences also.

If a null object is passed for the transaction parameter, the take operation is considered to be in its own transaction. This means that it is unable to take any objects involved in an incomplete transaction, which includes objects that are only read during the transaction. If a transaction object is used, the objects that are written by the transaction can be taken (along with any objects outside of a transaction). Objects that are only read during a transaction can be taken if they have not been read by another transaction.

The take( ) method can also be used to read all object entries that match a template. To accomplish this, create a new transaction, take all of the entries that match the required template until a null is returned, and abort the transaction. Since the objects are not removed from the space until the transaction commits, any other read operation will think that the entry objects still exist and wait for the take transaction to complete. Aborting the transaction will restore the objects into the space.

The "notify" Operation

There is a single method to register listeners to be informed of changes in the space:

```
public EventRegistration notify(Entry tmpl, Transaction txn,
    RemoteEventListener listener, long lease, MarshalledObject handback)
    throws TransactionException, RemoteException
```

This operation provides the calling application with the ability to be notified of newly written objects that match a particular template. Notification occurs after the entry is able to be read from the space, using the same semantics as the read( ) method. A notification will be sent if a newly written entry object can be read using the template and the transaction object that is specified.

This method takes five parameters: the Entry object that is to be used as a template, the transaction object for this operation, a remote event listener that will receive the remote events, a lease time for the registered listener, and a marshalled object that will be handed back to the remote event listener as part of the event.

This method returns a net.jini.core.event.EventRegistration object. The object includes the event ID that will be used for this notify request, the source of the events, a lease, and the starting sequence number (which is the sequence number the space last used for an event of this type). If the lease is cancelled or allowed to expire, no further notifications will be sent. If a transaction is provided, notification ends when the transaction completes.

When you receive a remote event, the sequence number in the event minus the starting sequence number will be the number of matching objects that have been added to the space since you registered. The JavaSpaces service can compress multiple events, which will cause the sequence number to skip.

The snapshot () Method

This method applies to all operations:

```
public Entry snapshot(Entry e) throws RemoteException
```

This method is provided as a means of optimizing certain loops. For example, if we want to delete from the space a large group of objects that match a particular template, we call the take() method in a loop until null is returned. For this loop, we will probably use the same template for each iteration. This means that the template object must be serialized and sent to the service many times.

If the template is a complex class, or if the loop is really large, repeated serialization and delivery of the template may take a lot of time. The snapshot() method will record the requested parameter and return another Entry object that will be easy to serialize and deliver. When we use this object in a subsequent method call, we are serializing and delivering to the space an opaque object that is used to refer to the original Entry object.

The object returned from the snapshot() method cannot be used as if it were the original object. The space has a copy of the original object, so changes to the original object do not affect the object held by the space. An object that is returned from one space should not be used in another space, since the spaces may use the same marker to refer to different objects. This means that if the same template is to be used with two spaces, the snapshot() method has to be called twice; each space will return a separate object that cannot be shared between the spaces.

A JavaSpaces Example

We'll use the JavaSpaces service to perform the same type of integer conversion that we've been using all along. For simplicity, we won't build this into a full-fledged Jini service. This is a common technique for applications that are built around the JavaSpaces service, which you can think of as a workflow manager. An employee reimbursement application built with the JavaSpaces service would start with the employee creating an entry that has the employee ID, the amount to be reimbursed, and an empty slot for the manager's approval. The employee puts that entry into the space. Periodically, the manager goes to the space and takes out all entries that have an empty approval slot; the manager approves the entries by filling that slot with a digital signature and puts the entries back into the space. Periodically, the controller goes to the space and takes out all entries that have a full approval slot and issues checks for those reimbursements. Even though there is one payroll application, the application is distributed into three concrete sets of work (each of which is a different executable).

This paradigm, where data flows from executable to executable and the application is the combined effect of all the executables, is the key benefit of the JavaSpaces service: it allows us to write distributed applications in a simple and natural way. So we'll follow this paradigm for our first example and develop two parties that act on data in order to create an integer conversion. The files required for this example are listed in Example 10-1.

Example 10–1: A JavaSpaces Example

```
Common classes
    Conversion (new)
    ServiceFinder (used in Example 8-3; listed in Example 6-2)
    ServiceFinderListener (used in Example 8-3; listed in Example 6-2)
Server classes
    Converter (new)
Client classes
    ConvertClient (modified from Example 8-3; listed in Example 6-1)
```

Note that our server now needs the ServiceFinder and ServiceFinderListener classes, because our server is now going to be a client of the JavaSpaces service. We've seen all along that servers are all clients of the Jini lookup service, and in general a Jini server can be the client of any other Jini service.

The Common Classes

In this example, we're not setting up a service, so we have no common service interfaces. We do have a new common class between server and client, however: the Conversion class. This class is the Entry class that we'll use to store data into the space:

```
import net.jini.core.entry.*;

public class Conversion implements Entry {
    public Integer value;   // The value to convert
    public String result;   // The answer
    public Boolean done;    // Whether or not the operation has happened

    // Required for all entry objects
    public Conversion() {
    }

    public Conversion(int v, boolean d) {
        value = new Integer(v);
        done = new Boolean(d);
    }

    public Conversion(boolean d) {
        done = new Boolean(d);
    }
}
```

We'll control the operation on the Entry objects by using the done variable. The client will insert a Conversion entry that has a false value for its done variable into the space to indicate that we want something to convert the integer. The client will retrieve answers by looking for entries where the done variable is true. And the server will look for objects to operate on by looking for entries where the done variable is false; when it has completed the conversion, it will set that done variable to true. Note that the value variable is an Integer and the done variable a Boolean, since Entry objects are not allowed to contain primitives.

The Client Code

Here's the code that we'll use on the client side:

```
import java.rmi.*;
import net.jini.core.lease.*;
import net.jini.space.*;
import com.sun.jini.lease.*;

public class ConvertClient {

    public static void main(String[] args) throws Exception {
        System.setSecurityManager(new RMISecurityManager());
        LeaseRenewalManager lrm = new LeaseRenewalManager();

        // Find the JavaSpaces service
        ServiceFinder sf = new ServiceFinder(JavaSpace.class);
        JavaSpace js = (JavaSpace) sf.getObject();

        Conversion request = new Conversion(5, true);
        Conversion result = (Conversion)
                    js.read(request, null, JavaSpace.NO_WAIT);
        if (result == null) {
            // There was no cached result. Make a new request
            // and retrieve that answer
            request.done = new Boolean(false);
            Lease l = js.write(request, null, Lease.FOREVER);
            lrm.renewUntil(l, Lease.FOREVER, null);
            request.done = new Boolean(true);
            result = (Conversion) js.read(request, null, Long.MAX_VALUE);
            lrm.cancel(l);
            lrm.remove(l);
        }
        // else just use the cached value

        System.out.println(result.result);
        System.exit(0);
    }
}
```

The client uses the `result` variable to search for entries in the space. First, it looks for an entry where the value is 5 and the `done` flag is `true`; if such an entry exists, that's the answer the client needs. Otherwise, it sets the done flag of the entry to `false` and writes it into the space; that triggers the server code to perform the conversion. Then the client sets the `done` flag back to `true` and waits forever until the matching entry is found.

When the client wrote the request to the space, it received a lease for the entry, which it renews until it gets a response. Cancelling the lease causes the space to delete the entry.

The Server Code

The server side of our code looks like this:

```
import java.rmi.*;
import net.jini.core.lease.*;
import net.jini.core.transaction.*;
```

```
import net.jini.core.transaction.server.*;
import net.jini.space.*;
import com.sun.jini.lease.*;

public class Converter {

    public static void main(String[] args) throws Exception {
        System.setSecurityManager(new RMISecurityManager());

        // Find the transaction manager
        ServiceFinder sf = new ServiceFinder(TransactionManager.class);
        TransactionManager txm = (TransactionManager)(sf.getObject());
        LeaseRenewalManager lrm = new LeaseRenewalManager();

        // Find the JavaSpaces
        ServiceFinder sfjs = new ServiceFinder(JavaSpace.class);
        JavaSpace js = (JavaSpace) sfjs.getObject();

        Conversion request = new Conversion(false);
        Conversion result;

        while (true) {
            Transaction.Created txn = null;
            try {
                // Take the request in a thread so that if the service
                // exits before it writes the answer the request is not
                // lost
                txn = TransactionFactory.create(txm, Lease.FOREVER);
                lrm.renewUntil(txn.lease, Lease.FOREVER, null);
                result = (Conversion) js.take(request,
                                    txn.transaction, Long.MAX_VALUE);

                // Calculate the answer
                try {
                    result.result = String.valueOf(result.value);
                } catch (Exception e) {
                    // If we can't calculate the answer, we have to
                    // abort the transaction, but we can go get the
                    // next request
                    txn.transaction.abort();
                    lrm.remove(txn.lease);
                    continue;
                }

                // Write the answer
                result.done = new Boolean(true);
                js.write(result, txn.transaction, 60 * 60 * 1000);
                txn.transaction.commit();
                lrm.remove(txn.lease);
            } catch (Exception e) {
                // These exceptions mean that we couldn't talk to the
                // space or transaction manager, which we can't
                // recover from.
                System.out.println("Unrecoverable error" + e);
                System.exit(-1);
            }
        }
    }
}
```

The server takes a predictable path: it takes the entry out of the space, performs the conversion, and writes the new entry (with the answer and the done flag set to true) to the space.

The most interesting thing about the server is that we now have a need for transactions. We don't want to remove a request from the space and crash; in that case, the client would wait forever for the answer to come. So we create a transaction that we use to take the data from the space; when we've put the answer back into the space we commit the entire transaction. If we get a recoverable error while calculating the conversion, we call the abort( ) method directly; if there is an unrecoverable error (such as not being able to talk to the JavaSpaces service at all), then we'll exit and the transaction's lease will not be renewed, in which case the transaction manager will abort the transaction. Either way, the JavaSpaces service will rollback such that the original request is back in the space and another server can fulfill it.

When the server writes the result back to the space, it requests a lease time of one hour. We do not care if we receive the requested time, nor do we even maintain the lease. This is fairly common. The point behind operations in a space is that the clients are uncoupled. One client may request that the value of 5 be converted, and in 30 minutes another client may need that value—even though the first client has since exited. So the lease in a space is really used only to ensure that unused objects in the space eventually will be removed.

Running the Example

Even though we haven't created a Jini service in this example, it must be run using the same procedure we have all along, including specifying the java.rmi.server.codebase property for both the client and server: both applications need to provide the lookup service with the stub object of ServiceFinderListener class in order to be notified when JavaSpaces services have joined the Jini community. In addition, to run this example you must have started both the transaction manager and the JavaSpaces service as we outlined in Chapter 2, *Getting Started with Jini*.

Embedding JavaSpaces in Services

In our last example, we developed two cooperating applications that together formed a distributed application used to convert integers. That's a common use of the JavaSpaces service. But there's no reason why we can't take this example one step further and implement our standard ConvertService interface by using the JavaSpaces service. In Example 10-2, we'll do just that.

Example 10–2: A Service with an Embedded JavaSpace Service

```
Common classes
    ConvertService (used in Example 6-2; listed in Example 6-1)
    ConvertServiceRegistration (used in Example 6-2; listed in Example 5-1)
    ConvertEvent (used in Example 6-2; listed in Example 6-1)
    ServiceFinder (used in Example 6-2)
    ServiceFinderListener (used in Example 6-2)
```

Example 10–2: A Service with an Embedded JavaSpace Service (continued)

```
Server classes
    ConvertServiceImpl (modified from Example 6-2)  .
    ConvertServiceRegistrationImpl (modified from Example 6-2;
             listed in Example 5-1)
    ConvertServiceProxy (modified from Example 6-2; listed in Example 5-1)
    ServerLandlord (used in Example 6-2; listed in Example 5-2)
    ServerResource (used in Example 6-2; listed in Example 5-1)
    ServerDelivery (used in Example 6-2; listed in Example 5-1)
    Conversion.java (used in Example 10-1)
Client classes
    ConvertEventHandler (used in Example 6-2; listed in Example 6-1)
    ConvertClient (used in Example 6-2; listed in Example 6-1)
```

We've gone back to Example 6-2 as the basis of our example. None of the code in the client needs to be changed for this example; in the server, we'll be incorporating the code from the Converter class into the service.

In Example 6-2, when the client downloaded the ConvertServiceRegistration object, that object contained a reference to the server. When the client called the convert( ) method, the registration object shipped the call back to the server, got the answer, and presented it to the client. Here, we'll do things differently:

```
import java.io.*;
import java.rmi.*;
import net.jini.core.lease.*;
import net.jini.space.*;

public class ConvertServiceRegistrationImpl
            implements ConvertServiceRegistration, Serializable {

    private JavaSpace js;

    private Lease lease;

    public ConvertServiceRegistrationImpl(JavaSpace js, Lease l) {
        this.js = js;
        this.lease = l;
    }

    // Code to convert. This code runs on the client and puts
    // the request into the JavaSpace and then reads out the result.
    // A previous result will be cached and we'll get that too.
    public String convert(int i) throws RemoteException {
        try {
            // See if there's a cached result (done == true) already
            Conversion request = new Conversion(5, true);
            Conversion result =
              (Conversion) js.read(request, null, JavaSpace.NO_WAIT);
            if (result == null) {
                // There was no cached result. Make a new request
                // and retrieve that answer
                request.done = new Boolean(false);
                js.write(request, null, Lease.FOREVER);
                request.done = new Boolean(true);
                result = (Conversion)
                            js.read(request, null, Long.MAX_VALUE);
            }
            // else just use the cached value
```

```
                return result.result;
            } catch (Exception e) {
                throw new RemoteException("convert", e);
            }
        }

        public Lease getLease() {
            return lease;
        }
    }
}
```

The code of the `convert( )` method is now the same as the code of the client in Example 10-1: it puts the request into the space and reads the result from the space. Remember that this class will downloaded by and executed on the client—so the client will be calling the JavaSpaces service directly, even though the client was originally programmed with no knowledge at all of the JavaSpaces service. We still need the server side code that takes the requests from the JavaSpaces service and processes it. We'll incorporate that code into our service implementation:

```
import java.util.*;
import java.io.*;
import java.rmi.*;
import java.rmi.server.*;
import net.jini.discovery.*;
import net.jini.core.lease.*;
import net.jini.core.event.*;
import net.jini.core.transaction.*;
import net.jini.core.transaction.server.*;
import net.jini.space.*;
import com.sun.jini.lookup.*;
import com.sun.jini.lease.*;

public class ConvertServiceImpl extends UnicastRemoteObject
                        implements ConvertServiceProxy, Runnable {

    private ServerLandlord lord;
    private ServerDelivery sender;
    private JavaSpace js;
    private ServiceFinder txsf;

    public ConvertServiceImpl() throws RemoteException {
        lord = new ServerLandlord();
        sender = new ServerDelivery(this, lord);
        // Get the JavaSpaces and Transaction Manager now so that
        // the thread doesn't have to deal with exceptions if they
        // can't be found
        try {
            ServiceFinder sf = new ServiceFinder(JavaSpace.class);
            js = (JavaSpace) sf.getObject();
            txsf = new ServiceFinder(TransactionManager.class);
        } catch (IOException ioe) {
            throw new RemoteException("Can't find java space", ioe);
        }

        // Start the thread to take and convert requests
        new Thread(this).start();

    }

    public ConvertServiceRegistration getInstance(long duration) {
```

```
        Hashtable ht = new Hashtable(13);
        return new ConvertServiceRegistrationImpl(js,
                                lord.newLease(ht, duration)));
    }

    public EventRegistration trackConversions(long duration,
                    RemoteEventListener rel, MarshalledObject key) {
        return sender.addListener(rel, duration, key);
    }

// This handles the conversions: the
// ConvertServiceRegistrationImpl class puts the request into the
// space; this thread takes the requests and calculates the
// answers
public void run() {
    TransactionManager txm =
                (TransactionManager) txsf.getObject();
    LeaseRenewalManager lrm = new LeaseRenewalManager();

    Conversion request = new Conversion(false);
    Conversion result;

    while (true) {
        Transaction.Created txn = null;
        try {
            // Take the request in a thread so that if the
            // service exits before it writes the answer the
            // request is not lost
            txn = TransactionFactory.create(txm, Lease.FOREVER);
            lrm.renewUntil(txn.lease, Lease.FOREVER, null);
            // Get a request (one with the done field == false)
            result = (Conversion) js.take(request,
                                txn.transaction, Long.MAX_VALUE);

            try {
                result.result = String.valueOf(result.value);
            } catch (Exception e) {
                // If we can't calculate the answer, we have to
                // abort the transaction, but we can go get the
                // next request
                txn.transaction.abort();
                lrm.remove(txn.lease);
                continue;
            }

            // Write the answer.
            result.done = new Boolean(true);
            js.write(result, txn.transaction, Long.MAX_VALUE);
            txn.transaction.commit();
            lrm.remove(txn.lease);

        } catch (Exception e) {
            // These exceptions mean that we couldn't talk to the
            // space or transaction manager, which we can't
            // recover from.
            System.out.println("Unrecoverable error" + e);
            return;
        }
    }
}
```

```
public static void main(String[] args) throws Exception {
    System.setSecurityManager(new RMISecurityManager());
    String[] groups = new String[] { "" };

    // Create the instance of the service; the JoinManager will
    // register it and renew its leases with the lookup service
    ConvertServiceImpl csi =
                (ConvertServiceImpl) new ConvertServiceImpl();
    JoinManager manager = new JoinManager(csi, null, groups,
                                null, null, null);
    }
}
```

The run( ) method here is essentially the same as the code we previously showed in the Converter class. We run this code in a separate thread because the client will no longer contact this class to do a conversion (you'll note that the convert( ) method has been removed from this class); it will put things into the space at arbitrary points in time, and so we need a thread to monitor the space and perform the conversions when they are required.

While it was convenient to add this logic to our ConvertServiceImpl class, there are other possible implementations that make sense. We could leave the Converter class alone and run that application; that achieves the same result. Or we could run the converter application on another machine, freeing resources from the machine running our service. And we could run multiple instances of the converter application throughout our Jini community; that would greatly increase the throughput of our conversion application. In fact, that type of scalability is another key benefit of building a distributed application by using the JavaSpaces service.

In Example 6-2, the ConvertServiceProxy interface contained a special convert( ) method that was used (without the client's knowledge) to send the request to the server. Since we no longer need that method, we've removed it from the ConvertServiceProxy interface:

```
import java.rmi.*;

public interface ConvertServiceProxy extends Remote, ConvertService {
}
```

Even though we have used the code we've been developing though the book, we now have a completely different implementation of the conversion service: one that uses the JavaSpaces service transparently to the client. And that's the idea behind Jini: you can use whatever implementation tools are at hand without affecting other members of the community.

Summary

The JavaSpaces service is very versatile. It is an ideal service to use to develop distributed applications since it is designed to allow data to flow between the pieces of such an application. While the basic API of the JavaSpaces service is simple, it can be used for a variety of complex tasks.

CHAPTER 11

Helper Services

In this chapter, we'll discuss the services that are included as part of the *Jini 1.1 Technology Helper Utilities and Services* specification. This specification defines new classes that assist developers of services and clients by abstracting some of the lower-level details of Jini; we've looked at those utilities throughout earlier chapters. The specification also defines three new Jini services. These services are optional within a Jini community, but if they do exist, they can help you build more useful Jini applications.

There are three services that are part of this specification:

The Lookup Discovery Service
> This service performs the discovery of lookup services on behalf of a Jini application. Sun's implementation of Jini comes with a version of this service called *fiddler*.

The Lease Renewal Service
> This service performs lease renewal on behalf of a Jini application. Sun's implementation of Jini comes with a version of this service called *norm*.

The Event Mailbox Service
> This service will listen for events on behalf of a Jini application; the application can later retrieve those events as desired. Sun's implementation of Jini comes with a version of this service called *mercury*.

We'll look at each of these services, and then we'll present two examples: an activatable Jini service that relies on the lookup discovery and lease renewal services, and a detachable Jini client that uses the event mailbox and lease renewal services.

Since these services are part of the 1.1 specification, Sun's implementation of them comes only in the 1.1 release. Information in this chapter is based on the 1.1 alpha release of the specification and is subject to change.

The Lookup Discovery Service

In our previous examples, we used the LookupDiscovery class to find lookup services. For Jini clients, we provided the ServiceFinder class, which uses the LookupDiscovery class directly. For services, we used the JoinManager class, which uses the LookupDiscovery class internally. In 1.1, we have the option of using any class that implements the DiscoveryManagement interface.

There are times when you want another entity to perform discovery for you. Take the example of a service that is rarely used. This service is still required to join any new lookup services that may appear within the Jini community, and it must discard any lookup services that it can no longer communicate with. Ideally, we want the rarely-used service to run only when it is needed, which reduces the amount of resources required on the machine running the service. This is a good use of the RMI activation facility.

In order to use activation in this scenario, something must perform lookup discovery while the service is not running. That something is the lookup discovery service. The lookup discovery service discovers lookup services on behalf of the activatable service; it notifies the activatable service whenever a new lookup service has been found. This activates the service, which can join the new lookup service and then deactivate itself.

The assumption here is that the addition or deletion of a lookup service from the Jini community is also a rare event: you don't want the activatable service to wake up every few minutes to manage changes to the lookup services. There is still an issue with the lease that the activatable service holds with the lookup service; that will have to be handled by the lease renewal service that we discuss below.

There are other times when the lookup discovery service is useful. The lookup discovery service can be used to extend the range over which you can discover lookup services. An application cannot discover a lookup service outside of its multicast radius. If lookup discovery services are placed at strategic points in the network, they can find all the lookup services on the network. Applications can search for lookup services within their multicast radius, search for lookup discovery services that are registered with those services, and ask those lookup discovery services to perform discovery. This allows the application to discover lookup services beyond its multicast radius.

Such a network is shown in Figure 11-1. The circles in this diagram show the multicast radii for the client, lookup discovery service, and service. The client cannot directly find the service, because the client and service have no common lookup service within their multicast radii. But the client can discover lookup service A; it can then locate the lookup discovery service. Once it registers with the lookup discovery service, it will be notified about lookup service B; it can then find the target service.

Another scenario occurs if your service is on a device that doesn't support multicasting, or if there are no lookup services at all within your multicast radius. In either case, your service must find lookup services using lookup locators: you use a lookup locator to find a known lookup service, find a lookup discovery service

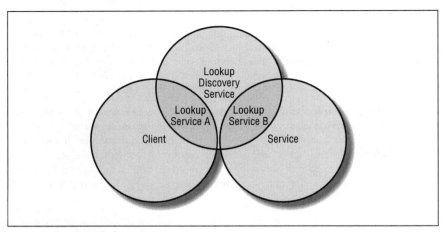

Figure 11–1: An application can discover far-away lookup services

registered with that lookup service, and ask the lookup discovery service to perform all other discovery.

The LookupDiscoveryService API

To use a lookup discovery service, you must find one registered with the Jini lookup service, using the `net.jini.discovery.LookupDiscoveryService` interface:

```
ServiceFinder sf = new ServiceFinder(LookupDiscoveryService.class);
LookupDiscoveryService lds = (LookupDiscoveryService) sf.getObject();
```

Once you have located the service, you must register with it by calling the `register()` method, which returns an object that implements the `net.jini.discovery.LookupDiscoveryRegistration` interface. This interface is very similar to the API presented by the `LookupDiscovery` class: there are methods to manipulate the groups that you are interested in discovering and the lookup locators that you want to use for unicast discovery. In addition, this interface contains a `getLease()` method: you must renew your lease to the lookup discovery service in the same way that you must renew a lease to other Jini services.

When you call the `register()` method, you must provide a remote event listener; the lookup discovery service will send a `net.jini.discovery.RemoteDiscoveryEvent` to the listener whenever a new lookup service is discovered or an existing lookup service goes away. The event contains one or more lookup services; these are returned by the `getRegistrars()` method. These may be newly discovered services or they may be services which have been discarded; the listener determines which case applies by calling the `isDiscarded()` method.

If the event represents discovery of new lookup services, the service should loop through the array of service registrars and join each lookup service. Remember that joining the lookup service involves receiving a lease from the lookup service which the service must renew; the service generally saves this lease locally so that it can renew it. If the event represents discarding of existing services, the service should no longer renew the lease associated with that service, and it should discard any other local state related to that lookup service. Remember that it is not a good idea to cancel the lease, since although we don't know why the lookup service was discarded, it probably doesn't exist anymore.

The remote event listener should also examine the sequence number of the remote discovery event. If this sequence number differs from the previously received sequence number by more than one, it's possible (but not guaranteed) that the listener has missed one or more events. In this case, the listener must call the getRegistrars() method of the lookup discovery service. This method will return all lookup services that the lookup discovery service has located for our service. The service can use this list to make sure that it has not missed any lookup services; if it has missed any, then it must join each of those services.

If you're using the lookup discovery service to extend the radius at which you can discover lookup services, that's all you need. If you want to use the lookup discovery service to allow your activatable service to become inactive and free its resources, there's another step involved: something must maintain all the leases to the lookup services and to the lookup discovery service. That something is the lease renewal service. In the examples at the end of this chapter, we'll show an activatable service that uses the lookup discovery service and the lease renewal service.

The Lease Renewal Service

In previous chapters, we used the LeaseRenewalManager class to renew any leases held by our applications. This allows the application to specify the duration of a lease; the lease renewal manager takes on the burden of renewing the lease until the specified duration has elapsed. The lease renewal service accomplishes the same task, but it does so as a remote service: the lease renewal manager runs as a thread within the application, where the lease renewal service is a separate Jini service.

There are two advantages to deferring lease renewals to a separate service. The first was implied in our discussion above: an activatable service cannot become inactive while it holds leases that need to be renewed. A similar situation exists for a client that must temporarily disconnect from the network. In either case, if the lease renewal service is charged with renewing the leases, when the application comes back online (or reconnects to the network), it has not lost any service registrations that it holds.

The second advantage involves lease batching. The lease renewal manager will automatically batch any leases that were issued by the same landlord and that expire near the same time, but it's unlikely that a single client will hold many leases that fit these criteria. The lease renewal service, on the other hand, can handle leases from many clients, increasing the chances that the leases can be batched. This can reduce the network traffic that leasing creates.

The LeaseRenewalService API

To use a lease renewal service, you must find one registered with the Jini lookup service, using the `net.jini.lease.LeaseRenewalService` interface:

```
ServiceFinder sf = new ServiceFinder(LeaseRenewalService.class);
LeaseRenewalService lrs = (LeaseRenwalService) sf.getObject();
```

Like other Jini services, you must register with this service in order to use it, but registration is slightly different in this case. You must call the `createLeaseRenewalSet()` method, which will return an object that implements the `net.jini.lease.LeaseRenewalSet` interface. This set is valid for the duration that is passed to the `createLeaseRenewalSet()` method.

In effect, this leases the lease renewal service itself. The lease renewal service can't issue a lease with a negotiated duration, since that would defeat its entire purpose. Instead, it allows the client to specify the amount of time for which the registration will be valid; unlike other services, the lease renewal service will honor whatever request the client makes (even if the client passes a duration of `Long.MAX_VALUE` or `Lease.FOREVER`).

A good application will not abuse this feature. An activatable service that asks the lease renewal service to renew its lease to a lookup service for a duration of `Lease.FOREVER` will remain forever registered in the lookup service, even if the activatable service is permanently removed from the Jini community. A better activatable service might use a duration of one day (e.g., `com.sun.jini.constants.TimeConstants.DAYS`); it can wake up once a day to extend its lease with the lease renewal service. If the activatable service is permanently removed from the Jini community, its registration will eventually be cancelled.

The lease renewal set contains methods that control the renewal of leases. A lease is added to the set with the `renewFor()` method; the lease renewal service will renew the lease until the duration specified as a parameter to this method has passed. Note that this duration is unrelated to the duration of the set itself, though if the duration of the set expires, all leases that are held by the set will no longer be renewed. A lease is removed from the set with the `remove()` method.

You can ask the lease renewal service to notify you before the set expires by registering a remote event listener via the `setExpirationWarningListener()` method. Unlike other sources of remote events, the lease renewal set allows only a single warning listener to be registered at one time; if you register a second listener, it will replace the existing listener. So an activatable service must register a listener so that it will be warned before the set's duration expires; the service can specify when the notification should occur. Even if nothing else activates the service, this ensures that the service will be activated before the lease renewal set expires. The listener will receive a `net.jini.lease.ExpirationWarningEvent` object.

When the service receives this notification, it must call the `getRenewalSetLease()` method to obtain the lease renewal set's lease and renew that lease for another day (or appropriate time period). As before, the lease time specified in the renewal will be granted by the lease renewal service. The set can also be cancelled by invoking the `cancel()` method on this lease.

When the lease renewal service cannot renew a lease, it will send a net.jini.lease.RenewalFailureEvent to the listener which has been registered with the setRenewalFailureListener() method. This method also allows only a single listener to be registered.

The Event Mailbox Service

We've seen several examples throughout this book that use a RemoteEventListener object to receive events from a Jini service. There are times when you might want to defer delivery of these events. You may want to do this for reasons we've explored so far in this chapter: an activatable service might not want to wake up just to receive an event, or an application may want to disconnect temporarily from the network without losing any events in its absence. You may additionally want to batch events: a billing service may register to be notified of particular events from a service and produce a bill based on those events. But there's no reason why billing has to occur as the events happen; if the events are saved somewhere, the billing service can operate on them as a batch.

The event mailbox service supports these cases by providing a remote event listener that receives events. The events are placed into a mailbox; at a later time, the application that wants to process the events connects to the mailbox and the events are delivered to the application.

The EventMailbox API

To use an event mailbox service, you must find one registered with the Jini lookup service, using the net.jini.event.EventMailbox interface:*

```
ServiceFinder sf = new ServiceFinder(EventMailbox.class);
EventMailbox em = (EventMailbox) sf.getObject();
```

Once you've obtained this service, you register with it by calling the register() method, which returns an object that implements the net.jini.event.MailboxRegistration interface. Using the mailbox is simple: you use the getListener() method of the mailbox registration object to obtain an object that implements the RemoteEventListener interface. You then register this event listener with whatever event source you're interested in. Events will be delivered to this listener, which is running inside of the event mailbox service.

The mailbox service will hold these events until you call the enableDelivery() method of the mailbox registration object. At that point, the mailbox will forward the events to the remote listener passed to the enableDelivery() method: it will forward any queued events as well as any new events. Event delivery will continue until the disableDelivery() method is called, at which point the mailbox service will begin to queue the events again for later delivery.

---

* The source for the EventMailbox and MailboxRegistration classes ships with Jini 1.1 alpha, and Sun's implementation of the mailbox service provides those classes to *mercury*. For some reason, however, the classes themselves are not included in the *jini-ext.jar* file; you must copy the source files into your directory and compile them with your application. This will be fixed in future releases.

Like most Jini service registrations, the mailbox registration contains a lease, which is returned from the getLease( ) method. The client must renew this lease; since the client is likely to be disconnected or not running, this is another good use of the lease renewal service.

An Activatable Service Example

In Chapter 3, *Remote Method Invocation*, we showed an activatable RMI service. In this example, there was a problem with registrations with the Jini lookup service: the service had to remain active to renew its leases to the lookup service and to discover new lookup services. In Example 11-1, we'll change our existing service to an activatable service that doesn't have these problems.

Example 11-1: An Activatable Jini Service

```
Common classes
    ConvertService (used in Example 8-3; listed in Example 6-1)
    ConvertServiceRegistration (used in Example 8-3; listed in Example 5-1)
    ConvertEvent (used in Example 8-3; listed in Example 6-1)
    ServiceFinder (used in Example 8-3; listed in Example 6-2)
    ServiceFinderListener (used in Example 8-3; listed in Example 6-2)
Server Classes
    ConvertServiceImpl (modified from Example 8-3)
    ConvertServiceRegistrationImpl (used in Example 8-3;
        listed in Example 5-1)
    ConvertServiceProxy (used in Example 8-3; listed in Example 5-1)
    ServerLandlord (modified from Example 8-3; listed in Example 8-2)
    ServerResource (used in Example 8-3; listed in Example 5-1)
    ServerDelivery (used in Example 8-3; listed in Example 8-1)
    ConvertServiceImpl (used in Example 8-3; listed in Example 6-1)
    Expirer (used in Example 8-3; listed in Example 8-2)
Client Classes
    ConvertEventHandler (used in Example 8-3; listed in Example 6-1)
    ConvertClient (used in Example 8-3; listed in Example 6-1)
```

All the changes in this example are confined to the server. The server now needs to find other services, so the ServiceFinder and ServiceFinderListener classes are now common classes. There are some small changes to the ServerLandlord class, but the bulk of the changes occur in the ConvertServiceImpl class.

The changes to the ServerLandlord class allow us to determine when the landlord is not holding any leases. When the landlord isn't holding any leases, we know it's a good time to deactivate our service. The landlord now looks like this:

```
import java.rmi.*;
import java.rmi.server.*;
import java.util.*;
import net.jini.core.lease.*;
import com.sun.jini.lease.landlord.*;

public class ServerLandlord extends UnicastRemoteObject
                    implements Landlord {
        // cookie -> ServerResource
    protected Hashtable resources = new Hashtable();
    protected long MAXLEASETIME = 10*60*1000;    // 10 Minutes
    protected LeasePolicy policy;
```

```
public ServerLandlord() throws RemoteException {
    policy = new LeaseDurationPolicy(MAXLEASETIME, MAXLEASETIME,
                            this, new Expirer(this), null);
}

public long renew(Object cookie, long duration)
        throws LeaseDeniedException,
                UnknownLeaseException, RemoteException {
    synchronized (this) {
        ServerResource sr = (ServerResource)resources.get(cookie);
        if (sr == null)
            throw new UnknownLeaseException();

        return policy.renew(sr, duration);
    }
}

public Landlord.RenewResults renewAll(Object[] cookie,
                    long[] duration) throws RemoteException {
    long[] granted = new long[cookie.length];
    Vector denied = new Vector();

    for (int i = 0; i < cookie.length; i++) {
        try {
            granted[i] = renew(cookie[i], duration[i]);
        } catch (LeaseException lex) {
            granted[i] = -1;
            denied.add(lex);
        }
    }
    return new Landlord.RenewResults(granted,
            denied.isEmpty() ? null : (Exception[]) denied.toArray());
}

public void cancel(Object cookie)
        throws UnknownLeaseException, RemoteException {
    synchronized (this) {
        ServerResource sr = (ServerResource)resources.get(cookie);
        if (sr == null)
            throw new UnknownLeaseException();

        resources.remove(cookie);
        if (resources.size() == 0)
            notifyAll();

    }

}

public void cancelAll(Object[] cookie)
        throws LeaseMapException, RemoteException {
    Map map = null;
    for (int i = 0; i < cookie.length; i++) {
        try {
            cancel(cookie[i]);
        } catch (LeaseException ex) {
            if (map == null)
                map = new HashMap();
            map.put(cookie[i], ex);
        }
    }
```

```
        if (map !=null)
            throw new LeaseMapException("Can't cancel all leases", map);
    }

    // The following methods are not part of the Landlord interface
    //     and can only be called by directly using this object.
    public Lease newLease(Object sessionData, long duration) {
        ServerResource sr = new ServerResource(sessionData);

        try {
            sr.lease = policy.leaseFor(sr, duration);
            synchronized(this) {
                resources.put(sr.getCookie(), sr);
            }
            return sr.lease;
        } catch (LeaseDeniedException e) {};
        return null;
    }

    // The cookie is an *internal* reference for the LandlordLease.
    // No one outside the lease can access it.
    public Object getSessionData(Lease lease) {
        Object sessiondata = null;
        synchronized (this) {
            for (Enumeration e = resources.elements();
                            e.hasMoreElements();) {
                ServerResource sr = (ServerResource) e.nextElement();
                if (lease.equals(sr.lease)) {
                    sessiondata = sr.sessionData;
                    break;
                }
            }
        }
        return sessiondata;
    }

    public synchronized void waitForEmpty() {
        while (resources.size() != 0) {
            try {
                wait();
            } catch (InterruptedException ie) {}
        }
    }

}
```

The landlord now has a new method: waitForEmpty( ). This method is used to tell
when there are no outstanding leases. When leases are cancelled, the landlord
notifies any threads that are waiting in this method.

The remaining changes in our example are in the ConvertServiceImpl class,
which has the following additions:

- It is now an activatable service, so it must register with *rmid*.

- The service uses lookup discovery to find lookup services while it is inactive.
  The lookup discovery service activates the service to notify it when a new
  lookup service is found. The service must be prepared to deal with out of
  sequence events from the lookup discovery service.

- The service uses the lease renewal service to renew its leases to the lookup discovery service and any discovered lookup services. It must also register to be notified when the lease renewal set is about to expire so that it can renew the set.

- The service now has a lot of state that it must save between invocations. This is important since the activatable service will exit and restart when it is needed, but don't think it's important only for activatable services: all services should save their state in order to survive crashes.

- The service must keep track of the leases it issues; when it has no outstanding leases, it can deactivate.

The `ConvertServiceImpl` class is now very large, but it contains all the features that are required to support a fully activatable Jini service, including a lot of error handling. The good news is that we can reuse this framework as a starting point for a real Jini service; if we add complex service logic to the example, it won't increase the size of the framework.

Here is the full listing:

```
import java.util.*;
import java.io.*;
import java.rmi.*;
import java.rmi.server.*;
import java.rmi.activation.*;
import net.jini.discovery.*;
import net.jini.lookup.*;
import net.jini.lease.*;
import net.jini.core.lookup.*;
import net.jini.core.lease.*;
import net.jini.core.event.*;
import com.sun.jini.constants.*;
import com.sun.jini.lookup.*;
import com.sun.jini.reliableLog.*;

public class ConvertServiceImpl extends Activatable
            implements ConvertServiceProxy, RemoteEventListener {

    private ServerLandlord lord;
    private ServerDelivery sender;
    private ConvertServiceLogHandler handler;
    private ReliableLog log;
    private long seqNo;
    private ServiceID serviceID;

    private ActivationID activeID;
    private LookupDiscoveryRegistration lookupReg;
    private LeaseRenewalSet leaseRenewal;
    private String[] groups = new String[] { "" };
    private Hashtable leases;
    private Thread waitThread;
    private long lastLookupSeqNo;
    private ServiceItem serviceItem;

    // This class holds the information necessary for an update to the
    // sequence number.
    private static class ConvertServiceUpdateRecord
```

```
                        implements Serializable {
    long seqNo;
}

private static class ConvertServiceUpdateLeases
                    implements Serializable {
    transient Hashtable leases;
    long seqNo;

    ConvertServiceUpdateLeases(Hashtable l, long seqNo) {
        leases = l;
        this.seqNo = seqNo;
    }

    // The leases hashtable contains service registrar objects, the
    // class definition for which we obtained dynamically from the
    // lookup service. In order to reread the class definition, we
    // must preserve the java.rmi.server.codebase from which we
    // loaded it; we save it as a marshalled object which preserves
    // that information.
    private void writeObject(ObjectOutputStream oos)
                            throws IOException {
        oos.defaultWriteObject();
        MarshalledObject[] keys =
                new MarshalledObject[leases.size()];
        MarshalledObject[] values =
                new MarshalledObject[leases.size()];
        int i = 0;
        for (Enumeration e = leases.keys(); e.hasMoreElements(); ) {
            Object key = e.nextElement();
            keys[i] = new MarshalledObject(key);
            values[i++] = new MarshalledObject(leases.get(key));
        }
        oos.writeObject(keys);
        oos.writeObject(values);
    }

    private void readObject(ObjectInputStream ois)
            throws NotActiveException, ClassNotFoundException,
                IOException {
        ois.defaultReadObject();
        MarshalledObject[] keys =
                (MarshalledObject[]) ois.readObject();
        MarshalledObject[] values =
                (MarshalledObject[]) ois.readObject();
        leases = new Hashtable(keys.length);
        for (int i = 0; i < keys.length; i++) {
            Object key = keys[i].get();
            Object value = values[i].get();
            leases.put(key, value);
        }
    }
}

// This class reads and writes the reliable log
class ConvertServiceLogHandler extends LogHandler {
    public void snapshot(OutputStream os) throws Exception {
        ObjectOutputStream oos = new ObjectOutputStream(os);
        Object target;
```

```
    if (serviceID == null)
        // write a dummy object
        target = new String();
    else target = serviceID;
    oos.writeObject(target);

    oos.writeLong(seqNo);

    if (leaseRenewal == null)
        target = new String();
    else target = new MarshalledObject(leaseRenewal);
    oos.writeObject(target);

    if (lookupReg == null)
        target = new String();
    else target = new MarshalledObject(lookupReg);
    oos.writeObject(target);

    oos.writeObject(new ConvertServiceUpdateLeases(leases,
                            lastLookupSeqNo));

    oos.flush();    // Make sure it all gets to disk
}

public void recover(InputStream is) throws Exception {
    ObjectInputStream ois = new ObjectInputStream(is);
    Object target;
    try {
        target = ois.readObject();
    } catch (Exception e) {
        // no log
        return;
    }
    if (target instanceof ServiceID)
        serviceID = (ServiceID) target;
    // else it was the dummy string

    seqNo = ois.readLong();

    target = ois.readObject();
    if (target instanceof MarshalledObject) {
        MarshalledObject mo = (MarshalledObject) target;
        leaseRenewal = (LeaseRenewalSet) mo.get();
    }
    // else it was the dummy string; we'll find it when
    // we first need it.

    target = ois.readObject();
    if (target instanceof MarshalledObject) {
        MarshalledObject mo = (MarshalledObject) target;
        lookupReg = (LookupDiscoveryRegistration) mo.get();
    }
    // else it was the dummy string
    else findLookupDiscoveryService();

    ConvertServiceUpdateLeases csul =
        (ConvertServiceUpdateLeases) ois.readObject();
    leases = csul.leases;
    lastLookupSeqNo = csul.seqNo;
```

```
        }

        // Called when reading an update; the update was written
        // as a ConvertServiceUpdateRecord
        public void applyUpdate(Object o) {
            if (o instanceof ConvertServiceUpdateRecord)
                seqNo = ((ConvertServiceUpdateRecord) o).seqNo;
            else if (o instanceof ConvertServiceUpdateLeases) {
                leases = ((ConvertServiceUpdateLeases) o).leases;
                lastLookupSeqNo =
                        ((ConvertServiceUpdateLeases) o).seqNo;
            }

            else throw new IllegalArgumentException("Unexpected update");
        }
    }

    public ConvertServiceImpl(ActivationID id, MarshalledObject data)
                        throws RemoteException {
        super(id, 0);
        activeID = id;

        try {
            String logDir = (String) data.get();

            handler = new ConvertServiceLogHandler();
            log = new ReliableLog(logDir, handler);
            log.recover();
            lord = new ServerLandlord();
            sender = new ServerDelivery(this, lord);
            if (lookupReg == null) {
                // First time we've run, so there is no
                // lookup discovery service yet
                leases = new Hashtable();
                findLookupDiscoveryService();
            }

            log.snapshot();
        } catch (Exception e) {
            throw new RemoteException("Can't construct service", e);
        }
    }

    public ConvertServiceRegistration getInstance(long duration) {
        Hashtable ht = new Hashtable(13);
        Lease l = lord.newLease(ht, duration);
        startWaitThread();

        return new ConvertServiceRegistrationImpl(this, l);
    }

    // To convert, first check the cache for previous results. If
    // there's no cache, the landlord has expired the lease. If
    // there's no data in the cache, calculcate the data and put it there
    public String convert(Lease l, int i) throws LeaseDeniedException {
        Hashtable cache = (Hashtable) lord.getSessionData(l);
        if (cache == null)
            throw new LeaseDeniedException("Lease expired");
        Integer I = new Integer(i);
        String s;
        s = (String) cache.get(I);
```

```
            if (s == null) {
                s = I.toString();
                cache.put(I, s);
            }
        sender.deliver(i, getNextSeq());
        return s;
    }

    public synchronized EventRegistration
                        trackConversions(long duration,
                            RemoteEventListener rel, MarshalledObject key) {
        return sender.addListener(rel, duration, key, seqNo);
    }

    private synchronized long getNextSeq() {
        seqNo++;
        try {
            // Update the log with the new seq no; we must wrap
            // this into an object for the update method
            ConvertServiceUpdateRecord csur =
                        new ConvertServiceUpdateRecord();
            csur.seqNo = this.seqNo;
            log.update(csur, true);
        } catch (Exception e) {
            e.printStackTrace();
        }
        return seqNo;
    }

    // This must only be called from a synchronized method
    private void unregister(ServiceRegistrar sr) {
        // Remove the registration. If the lookup service comes
        // back later, we'll re-register at that time.
        // Tell the lease renewal to let the lease expire
        // and remove it from our internal table too.
        try {
            leaseRenewal.remove((Lease) leases.get(sr));
        } catch (Exception cnfe) {
        }           leases.remove(sr);
    }

    // This must only be called from a synchronized method
    private void register(ServiceRegistrar sr) {
        try {
            if (serviceItem == null)
                serviceItem = new ServiceItem(serviceID, this, null);
            ServiceRegistration ret =
                        sr.register(serviceItem, Lease.FOREVER);
            if (serviceID == null) {
                serviceID = ret.getServiceID();
                try {
                    log.snapshot();
                } catch (Exception e) {
                    System.out.println("Can't take snapshot" + e);
                }
            }
            // Save this registration
            try {
                leases.put(sr, ret.getLease());
                renewLease(ret.getLease());
```

```
                } catch (IOException ioe) {
                    // Can't really happen -- renewLease only throws
                    // IOException when it finds the service, and we
                    // already know the service has been found
                }
        } catch (RemoteException rex) {
            System.out.println("Can't register with service " + rex);
            try {
                lookupReg.discard(sr);
            } catch (RemoteException rExp) {
            }
        }
    }
}

// We may have dropped an event.
// We must retrieve the entire set and compare it to what
// we have, cancelling and adding registrars as necessary.
// Getting the entire list is an expensive operation, so we
// don't do it unless we have to.
private synchronized void resyncHashtable(long seq) {
    // Because this runs in another thread, it's conceivable that
    // the another event has superceded this.
    if (seq <= lastLookupSeqNo)
        return;
    ServiceRegistrar[] current = new ServiceRegistrar[0];
    try {
        current = lookupReg.getRegistrars();
    } catch (Exception exp) {
        // There's no way in the LookupDiscoveryService interface
        // to find just the successful ones -- best we can do
        // is to drop the event and try again when the next
        // event comes.
        return;
    }
    Hashtable newLeases = new Hashtable();
    for (int i = 0; i < current.length; i++)  {
        Object o = leases.get(current[i]);
        if (o == null) {
            // We haven't registered this one yet
            register(current[i]);
        }
        else {
            // We have registered; just move the registration
            newLeases.put(current[i], o);
            leases.remove(current[i]);
        }
    }
    for (Enumeration e = leases.keys(); e.hasMoreElements(); ) {
        unregister((ServiceRegistrar) e.nextElement());
    }
    leases = newLeases;
    lastLookupSeqNo = seq;
    try {
        log.update(new
                ConvertServiceUpdateLeases(leases, seq), true);
    } catch (IOException ioe) {
        System.out.println("Update failed " + ioe);
    }
    startWaitThread();
}
```

```
public synchronized void notify(RemoteEvent re)
                        throws UnknownEventException {
    if (re instanceof ExpirationWarningEvent) {
        try {
            ExpirationWarningEvent ewe =
                    (ExpirationWarningEvent) re;
            Lease l = ewe.getLease();
            l.renew(TimeConstants.DAYS);
        } catch (Exception e) {
            // We should take over lease renewal ourselves,
            // using a lease renewal manager.
        }
        startWaitThread();
        return;
    }
    if (!(re instanceof RemoteDiscoveryEvent)) {
        System.out.println("Unexpected event " + re);
        throw new UnknownEventException("ConvertServiceImpl");
    }
    RemoteDiscoveryEvent rde = (RemoteDiscoveryEvent) re;
    long seq = rde.getSequenceNumber();
    if (seq <= lastLookupSeqNo) {
        // This event was delivered out of order. We noticed
        // at the time that we had dropped it, so we can
        // just ignore it.
        return;
    }
    if (seq != lastLookupSeqNo + 1) {
        // We may have dropped an event. In order to tell, we
        // have to check with the lookup discovery service. Since
        // we're in a callback from that service, we can't call
        // it in this thread or deadlock will occur.
        class runResync implements Runnable {
            long seq;
            runResync(long l) {
                seq = l;
            }
            public void run() {
                resyncHashtable(seq);
            }
        };
        new Thread(new runResync(seq)).start();
        return;
    }
    else {
        // Else the sequence number was as expected;
        // get the registrars and process them
        ServiceRegistrar[] sr = null;
        try {
            sr = rde.getRegistrars();
        } catch (LookupUnmarshalException lue) {
            // Get the ones that we can; ignore the rest
            sr = lue.getUnmarshalledRegs();
        }
        if (rde.isDiscarded()) {
            for (int i = 0; i < sr.length; i++) {
                if (leases.containsKey(sr[i])) {
                    unregister(sr[i]);
                }
            }
```

```
        }
        else {
            for (int i = 0; i < sr.length; i++) {
                if (leases.containsKey(sr[i]) == false) {
                    register(sr[i]);
                }
            }
            // else we were already registered in this service
        }
    }

    // All done -- update the log with the new leases and seq no
    lastLookupSeqNo = seq;
    try {
        log.update(new ConvertServiceUpdateLeases(
                            leases, lastLookupSeqNo), true);
    } catch (Exception e) {
        System.out.println("Update failed " + e);
    }
    startWaitThread();
}

private void findLookupDiscoveryService()
            throws IOException, RemoteException {
    ServiceFinder sf =
            new ServiceFinder(LookupDiscoveryService.class);
    LookupDiscoveryService lds =
            (LookupDiscoveryService) sf.getObject();
    lookupReg = lds.register(groups, null, this,
                    new MarshalledObject("dummy"), Lease.FOREVER);
    EventRegistration er = lookupReg.getEventRegistration();
    lastLookupSeqNo = er.getSequenceNumber();
    renewLease(lookupReg.getLease());
}

private void renewLease(Lease l)
            throws IOException, RemoteException {
    ServiceFinder sf = null;
    LeaseRenewalService lrs = null;
    while (true) {
        // If leaseRenewal is null, we have to find one. It will
        // be null the first time we run the code; if we get an
        // error talking to a leaseRenewal object, we set it to
        // null so that we find another one here.
        // If we've just be re-activated, then leaseRenewal will
        // be set from the log.
        if (leaseRenewal == null) {
            // Only set sf the first time we need it.
            if (sf == null)
                sf = new ServiceFinder(
                            LeaseRenewalService.class);
            lrs = (LeaseRenewalService) sf.getObject();
            leaseRenewal = lrs.createLeaseRenewalSet(
                            TimeConstants.DAYS);
            leaseRenewal.setExpirationWarningListener(
                            this, TimeConstants.HOURS, null);
        }
        try {
            leaseRenewal.renewFor(l, Lease.FOREVER);
            break;
```

```
            } catch (RemoteException re) {
                // If we were talking to a leaseRenewal from a
                // previous activation, sf will be null. We'll create
                // sf the next time through the loop.
                if (sf != null)
                    sf.errored(lrs);
                leaseRenewal = null;
            }
        }
    }

    private synchronized void startWaitThread() {
        if (waitThread != null)
            return;

        Runnable doWait = new Runnable() {
            public void run() {
                while (true) {
                    // There's a possibility that the client is
                    // connecting, but has not yet been granted a
                    // lease (or isn't even getting a lease if we
                    // became active as a result of a lookup
                    // discovery service event).
                    // Wait a bit to let that settle down, and
                    // then wait for the lease to be empty again.
                    try {
                        Thread.sleep(60 * 1000);
                    } catch (Exception e) {}
                    // Wait until there are no clients with an
                    // active lease and exit when that happens.
                    lord.waitForEmpty();
                    try {
                        if (Activatable.inactive(activeID)) {
                            try {
                                log.snapshot();
                            } catch (Exception e) {
                            }
                            System.exit(0);
                        }
                    } catch (Exception e) {
                        // inactive() threw an exception -- simply
                        // exit, because rmid is confused, but it
                        // will restart and recover (and then restart
                        // us if needed)
                        System.exit(0);
                    }
                }
            }
        };
        waitThread = new Thread(doWait);
        waitThread.start();
    }

    public static void main(String[] args) throws Exception {
        System.setSecurityManager(new RMISecurityManager());

        Properties props = new Properties();
        props.put("java.security.policy", args[1]);
        props.put("java.class.path",
                System.getProperty("java.class.path"));
        props.put("java.rmi.server.codebase", args[0]);
```

```
ActivationGroupDesc agd =
        new ActivationGroupDesc(props, null);
ActivationGroupID agi =
        ActivationGroup.getSystem().registerGroup(agd);
ActivationGroup.createGroup(agi, agd, 0);
ActivationDesc ad = new ActivationDesc("ConvertServiceImpl",
        args[0], new MarshalledObject(args[2]));
ConvertService cs =
        (ConvertService) Activatable.register(ad);
cs.getInstance(0);
System.exit(0);


    }
}
```

We'll talk about these changes in terms of the five additions that we listed earlier.

Changes to Support Activation

Most of the changes to support activation occur in the main( ) method. Following the code that we used in Example 3-3, the service now sets up the appropriate environment to register with *rmid*. The only difference in the main( ) method is that we invoke the getInstance( ) method on the service object before we exit. This bootstraps the object so that it will find the lookup discovery service and register with that service; this replaces the call that registered with the RMI registry.

Because the service is activatable, it now extends the Activatable class and has the standard activatable service constructor. The marshalled data object that gets passed to the constructor is the third argument on the command line (args[2]), which we'll use as the directory name where the service should store its reliable log.

There's one more addition to this example: we now set the java.class.path and java.rmi.server.codebase properties in the properties that we register with *rmid*. We didn't need that in our previous example, because the code in our previous example had no external dependencies. In this example, *rmid* must know where to find all the classes that the ConvertServiceImpl class depends upon (e.g., all the Jini classes).

Changes to Support the Lookup Discovery Service

Instead of using a join manager, our service now uses the lookup discovery service to manage the discovery of lookup services. The registration to that service is held in the lookupReg variable. When the service is constructed, it attempts to recover the value of that variable from the reliable log. If it cannot (e.g., the first time the service runs), it will invoke the findLookupDiscoveryService( ) method. That method uses our standard technique to locate a lookup service and lookup the target service (i.e, the lookup discovery service). Once it finds the lookup discovery service, it registers with that service and saves the registration. The service passes its lease to the lookup discovery service with the lease renewal service, which we'll discuss later.

The lookup discovery service does not participate in the join protocol, so the convert service must do that. It registers a listener (itself) with the lookup discovery service; when the lookup discovery service discovers or discards lookup services, it will call the listener. The notify( ) method processes the RemoteDiscoveryEvent by examining it to see what lookup services are involved and what type of event it is. If its a discard event, the notify( ) method removes the lookup services from its locally held set of lookup services (the leases hashtable). If it is a discover event, the notify( ) method joins that lookup service and adds the lookup service to its locally held set. This code is implemented in the register( ) and unregister( ) methods and is very similar to the ServerListener class we showed in Example 4-2, before we introduced the join manager.

The notify( ) method must pay attention to the sequence number held in the remote discovery event. If there is a gap in sequence numbers, it means that we might have dropped an event. In that case, the notify( ) method must retrieve the entire list of lookup services from the lookup discovery service, and it must reconcile that list with the locally held set of lookup services. It does that in the resyncHashtable( ) method. If the sequence number is earlier than one we've already processed, then it is the dropped event; since we've already handled the gap, we can safely discard this event.

The notify( ) method changes a lot of important state, so it interacts with the reliable log. It also registers with lookup services, which means that it must pass the lease contained in those registrations to the lease renewal service. We'll give more details on those two issues next.

Changes to Support the Lease Renewal Service

Instead of using a lease renewal manager, our service now uses the lease renewal service to renew its leases, so that the leases will continue to be renewed while the service is inactive. The registration to the lease renewal service (i.e., the LeaseRenewalSet) is held in the leaseRenewal variable. In the service constructor, we attempt to load that registration from our reliable log. If we cannot load the previous registration, then the first time that we attempt to renew a lease, we'll lookup the lease renewal service and create a new lease renewal set.

All leases that our service needs to renew are passed to the renewLease( ) method, which passes the lease to the lease renewal service. In addition to finding the lease renewal service (if necessary) and passing it the lease, this method also handles our registration with the lease renewal service. We create the lease renewal set with a duration of one day, and we register our listener so that it will be notified one hour before the lease renewal set expires.

In the notify( ) method, when we receive the ExpirationWarningEvent, we obtain the lease from the event. This is the lease associated with the lease renewal set; we renew the lease for another day. We're still registered to be notified when the new duration is about to expire, at which point we'll renew it again. This is necessary because there's no guarantee that a client will call us during the day; receiving this notification may be the only event that causes us to become active.

Changes to Support Logging

The logging performed by this class is conceptually the same as we saw in Example 8-3; this class just has a lot more state to log, which requires a lot more code. In addition to saving the serviceID and sequence number, we must now save the lease renewal set, the lookup discovery registration, the local set of discovered lookup services (i.e., the leases hashtable), and the last sequence number that we received in a lookup discovery event. This data is all saved during a snapshot and retrieved during a recover.

In addition, every time we receive a lookup discovery event, we must update the leases hashtable and the last lookup discovery event sequence number. That data is held in the ConvertServiceUpdateLeases object. Note that this class has special handling for the leases hashtable. The leases hashtable contains service registrations and leases, but the classes that define those objects are classes that we loaded dynamically from the lookup service. If we serialize those objects as is to the log file, we will be unable to recover them, because we don't know which codebase we loaded them from. So we must save them as marshalled objects, which preserves the codebase; when we recover these objects, we'll contact the lookup service in order to retrieve the necessary class files. This same rule applies to the lookup discovery registration and the lease renewal set, which is why they are saved as marshalled objects in the snapshot( ) method.

Logging occurs frequently in our class; it must occur anytime data that we're interested in changes. When we first construct the object, we take a snapshot so that we have a clean beginning state. We also take a snapshot when we are assigned a service ID (just as we did in previous examples). And we take a snapshot before we exit so that recovery is quicker, since it won't have any updates to process.

There are frequent updates as well. We take an update of the leases hashtable and last lookup discovery event sequence number every time a lookup discovery event occurs, since processing that event changes those two pieces of data. Finally, as before, every time the sequence number for events that we generate changes, we write that update to the log as well.

Changes to Support Deactivation

Finally, we need a mechanism to know when the service can deactivate itself. We do this by keeping track of the leases that we've issued to clients; if we have no outstanding leases, then we shut down. This is accomplished in the startWaitThread( ) method, which creates a new thread that waits for notification from the landlord that there are no outstanding leases.

When the lookup discovery service or lease renewal service sends us an event, we'll also be activated, and we can shutdown after we process the event (if there are no outstanding leases). So the notify( ) method also starts the wait thread. If there are no outstanding leases, the waitForEmpty( ) method will immediately return, and the wait thread will call the inactive( ) method to see if the service can shutdown. But the call to the notify( ) method may not have completed yet, so the inactive( ) method might return false. This is why the wait thread sleeps for one minute before calling the inactive( ) method; this allows the notification call to complete. When the `inactive( )` method indicates that there are no pending calls, we call `System.exit( )`.

Running the Example

Because of the introduction of *rmid*, running this example takes a little more work than our previous examples. The server must supply its entire environment to *rmid*, including the Jini classes that are required to instantiate the service. *rmid* does not have the Jini classes in its classpath, and it is an error to put them in *rmid*'s classpath because that confuses recovery: if *rmid* loads classes through its classpath that the service originally loaded through its own classpath, recovery will fail. This is why *rmid* cannot be allowed to load anything through its local classpath: it must always load classes from the service's `java.rmi.server.codebase` property.

Since the service depends upon the Jini classes, those classes must be in the server's codebase. The simplest way to do this is to put all required files into an executable jar file. That's the path taken by Sun's implementations of the Jini services, and though it may seem like more work, it is really the simplest way to get everything running correctly.

To do this, you must unjar each of the three Jini jar files into the directory that contains your service classes. Then you must create a jar file containing all those classes; the manifest of the jar file should contain the main class that you want to execute. Then you can use this jar file as both the classpath that is used to run the service and as the value of the `java.rmi.server.codebase` property so that *rmid* and clients can download the necessary files.

Here's a summary of all the steps required:

1. Create a manifest file. For our example, the manifest file contains a single line:

```
Main-Class: ConvertServiceImpl
```

Call this file *manifest* and save it in the directory with all your service classes.

2. Unjar each of the Jini jar files:

```
server% jar xf /files/jini1_1/lib/jini-ext.jar
server% jar xf /files/jini1_1/lib/jini-core.jar
server% jar xf /files/jini1_1/lib/sun-util.jar
```

3. Compile your code as usual, and generate the stubs for each required class (`ServerLandlord`, `ServiceFinderListener`, and `ConvertServiceImpl`).

4. Create the executable jar file:

```
server% jar cfm server.jar manifest *.class net com
```

This creates a jar file containing the given manifest, all the class files in the current directory, and all the class files in the *net* and *com* directories (which are the class files that you unjared in step 2).

5. Start the required services: *rmid, reggie, fiddler, norm,* and the service's HTTP server.

6. Run the server, specifying the usual codebase and the executable jar file as the classpath:

```
server% java -Djava.rmi.server.codebase=http://server:8086/
             -Djava.security.policy=/files/jini1_1/java.policy.all
             -jar path_to_jar_file
             http://server:8086/ /files/jini1_1/java.policy.all
             /tmp/csiLog
```

This command looks very similar to the commands used to start Sun's activatable services. The given policy file will be used to run the service, the given directory will be used to store the log, and so on. The only difference is that you must supply the full pathname to the executable jar file; you can't simply specify *server.jar.* This is because *rmid* is running in a different directory, and it won't find the executable jar file when it restarts the service if the pathname is not fully-qualified.

Strictly speaking, there is no need to include *all* the Jini class files in the executable jar file you create: you need to include only the ones required to run your service. In addition, we've used the same jar file as the classpath and the codebase, but you can specify different jar files, because the codebase requires fewer classes than the classpath. The classpath requires all the classes to instantiate and run the service; the codebase requires only those classes to instantiate the service stubs and any serialized objects passed to clients. That's the difference between jar files in Sun's implementation of Jini: *reggie.jar* contains all the server code to run *reggie,* and *reggie-dl.jar* contains all the code that clients need to talk to *reggie.*

Figuring out just what goes into each jar file is difficult, however. There are no tools in Jini (or Java) that determine what classes are required to support a particular class, and you're generally left to figure this out by trial and error. That's a tedious procedure, and though it's less efficient to have one big jar file as we do, it's certainly easier.

No changes are required to run the client.

A Detachable Client

For our final example, we'll use the event mailbox service to show how a client can detach from the network, reattach to the network, and process events that were delivered during its absence. This example shows a different client, one that we'll call a billing client. This client registers with our convert service to be notified whenever the service performs a conversion. It then generates a billing record based on the number of events it receives. There's no point in having the billing client run all time: it can use the event mailbox service to hold events, and then run every day to read the queued events and create the billing record. The classes to run this example are listed in Example 11-2.

Example 11-2: A Detachable Client

```
Common classes
    ConvertService (used in Example 11-1; listed in Example 6-1)
```

Example 11–2: A Detachable Client (continued)

```
ConvertServiceRegistration (used in Example 11-1; listed in Example 5-1)
ConvertEvent (used in Example 11-1; listed in Example 6-1)
ServiceFinder (used in Example 11-1; listed in Example 6-2)
ServiceFinderListener (used in Example 11-1; listed in Example 6-2)
```
Server Classes
```
ConvertServiceImpl (used in Example 11-1)
ConvertServiceRegistrationImpl (used in Example 11-1;
    listed in Example 5-1)
ConvertServiceProxy (used in Example 11-1; listed in Example 5-1)
ServerLandlord (used in Example 11-1)
ServerResource (used in Example 11-1; listed in Example 5-1)
ServerDelivery (used in Example 11-1; listed in Example 8-1)
ConvertServiceImpl (used in Example 11-1; listed in Example 6-1)
Expirer (used in Example 11-1; listed in Example 8-2)
```
Client Classes
```
ConvertEventHandler (used in Example 11-1; listed in Example 6-1)
ConvertClient (used in Example 11-1; listed in Example 6-1)
```
Billing Client Classes
```
ConvertEventHandler (used in Example 11-1; listed in Example 6-1)
BillingClient (new)
```

The billing client for this example is a new class. Note that we need the original client for this example as well. We have to run instances of the original client, which will make the requests to the conversion service, which in turn will generate the events that our billing client will process. No other changes are required to support this example. Here's our billing client:

```java
import java.io.*;
import java.rmi.*;
import java.rmi.server.*;
import net.jini.core.lease.*;
import net.jini.core.event.*;
import net.jini.discovery.*;
import net.jini.lease.*;
import net.jini.event.*;
import com.sun.jini.lease.*;
import com.sun.jini.reliableLog.*;
import com.sun.jini.constants.*;

public class BillingClient extends UnicastRemoteObject
                            implements RemoteEventListener {

    MailboxRegistration mailbox;
    LeaseRenewalSet renewalSet;
    boolean doneProcessing;
    int numRecords = 0;

    class BillingClientLogHandler extends LogHandler {
        public void snapshot(OutputStream os) throws Exception {
            ObjectOutputStream oos = new ObjectOutputStream(os);
            Object target;

            if (mailbox == null)
                target = new String();
            else target = new MarshalledObject(mailbox);
            oos.writeObject(target);

            if (renewalSet == null)
```

```
                    target = new String();
                else target = new MarshalledObject(renewalSet);
                oos.writeObject(target);
        }

        public void recover(InputStream is) throws Exception {
            ObjectInputStream ois = new ObjectInputStream(is);
            Object target;

            target = ois.readObject();
            if (target instanceof MarshalledObject) {
                MarshalledObject mo = (MarshalledObject) target;
                mailbox = (MailboxRegistration) mo.get();
            }
            // else it was the dummy string

            target = ois.readObject();
            if (target instanceof MarshalledObject) {
                MarshalledObject mo = (MarshalledObject) target;
                renewalSet = (LeaseRenewalSet) mo.get();
            }
            // else it was the dummy string
        }

        public void applyUpdate(Object o) {
            // we never write updates
        }
    }

    public BillingClient(String logDir)
                         throws RemoteException, IOException {
        BillingClientLogHandler bclh = new BillingClientLogHandler();
        ReliableLog log = new ReliableLog(logDir, bclh);
        log.recover();
        if (mailbox == null)
            initServices();
        renewalSet.renewFor(mailbox.getLease(), TimeConstants.DAYS * 3);
        processRecords();
        log.snapshot();
        System.exit(0);
    }

    private void initServices() throws IOException, RemoteException {
        if (mailbox == null) {
            // First time we've run -- find all the services and ask for
            // conversion events to be send to us

            // Find the event mailbox service and register with it
            ServiceFinder sfem = new ServiceFinder(EventMailbox.class);
            EventMailbox em = (EventMailbox) sfem.getObject();
            mailbox = em.register(Long.MAX_VALUE);

            // Find the lease renewal service, and use it to renew the
            // mailbox lease. We intend to run every day, but set the
            // renewal time to 3 days if we don't run over a weekend.
            ServiceFinder sflrs =
                    new ServiceFinder(LeaseRenewalService.class);
            LeaseRenewalService lrs =
                    (LeaseRenewalService) sflrs.getObject();
            renewalSet = lrs.createLeaseRenewalSet(
```

```
                        TimeConstants.DAYS * 3);

        // Find the convert service and ask that it send events
        // to the mailbox forever (when we cancel the lease
        // renewal set, this lease will get cancelled).
        ServiceFinder sf = new ServiceFinder(ConvertService.class);
        ConvertService cs = (ConvertService) sf.getObject();
        EventRegistration er = cs.trackConversions(Long.MAX_VALUE,
                            mailbox.getListener(), null);
        renewalSet.renewFor(er.getLease(), Long.MAX_VALUE);
    }
}

// Turn on the mailbox to send us events; they'll be sent to
// our notify method. If 30 seconds elapse without us getting an
// event from the mailbox, we assume that we've drained the mailbox
// and that we're done.
private void processRecords() {
    try {
        mailbox.enableDelivery(this);
    } catch (RemoteException re) {
        System.out.println("Can't enable mailbox delivery");
        System.exit(0);
    }
    doneProcessing = false;
    synchronized(this) {
        while (!doneProcessing) {
            // Set done to true; if it's still true after 30 seconds
            // then we're done. The notify() method will set it to
            // false, in which case we'll try again.
            doneProcessing = true;
            try {
                wait(30 * 1000);
            } catch (InterruptedException ie) {}
        }
    }
    System.out.println("Processed " + numRecords + " records");
    try {
        mailbox.disableDelivery();
    } catch (RemoteException re) {
    }
}

public synchronized void notify(RemoteEvent re)
                throws UnknownEventException {
    if (!(re instanceof ConvertEvent))
        throw new UnknownEventException("BillingClient");
    doneProcessing = false;
    ConvertEvent ce = (ConvertEvent) re;
    long seq = ce.getSequenceNumber();
    int val = ce.getValue();
    System.out.println("Convert #" + seq + ": " + val);
    numRecords++;
}

public static void main(String[] args) throws Exception {
    System.setSecurityManager(new RMISecurityManager());
    new BillingClient(args[0]);
}
}
```

This application is run every day to process the queued events. When the application runs, it attempts to retrieve an event mailbox registration from its reliable log; if it doesn't find one, then it creates a new mailbox and registers that mailbox with the convert service. This all happens in the initServices( ) method.

Once it has a mailbox, the application calls the processEvents( ) method, which is the interesting method of this example. This method registers a listener (the billing client itself) with the event mailbox. At this point, any events that the mailbox is holding will be sent to the client's notify( ) method. The processEvents( ) method then enters a loop where it wakes up every 30 seconds to see if these event notifications have stopped: if we run for 30 seconds without receiving a notification, we assume that we're done. We unregister the listener from the mailbox, which means that when the mailbox receives further events from the convert service, they'll be held in the mailbox until this application runs again.

The notify( ) method simply prints out the event and increments the numRecords indicator. When we've completed processing events, we print out the total number of conversion records we've processed (that's the number we could use to create an actual bill).

The lease to the mailbox is maintained by the lease renewal service. We lease the lease renewal set for a period of three days, and we renew that lease for three days every time the billing client runs. In this example, there's nothing for the lease renewal service to notify if the lease set is about to expire (we're not an activatable service), so we have to make sure that procedures are in place to run this client at least every three days, or the mailbox registration will be cancelled. If that happens, the client could simply create a new mailbox, but it will have lost the events associated with the old mailbox.

Running the Example

The billing client is an RMI service, since it is a remote event listener. To run it, you must compile it, generate its stub, and place the stub (plus the stub of the service finder listener) on a web server. The command line to run the billing client is the same as the command line to run all our other clients, except that the target class name has changed from ConvertClient to BillingClient.

In addition to whatever is required by the service, this client requires that *mercury* and *norm* are running. Of course, to receive interesting output, you must run the convert client from time to time to generate events. As a quick test, you can run the billing client, run the convert client a few times, and then run the billing client again.

Remember that it doesn't matter what service implementation or convert client implementation is running. You can run the service implementations from a previous chapter (e.g., one that doesn't require *rmid*) if that's easier; you can use any client as well. As long as the service and clients agree on the service interfaces, you can freely substitute implementations.

Summary

The services specified in the *Jini 1.1 Technology Helper Utilities and Services* specification allow us to write more useful and robust Jini applications. Jini is designed for an environment where applications are able to disconnect and reconnect, or deactivate and reactivate as necessary. Without the services discussed in this chapter, a Jini service can still recover when it reconnects to the network, but these services make that process much simpler. An application that reconnects or restarts can easily retrieve events that it may have missed, find out the state of lookup services that may have changed in its absence, and be confident that any leases its holds will be renewed during its absence.

Helper Services

CHAPTER 12

Security in Jini

Jini services presently use the same security model as all Java 2 programs. This model is very flexible and configurable. We'll give a brief overview of the default operation of this model, though you should be aware that the model can be configured in many different ways. For more information on security in Java, see *Java in a Nutshell* or *Java Security*, both published by O'Reilly.

The Java 2 security model operates only when a security manager is installed into your application; by default, applications do not have a security manager. However, in order for RMI clients to be able to download code from RMI servers, a security manager must be installed. As a result, all of our services have such a security manager. Remember that even though we may write a generic server, we're still an RMI client of the lookup service, so we can assume that all Jini applications have a security manager installed into them.

In the Java 2 security model, all code is given a set of permissions. This set is determined by a combination of the URL from which the code was loaded (including file-based URLs for code that is loaded from the classpath) and the entities (if any) that signed the jar file containing the class. The URL in this context is referred to as the codebase (it actually appears as *codeBase* in policy files); don't confuse this with the java.rmi.server.codebase property, since they may or may not be the same.

When a Java API attempts to perform a sensitive operation (such as opening a file), it checks the stack of the thread attempting the operation: all classes that are on the current stack must have permission to perform the operation if the operation is to be allowed. Classes that are part of the core Java platform—that is, classes that are loaded from the *rt.jar* file—are given permission to perform any operation. Classes that are installed into the standard Java extensions directory (*$JAVAHOME/lib/ext*) are also given permission to perform any operation. All other classes, including classes on the classpath, are by default given a very limited set of permissions: to listen on a server socket that operates on a non-privileged port, and to read a limited set of system properties.

The set of permissions associated with a particular class is loaded from two files: *$JAVAHOME/lib/security/java.policy* and *$HOME/.java.policy* (on most Windows systems *C:\WINDOWS\.java.policy*). There are many ways to specify additional files from which to load sets of permissions, and the most common method is to specify a file on the command line by associating it with the `java.security.policy` property. Hence, to include the permissions located in the file called *policy* in the current directory, include the command-line argument `-Djava.security.policy=policy`.

Policy files are created and edited with the *policytool* command (although their syntax is very straightforward, and we generally use our favorite text editor to edit them). A policy file contains a set of very specific permissions—we'll list some simple examples here, but the entire list of possible permissions and how to create new permissions is beyond the scope of this book.

Sample Policy Files

The path of least resistance in all of this is to use a policy file that gives all code permission to perform all operations. Such a policy file looks like this:

```
grant {
    permission java.security.AllPermission;
};
```

This file grants all permissions to all classes, since we have not specified either a codebase or a signer for the code. The `AllPermission` permission is a special object that grants, as you might guess, all permissions.

To use this file, save it somewhere. Don't save it as *$JAVAHOME/lib/security/ java.policy* or as *$HOME/.java.policy*, since then the permissions would apply to any Java program. A common technique is to save this file as */files/ jini1_0/java.policy.all* and then to start a Java program like this:

```
piccolo% java -Djava.security.policy=/files/jini1_0/java.policy.all  ...
```

Clearly this is a potentially dangerous policy file; if it is misused, then you'll lose all benefits of Java's security model. A better alternative is to specify the codebase that you're interested in applying the permissions to. That is sometimes hard: if you're running lots of programs from lots of locations, you need lots of entries in your policy file.

A good compromise in this case is to set up each of your applications to run from a classpath that contains a single directory (it can be different for each application), or to run all your applications from executable jar files. Then you can use the following file:

```
grant codeBase "file:${java.class.path}" {
    permission java.security.AllPermission;
};

grant {
    // Let the code connect to and accept connections from
    // non-privileged ports
    permission java.net.SocketPermission "*:1024-", "connect,accept";
```

```
        // Let the code talk to the standard HTTP server port
        permission java.net.SocketPermission "80", "connect";
};
```

This file has two policy entries. The first grants all permissions to everything on your classpath, but its syntax will not work if your classpath contains more than one directory. In that case, you have no alternative but to list each directory as a separate entry in the policy file.

The second entry in this file will apply to code that is downloaded from a Jini service. In that case, you probably don't even know where the server is; that's part of the reason behind Jini. So we've given that code the ability to operate on any network socket on an unprivileged port and to open a socket (but not create a server socket) on port 80. This works as long as the downloaded code does not need access to any local resources; it works for all the example services we show in this book and for the services that come with Sun's implementation of Jini. It may not work for third-party Jini services.

To summarize, there are two viable options:

Use a wide-open policy file
>   This runs the risk that the downloaded code may perform an unwanted operation on your network. Because you're most likely running Jini on your local network, this is a minimal risk, as long as you make sure not to run other programs (and certainly not your Java-enabled browser) with that policy file.

Use the classpath-based policy file
>   This is a better choice, but it won't work if the Jini services require access to local resources. It also requires that you have a single directory as your classpath, which means that you must either bundle all Jini classes and your service classes into a single jar file (as we did in Chapter 11) or you must unpack the Jini classes into the same directory as your service classes. If you're in an environment where you feel you cannot trust Jini services, this is the choice to make.

Several security enhancements are scheduled for Jini 1.2.

Jini Policy Files

If you're interested in the specific permissions that each service requires, you can check some of the example files that Sun's implementation of Jini comes with; these are located in *$JINIHOME /examples*. We'll look at some of these briefly.

Policies for the HTTP Server

The HTTP server does not actually install a security manager, so it needs no special entries in policy files.

Policies for reggie

At a minimum, *reggie* requires the permissions that can be found in *$JINIHOME /examples/lookup/policy*. Note that this file has an error; it lists permissions to read and write its reliable log as:

```
permission java.io.FilePermission "/tmp/reggie_log", "read,write,delete";
permission java.io.FilePermission
    "/tmp/reggie_log/-", "read,write,delete";
```

The forward slashes in these two entries should be replaced with ${file.separator}, and the name listed there must match the name of the log that you specify when you run *reggie*. In addition, the entry

```
permission java.net.SocketPermission "*:80", "connect";
```

assumes that the HTTP server is running on port 80. You can either hardwire the port number, or change the entry so that it can connect to all ports:

```
permission java.net.SocketPermission "*:1-", "connect";
```

In either case, you'll need the ability to connect to ports greater than 1024: RMI uses anonymous ports for its connections, so you can't specify a particular port for those connections.

Sun's implementation of Java also provides a file called *$JINIHOME/examples/ lookup/policy.all*, which grants all permissions to all classes. That's the file that the start service tool will by default use to start *reggie*.

Policies for mahalo

The default policy file for *mahalo* (*$JINIHOME/examples/txn/policy*) lists all permissions for all classes. An alternative is to use this file, which has the minimum permission required to start *mahalo*:

```
grant codebase "file:${java.class.path}" {
    permission java.io.FilePermission "-", "read,write,delete";
    permission java.net.SocketPermission "*:1-","connect,resolve";
    permission java.lang.RuntimePermission
        "accessClassInPackage.sun.rmi.server";
    permission java.util.PropertyPermission
        "com.sun.jini.thread.debug", "read";
    permission java.util.PropertyPermission
        "com.sun.jini.mahalo.*", "read";
    permission java.util.PropertyPermission "com.sun.jini.use.*", "read";
    permission net.jini.discovery.DiscoveryPermission "*";
};
```

Policies for outrigger

Similarly, the example policy file (*$JINIHOME/examples/books/policy.all*) for Sun's implementation of the JavaSpaces service contains all permissions. A reduced file would look like this:

```
grant {
    // This section is needed for both types of JavaSpaces.
    permission java.util.PropertyPermission
```

```
            "com.sun.jini.outrigger.basicspace.*", "read";
    permission java.util.PropertyPermission
            "com.sun.jini.outrigger.*", "read";
    permission java.util.PropertyPermission "com.sun.jini.use.*", "read";
    permission java.net.SocketPermission "*:1-", "connect,resolve";
    permission net.jini.discovery.DiscoveryPermission "*";

    // The remainder of this file is needed only for
    //     persistent JavaSpaces.
    // Change this entry to point to the location where you actually
    //     have Jini installed.
    permission java.io.FilePermission
            "${file.separator}jini1_0${file.separator}lib${file.separator}-",
            "read";
    permission java.io.FilePermission
            "${file.separator}tmp${file.separator}javaspaces", "read,write";
    permission java.io.FilePermission
        "${file.separator}tmp${file.separator}javaspaces${file.separator}-",
        "read,write,delete";
    permission java.lang.RuntimePermission
            "accessClassInPackage.sun.rmi.server";
};
```

Jini Security Classes

Jini defines a new security permission class: the net.jini.discovery.Discov-eryPermission class. This class signifies permission to connect to a Jini lookup service that is serving a particular group. The group is the permission name for the class; this class has no associated list of actions. The name can be "*" to signify all groups, the empty string " " to specify the public group, or a specific group name. This permission supports wildcard matching, so that the string "*.sun.com" will match any group that ends in sun.com. Like all Java permission classes, you do not use this class as a developer, but you do need to know the details of this class so that you can use it in policy files (as we have in several of our examples).

Summary

Java has a strong security model that is based in part upon knowing where code comes from and the specific permissions that code needs. This model isn't the best choice for Jini, where code comes from unknown places but still needs specific permissions. For the time being, it's easiest to run Jini services and clients in an environment that grants them permission to perform any operation; that's the approach that we've taken in our examples.

PART II

Quick Reference

Part II is quick-reference material for the services and APIs of the Jini platform. Please read the following section, *How To Use This Quick Reference*, to learn how to get the most out of this material.

How To Use This Quick Reference

The quick-reference section that follows packs a lot of information into a small space. This introduction explains how to get the most out of that information. It describes how the quick reference is organized and how to read the individual quick-ref entries.

Finding a Quick-Reference Entry

The quick reference is organized into five chapters. Chapter 13, *Service Reference*, provides manual pages for the services that ship with Sun's implementation of Jini. Chapter 14, *The com.sun.jini Packages*, documents the Jini "helper" packages in the com.sun.jini hierarchy. These are not part of the Jini specification, but can be quite useful to Jini programmers. Chapter 15, *The net.jini.core Package*, documents the net.jini.core packages, which comprise the "Jini Core Platform" or JCP. Chapter 16, *The net.jini Packages*, documents the non-core net.jini packages—the "Jini Extended Platform" or JXP. Finally, Chapter 17, *The java Packages*, documents selected classes and packages from the core Java API. These java.io and java.rmi classes are not part of Jini itself, but they are commonly used in Jini programming, and are documented here for your convenience.

Chapters 14 through 17 begin with a short introduction to the packages documented in that chapter. This is followed by a series of sections, each of which covers one package. Each section begins with an overview and class hierarchy diagram of the package. Following this overview are quick-reference entries for all of the public classes and interfaces in the package.

Entries are organized alphabetically by class *and* package name, so that related classes are grouped near each other. Thus, in order to look up a quick reference entry for a particular class, you must also know the name of the package that contains that class. Usually, the package name is obvious from the context, and you should have no trouble looking up the quick-reference entry you want. Use the tabs on the outside edge of the book and the dictionary-style headers on the upper outside corner of each page to help you find the package and class you are looking for.

Packages are listed in alphabetical order within each chapter. Note, however, that because of the way packages are grouped together into chapters, packages do not appear in strictly global alphabetical order. Specifically, the net.jini.admin package appears at the beginning of Chapter 16, although if the book were in strict alphabetical order, it would appear before the packages of Chapter 15.

Occasionally, you may need to look up a class for which you do not already know the package. In this case, refer to Chapter 18, *Class, Method, and Field Index*. This index allows you to look up a class by class name and find out what package it is part of.

Reading a Quick-Reference Entry

Each quick-reference entry contains quite a bit of information. The sections that follow describe the structure of a quick-reference entry, explaining what information is available, where it is found, and what it means. While reading the descriptions that follow, you will find it helpful to flip through the reference section itself to find examples of the features being described.

Class Name, Package Name, Availability, and Flags

Each quick-reference entry begins with a four-part title that specifies the name, package, and availability of the class, and may also specify various additional flags that describe the class. The class name appears in bold at the upper left of the title. The package name appears, in smaller print, in the lower left, below the class name.

The upper-right portion of the title indicates the availability of the class; it specifies the earliest release that contained the class. If a class was introduced in Jini 1.0, for example, this portion of the title reads "Jini 1.0". If a class was introduced in Jini 1.1, the availability reads "Jini 1.1". The availability section of the title is also used to indicate whether a class has been deprecated, and, if so, in what release. For example, it might read "Jini 1.0; Deprecated in Jini 1.1". In Chapter 17, which documents classes from the core Java APIs, the availability section will contain a Java version number rather than a Jini version number.

In the lower-right corner of the title you may find a list of flags that describe the class. The possible flags and their meanings are as follows:

checked
> The class is a checked exception, which means that it extends java.lang.Exception, but not java.lang.RuntimeException. In other words, it must be declared in the throws clause of any method that may throw it.

cloneable
> The class, or a superclass, implements java.lang.Cloneable.

collection
> The class, or a superclass, implements java.util.Collection or java.util.Map.

comparable

The class, or a superclass, implements java.lang.Comparable.

entry

The class, or a superclass, implements net.jini.core.entry.Entry.

error

The class extends java.lang.Error.

event

The class extends java.util.EventObject, but does not extend net.jini.core.event.RemoteEvent.

event adapter

The class, or a superclass, implements java.util.EventListener, and the class name ends with "Adapter".

event listener

The class, or a superclass, implements java.util.EventListener.

remote event

The class extends net.jini.core.event.RemoteEvent.

remote event listener

The class extends net.jini.core.event.RemoteEventListener.

runnable

The class, or a superclass, implements java.lang.Runnable.

serializable

The class, or a superclass, implements java.io.Serializable and may be serialized.

unchecked

The class is an unchecked exception, which means it extends java.lang.RuntimeException and therefore does not need to be declared in the throws clause of a method that may throw it.

Description

The title of each quick-reference entry is followed by a short description of the most important features of the class or interface. This description may be anywhere from a couple of sentences to several paragraphs long.

Synopsis

The most important part of every quick-reference entry is the class synopsis, which follows the title and description. The synopsis for a class looks a lot like the source code for the class, except that the method bodies are omitted and some additional annotations are added. If you know Java syntax, you know how to read the class synopsis.

The first line of the synopsis contains information about the class itself. It begins with a list of class modifiers, such as public, abstract, and final. These modifiers are followed by the class or interface keyword and then by the name of the class. The class name may be followed by an extends clause that specifies the superclass and an implements clause that specifies any interfaces the class implements.

The class definition line is followed by a list of the fields and methods that the class defines. Once again, if you understand basic Java syntax, you should have no trouble making sense of these lines. The listing for each member includes the modifiers, type, and name of the member. For methods, the synopsis also includes the type and name of each method parameter and an optional throws clause that lists the exceptions the method can throw. The member names are in boldface, so it is easy to scan the list of members looking for the one you want. The names of method parameters are in italics to indicate that they are not to be used literally. The member listings are printed on alternating gray and white backgrounds to keep them visually separate.

Member availability and flags

Each member listing is a single line that defines the API for that member. These listings use Java syntax, so their meaning is immediately clear to any Java programmer. There is some auxiliary information associated with each member synopsis, however, that requires explanation.

Recall that each quick-reference entry begins with a title section that includes the release in which the class was first defined. When a member is introduced into a class after the initial release of the class, the version in which the member was introduced appears, in small print, to the left of the member synopsis. For example, if a class was first introduced in Jini 1.0, but had a new method added in Jini 1.1, the title contains the string "Jini 1.0", and the listing for the new member is preceded by the number "1.1". Furthermore, if a member has been deprecated, that fact is indicated with a hash mark (#) to the left of the member synopsis.

The area to the right of the member synopsis is used to display a variety of flags that provide additional information about the member. Some of these flags indicate additional specification details that do not appear in the member API itself. Other flags contain implementation-specific information. This information can be quite useful in understanding the class and in debugging your code, but be aware that it may differ between implementations. The implementation-specific flags displayed in this book are based on Sun's implementation of Java for Microsoft Windows.

The following flags may be displayed to the right of a member synopsis:

native
> An implementation-specific flag that indicates that a method is implemented in native code. Although native is a Java keyword and can appear in method signatures, it is part of the method implementation, not part of its specification. Therefore, this information is included with the member flags, rather than as part of the member listing. This flag is useful as a hint about the expected performance of a method.

synchronized
> An implementation-specific flag that indicates that a method implementation is declared synchronized, meaning that it obtains a lock on the object or class before executing. Like the native keyword, the synchronized keyword is part of the

method implementation, not part of the specification, so it appears as a flag, not in the method synopsis itself. This flag is a useful hint that the method is probably implemented in a thread-safe manner.

Whether or not a method is thread-safe is part of the method specification, and this information *should* appear (although it often does not) in the method documentation. There are a number of different ways to make a method thread-safe, however, and declaring the method with the synchronized keyword is only one possible implementation. In other words, a method that does not bear the synchronized flag can still be thread-safe.

Overrides:

Indicates that a method overrides a method in one of its superclasses. The flag is followed by the name of the superclass that the method overrides. This is a specification detail, not an implementation detail. As we'll see in the next section, overriding methods are usually grouped together in their own section of the class synopsis. The Overrides: flag is only used when an overriding method is not grouped in that way.

Implements:

Indicates that a method implements a method in an interface. The flag is followed by the name of the interface that is implemented. This is a specification detail, not an implementation detail. As we'll see in the next section, methods that implement an interface are usually grouped into a special section of the class synopsis. The Implements: flag is only used for methods that are not grouped in this way.

empty

Indicates that the implementation of the method has an empty body. This can be a hint to the programmer that the method may need to be overridden in a subclass.

constant

An implementation flag that indicates that a method has a trivial implementation. Only methods with a void return type can be truly empty. Any method declared to return a value must have at least a return statement. The "constant" flag indicates that the method implementation is empty except for a return statement that returns a constant value. Such a method might have a body like return null; or return false;. Like the "empty" flag, this flag indicates that a method may need to be overridden.

default:

This flag is used with property accessor methods that read the value of a property (i.e., methods whose names begins with "get" and take no arguments). The flag is followed by the default value of the property. Strictly speaking, default property values are a specification detail. In practice, however, these defaults are not always documented, and care should be taken, because the default values may change between implementations.

Not all property accessors have a "default:" flag. A default value is determined by dynamically loading the class in question, instantiating it using a no-argument constructor, and then calling the method to find out what it returns. This technique can be used only on classes that can be dynamically loaded and instantiated and that have no-argument constructors, so default values are shown for those classes only. Furthermore, note that when a class is instantiated using a different constructor, the default values for its properties may be different.

=   For static final fields, this flag is followed by the constant value of the field. Only constants of primitive and String types and constants with the value null are displayed. Some constant values are specification details, while others are implementation details. The reason that symbolic constants are defined, however, is so you can write code that does not rely directly upon the constant value. Use this flag to help you understand the class, but do not rely upon the constant values in your own programs.

Functional grouping of members

Within a class synopsis, the members are not listed in strict alphabetical order. Instead, they are broken down into functional groups and listed alphabetically within each group. Constructors, methods, fields, and inner classes are all listed separately. Instance methods are kept separate from static (class) methods. Constants are separated from non-constant fields. Public members are listed separately from protected members. Grouping members by category breaks a class down into smaller, more comprehensible segments, making the class easier to understand. This grouping also makes it easier for you to find a desired member.

Functional groups are separated from each other in a class synopsis with Java comments, such as "// Public Constructors", "// Inner Classes", and "// Methods Implementing Lease". The various functional categories are as follows (in the order in which they appear in a class synopsis):

Constructors
> Displays the constructors for the class. Public constructors and protected constructors are displayed separately in subgroupings. If a class defines no constructor at all, the Java compiler adds a default no-argument constructor that is displayed here. If a class defines only private constructors, it cannot be instantiated, so a special, empty grouping entitled "No Constructor" indicates this fact. Constructors are listed first because the first thing you do with most classes is instantiate them by calling a constructor.

Constants
> Displays all of the constants (i.e., fields that are declared static and final) defined by the class. Public and protected constants are displayed in separate subgroups. Constants are listed here, near the top of the class synopsis, because constant values are often used throughout the class as legal values for method parameters and return values.

Inner Classes
> Groups all of the inner classes and interfaces defined by the class or interface. For each inner class, there is a single-line synopsis. Each inner class also has its own quick-reference entry that includes a full class synopsis for the inner class. Like constants, inner classes are listed near the top of the class synopsis because they are often used by a number of other members of the class.

Static Methods

Lists the static methods (class methods) of the class, broken down into sub-groups for public static methods and protected static methods.

Event Listener Registration Methods

Lists the public instance methods that register and deregister event listener objects with the class. The names of these methods begin with the words "add" and "remove" and end in "Listener". These methods are always passed a java.util.EventListener object. The methods are typically defined in pairs, so the pairs are listed together. The methods are listed alphabetically by event name rather than by method name.

Property Accessor Methods

Lists the public instance methods that set or query the value of a property or attribute of the class. The names of these methods begin with the words "set," "get," and "is," and their signatures follow the patterns set out in the Java-Beans specification. Although the naming conventions and method signature patterns are defined for JavaBeans, classes and interfaces throughout the Java platform define property accessor methods that follow these conventions and patterns. Looking at a class in terms of the properties it defines can be a powerful tool for understanding the class, so property methods are grouped together in this section. Property accessor methods are listed alphabetically by property name, not by method name. This means that the "set," "get," and "is" methods for a property all appear together.

Public Instance Methods

Contains all public instance methods that aren't grouped elsewhere.

Implementing Methods

Groups the methods that implement the same interface. There is one sub-group for each interface implemented by the class. Methods that are defined by the same interface are almost always related to each other, so this is a useful functional grouping of methods.

Note that if an interface method is also an event registration method or a property accessor method, it is listed both in this group and in the event or property group. This situation does not arise often, but when it does, all of the functional groupings are important and useful enough to warrant the duplicate listing. When an interface method is listed in the event or property group, it displays an "Implements:" flag that specifies the name of the interface of which it is part.

Overriding Methods

Groups the methods that override methods of a superclass broken down into subgroups by superclass. This is typically a useful grouping, because it helps to make it clear how a class modifies the default behavior of its superclasses. In practice, it is also often true that methods that override the same superclass are functionally related to each other.

Sometimes a method that overrides a superclass is also a property accessor method or (more rarely) an event registration method. When this happens, the method is grouped with the property or event methods and displays a flag that indicates which superclass it overrides. The method is not listed with other overriding methods, however. Note that this is different from interface methods, which, because they are more strongly functionally related, may have duplicate listings in both groups.

Protected Instance Methods
    Contains the protected instance methods that aren't grouped elsewhere.

Fields
    Lists all the non-constant fields of the class, breaking them down into subgroups for public and protected static fields and public and protected instance fields. Many classes do not define any publicly accessible fields. For those that do, many object-oriented programmers prefer not to use those fields directly, but instead to use accessor methods when such methods are available.

Deprecated Members
    Deprecated methods and deprecated fields are grouped at the very bottom of the class synopsis. Use of these members is strongly discouraged.

Class Hierarchy

For any class or interface that has a non-trivial class hierarchy, the class synopsis is followed by a "Hierarchy" section. This section lists all of the superclasses of the class, as well as any interfaces implemented by those superclasses. It may also list any interfaces extended by an interface. In the hierarchy listing, arrows indicate superclass to subclass relationships, while the interfaces implemented by a class follow the class name in parentheses. For example, the quickref entry for jini.net.core.event.RemoteEvent includes the following hierarchy:

Object→java.util.EventObject(Serializable)→RemoteEvent

This hierarchy indicates that RemoteEvent extends java.util.EventObject (which implements java.io.Serializable), and that java.util.EventObject extends java.lang.Object.

If a class has subclasses, the "Hierarchy" section is followed by a "Subclasses" section that lists those subclasses. If an interface has implementations, the "Hierarchy" section is followed by an "Implementations" section that lists those implementations. While the "Hierarchy" section shows ancestors of the class, the "Subclasses" or "Implementations" section shows descendants.

Cross References

The class hierarchy section of a quick-reference entry is followed by a number of optional "cross reference" sections that indicate other, related classes and methods that may be of interest. These sections are the following:

Passed To
    This section lists all of the methods and constructors that are passed an object of this type as an argument. This is useful when you have an object of a given type and want to figure out what you can do with it.

Returned By

> This section lists all of the methods (but not constructors) that return an object of this type. This is useful when you know that you want to work with an object of this type, but don't know how to obtain one.

Thrown By

> For checked exception classes, this section lists all of the methods and constructors that throw exceptions of this type. This material helps you figure out when a given exception or error may be thrown. Note, however, that this section is based on the exception types listed in the throws clauses of methods and constructors. Subclasses of RuntimeException and Error do not have to be listed in throws clauses, so it is not possible to generate a complete cross reference of methods that throw these types of unchecked exceptions.

Type Of

> This section lists all of the fields and constants that are of this type, which can help you figure out how to obtain an object of this type.

A Note About Class Names

Throughout the quick reference, you'll notice that classes are sometimes referred to by class name alone and at other times referred to by class name and package name. If package names were always used, the class synopses would become long and hard to read. On the other hand, if package names were never used, it would be difficult to know what class was being referred to (especially because of the complex Jini package hierarchy). Package names are omitted for all classes in the java.lang package, for java.io.Serializable, and for any classes that are in the same package as the current class being documented.

CHAPTER 13

Service Reference

This chapter contains reference pages for all the services that ship with Sun's implementation of Jini. Chapter 2, *Getting Started with Jini*, shows the basic commands used to start these services; this chapter contains their complete set of options.

fiddler

Synopsis

```
java [setup_jvm_options] -jar $JINIHOME/lib/fiddler.jar
        server_codebase policy_file log_directory
        [groups] [server_jvm] [server_jvm_options]
```

or

```
java -Djava.rmi.server.codebase=<server_codebase>
    -Djava.security.policy=<policy_file>
    [setup_jvm_options] [server_jvm_options]
    -cp $JINIHOME/lib/fiddler.jar com.sun.jini.fiddler.TransientFiddler
    log_directory [groups]
```

Description

fiddler is Sun's implementation of the Jini lookup discovery service. Two implementations are available. The first command line shows how to start the activatable version of *fiddler* which runs under the control of *rmid*. The command line for this version of *fiddler* is used to register it with *rmid* and to provide *rmid* with the options it should use to invoke the VM in which *fiddler* will run.

Like all activatable services, the first command involves two VMs: the one which is used to register the service with *rmid*, and the one that *rmid* will start to run the service. These are referred to as the setup and server VMs respectively.

The second command line shows how to run *fiddler* in transient mode, in which case it is not an activatable service. It runs in the VM started from the command line and does not automatically restart. It is faster to start and easier to configure, although its data cannot survive between invocations.

Options

setup_jvm_options

> The Java options used for the VM that will register the service with *rmid*. You may specify any option for the Java command here; you should specify a policy file (*-Djava.security.policy=somefile*) that has sufficient permissions to register a service with *rmid*. For the transient version, the *setup_jvm_options* are used to specify system properties for its VM.

-jar $JINIHOME/lib/fiddler.jar

> The jar file containing the code for *fiddler*. The manifest for this jar file lists the class for the persistent version as the main class.

-cp $JINIHOME/lib/fiddler.jar com.sun.jini.fiddler.TransientFiddler

> To run the transient version of *fiddler*, you must specify the class name since the jar file can list only a single class as its main class.

server_codebase

> The argument that the server VM should use for the java.rmi.server.codebase property. This codebase must contain the *fiddler-dl.jar* file, e.g., *http://server:8080/fiddler-dl.jar*.

policy_file

> The security policy that the server VM should run with by using the *-Djava.security.policy* property.

log_directory

> The directory in which the persistent version of *fiddler* will keep its persistent storage. If this directory exists, *fiddler* will attempt to read the log files in that directory and recreate its previous state from that log.

groups

> This optional argument specifies the groups that lookup services must support for *fiddler* to join them. The default is to join the public group (i.e., the group " ", which is also specified as "public"). Multiple groups may be specified by separating the group names with a comma (e.g., "NY/02,public").

server_jvm_args

> Any remaining arguments must start with a hyphen ("-"); they will be passed to the persistent server's VM (or they will apply to the VM running the transient version). There may be multiple arguments here; in addition to passing arguments for the *java* command, you may specify system properties here.

System Properties

fiddler uses properties to override certain aspects of its behavior. These properties are set by specifying *-DpropertyName=propertyValue* as a *server_jvm_arg* or a *setup_jvm_arg* as indicated. The properties supported by *fiddler* are:

com.sun.jini.fiddler.server.debug

If set, this property causes *fiddler* to print debugging output. The format of the value of this property is:

```
subsystem0[:subsystemLog0],subsystem1[:subsystemLog1],...
```

For each listed subsystem (chosen from the list below), debugging output will be sent to the associated file. The file is optional; if it is left out, the debugging output will be sent to System.out. No output will be generated for subsystems not included in the property setting.

The subsystems that *fiddler* currently supports are:

- all—writes all diagnostic information

- startup—writes information pertaining to service startup

- tasks—writes information pertaining to service tasks

- events—writes information pertaining to events generated

- groups—writes information about the managed set of groups

- locators—writes information about the managed set of locators

- discard—writes information about discard processing

- registration—writes information about the registrations granted

- lease—writes information about leases on registrations

- log—writes information pertaining to logging system state

- off—turns off the writing of diagnostic information

These subsystems may also be set through the setDebugProperty( ) method of the FiddlerAdmin interface.

This is a *server_jvm_arg*.

net.jini.discovery.debug

If this property is set to any value, *fiddler* will print to *System.err* any exceptions received by the LookupDiscovery class. This is a *server_jvm_arg*.

net.jini.discovery.mtu

The size defined by this property is used as the packet size of the multicast request to discover a lookup service. The lower limit of this value is 512, and its upper limit is set by the operating system. The default value is 512. This is a *server_jvm_arg*.

net.jini.discovery.timeout

As part of the lookup request protocol, a unicast connection is made from the client or service to the lookup service. The socket connection involved in this unicast connection has a timeout value of one minute. This property defines the number of milliseconds for this timeout (the default value is 60,000 milliseconds). This is a *server_jvm_arg*.

net.jini.discovery.ttl

> This property will set the TTL (time to live) value used in UDP multicast requests. This will affect the multicast announcement and multicast request protocols used by the lookup/discovery system. The TTL determines the number of routers that a multicast packet will be sent through. Each handling by a router is considered a hop, and this value is decremented with each hop. The default value is 15. This is a *server_jvm_arg*.

mahalo

Synopsis

```
java [setup_jvm_options] -jar $JINIHOME/lib/mahalo.jar
        server_codebase policy_file log_directory
        [groups] [server_jvm] [server_jvm_args]
```

Description

mahalo is Sun's implementation of the Jini transaction service. It is an activatable service, which means that it runs under the control of *rmid*. The command line for *mahalo* is used to register it with *rmid* and to provide *rmid* with the options it should use to invoke the VM in which *mahalo* will run.

Like all activatable services, two VMs are involved: the one which is used to register the service with *rmid*, and the one that *rmid* will start to run the service. These are referred to as the setup and server VMs respectively.

Options

setup_jvm_options

> The Java options used for the VM that will register the service with *rmid*. You may specify any option for the Java command here; you should specify a policy file (*-Djava.security.policy=somefile*) that has sufficient permissions to register a service with *rmid*.

-jar $JINIHOME/lib/mahalo.jar

> The jar file containing the code for *mahalo*.

server_codebase

> The argument that the server VM should use for the java.rmi.server.codebase property. This codebase must contain the *mahalo-dl.jar* file, e.g., *http://server:8080/mahalo-dl.jar*.

policy_file

> The security policy that the server VM should run with by using the *-Djava.security.policy* property. This policy file must have sufficient permissions for *mahalo* to run. An example policy file may be found in *$JINIHOME/example/txn/policy.all*.

log_directory

The directory in which *mahalo* will keep its persistent storage. If this directory exists, *mahalo* will attempt to read the log files in that directory and recreate its previous state from that log. On Windows, this directory must include a drive specifier (e.g., *C:*).

groups

This optional argument specifies the groups that lookup services must support for *mahalo* join them. The default is to join the public group (i.e., the group " ", which is also specified as "public"). Multiple groups may be specified by separating the group names with a comma (e.g., "NY/02,public").

You may specify the string "none" for the group, which indicates that *mahalo* should not use the Jini lookup service at all. In this case, *mahalo* should be configured to register itself with the RMI registry. That functionality will be removed from *mahalo* in a future release.

server_jvm

This optional argument specifies a path to the virtual machine used to run the service. The default is to use the command *java* in the user's PATH.

server_jvm_args

Any remaining arguments must start with a hyphen ("-"); they will be passed to the server VM. There may be multiple arguments here; in addition to passing arguments for the *java* command, you may specify system properties here.

System Properties

mahalo uses properties to override the behavior of certain aspects of the transaction manager. These properties are set by specifying *-DpropertyName=property-Value* as a *server_jvm_arg* or as a *setup_jvm_arg* as indicated. The properties supported by *mahalo* are:

com.sun.jini.use.registry

If this property is set to any value, *mahalo* will bind itself into the RMI registry instead of the Jini lookup service. This functionality will be removed from *mahalo* in a future release. This property is a *setup_jvm_arg*.

com.sun.jini.rmiRegistryPort

If the RMI registry is being used, this property is used to set the network port that *rmiregistry* is listening on, which by default is 1099. This property is a *setup_jvm_arg*.

com.sun.jini.mahalo.managerName

This property defines the name that is associated with the transaction manager. When using the RMI registry, this is the name that is used to refer to the service. When used with the Jini lookup service, this is the name that is assigned to the Name attribute that is associated with the transaction manager. This allows clients of the transaction service to use a particular transaction manager. This property is a *setup_jvm_arg*.

net.jini.discovery.debug

> If this property is set to any value, *mahalo* will print to *System.err* any excep-
> tions received by the LookupDiscovery class. This property is a
> *server_jvm_arg*.

net.jini.discovery.mtu

> The size defined by this property is used as the packet size of the multicast
> request to discover a lookup service. The lower limit of this value is 512, and
> its upper limit is set by the operating system. The default value is 512. This
> property is a *server_jvm_arg*.

net.jini.discovery.timeout

> As part of the lookup request protocol, a unicast connection is made from the
> client or service to the lookup service. The socket connection involved in this
> unicast connection has a timeout value of one minute. This property defines
> the number of milliseconds for this timeout (the default value is 60,000 mil-
> liseconds). This property is a *server_jvm_arg*.

net.jini.discovery.ttl

> This property will set the TTL (time to live) value used in UDP multicast
> requests. This will affect the multicast announcement and multicast request
> protocols used by the lookup/discovery system. The TTL determines the num-
> ber of routers that a multicast packet will be sent through. Each handling by a
> router is considered a hop, and this value is decremented with each hop. The
> default value is 15. This property is a *server_jvm_arg*.

mercury

Synopsis

```
java [setup_jvm_options] -jar $JINIHOME/lib/mercury.jar
        server_codebase policy_file log_directory
        [groups] [server_jvm] [server_jvm_options]
```

Description

mercury is Sun's implementation of the Jini event mailbox. *mercury* is an activatable service, which means that it runs under the control of *rmid*. The command
line for *mercury* is used to register it with *rmid* and to provide *rmid* with the
options it should use to invoke the VM in which *mercury* will run.

Like all activatable services, two VMs are involved: the one which is used to register the service with *rmid*, and the one that *rmid* will start to run the service. These
are referred to as the setup and server VMs respectively.

Options

setup_jvm_options

> The Java options used for the VM that will register the service with *rmid*. You
> may specify any option for the Java command here; you should specify a pol-
> icy file (*-Djava.security.policy=somefile*) that has sufficient permissions to reg-
> ister a service with *rmid*.

-jar $JINIHOME/lib/mercury.jar
> The jar file containing the code for *mercury*.

server_codebase
> The argument that the server VM should use for the `java.rmi.server.code-base` property. This codebase must contain the *mercury-dl.jar* file, e.g., *http://server:8080/mercury-dl.jar*.

policy_file
> The security policy that the server VM should run with by using the *-Djava.security.policy* property.

log_directory
> The directory in which the persistent version of *mercury* will keep its persistent storage. If this directory exists, *mercury* will attempt to read the log files in that directory and recreate its previous state from that log.

groups
> This optional argument specifies the groups that lookup services must support for *mercury* to join them. The default is to join the public group (i.e., the group " ", which is also specified as "public"). Multiple groups may be specified by separating the group names with a comma (e.g., "NY/02,public").

server_jvm_args
> Any remaining arguments must start with a hyphen ("-"); they will be passed to the persistent server's VM (or they will apply to the VM running the transient version). There may be multiple arguments here; in addition to passing arguments for the *java* command, you may specify system properties here.

System Properties

mercury uses properties to override certain aspects of its behavior. These properties are set by specifying *-DpropertyName=propertyValue* as a *server_jvm_arg* or a *setup_jvm_arg* as indicated. The properties supported by *mercury* are:

com.sun.jini.mercury.server.debug
> If set, this property causes *mercury* to print debugging output. The format of the value of this property is:
>
> ```
> subsystem0[:subsystemLog0],subsystem1[:subsystemLog1],...
> ```

For each listed subsystem (chosen from the list below), debugging output will be sent to the associated file. The file is optional; if it is left out, the debugging output will be sent to `System.out`. No output will be generated for subsystems not included in the property setting.

The subsystems that *mercury* currently supports are:

- leases—for lease-related debugging information

- delivery—for event delivery-related debugging information

- admin—for administrative-related debugging messages

- init—for service initialization-related debugging messages

- receive—for event reception-related debugging messages

- expiration—for registration expiration-related debugging messages

- recovery—for state recovery-related debugging messages

This is a *server_jvm_arg*.

net.jini.discovery.debug

If this property is set to any value, *mercury* will print to *System.err* any exceptions received by the LookupDiscovery class. This is a *server_jvm_arg*.

net.jini.discovery.mtu

The size defined by this property is used as the packet size of the multicast request to discover a lookup service. The lower limit of this value is 512, and its upper limit is set by the operating system. The default value is 512. This is a *server_jvm_arg*.

net.jini.discovery.timeout

As part of the lookup request protocol, a unicast connection is made from the client or service to the lookup service. The socket connection involved in this unicast connection has a timeout value of one minute. This property defines the number of milliseconds for this timeout (the default value is 60,000 milliseconds). This is a *server_jvm_arg*.

net.jini.discovery.ttl

This property will set the TTL (time to live) value used in UDP multicast requests. This will affect the multicast announcement and multicast request protocols used by the lookup/discovery system. The TTL determines the number of routers that a multicast packet will be sent through. Each handling by a router is considered a hop, and this value is decremented with each hop. The default value is 15. This is a *server_jvm_arg*.

norm

Synopsis

```
java [setup_jvm_options] -jar $JINIHOME/lib/norm.jar
        server_codebase policy_file log_directory
        [groups] [server_jvm] [server_jvm_options]
```

Description

norm is Sun's implementation of the Jini lease renewal service. *norm* is an activatable service, which means that it runs under the control of *rmid*. The command line for *norm* is used to register it with *rmid* and to provide *rmid* with the options it should use to invoke the VM in which *norm* will run.

Like all activatable services, two VMs are involved: the one which is used to register the service with *rmid*, and the one that *rmid* will start to run the service. These are referred to as the setup and server *VMs* respectively.

Options

setup_jvm_options

The Java options used for the VM that will register the service with *rmid*. You may specify any option for the Java command here; you should specify a policy file (*-Djava.security.policy=somefile*) that has sufficient permissions to register a service with *rmid*.

-jar $JINIHOME/lib/norm.jar

The jar file containing the code for *norm*.

server_codebase

The argument that the server VM should use for the java.rmi.server.codebase property. This codebase must contain the *norm-dl.jar* file, e.g., *http://server:8080/norm-dl.jar*.

policy_file

The security policy that the server VM should run with by using the *-Djava.security.policy* property.

log_directory

The directory in which the persistent version of *norm* will keep its persistent storage. If this directory exists, *norm* will attempt to read the log files in that directory and recreate its previous state from that log.

groups

This optional argument specifies the groups that lookup services must support for *norm* to join them. The default is to join the public group (i.e., the group " ", which is also specified as "public"). Multiple groups may be specified by separating the group names with a comma (e.g., "NY/02,public").

server_jvm_args

Any remaining arguments must start with a hyphen ("-"); they will be passed to the persistent server's VM (or they will apply to the VM running the transient version). There may be multiple arguments here; in addition to passing arguments for the *java* command, you may specify system properties here.

System Properties

norm uses properties to override certain aspects of its behavior. These properties are set by specifying *-DpropertyName=propertyValue* as a *server_jvm_arg* or a *setup_jvm_arg* as indicated. The properties supported by *norm* are:

net.jini.discovery.debug

If this property is set to any value, *norm* will print to *System.err* any exceptions received by the LookupDiscovery class. This is a *server_jvm_arg*.

net.jini.discovery.mtu

The size defined by this property is used as the packet size of the multicast request to discover a lookup service. The lower limit of this value is 512, and its upper limit is set by the operating system. The default value is 512. This is a *server_jvm_arg*.

net.jini.discovery.timeout

> As part of the lookup request protocol, a unicast connection is made from the client or service to the lookup service. The socket connection involved in this unicast connection has a timeout value of one minute. This property defines the number of milliseconds for this timeout (the default value is 60,000 milliseconds). This is a *server_jvm_arg*.

net.jini.discovery.ttl

> This property will set the TTL (time to live) value used in UDP multicast requests. This will affect the multicast announcement and multicast request protocols used by the lookup/discovery system. The TTL determines the number of routers that a multicast packet will be sent through. Each handling by a router is considered a hop, and this value is decremented with each hop. The default value is 15. This is a *server_jvm_arg*.

outrigger

Synopsis

```
java [setup_jvm_options] -jar $JINIHOME/lib/outrigger.jar
        server_codebase policy_file log_directory
        [groups] [server_jvm_options]
```

or

```
java -Djava.rmi.server.codebase=<server_codebase>
    -Djava.security.policy=<policy_file>
    [setup_jvm_options] [server_jvm_options]
    -jar $JINIHOME/lib/transient-outrigger.jar [groups]
```

Description

outrigger is Sun's implementation of the Jini JavaSpaces service. Two implementations are available. The first command line shows how to start the *FrontEndSpace*. The *FrontEndSpace* is an activatable service, which means that it runs under the control of *rmid*. The command line for the *FrontEndSpace* is used to register it with *rmid* and to provide *rmid* with the options it should use to invoke the VM in which the space will run.

Like all activatable services, two VMs are involved: the one which is used to register the service with *rmid*, and the one that *rmid* will start to run the service. These are referred to as the setup and server *VMs* respectively.

The second command line shows how to run the *TransientSpace*, which is not an activatable service. It runs in the VM started from the command line and does not automatically restart. It is faster to start and easier to configure, although its data cannot survive between invocations.

Options

setup_jvm_options

The Java options used for the VM that will register the service with *rmid*. You may specify any option for the Java command here; you should specify a policy file (*-Djava.security.policy=somefile*) that has sufficient permissions to register a service with *rmid*. For the *TransientSpace*, the *setup_jvm_options* are used to specify system properties for its VM.

-jar $JINIHOME/lib/outrigger.jar

The jar file containing the code for the *FrontEndSpace*.

-jar $JINIHOME/lib/transient-outrigger.jar

The jar file containing the code for the *TransientSpace*.

server_codebase

The argument that the server VM should use for the java.rmi.server.codebase property. This codebase must contain the *outrigger-dl.jar* file, e.g. *http://server:8080/outrigger-dl.jar*. Note that both versions of *outrigger* use the same jar file as their server codebase.

policy_file

The security policy that the server VM should run with by using the *-Djava.security.policy* property. This policy file must have sufficient permissions for the JavaSpaces service to run. An example policy file may be found in *$JINIHOME/example/books/policy.all*.

log_directory

The directory in which the *FrontEndSpace* will keep its persistent storage. If this directory exists, the *FrontEndSpace* will attempt to read the log files in that directory and recreate its previous state from that log. On Windows, this directory must include a drive specifier (e.g., *C:*). The *TransientSpace* does not use a log directory.

groups

This optional argument specifies the groups that lookup services must support for *outrigger* to join them. The default is to join the public group (i.e., the group " ", which is also specified as "public"). Multiple groups may be specified by separating the group names with a comma (e.g., "NY/02,public").

You may specify the string "none" for the group, which indicates that *outrigger* should not use the Jini lookup service at all. In this case, *outrigger* should be configured to register itself with the RMI registry. That functionality will be removed from *outrigger* in a future release.

server_jvm_args

Any remaining arguments must start with a hyphen ("-"); they will be passed to the *FrontEndSpace* server's VM (or run the *TransientSpace* VM). There may be multiple arguments here; in addition to passing arguments for the *java* command, you may specify system properties here.

System Properties

outrigger uses properties to override certain aspects of its behavior. These properties are set by specifying *-DpropertyName=propertyValue* as a *server_jvm_arg* or a *setup_jvm_arg* as indicated. The properties supported by *outrigger* are:

com.sun.jini.use.registry

If this property is set to any value, *outrigger* will bind itself into the RMI registry instead of the Jini lookup service. This functionality will be removed from *outrigger* in a future release. This is a *setup_jvm_arg*.

com.sun.jini.rmiRegistryPort

If the RMI registry is being used, this property is used to set the network port that *rmiregistry* is listening on, which by default is 1099. This is a *setup_jvm_arg*.

com.sun.jini.outrigger.spaceName

This property defines the name that is associated with the JavaSpaces service. When using the RMI registry, this is the name that is used to refer to the service. When running with the Jini lookup service, this is the name that is assigned to the Name attribute that is associated with the service. This allows clients of the transaction service to use a particular Java space. This is a *setup_jvm_arg*.

net.jini.discovery.debug

If this property is set to any value, *outrigger* will print to *System.err* any exceptions received by the LookupDiscovery class. This is a *server_jvm_arg*.

net.jini.discovery.mtu

The size defined by this property is used as the packet size of the multicast request to discover a lookup service. The lower limit of this value is 512, and its upper limit is set by the operating system. The default value is 512. This is a *server_jvm_arg*.

net.jini.discovery.timeout

As part of the lookup request protocol, a unicast connection is made from the client or service to the lookup service. The socket connection involved in this unicast connection has a timeout value of one minute. This property defines the number of milliseconds for this timeout (the default value is 60,000 milliseconds). This is a *server_jvm_arg*.

net.jini.discovery.ttl

This property will set the TTL (time to live) value used in UDP multicast requests. This will affect the multicast announcement and multicast request protocols used by the lookup/discovery system. The TTL determines the number of routers that a multicast packet will be sent through. Each handling by a router is considered a hop, and this value is decremented with each hop. The default value is 15. This is a *server_jvm_arg*.

com.sun.jini.outrigger.backend.vm.options

This option only applies to the *FrontEndSpace*. The value of this property is treated as extra command line arguments for the backend process. This is a *server_jvm_arg*.

com.sun.jini.outrigger.java

> The property is used to specify the VM used to execute the backend process. This option only applies to the *FrontEndSpace*. This is a *server_jvm_arg*.

com.sun.jini.outrigger.backend.gcInterval

> This property controls how aggressive *outrigger* will be when garbage collecting the persistent store. This is a *server_jvm_arg*.

com.sun.jini.outrigger.basicspace.reapingInterval

> This property controls how often unused entry objects are reaped. The default value for this interval is 300000 milliseconds (five minutes). Reducing this value helps reduce the memory footprint of a heavily-loaded space. This is a *server_jvm_arg*.

reggie

Synopsis

```
java [setup_jvm_options] -jar $JINIHOME/lib/reggie.jar
        server_codebase policy_file log_directory
        [groups] [server_jvm] [server_jvm_args]
```

Description

reggie is Sun's implementation of the Jini lookup service. It is an activatable service, which means that it runs under the control of *rmid*. The command line for *reggie* is used to register it with *rmid* and to provide *rmid* with the options it should use to invoke the VM in which *reggie* will run.

Like all activatable services, two VMs are involved: the one which is used to register the service with *rmid*, and the one that *rmid* will start to run the service. These are referred to as the setup and server *VMs* respectively.

Options

setup_jvm_options

> The Java options used for the VM that will register the service with *rmid*. You may specify any option for the Java command here; you should specify a policy file (*-Djava.security.policy=somefile*) that has sufficient permissions to register a service with *rmid*.

-jar $JINIHOME/lib/reggie.jar

> The jar file containing the code for *reggie*.

server_codebase

> The argument that the server VM should use for the `java.rmi.server.codebase` property. This codebase must contain the *reggie-dl.jar* file, e.g., *http://server:8080/reggie-dl.jar*.

policy_file

The security policy that the server VM should run with by using the *-Djava.security.policy* property. This policy file must have sufficient permissions for *reggie* to run. An example policy file may be found in *$JINIHOME/example/lookup/policy.all*.

log_directory

The directory in which *reggie* will keep its persistent storage. If this directory exists, *reggie* will attempt to read the log files in that directory and recreate its previous state from that log.

groups

This optional argument specifies the groups that *reggie* should support. The default is to support the public group (i.e., the group " ", which is also specified as "public"). Multiple groups may be specified by separating the group names with a comma (e.g., "NY/02,public").

server_jvm

This optional argument specifies a path to the virtual machine used to run the service. The default is to use the command *java* in the user's PATH.

server_jvm_args

Any remaining arguments must start with a hyphen ("-"); they will be passed to the server VM. There may be multiple arguments here; in addition to passing arguments for the *java* command, you may specify system properties here.

System Properties

reggie uses properties to override the behavior of certain aspects of the lookup process. These properties are set by specifying *-DpropertyName=propertyValue* as a *server_jvm_arg*. The properties supported by *reggie* are:

com.sun.jini.reggie.unicastTimeout

As part of the discover protocol, a unicast connection is made to the client or server that is trying to discover the lookup service. This socket connection has a timeout value in milliseconds defined by this property (the default value is 60,000 milliseconds, or 1 minute).

com.sun.jini.reggie.proxy.debug

If this value is set to any value, the lookup's service proxy will send debugging information to System.err. Clients who set this property will obtain information on the execution of the lookup service.

net.jini.discovery.announce

This property defines the number of milliseconds in the interval to send out the multicast packet announcing the existence of the lookup service. The default value is 120,000 milliseconds, which means that *reggie* will send out multicast packets every two minutes to inform services of its existence.

net.jini.discovery.debug

If this property is set to any value, *reggie* will print to *System.err* any exceptions received by the LookupDiscovery class.

net.jini.discovery.mtu

The size defined by this property is used as the packet size of the multicast request to discover a lookup service. The lower limit of this value is 512, and its upper limit is set by the operating system. The default value is 512.

net.jini.discovery.ttl

This property will set the TTL (time to live) value used in UDP multicast requests. This will affect the multicast announcement and multicast request protocols used by the lookup/discovery system. The TTL determines the number of routers that a multicast packet will be sent through. Each handling by a router is considered a hop, and this value is decremented with each hop. The default value is 15.

CHAPTER 14

The com.sun.jini Packages

The com.sun.jini package hierarchy contains two types of packages. The first category includes packages that extend Jini's basic functionality at an API level. For the most part, these classes provide APIs that help developers write Jini services and clients by abstracting some of the low-level details of the core or extended Jini interfaces. This allows, for example, a service to discover and register with all lookup services on a local network simply by creating an object to perform that operation. Since most services don't need to interact with the lookup and discovery protocol at the level defined by the core Jini APIs, these helper classes are useful to a great many services.

The APIs in this category are not part of the official Jini specification, and there is no guarantee that they will continue to be distributed in the future or that they won't change. In fact, many of these APIs make up the proposed *Jini Technology Helper Utilities and Services Specification*, which is part of Jini 1.1. As this book goes to press, this specification is in alpha review. That means that many of the APIs in this category may go through changes during the specification process; it also means that the APIs in this category may never become official Jini APIs. In general, in Jini 1.1 you can expect to see several of the classes described in this section moved into the net.jini package, and generally with the same interface. The class diagram for each package are based on 1.1; the classes that have moved are marked as deprecated.

Because these APIs are implemented completely in Java, however, you can use them without concern: if they become official APIs, you can migrate your services and clients to use them as you need to, or you can continue to use their current implementation simply by downloading the code to your service or client.

The packages that fall into this first category are:

- com.sun.jini.admin

- com.sun.jini.collections

- com.sun.jini.constants

- com.sun.jini.debug

- com.sun.jini.discovery

- com.sun.jini.lease

- com.sun.jini.lease.landlord

- com.sun.jini.lookup

- com.sun.jini.lookup.entry

- com.sun.jini.proxy

- com.sun.jini.reliableLog

- com.sun.jini.system

- com.sun.jini.thread

In this chapter, we'll provide a quick reference for all of these packages.

The second category of packages includes the code that provides Sun's implementation of core Jini services: the Jini lookup service, the Jini transaction manager, parts of the JavaSpaces service, and so on. We will not provide a quick reference for these packages, because they do not include code that you would commonly use in your own service or client. If you're really interested in writing your own Jini lookup service, the code in these packages may be of use to you, but an examination of writing such services is beyond the scope of this book.

Hence, we will not look into the following packages:

- com.sun.jini.example (implementations of the Jini browser and start services GUI)

- com.sun.jini.fiddler (an implementation of the Jini lookup discovery service; 1.1 only)

- com.sun.jini.mahalo (an implementation of the Jini transaction manager)

- com.sun.jini.mahout (utilities for *outrigger*, *mahalo*, and *reggie*)

- com.sun.jini.mercury (an implementation of the Jini event mailbox service; 1.1 only)

- com.sun.jini.norm (an implementation of the Jini lease renewal service; 1.1 only)

- com.sun.jini.outrigger (parts of Sun's implementation of the JavaSpaces service)

- com.sun.jini.reggie (an implementation of the Jini lookup service)

The com.sun.jini.admin Package

The com.sun.jini.admin package defines two interfaces for administrable services. Services that implement an administrable interface are encouraged to implement both of these interfaces as well. To test if a particular administration object (returned from the net.jini.admin.Administrable.getAdmin( ) method) implements one of these interfaces, use the instanceof operator. If the object implements the interface in question, cast the object to the interface type and invoke the desired methods on the object.

Figure 14-1 shows the class hierarchy for this package. Use the DestroyAdmin interface to allow clients to destroy (completely remove) your service; use the StorageLocationAdmin interface to allow clients to change the location where the service keeps its persistent storage.

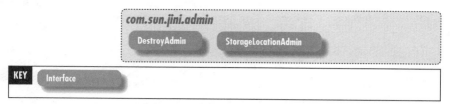

Figure 14–1: The com.sun.jini.admin package

DestroyAdmin   Jini 1.0
com.sun.jini.admin

A client that wants to destroy a service invokes the destroy( ) method on the service's administrable object. On the server side, the implementation of this method is required to delete all persistent storage associated with the service, unregister the service from the RMI activation framework (if applicable), and exit the VM that the service is running in.

Note that the server-side implementation of the destroy( ) method cannot afford to exit the VM immediately; that would cause the client to receive a RemoteException since the call into the service will not complete. The destroy( ) method typically arranges to start another thread that exits the VM after allowing a few seconds for the method invocation to complete.

```
public interface DestroyAdmin {
// Public Instance Methods
    public abstract void destroy() throws java.rmi.RemoteException;
}
```

StorageLocationAdmin   Jini 1.0
com.sun.jini.admin

This interface allows administrative clients to specify the location where a service keeps its persistent data. The argument to the setStorageLocation( ) method should be the name of a directory that should be used for the service's persistent storage.

This method should create a new log in the given directory and make a snapshot to that log. Only after that succeeds should it destroy the original log. Activatable services must construct a new activation descriptor and use the setActivationDesc( ) method of the java.rmi.activation.ActivationSystem class to arrange for the new string to be passed as its marshalled data.

```
public interface StorageLocationAdmin {
// Public Instance Methods
    public abstract String getStorageLocation() throws java.rmi.RemoteException;
    public abstract void setStorageLocation(String location) throws java.io.IOException, java.rmi.RemoteException;
}
```

The com.sun.jini.collection Package

The com.sun.jini.collection package defines new collection-style classes that are useful for the Jini framework. These classes do not implement the java.util.Collection interface; they cannot be used as a general collection class.

Figure 14-2 shows the class hierarchy for this package. The FastList class is self-contained, but the remaining classes rely upon the java.lang.ref.WeakReference class. A weak reference is like any other Java object reference, except that the garbage collector (if it is pressed for memory) may free an object that only has weak references.

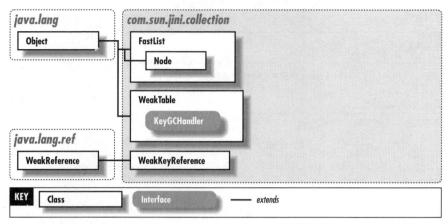

Figure 14–2: The com.sun.jini.collection package

FastList

com.sun.jini.collection

This class implements a doubly-linked list. It is faster than other implementations of linked lists because it uses "weak" synchronization: no synchronization is performed when nodes are read out of the list.

A thread is free to delete a node from the list even while another thread is iterating through the list; developers must explicitly synchronize a node in order to prevent it from being deleted. Similarly, a thread that walks through the list deleting nodes must check the return value of the remove( ) method, since it is possible for two threads to remove a node at the same time. A false value indicates that another thread has already removed the node.

At any point in time, the list may maintain references to nodes that have been removed from the list. These nodes are automatically deleted when the list is traversed (using methods of the FastList.Node class). In 1.0, you may reap these nodes explicitly with the reapAll( ) method or arrange for a daemon thread to periodically remove them with the globalReap( ) method; this latter methods affects all instances of the FastList class. Global reaping was deprecated in 1.0.1.

A fast list holds objects of type FastList.Node; that class contains the iteration methods for the list. By default, nodes are added to the end of the list.

```
public class FastList {
// Public Constructors
    public FastList();
// Inner Classes
    public static class Node;
// Public Instance Methods
    public void add(FastList.Node node);
    public void addAfter(FastList.Node after, FastList.Node node);
    public void dump(java.io.PrintWriter out);
    public FastList.Node head();
```

```
    public void reap();
    public final int reapCnt();
    public boolean remove(FastList.Node node);
    public FastList.Node tail();
}
```

FastList.Node

com.sun.jini.collection

This class represents objects that can be held in a FastList. Since there is no place in this class to hold data, you will usually subclass it. Iteration through the list occurs using the methods of this class.

```
public static class FastList.Node {
// Public Constructors
    public Node();
// Public Instance Methods
    public final FastList.Node next();
    public final FastList.Node prev();
    public final boolean removed();
// Public Instance Fields
    public FastList.Node next;
}
```

Passed To: FastList.{add(), addAfter(), remove()}

Returned By: FastList.{head(), tail()}, FastList.Node.{next(), prev()}

Type Of: FastList.Node.next

WeakKeyReference

com.sun.jini.collection

This class allows keys that are weak references to be held in java.util.Collection objects by correctly implementing the hashValue() and equals() methods to refer to the key (rather than to the reference).

```
public class WeakKeyReference extends java.lang.ref.WeakReference {
// Public Constructors
    public WeakKeyReference(Object key);
    public WeakKeyReference(Object key, java.lang.ref.ReferenceQueue refQueue);
// Public Methods Overriding Object
    public boolean equals(Object other);
    public int hashCode();
}
```

Hierarchy: Object→ java.lang.ref.Reference→ java.lang.ref.WeakReference→ WeakKeyReference

WeakTable

com.sun.jini.collection

This class creates an internal table that maps a weak key reference to a weak object reference. Objects are added to the table with the getOrAdd() method: if the key passed to that method is already in the table, the method returns the object associated with the key. Otherwise, it updates the table to map the key to the proxy and returns the proxy.

```
public class WeakTable {
// Public Constructors
```

```
   public WeakTable();
   public WeakTable(WeakTable.KeyGCHandler handler);
// Inner Classes
   public static interface KeyGCHandler;
// Public Instance Methods
1.1 public Object get(Object key);                                    synchronized
   public Object getOrAdd(Object key, Object proxy);                  synchronized
   public Object remove(Object key);                                  synchronized
   public void removeBlanks();                                        synchronized
}
```

WeakTable.KeyGCHandler   Jini 1.0

com.sun.jini.collection

If you need to know when a key in a WeakTable has been removed, create an object that implements this interface and pass that object to the constructor of the WeakTable() class. If the object that a weak key references is garbage collected, the key will be removed from the table at some point. When that happens, the weak reference to the value in the table is retrieved; if that weak reference points to a still-valid object, the keyGC() method will be called with the strongly-referenced value as its parameter.

```
public static interface WeakTable.KeyGCHandler {
// Public Instance Methods
   public abstract void keyGC(Object value);
}
```

Passed To: WeakTable.WeakTable()

The com.sun.jini.constants Package

The com.sun.jini.constants package contains classes that define constants useful in the Jini environment. Figure 14-3 shows the class hierarchy for this package.

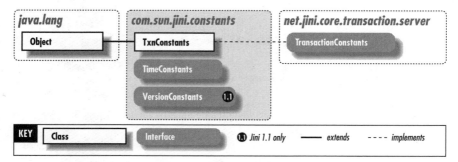

Figure 14-3: The com.sun.jini.constants package

TimeConstants   Jini 1.0

com.sun.jini.constants

This interface contains constants in terms of milliseconds. These constants can be used in calls to Thread.sleep( ) or in methods that deal with lease times.

```
public interface TimeConstants {
// Public Constants
```

public static final long **DAYS**;	=86400000
public static final long **HOURS**;	=3600000
public static final long **MINUTES**;	=60000
public static final long **SECONDS**;	=1000
}	

Implementations: com.sun.jini.thread.RetryTask, com.sun.jini.thread.WakeupManager

TxnConstants
Jini 1.0

com.sun.jini.constants

This class provides a mapping between the integer state values defined in the net.jini.core.transaction.server.TransactionConstants interface and human-readable strings. For example, calling the getName(ABORTED) method will return the string "aborted."

See also net.jini.core.transaction.server.TransactionConstants.

```
public class TxnConstants implements net.jini.core.transaction.server.TransactionConstants {
// Public Constructors
    public TxnConstants();
// Public Class Methods
    public static String getName(int state);
}
```

Hierarchy: Object→ TxnConstants(net.jini.core.transaction.server.TransactionConstants)

VersionConstants
Jini 1.1 Alpha

com.sun.jini.constants

This interface defines a string that indicates the version of the Jini API that is in use.

```
public interface VersionConstants {
// Public Constants
    public static final String SERVER_VERSION;                              ="1.1 alpha"
}
```

The com.sun.jini.debug Package

The com.sun.jini.debug package contains a single class that defines a property-enabled tracing facility. Figure 14-4 shows the class hierarchy for this package.

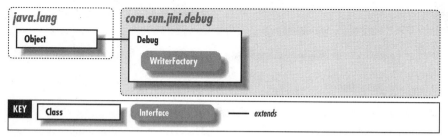

Figure 14-4: The com.sun.jini.debug package

Debug

Jini 1.0

com.sun.jini.debug

This class implements a tracing facility. Tracing is based on a *property name* and *subsystem*: an application uses the property name to construct the Debug object and the subsystem name as the argument to the getWriter( ) method. If the returned Writer object is not null, the application should print output to it.

Tracing for a particular property name and subsystem is enabled through command-line properties that set the property name to the list of subsystems for which to enable tracing. The subsystem may optionally specify a particular file name by following it with a colon; otherwise, data will be sent to System.out. Given the property:

```
-DmyServiceDebug=init:init.log,term
```

A Debug object constructed with the string *myServiceDebug* will return a writer to the *init.log* file when the getWriter( ) method is called with the string *init;* a writer to System.out when that method is called with the string *term*; and null in all other cases.

```
public class Debug {
// Public Constructors
    public Debug(String propertyName);
    public Debug(String propertyName, Debug.WriterFactory factory);
// Inner Classes
    public static interface WriterFactory;
// Public Instance Methods
    public String getPropertyName();
    public java.io.PrintWriter getWriter(String subsystem);
// Public Methods Overriding Object
    public String toString();
}
```

Debug.WriterFactory

Jini 1.0

com.sun.jini.debug

By default, the Debug class generates PrintStream objects for a given subsystem according to the rules outlined above. If you want to use a different set of rules to generate those objects, create an object that implements this interface and pass it to the constructor of the Debug class. The WriterFactory is responsible for creating the correct PrintWriter object for the given subsystem and argument. The *arg* parameter will be the string in the debug property following a colon (e.g., log for -DjavaDebug=init:log); if no argument is given for a particular subsystem then the *arg* parameter will be the empty string.

```
public static interface Debug.WriterFactory {
// Public Instance Methods
    public abstract java.io.PrintWriter writer(String subsystem, String arg) throws java.io.IOException;
}
```

Passed To: Debug.Debug()

The com.sun.jini.discovery Package

The com.sun.jini.discovery package contains a single class that provides a utility class used with the unicast discovery protocol. Figure 14-5 shows its class hierarchy.

Figure 14–5: The com.sun.jini.discovery package

LookupLocatorDiscovery
Jini 1.0; Deprecated in Jini 1.1 Alpha

com.sun.jini.discovery

This class uses a daemon thread to find the lookup service at each specified net.jini.core.discovery.LookupLocator. The daemon thread calls the getServiceRegistrar( ) method of each lookup locator. After constructing the LookupLocatorDiscovery object, the service should add to it a net.jini.discovery.DiscoveryListener object. The listener will be called immediately with an event containing the list of all registrars that the background thread has already discovered, and it will be called with additional events each time the background thread locates a new registrar.

When the service receives an error while talking to a particular registrar, it should call the discard( ) method with that registrar. The discovery listener will also be notified whenever a service registrar is discarded.

The daemon threads of this class are stopped when the terminate( ) method is called. After this method has been called, no further operations should be performed on the LookupLocatorDiscovery object.

See also net.jini.discovery.LookupLocatorDiscovery.

```
public final class LookupLocatorDiscovery {
// Public Constructors
    public LookupLocatorDiscovery(net.jini.core.discovery.LookupLocator[ ] locators);
// Event Registration Methods (by event name)
    public void addDiscoveryListener(net.jini.discovery.DiscoveryListener l);
    public void removeDiscoveryListener(net.jini.discovery.DiscoveryListener l);              synchronized
// Property Accessor Methods (by property name)
    public net.jini.core.discovery.LookupLocator[ ] getDiscoveredLocators();                 synchronized
    public net.jini.core.discovery.LookupLocator[ ] getLocators();                           synchronized
    public void setLocators(net.jini.core.discovery.LookupLocator[ ] locators);
    public net.jini.core.discovery.LookupLocator[ ] getUndiscoveredLocators();               synchronized
// Public Instance Methods
    public void addLocators(net.jini.core.discovery.LookupLocator[ ] locators);              synchronized
    public void discard(net.jini.core.lookup.ServiceRegistrar proxy);
    public void removeLocators(net.jini.core.discovery.LookupLocator[ ] locators);
    public void terminate();                                                                 synchronized
}
```

The com.sun.jini.lease Package

The com.sun.jini.lease package contains lease-related classes. Most of these classes are used by the com.sun.jini.lease.landlord package to implement the landlord leasing protocol; they can also be used in other leasing protocols that you might devise. Figure 14-6 shows the class hierarchy for this package.

The AbstractLease and AbstractLeaseMap classes provide the basis of a lease implementation. The LeaseRenewalManager provides a generic mechanism to renew any lease

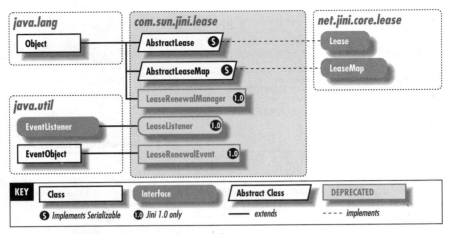

Figure 14–6: The com.sun.jini.lease package

continually; it uses the LeaseListener and LeaseEvent classes to pass events based upon the failure to renew a lease.

AbstractLease   Jini 1.0

com.sun.jini.lease   *serializable*

This class provides the following basic lease features:

- It stores the expiration time of the lease.

- It serializes the lease expiration. By default, the serialization format is Lease.DURA-TION, which means that the lease expiration is serialized as a relative value. This is the preferred format, since it means that the clocks between the two systems do not need to be synchronized.

- It provides an implementation of the renew( ) method that correctly takes into account the possibility of overflow of the lease expiration time. However, the actual renewal of the lease is deferred to the abstract doRenew( ) method.

The remaining methods of the net.jini.core.lease.Lease interface remain undefined; it is the responsibility of the concrete subclass to implement those methods.

```
public abstract class AbstractLease implements net.jini.core.lease.Lease, Serializable {
// Protected Constructors
    protected AbstractLease(long expiration);
// Methods Implementing Lease
    public abstract boolean canBatch(net.jini.core.lease.Lease lease);
    public abstract void cancel() throws net.jini.core.lease.UnknownLeaseException, java.rmi.RemoteException;
    public abstract net.jini.core.lease.LeaseMap createLeaseMap(long duration);
    public long getExpiration();
    public int getSerialFormat();
    public void renew(long duration) throws net.jini.core.lease.UnknownLeaseException,
        net.jini.core.lease.LeaseDeniedException, java.rmi.RemoteException;
    public void setSerialFormat(int format);
// Protected Instance Methods
    protected abstract long doRenew(long duration) throws net.jini.core.lease.UnknownLeaseException,
        net.jini.core.lease.LeaseDeniedException, java.rmi.RemoteException;
```

```
// Protected Instance Fields
    protected transient long expiration;
    protected int serialFormat;
}
```

Hierarchy: Object→ AbstractLease(net.jini.core.lease.Lease, Serializable)

Subclasses: com.sun.jini.lease.landlord.LandlordLease

AbstractLeaseMap

Jini 1.0

com.sun.jini.lease

serializable collection

This class provides the basis of an implementation of the net.jini.core.lease.LeaseMap interface. This class implements all the methods specified by the Map interface; concrete
subclasses of this class are required to implement the methods specified by the
LeaseMap interface.

```
public abstract class AbstractLeaseMap implements net.jini.core.lease.LeaseMap, Serializable {
// Protected Constructors
    protected AbstractLeaseMap(net.jini.core.lease.Lease lease, long duration);
    protected AbstractLeaseMap(java.util.Map map, net.jini.core.lease.Lease lease, long duration);
// Protected Class Methods
    protected static void checkValue(Object value);
// Methods Implementing LeaseMap
    public abstract void cancelAll() throws net.jini.core.lease.LeaseMapException, java.rmi.RemoteException;
    public abstract boolean canContainKey(Object key);
    public abstract void renewAll() throws net.jini.core.lease.LeaseMapException, java.rmi.RemoteException;
// Methods Implementing Map
    public void clear();
    public boolean containsKey(Object key);
    public boolean containsValue(Object value);
    public java.util.Set entrySet();
    public boolean equals(Object o);
    public Object get(Object key);
    public int hashCode();
    public boolean isEmpty();
    public java.util.Set keySet();
    public Object put(Object key, Object value);
    public void putAll(java.util.Map m);
    public Object remove(Object key);
    public int size();
    public java.util.Collection values();
// Protected Instance Methods
    protected void checkKey(Object key);
// Protected Instance Fields
    protected final java.util.Map map;
}
```

Hierarchy: Object→ AbstractLeaseMap(net.jini.core.lease.LeaseMap(java.util.Map), Serializable)

Subclasses: com.sun.jini.lease.landlord.LandlordLeaseMap

LeaseListener

Jini 1.0; Deprecated in Jini 1.1 Alpha

com.sun.jini.lease

event listener

This interface defines a listener for lease renewals. When used in conjunction with the
LeaseRenewalManager class, the notify() method of an object that implements this interface
is called when a lease under management fails to renew.

See also net.jini.lease.LeaseListener.

```
public interface LeaseListener extends java.util.EventListener {
// Public Instance Methods
    public abstract void notify(com.sun.jini.lease.LeaseRenewalEvent e);
}
```

Hierarchy: (com.sun.jini.lease.LeaseListener(java.util.EventListener))

Passed To: com.sun.jini.lease.LeaseRenewalManager.{LeaseRenewalManager(), renewFor(), renewUntil()}

LeaseRenewalEvent

Jini 1.0; Deprecated in Jini 1.1 Alpha

com.sun.jini.lease

serializable event

This event class provides the implementation of the lease event that is delivered by the LeaseRenewalManager class. This class is only used to indicate lease renewal failures; the LeaseRenewalManager class does not deliver any event when a lease is renewed.

The getSource( ) method will return the lease renewal manager that was responsible for the lease that failed to renew; other pertinent information is encapsulated into the event itself.

See also net.jini.lease.LeaseRenewalEvent.

```
public class LeaseRenewalEvent extends java.util.EventObject {
// Public Constructors
    public LeaseRenewalEvent(com.sun.jini.lease.LeaseRenewalManager source, net.jini.core.lease.Lease lease,
                    long expiration, Exception ex);
// Property Accessor Methods (by property name)
    public Exception getException();
    public long getExpiration();
    public net.jini.core.lease.Lease getLease();
}
```

Hierarchy: Object→ java.util.EventObject(Serializable) → com.sun.jini.lease.LeaseRenewalEvent

Passed To: com.sun.jini.lease.LeaseListener.notify()

LeaseRenewalManager

Jini 1.0; Deprecated in Jini 1.1 Alpha

com.sun.jini.lease

Instances of this class may be used to renew one or more leases automatically. Lease renewal operations occur in a daemon thread that is managed by this class. You may request that a lease be renewed for a particular duration (via the renewFor( ) method) or until a particular point of time (via the renewUntil( ) method). The manager will renew the lease as often as needed to satisfy the request.

The lease renewal manager will renew a lease early in order to account for network delays. The details of this are specific to the implementation of this class and vary according to the duration of the lease; a lease is renewed on the following schedule:

- Immediately if the lease expires in the next 10 seconds

- 10 seconds early if the lease expires in the next 20 seconds

- In half the lease duration if the lease expires in the next 80 seconds

- In seven-eighths of the lease duration if the lease expires in the next week

- A day early if the lease expires in the next two weeks

- Three days early if none of the previous conditions apply

There is a bug in the 1.0 implementation of the renewFor( ) method: do not use Lease.FOREVER to specify the duration of the lease; use the renewUntil(. . . , Lease.FOREVER, . . .) method instead. This bug is fixed in 1.0.1.

When the lease renewal manager attempts to renew a particular lease, it will check its list of leases for any others that can be batched into a lease map with the expiring lease and that also need to be renewed within the next five minutes. A new lease map is created containing these leases, and they are renewed in a single call to the service.

See also net.jini.lease.LeaseRenewalManager.

```
public class LeaseRenewalManager {
// Public Constructors
    public LeaseRenewalManager();
    public LeaseRenewalManager(net.jini.core.lease.Lease lease, long expiration,
                               com.sun.jini.lease.LeaseListener listener);
// Public Instance Methods
    public void cancel(net.jini.core.lease.Lease lease) throws net.jini.core.lease.UnknownLeaseException,
        java.rmi.RemoteException;
    public void clear();                                                             synchronized
    public long getExpiration(net.jini.core.lease.Lease lease)                       synchronized
        throws net.jini.core.lease.UnknownLeaseException;
    public void remove(net.jini.core.lease.Lease lease)                              synchronized
        throws net.jini.core.lease.UnknownLeaseException;
    public void renewFor(net.jini.core.lease.Lease lease, long duration, com.sun.jini.lease.LeaseListener listener);
    public void renewUntil(net.jini.core.lease.Lease lease, long expiration, com.sun.jini.lease.LeaseListener listener);
    public void setExpiration(net.jini.core.lease.Lease lease, long expiration)      synchronized
        throws net.jini.core.lease.UnknownLeaseException;
}
```

Passed To: com.sun.jini.lease.LeaseRenewalEvent.LeaseRenewalEvent(), com.sun.jini.lookup.JoinManager.JoinManager()

The com.sun.jini.lease.landlord Package

The com.sun.jini.lease.landlord package contains the server-side implementation of Sun's landlord leasing protocol. Services can use these classes if they need to grant leases to their clients, though the client sees only an object that implements the net.jini.core.lease.Lease interface. Figure 14-7 shows the class hierarchy for this package.

A service that wants to grant leases that participate in the landlord leasing protocol must do the following:

- Define a method in their service interface that returns the lease to the client. This is often done as part of a service registration class where the lease is an instance variable within the class.

- Implement the method that returns the lease to the client. Creating the lease can be accomplished by:

    - Creating an object that implements the LeasedResource interface to hold client-specific data.

    - Using a LeaseDurationPolicy object to create a new lease associated with that leased resource.

The lease can then be returned directly or as part of the service interface.

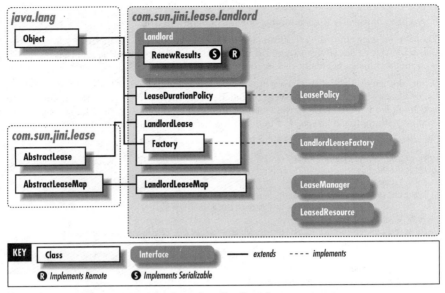

Figure 14-7: The com.sun.jini.lease.landlord package

- Define a Remote object that implements the Landlord interface. This object will be called by the client whenever the client wants to renew or cancel a lease (or a set of leases). The landlord should forward the renewals of the lease to the LeaseDurationPolicy object.

- Optionally, create an object that implements the LeaseManager interface to be notified when leases are created and renewed.

Use of the LeaseDurationPolicy class is optional; the service can choose to implement all the details of lease creation and renewal itself.

Landlord   Jini 1.0

com.sun.jini.lease.landlord   *remote*

Implementations of this interface receive lease messages from clients. The messages follow a predictable path: the renew( ) method of the Lease object calls the renew( ) method of the Landlord object, the renewAll( ) method of the LeaseMap object calls the renewAll( ) method of the Landlord object, and so on.

The methods of this class all receive a parameter of type Object; this parameter is the object passed as the first parameter when the LandlordLease object was created. This, in turn, is typically the cookie object of the LeasedResource class that is associated with the lease.

When the landlord cancels multiple leases in the cancelAll( ) method, it must throw a LeaseMapException if cancelling any lease failed. The exception is constructed with a Map object that maps cookies to exceptions. The LandlordLeaseMap class will turn this into an object that maps leases to exceptions; that object is returned so that the client can find out the particular exception for a particular lease by examining the map.

```
public interface Landlord extends java.rmi.Remote {
// Inner Classes
    public static class RenewResults implements Serializable;
// Public Instance Methods
    public abstract void cancel(Object cookie) throws net.jini.core.lease.UnknownLeaseException,
        java.rmi.RemoteException;
    public abstract void cancelAll(Object[ ] cookie) throws net.jini.core.lease.LeaseMapException,
        java.rmi.RemoteException;
    public abstract long renew(Object cookie, long extension) throws net.jini.core.lease.LeaseDeniedException,
        net.jini.core.lease.UnknownLeaseException, java.rmi.RemoteException;
    public abstract Landlord.RenewResults renewAll(Object[ ] cookie, long[ ] extension)
        throws java.rmi.RemoteException;
}
```

Hierarchy: (Landlord(java.rmi.Remote))

Passed To: LandlordLease.Factory.newLease(), LandlordLeaseFactory.newLease(),
LeaseDurationPolicy.LeaseDurationPolicy()

Landlord.RenewResults

Jini 1.0

serializable

When the landlord renews multiple leases in the renewAll( ) method, it must return an
instance of this class. The granted array holds the actual duration granted for each lease;
for leases that failed to renew, that duration must be set to –1. The denied array holds
one entry for each lease that failed to renew: if leases 1 and 3 failed to renew, then
denied[0] would be the exception for lease 1 and denied[1] would be the exception for
lease 3.

```
public static class Landlord.RenewResults implements Serializable {
// Public Constructors
    public RenewResults(long[ ] granted);
    public RenewResults(long[ ] granted, Exception[ ] denied);
// Public Instance Fields
    public Exception[ ] denied;
    public long[ ] granted;
}
```

Returned By: Landlord.renewAll()

LandlordLease

com.sun.jini.lease.landlord

Jini 1.0

serializable

Instances of this class are usually created by the LeasePolicy class; this is transparent to
the service developer. A LandlordLease object contains a reference to the landlord that
created it; most of the methods of this class are implemented by calling an appropriate
method of the embedded landlord. Landlord lease objects will return true from the
canBatch( ) method if their embedded landlord is the same.

```
public class LandlordLease extends com.sun.jini.lease.AbstractLease {
// No Constructor
// Inner Classes
    public static class Factory implements LandlordLeaseFactory;
// Public Methods Overriding AbstractLease
    public boolean canBatch(net.jini.core.lease.Lease lease);
    public void cancel() throws net.jini.core.lease.UnknownLeaseException, java.rmi.RemoteException;
    public net.jini.core.lease.LeaseMap createLeaseMap(long duration);
```

```
// Protected Methods Overriding AbstractLease
    protected long doRenew(long renewDuration) throws net.jini.core.lease.LeaseDeniedException,
        net.jini.core.lease.UnknownLeaseException, java.rmi.RemoteException;
// Public Methods Overriding Object
    public boolean equals(Object other);
    public int hashCode();
    public String toString();
}
```

Hierarchy: Object→ com.sun.jini.lease.AbstractLease(net.jini.core.lease.Lease, Serializable) →
LandlordLease

LandlordLease.Factory   Jini 1.0
com.sun.jini.lease.landlord

This class implements the LandlordLeaseFactory interface and is the mechanism by which
new LandlordLease objects are created. This is the default class that is used (transparently
to the developer) by the LeasePolicy class to create new leases.

```
public static class LandlordLease.Factory implements LandlordLeaseFactory {
// Public Constructors
    public Factory();
// Methods Implementing LandlordLeaseFactory
    public net.jini.core.lease.Lease newLease(Object cookie, Landlord landlord, long expiration);
}
```

LandlordLeaseFactory   Jini 1.0
com.sun.jini.lease.landlord

This interface defines a mechanism for creating new leases. These leases must follow
the landlord protocol, though strictly speaking they need not be an instance of the
LandlordLease class. Developers will rarely need to work with this interface directly; it is
generally used by implementations of the LeasePolicy interface.

```
public interface LandlordLeaseFactory {
// Public Instance Methods
    public abstract net.jini.core.lease.Lease newLease(Object cookie, Landlord landlord, long duration)
        throws net.jini.core.lease.LeaseDeniedException;
}
```

Implementations: LandlordLease.Factory

Passed To: LeaseDurationPolicy.LeaseDurationPolicy()

LandlordLeaseMap   Jini 1.0
com.sun.jini.lease.landlord   *serializable collection*

This class provides a concrete implementation of the net.jini.core.lease.LeaseMap interface.
Instances of this class are created by the createLeaseMap( ) method of the LandlordLease
class. Since its constructor is package protected, you cannot create instances of this
class directly, nor can you use this class as the basis of your own lease map class.

This class contains the necessary logic to convert between the landlord interface and
the net.jini.core.lease.LeaseMap interface. In particular, the renewAll( ) method will convert
the Landlord.RenewResults object it receives into the appropriate LeaseMapException.

```
public class LandlordLeaseMap extends com.sun.jini.lease.AbstractLeaseMap {
// No Constructor
```

```
// Public Methods Overriding AbstractLeaseMap
    public void cancelAll() throws net.jini.core.lease.LeaseMapException, java.rmi.RemoteException;
    public boolean canContainKey(Object key);
    public void renewAll() throws net.jini.core.lease.LeaseMapException, java.rmi.RemoteException;
}
```

Hierarchy: Object→
com.sun.jini.lease.AbstractLeaseMap(net.jini.core.lease.LeaseMap(java.util.Map), Serializable) →
LandlordLeaseMap

LeasedResource

Jini 1.0

com.sun.jini.lease.landlord

Classes that implement this interface are used to associate data specific to a particular lease with the lease itself. The cookie held by this class is an object that must uniquely identify a particular lease—the cookie is passed between the lease holder and the landlord, so the landlord must be able to use the cookie to find all the data it needs about a particular lease.

The expiration time that is held by the leased resource is the same as the expiration time of the lease itself. When a lease is renewed, the expiration time of the leased resource must be updated as well as the expiration time within the lease, but in standard usage this all happens transparently: the renew() method of the LandlordLease class sets the lease's expiration time, and the renew() method of the LeaseDurationPolicy sets the resource's expiration time.

```
public interface LeasedResource {
// Public Instance Methods
    public abstract Object getCookie();
    public abstract long getExpiration();
    public abstract void setExpiration(long newExpiration);
}
```

Passed To: LeaseDurationPolicy.{calculateDuration(), ensureCurrent(), leaseFor(), renew()},
LeaseManager.{register(), renewed()}, LeasePolicy.{ensureCurrent(), leaseFor(), renew()}

LeaseDurationPolicy

Jini 1.0

com.sun.jini.lease.landlord

This class provides the standard implementation of the LeasePolicy interface. Services that want to issue leases that use the landlord protocol can instantiate a LeaseDurationPolicy object and call its leaseFor() method to create LandlordLease objects. The leaseFor() method uses the LandlordLeaseFactory object passed to the constructor of this class to create the lease; in typical usage, that argument is null, in which case an internal instance of the LandlordLease.Factory class will be used.

The landlord should forward requests to renew a lease to the renew() method of this class. The policy for this class has two values: a default and a maximum duration. The default time will be used any time that Lease.ANY is specified as the duration for creating or renewing a lease. The maximum time will be used any time that Lease.FOREVER is specified; it will also be used any time a requested duration exceeds the maximum duration.

If a lease manager is passed to the constructor of this class, the register() method of that manager will be called every time a lease is handed out from the leaseFor() method. The manager's renewed() method will be called every time a lease is successfully renewed.

The LeaseDurationPolicy class does not automatically cancel leases when they expire. If a client attempts to renew an expired lease, an exception will be thrown at that point, but otherwise the policy class will hold all leases internally. If explicit lease cancellation is required, you must write a separate class to do that (using the LeaseManager interface to know when leases have been renewed and created).

```
public class LeaseDurationPolicy implements LeasePolicy {
// Public Constructors
    public LeaseDurationPolicy(long maximum, long defaultLength, Landlord landlord, LeaseManager mgr,
                    LandlordLeaseFactory factory);
// Methods Implementing LeasePolicy
    public boolean ensureCurrent(LeasedResource resource);
    public net.jini.core.lease.Lease leaseFor(LeasedResource resource, long requestedDuration)
        throws net.jini.core.lease.LeaseDeniedException;
    public long renew(LeasedResource resource, long requestedDuration);
// Protected Instance Methods
    protected long calculateDuration(LeasedResource resource, long requestedDuration);
    protected long currentTime();
}
```

Hierarchy: Object→ LeaseDurationPolicy(LeasePolicy)

LeaseManager   Jini 1.0

com.sun.jini.lease.landlord

The LeaseManager interface is used by the LeasePolicy class to notify interested parties that a particular lease has been created or renewed. Notification in this case does not imply Java's normal event mechanism: the LeaseManager is not a listener class, and it does not receive events (distributed or local). Instead, the lease manager is passed to the constructor of the lease policy, which then directly invokes the appropriate methods on it at the appropriate times.

```
public interface LeaseManager {
// Public Instance Methods
    public abstract void register(LeasedResource resource, long duration);
    public abstract void renewed(LeasedResource resource, long duration, long oldExpiration);
}
```

Passed To: LeaseDurationPolicy.LeaseDurationPolicy()

LeasePolicy   Jini 1.0

com.sun.jini.lease.landlord

This interface simplifies the implementation of landlords, since it allows the landlord to defer lease creation and renewal to another object. The policy object can contain the necessary information about how leases should be created and renewed; for example, the policy object could contain logic such that a particular lease can only be renewed five times. Separating this interface allows the developer to substitute a different policy without changing the implementation of the landlord.

The renew( ) method must calculate the renewal time for the lease based upon its own internal logic and the requested lease duration; this renewal time must be returned to the landlord. The lease policy is also responsible for setting the new expiration of the leased resource after it renews a lease.

```
public interface LeasePolicy {
// Public Instance Methods
    public abstract boolean ensureCurrent(LeasedResource resource);
```

```
     public abstract net.jini.core.lease.Lease leaseFor(LeasedResource resource, long requestedDuration)
          throws net.jini.core.lease.LeaseDeniedException;
     public abstract long renew(LeasedResource resource, long requestedDuration)
          throws net.jini.core.lease.LeaseDeniedException, net.jini.core.lease.UnknownLeaseException;
}
```

Implementations: LeaseDurationPolicy

The com.sun.jini.lookup Package

The com.sun.jini.lookup package contains utilities that help to manage Jini's lookup and discovery protocol. Figure 14-8 shows the class hierarchy for this package.

Figure 14–8: The com.sun.jini.lookup package

The JoinManager class manages the lookup and discovery protocol. It provides a simple way for services to discover lookup services, register with those services, and automatically renew their lease to each lookup service. The ServiceIDListener class can be used to find out which ID the lookup service assigned to the service; this ID should be saved and used the next time the service creates a JoinManager object.

JoinManager
Jini 1.0; Deprecated in Jini 1.1 Alpha

com.sun.jini.lookup

The join manager participates in the multicast discovery protocol and discovers all lookup services on its local network (or possibly farther, if multicast routing is in effect). In addition, it participates in the unicast discovery protocol with the lookup service represented by each lookup locator. So the join manager finds lookup services both dynamically and statically. The join manager then joins each lookup service it finds.

The set of lookup services to discover by unicast discovery can be changed via the addLocators( ), removeLocators( ), and setLocators( ) methods. The groups which the lookup service must support can by changed via the addGroups( ), removeGroups( ), and setGroups( ) methods. In either case, the service is automatically registered with any new or removed from any discarded lookup services.

The join manager automatically renews the lease to any lookup service it registers with. If you construct the join manager with a com.sun.jini.lease.LeaseRenewalManager object, that manager will be used to perform the renewals. If you pass null as the lease renewal manager, the join manager will construct a new LeaseRenewalManager object to use for that purpose.

The join manager also propagates to all discovered lookup services any changes to a service's attributes that are are result of the addAttributes( ) or modifyAttributes( ) methods.

See also net.jini.lookup.JoinManager.

```
public class JoinManager {
// Public Constructors
    public JoinManager(Object obj, net.jini.core.entry.Entry[ ] attrSets, com.sun.jini.lookup.ServiceIDListener callback,
                com.sun.jini.lease.LeaseRenewalManager leaseMgr) throws java.io.IOException;
    public JoinManager(net.jini.core.lookup.ServiceID serviceID, Object obj, net.jini.core.entry.Entry[ ] attrSets,
                String[ ] groups, net.jini.core.discovery.LookupLocator[ ] locators,
                com.sun.jini.lease.LeaseRenewalManager leaseMgr) throws java.io.IOException;
    public JoinManager(Object obj, net.jini.core.entry.Entry[ ] attrSets, String[ ] groups,
                net.jini.core.discovery.LookupLocator[ ] locators,
                com.sun.jini.lookup.ServiceIDListener callback,
                com.sun.jini.lease.LeaseRenewalManager leaseMgr) throws java.io.IOException;
// Property Accessor Methods (by property name)
    public net.jini.core.entry.Entry[ ] getAttributes();
    public void setAttributes(net.jini.core.entry.Entry[ ] attrSets);
    public String[ ] getGroups();
    public void setGroups(String[ ] groups) throws java.io.IOException;
    public net.jini.core.lookup.ServiceRegistrar[ ] getJoinSet();
    public net.jini.core.discovery.LookupLocator[ ] getLocators();
    public void setLocators(net.jini.core.discovery.LookupLocator[ ] locators);
// Public Instance Methods
    public void addAttributes(net.jini.core.entry.Entry[ ] attrSets);
    public void addAttributes(net.jini.core.entry.Entry[ ] attrSets, boolean checkSC);
    public void addGroups(String[ ] groups) throws java.io.IOException;
    public void addLocators(net.jini.core.discovery.LookupLocator[ ] locators);
    public void modifyAttributes(net.jini.core.entry.Entry[ ] attrSetTemplates, net.jini.core.entry.Entry[ ] attrSets);
    public void modifyAttributes(net.jini.core.entry.Entry[ ] attrSetTemplates, net.jini.core.entry.Entry[ ] attrSets,
                boolean checkSC);
    public void removeGroups(String[ ] groups) throws java.io.IOException;
    public void removeLocators(net.jini.core.discovery.LookupLocator[ ] locators);
    public void terminate();
}
```

ServiceIDListener   Jini 1.0; Deprecated in Jini 1.1 Alpha

com.sun.jini.lookup   *event listener*

Objects that implement this interface are used in conjunction with a join manager: when the join manager discovers a lookup service, it calls the serviceIDNotify( ) method of its associated ServiceIDListener. The implementation of this method should save the service ID to persistent store so that it may be read and reused when the service restarts.

See also net.jini.lookup.ServiceIDListener.

```
public interface ServiceIDListener extends java.util.EventListener {
// Public Instance Methods
    public abstract void serviceIDNotify(net.jini.core.lookup.ServiceID serviceID);
}
```

Hierarchy: (com.sun.jini.lookup.ServiceIDListener(java.util.EventListener))

Passed To: com.sun.jini.lookup.JoinManager.JoinManager()

The *com.sun.jini.lookup.entry* Package

The com.sun.jini.lookup.entry package defines utility implementations for various lookup entry classes. Figure 14-9 shows the class hierarchy for this package.

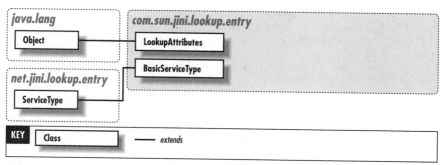

Figure 14–9: The com.sun.jini.lookup.entry package

A BasicServiceType object is a net.jini.core.entry.Entry object that provides human-readable information about the service—its name, icon, and description. The implementation in this package uses Java's resource bundle facility to provide that information. The LookupAttributes class provides a series of methods that operate on arrays of Entry objects.

BasicServiceType

Jini 1.0

com.sun.jini.lookup.entry

serializable entry

Services create a BasicServiceType entry by passing to the constructor of this class the name of the resource bundle from which information should be retrieved. Internally, the resource bundle name is passed to the getBundle( ) method of the ResourceBundle class in order to find the bundle. If the resource bundle name does not contain a . then the string net.jini.lookup.entry.servicetype. will be prepended to the name.

Calls to the methods of this class attempt to look up a resource in the bundle. The getIcon( ) method returns the object in the bundle named icon.<icon type> where <icon type> is the parameter passed to the getIcon( ) method. The getDisplayName( ) method returns the string in the bundle named name; if there is no such item in the bundle (or if the bundle itself can't be found), this method returns the last element of the name with which the basic service type was created. The getShortDescription( ) method returns the string in the bundle named desc.

It is an error to use the no-argument constructor of this class; a NullPointerException will be thrown when the first method is invoked on the resulting object.

```
public class BasicServiceType extends net.jini.lookup.entry.ServiceType {
// Public Constructors
    public BasicServiceType();
    public BasicServiceType(String type);
// Public Methods Overriding ServiceType
    public String getDisplayName();
    public java.awt.Image getIcon(int iconKind);
    public String getShortDescription();
// Public Instance Fields
    public String type;
}
```

Hierarchy: Object→ net.jini.entry.AbstractEntry(net.jini.core.entry.Entry(Serializable)) →
net.jini.lookup.entry.ServiceType(net.jini.lookup.entry.ServiceControlled) → BasicServiceType

LookupAttributes Jini 1.0

com.sun.jini.lookup.entry

This class contains a number of static methods that can be used to work with arrays of Entry objects. In general, these methods operate on arrays of entries and return a new array; the parameter arrays are not modified by these methods. Whenever these methods need to test fields for equality, they will do so according to the rules of the equal( ) method of this class described below.

The add( ) method calculates the union of the two parameter arrays. Only a single Entry object appears in the result for those entries that are represented in both parameter arrays. If the checkSC parameter is true, a security exception will be thrown if any entry in the addAttrSets array implements the ServiceControlled interface. The attrSets array is not subject to that security check.

The modify( ) method returns a clone of the attrSets parameter where each item in the array has been subject to possible modification. Each item in the array is tested in turn against each item in the attrSetTmpls array, and modification proceeds as follows:

- If the item and the template do not match, then continue to the next template.

- Otherwise, if the current template has an index of j, find the value of modAttrSets[j]:

    – If that value is null, delete the entry from the set of entries to be returned.

    – Otherwise obtain the field names for the original entry and the modified entry. For each field name that is the same and for which the modified entry has a non-null value, copy the value of the modified entry to the original entry.

- Continue with the next template.

The equal( ) method tests to see if the two objects have the same type. If they do, then the public fields of each entry are compared. If the type of the public field is a primitive wrapper type (e.g., Integer), then the standard equals( ) method is used to determine if the fields are equal. Otherwise, the value for each field is wrapped into a MarshalledObject, and the equals( ) method is used to determine if the two marshalled object are the same. If all fields are equal, this method returns true. Note the somewhat unfortunate name of this method: it is equal (without an s), not to be confused with the standard equals( ) method.

The matches( ) method tests to see if the entry matches the template. To match, the entry class must be the same class or a subclass of the template class, and each non-null public field of the template has the same value as the corresponding field in the entry.

```
public class LookupAttributes {
// No Constructor
// Public Class Methods
    public static net.jini.core.entry.Entry[ ] add(net.jini.core.entry.Entry[ ] attrSets,
                                net.jini.core.entry.Entry[ ] addAttrSets);
    public static net.jini.core.entry.Entry[ ] add(net.jini.core.entry.Entry[ ] attrSets, net.jini.core.entry.Entry[ ] addAttrSets,
                                boolean checkSC);
1.1 public static boolean equal(net.jini.core.entry.Entry[ ] attrSet1, net.jini.core.entry.Entry[ ] attrSet2);
    public static boolean equal(net.jini.core.entry.Entry e1, net.jini.core.entry.Entry e2);
    public static boolean matches(net.jini.core.entry.Entry tmpl, net.jini.core.entry.Entry e);
    public static net.jini.core.entry.Entry[ ] modify(net.jini.core.entry.Entry[ ] attrSets,
                                net.jini.core.entry.Entry[ ] attrSetTmpls,
```

```
                        net.jini.core.entry.Entry[ ] modAttrSets);
public static net.jini.core.entry.Entry[ ] modify(net.jini.core.entry.Entry[ ] attrSets,
                        net.jini.core.entry.Entry[ ] attrSetTmpls,
                        net.jini.core.entry.Entry[ ] modAttrSets, boolean checkSC);
}
```

The com.sun.jini.proxy Package

The com.sun.jini.proxy package contains classes that are used between clients and service proxies. The ThrowThis class provides a wrapper for exceptions between RMI servers and proxies. The UUID and UUIDFactory classes provide a mechanism to create and use a Unique Universal IDentifier. The class hierarchy for this package is shown in Figure 14-10.

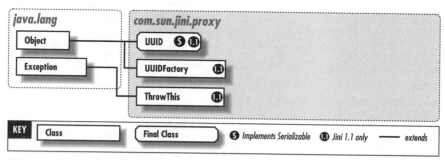

Figure 14–10: The com.sun.jini.proxy package

ThrowThis

Jini 1.1 Alpha

com.sun.jini.proxy

serializable checked

The ThrowThis class provides an exception wrapper for use between RMI servers and their proxies. When an RMI server throws a RemoteException (such as the NoSuchObjectException thrown by some service registration objects), that exception is always wrapped in a ServerException. If instead the server wraps the NoSuchObjectException in a ThrowThis exception, the proxy can call the throwRemoteException( ) method to throw the correct exception back to the client.

```
public class ThrowThis extends Exception {
// Public Constructors
    public ThrowThis(java.rmi.RemoteException toThrow);
    public ThrowThis(java.rmi.RemoteException toThrow, String message);
// Public Instance Methods
    public void throwRemoteException() throws java.rmi.RemoteException;
// Public Methods Overriding Throwable
    public String getMessage();
    public void printStackTrace();
    public void printStackTrace(java.io.PrintStream ps);
    public void printStackTrace(java.io.PrintWriter pw);
}
```

Hierarchy: Object→ Throwable(Serializable) → Exception→ ThrowThis

UUID

com.sun.jini.proxy
serializable

The UUID class models a universal unique identifier. UUIDs can be used as a global identification tag for participants in a Jini community. Despite the public constructors, you should only obtain instances of this class from a UUID factory.

```
public final class UUID implements Serializable {
// Public Constructors
    public UUID(java.io.DataInput in) throws java.io.IOException;
    public UUID(long mostSig, long leastSig);
// Public Instance Methods
    public long getLeastSignificantBits();
    public long getMostSignificantBits();
    public void writeBytes(java.io.DataOutput out) throws java.io.IOException;
// Public Methods Overriding Object
    public boolean equals(Object obj);
    public int hashCode();
    public String toString();
}
```

Hierarchy: Object→ UUID(Serializable)

Returned By: UUIDFactory.newUUID()

UUIDFactory

com.sun.jini.proxy

Instances of the UUIDFactory class are used to generate UUID objects via the newUUID( ) method.

```
public class UUIDFactory {
// Public Constructors
    public UUIDFactory();
// Public Instance Methods
    public UUID newUUID();
}
```

The com.sun.jini.reliableLog Package

The com.sun.jini.reliableLog package contains a set of classes that implement a reliable log. Figure 14-11 shows the class hierarchy for this package.

The log is called reliable because writes to the log can be made atomic: a call to update the log will not return until the data has actually been committed to disk. Further, the classes that read the log are smart enough to skip entries that have not been fully written. Hence, if a system crash occurs while the log is in the middle of updating, you'll still be able to recover all previous updates to the log.

Logs are held in a directory; it is an error for two instances of the ReliableLog class to write a log into the same directory. Within this directory, the log creates three files: *Logfile.<n>*, *Snapshot.<n>*, and *Version_Number*, where *<n>* is the snapshot version contained in the log. From a programmatic point of view, only the directory name is significant.

The reliable log is used by the activatable version of Sun's sample implementations of the Jini services; the location of the log for these services must be specified on their command line. A version of it is also used by *rmid*, which by default will create its log in the directory called *log* located in the current working directory.

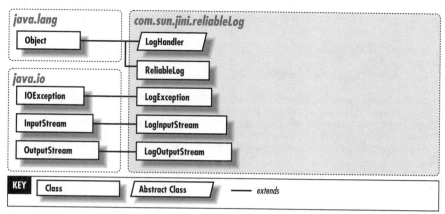

Figure 14–11: The com.sun.jini.reliableLog package

An example that uses the reliable log is found in Chapter 8, *Miscellaneous Classes*.

LogException
Jini 1.0

com.sun.jini.reliableLog
serializable checked

This exception indicates that the reliable log classes encountered an exception while reading or writing to the log. If critical log operations encounter an exception, they will wrap that exception into a LogException and throw that LogException back to their caller. However, certain methods may throw a LogException when no underlying exception has occurred; in this case, the value of the detail instance variable will be null.

```
public class LogException extends java.io.IOException {
// Public Constructors
    public LogException();
    public LogException(String s);
    public LogException(String s, Throwable ex);
// Public Methods Overriding Throwable
    public String getMessage();                                          default:null
// Public Instance Fields
    public Throwable detail;
}
```

Hierarchy: Object→ Throwable(Serializable) → Exception→ java.io.IOException→ LogException

Thrown By: LogInputStream.{read(), skip()}, ReliableLog.{recover(), ReliableLog(), snapshot(), update()}

LogHandler
Jini 1.0

com.sun.jini.reliableLog

Services that wish to implement a reliable log must create a concrete instance of this class that is responsible for log operations. Methods of this class should not be invoked directly; they are called in response to operations on the ReliableLog class. The snapshot( ) method should write all data to the given output stream; the recover( ) method should read the data from the given input stream and update the program's variables with that data. The data read by the recover( ) method will match the data written by the snapshot( ) method.

The applyUpdate( ) method should update the program's variables with data passed in the parameter object, which will match data that was previously saved in a call to the reliable log's update( ) method.

```
public abstract class LogHandler {
// Public Constructors
    public LogHandler();
// Public Instance Methods
    public abstract void applyUpdate(Object update) throws Exception;
    public void readUpdate(java.io.InputStream in) throws Exception;
    public abstract void recover(java.io.InputStream in) throws Exception;
    public abstract void snapshot(java.io.OutputStream out) throws Exception;
    public void writeUpdate(java.io.OutputStream out, Object value) throws Exception;
}
```

Passed To: ReliableLog.ReliableLog()

LogInputStream   Jini 1.0

com.sun.jini.reliableLog

This class implements the input stream that is used by the reliable log. In development, you do not use this stream directly. The implementation of this class is able to cope with the situation caused when a machine crashed in the middle of writing data to the log, in which case the last data written to the log is corrupt. In that case, this class ignores that partial data.

```
public class LogInputStream extends java.io.InputStream {
// Public Constructors
    public LogInputStream(java.io.InputStream in, int length) throws java.io.IOException;
// Public Methods Overriding InputStream
    public int available();
    public void close();
    public int read() throws java.io.IOException, LogException;
    public int read(byte[ ] b) throws java.io.IOException, LogException;
    public int read(byte[ ] b, int off, int len) throws java.io.IOException, LogException;
    public long skip(long n) throws java.io.IOException, LogException;
// Protected Methods Overriding Object
    protected void finalize() throws java.io.IOException;
}
```

Hierarchy: Object→ java.io.InputStream→ LogInputStream

LogOutputStream   Jini 1.0

com.sun.jini.reliableLog

This class implements the output stream used by the reliable log; it is not something developers need to access directly. This output stream writes special data to the file so that the LogInputStream can determine if a partial write occurred.

```
public class LogOutputStream extends java.io.OutputStream {
// Public Constructors
    public LogOutputStream(java.io.RandomAccessFile raf) throws java.io.IOException;
// Public Methods Overriding OutputStream
    public final void close() throws java.io.IOException;                          empty
    public void write(byte[ ] b) throws java.io.IOException;
    public void write(int b) throws java.io.IOException;
    public void write(byte[ ] b, int off, int len) throws java.io.IOException;
}
```

Hierarchy: Object→ java.io.OutputStream→ LogOutputStream

ReliableLog
com.sun.jini.reliableLog

Services that want to use a reliable log instantiate an object of this class, passing to the constructor the name of the directory that holds the log and the log handler that will read and write data in the log.

The update() method has two signatures; the additional boolean value in the second signature specifies whether or not the update() method should ensure that its data has been committed to disk. It is recommended that this signature is used with a value of true so that all writes to the log are atomic. The default value for this parameter is false. However, be aware that committing data to disk is a potentially time-consuming operation, so if you must make frequent updates, you may want to use the default update() method. Using the default value is a trade-off, though, since the machine could crash after the update() method returns but before data is actually written, which could lead to inconsistent behavior in your service.

```
public class ReliableLog {
// Public Constructors
    public ReliableLog(String dirPath, LogHandler handler) throws java.io.IOException, LogException;
// Public Instance Methods
    public void close() throws java.io.IOException;
    public void deletePersistentStore();
    public long logSize();
    public void recover() throws java.io.IOException, LogException;
    public void snapshot() throws java.io.IOException, LogException;
    public long snapshotSize();
    public void update(Object value) throws java.io.IOException, LogException;
    public void update(Object value, boolean forceToDisk) throws java.io.IOException, LogException;
}
```

The com.sun.jini.system Package

The classes in the com.sun.jini.system package are used to perform miscellaneous system utilities. The MultiCommandLine and POSIXCommandLine classes are concerned with parsing command-line arguments; there is also a class (the Filesystem class) that performs generic filesystem functions. Figure 14-12 shows the class hierarchy for this package.

For an example of command-line parsing, see Chapter 8.

CommandLine
com.sun.jini.system

The methods of this class all work the same: they take as arguments a string value and a default value. The string value should be the string that was passed on the command line; if that string is null, the default value is returned. Otherwise, the string is parsed into the desired primitive (or the desired object is created based on the value of the string). Unless you're creating a concrete subclass of this class, you do not call these methods directly.

The parseInt() and parseLong() methods will parse the string value according to the following rules: if the string begins with 0x or # then the number is assumed to be in hexadecimal; if it begins with 0 then it is assumed to be in octal; otherwise, it is assumed to be in decimal.

The methods of this class that return I/O classes (input streams, output streams, readers, or writers) all accept the special token "-" as their path, in which case the

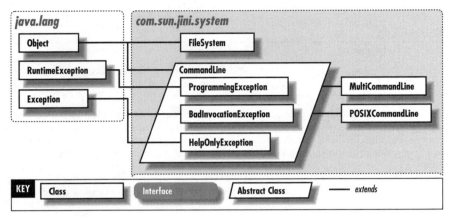

Figure 14-12: The com.sun.jini.system package

appropriate stream (System.in for reading, System.out for writing) will be returned (wrapped into a reader or writer if appropriate).

The parsing classes have the same interface, but they accept command lines that use different syntaxes. The command line is divided into two pieces: optional arguments and operands.

Optional arguments are those that are preceded with a hyphen; they may have a target (e.g., *-port 8080*) or they may be boolean options (e.g., *-verbose*). Operands are all strings on the command line that are not targets and are not preceded with a hyphen. Command line parsers usually allow an optional double hyphen (--) to separate options from operands.

To use a parser, you construct it with the arguments that were passed to the main method of your service. You may optionally include a program name in one of the constructors; this program name is only used in the output of the usage() method. Then call the appropriate get* methods to test each possible parameter.

To conclude, you must call the getOperands() method. This method will return the remaining arguments on the command line; that is, those that appear after the optional arguments. Even if you are not expecting operands, you must call this method to complete the error checking performed by this class.

When the getOperands() method is called, the parsing class performs error checking. If the command line contained options that you did not test, or if the options -? or -*help* appear on the command line, the usage() method will be called. This method prints the program name (if one was specified) followed by a list of all the valid options and the type of their target (if any); this list of valid options is constructed dynamically based on the arguments that you attempted to parse.

```
public abstract class CommandLine {
// Public Constructors
    public CommandLine();
// Inner Classes
    public static class BadInvocationException extends Exception;
    public static class HelpOnlyException extends Exception;
    public static class ProgrammingException extends RuntimeException;
// Public Class Methods
```

```
public static double parseDouble(String str, double defaultValue) throws NumberFormatException;
public static java.io.InputStream parseInputStream(String path, String defaultPath) throws java.io.IOException;
public static java.io.InputStream parseInputStream(String path, java.io.InputStream defaultValue)
     throws java.io.IOException;
public static int parseInt(String str, int defaultValue) throws NumberFormatException;
public static long parseLong(String str, long defaultValue) throws NumberFormatException;
public static java.io.OutputStream parseOutputStream(String path, String defaultPath)
     throws java.io.IOException;
public static java.io.OutputStream parseOutputStream(String path, java.io.OutputStream defaultValue)
     throws java.io.IOException;
public static java.io.RandomAccessFile parseRandomAccessFile(String path, String defaultPath, String mode)
     throws java.io.IOException;
public static java.io.RandomAccessFile parseRandomAccessFile(String path,
                                           java.io.RandomAccessFile defaultValue, String mode)
     throws java.io.IOException;
public static java.io.Reader parseReader(String path, String defaultPath) throws java.io.IOException;
public static java.io.Reader parseReader(String path, java.io.Reader defaultValue) throws java.io.IOException;
public static String parseString(String str, String defaultValue);
public static java.io.Writer parseWriter(String path, String defaultPath) throws java.io.IOException;
public static java.io.Writer parseWriter(String path, java.io.Writer defaultValue) throws java.io.IOException;
}
```

Subclasses: MultiCommandLine, POSIXCommandLine

CommandLine.BadInvocationException

Jini 1.0

com.sun.jini.system

serializable checked

This exception indicates that the command line is not well-formed because the user specified an unknown option or failed to provide a target for a non-boolean option.

```
public static class CommandLine.BadInvocationException extends Exception {
// Public Constructors
   public BadInvocationException(String str);
   public BadInvocationException(Object opt);
}
```

Thrown By: Too many methods to list.

CommandLine.HelpOnlyException

Jini 1.0

com.sun.jini.system

serializable checked

This exception indicates that the user invoked a help-only flag (i.e., -?); the program is expected to catch this exception and quietly exit. The parsing class will already have printed the usage message.

```
public static class CommandLine.HelpOnlyException extends Exception {
// Public Constructors
   public HelpOnlyException();
}
```

Thrown By: MultiCommandLine.getOperands(), POSIXCommandLine.getOperands()

CommandLine.ProgrammingException

Jini 1.0

com.sun.jini.system

serializable unchecked

This exception indicates that the command line is not well-formed according to the rules of the parsing class because it contains options after the operands.

```
public static class CommandLine.ProgrammingException extends RuntimeException {
// Public Constructors
    public ProgrammingException(String str);
}
```

FileSystem   Jini 1.0

com.sun.jini.system

This class provides basic utilities on directories in the filesystem. The destroy( ) method will recursively remove the named directory; if the proceed variable is false, it will stop removing entries as soon as it encounters an exception. Otherwise, exceptions are ignored.

The makeNewDir( ) and ensureDir( ) methods create the named directory, which must be an absolute pathname. The ensureDir( ) method will succeed if the directory already exists; the makeNewDir( ) method will throw an exception in that case. These methods will use the File.mkdirs( ) method to create any required intermediate directories.

```
public class FileSystem {
// Public Constructors
    public FileSystem();
// Public Class Methods
    public static void destroy(java.io.File file, boolean proceed) throws java.io.IOException;
    public static void ensureDir(String path) throws IllegalArgumentException;
    public static void makeNewDir(String path) throws IllegalArgumentException;
}
```

MultiCommandLine   Jini 1.0

com.sun.jini.system

This class allows you to parse command lines where the options may have multiple characters (e.g., *-dir /files/jini1_0* or *-verbose*). To be well-formed, a command line parsed by this class must have zero or more options followed by zero or more operands. Options that appear after the first operand will be parsed, but they will also be returned in the operand list (which is a bug; you should expect them to be treated only as an operand).

```
public class MultiCommandLine extends CommandLine {
// Public Constructors
    public MultiCommandLine(String[ ] args);
    public MultiCommandLine(String prog, String[ ] args);
// Public Instance Methods
    public boolean getBoolean(String opt);                                            synchronized
    public double getDouble(String opt, double defaultValue)                          synchronized
        throws CommandLine.BadInvocationException, NumberFormatException;
    public java.io.InputStream getInputStream(String opt, String path) throws java.io.IOException,   synchronized
        CommandLine.BadInvocationException;
    public java.io.InputStream getInputStream(String opt, java.io.InputStream defaultValue)         synchronized
        throws java.io.IOException, CommandLine.BadInvocationException;
    public int getInt(String opt, int defaultValue) throws CommandLine.BadInvocationException,      synchronized
        NumberFormatException;
    public long getLong(String opt, long defaultValue) throws CommandLine.BadInvocationException,   synchronized
        NumberFormatException;
    public String[ ] getOperands() throws CommandLine.BadInvocationException, CommandLine.HelpOnlyException;
    public java.io.OutputStream getOutputStream(String opt, String path) throws java.io.IOException, synchronized
        CommandLine.BadInvocationException;
```

public java.io.OutputStream **getOutputStream**(String *opt*, java.io.OutputStream *defaultValue*)   *synchronized*
    throws java.io.IOException, CommandLine.BadInvocationException;
public java.io.RandomAccessFile **getRandomAccessFile**(String *opt*,   *synchronized*
                                java.io.RandomAccessFile *defaultValue*,
                                String *mode*) throws java.io.IOException,
    CommandLine.BadInvocationException;
public java.io.RandomAccessFile **getRandomAccessFile**(String *opt*, String *path*, String *mode*)   *synchronized*
    throws java.io.IOException, CommandLine.BadInvocationException;
public java.io.Reader **getReader**(String *opt*, String *path*) throws java.io.IOException,   *synchronized*
    CommandLine.BadInvocationException;
public java.io.Reader **getReader**(String *opt*, java.io.Reader *defaultValue*) throws java.io.IOException,   *synchronized*
    CommandLine.BadInvocationException;
public String **getString**(String *opt*, String *defaultValue*)   *synchronized*
    throws CommandLine.BadInvocationException;
public java.io.Writer **getWriter**(String *opt*, java.io.Writer *defaultValue*) throws java.io.IOException,   *synchronized*
    CommandLine.BadInvocationException;
public java.io.Writer **getWriter**(String *opt*, String *path*) throws java.io.IOException,   *synchronized*
    CommandLine.BadInvocationException;
public void **usage**();
}

Hierarchy: Object→ CommandLine→ MultiCommandLine

POSIXCommandLine   Jini 1.0

com.sun.jini.system

This class parses command lines according to POSIX rules. Valid options in this class
contain a single letter (e.g., *-p*). Multiple boolean options may be combined into a single string; the string *-xvf* is three separate options: *-x*, *-v*, and *-f*. Options that require
targets may not be combined in this manner (unlike many Unix command lines).

public class **POSIXCommandLine** extends CommandLine {
// *Public Constructors*
    public **POSIXCommandLine**(String[ ] *args*);
    public **POSIXCommandLine**(String *prog*, String[ ] *args*);
// *Public Instance Methods*
    public boolean **getBoolean**(char *opt*);   *synchronized*
    public double **getDouble**(char *opt*, double *defaultValue*)   *synchronized*
        throws CommandLine.BadInvocationException, NumberFormatException;
    public java.io.InputStream **getInputStream**(char *opt*, String *path*) throws java.io.IOException,   *synchronized*
        CommandLine.BadInvocationException;
    public java.io.InputStream **getInputStream**(char *opt*, java.io.InputStream *defaultValue*)   *synchronized*
        throws java.io.IOException, CommandLine.BadInvocationException;
    public int **getInt**(char *opt*, int *defaultValue*) throws CommandLine.BadInvocationException,   *synchronized*
        NumberFormatException;
    public long **getLong**(char *opt*, long *defaultValue*) throws CommandLine.BadInvocationException,   *synchronized*
        NumberFormatException;
    public String[ ] **getOperands**() throws CommandLine.BadInvocationException, CommandLine.HelpOnlyException;
    public java.io.OutputStream **getOutputStream**(char *opt*, String *path*) throws java.io.IOException,   *synchronized*
        CommandLine.BadInvocationException;
    public java.io.OutputStream **getOutputStream**(char *opt*, java.io.OutputStream *defaultValue*)   *synchronized*
        throws java.io.IOException, CommandLine.BadInvocationException;
    public java.io.RandomAccessFile **getRandomAccessFile**(char *opt*,   *synchronized*
                                java.io.RandomAccessFile *defaultValue*,
                                String *mode*) throws java.io.IOException,
        CommandLine.BadInvocationException;

com.sun.jini
Packages

```
public java.io.RandomAccessFile getRandomAccessFile(char opt, String path, String mode)    synchronized
    throws java.io.IOException, CommandLine.BadInvocationException;
public java.io.Reader getReader(char opt, String path) throws java.io.IOException,           synchronized
    CommandLine.BadInvocationException;
public java.io.Reader getReader(char opt, java.io.Reader defaultValue) throws java.io.IOException,    synchronized
    CommandLine.BadInvocationException;
public String getString(char opt, String defaultValue) throws CommandLine.BadInvocationException;    synchronized
public java.io.Writer getWriter(char opt, java.io.Writer defaultValue) throws java.io.IOException,    synchronized
    CommandLine.BadInvocationException;
public java.io.Writer getWriter(char opt, String path) throws java.io.IOException,            synchronized
    CommandLine.BadInvocationException;
public void usage();
}
```

Hierarchy: Object→ CommandLine→ POSIXCommandLine

The com.sun.jini.thread Package

The com.sun.jini.thread package contains thread-related utilities. These utilities use the built-in primitive thread operations in Java's standard thread model to provide more useful semantics: different types of synchronization primitives and task-scheduling operations. Figure 14-13 shows the class hierarchy for this package. Examples of many of these classes are given in Chapter 8.

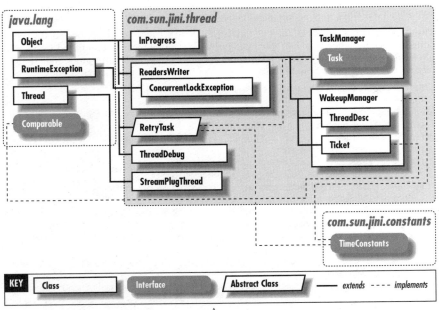

Figure 14-13: The com.sun.jini.thread package

InProgress   Jini 1.0

com.sun.jini.thread

This class implements a synchronization primitive that can be used by cooperating threads to protect critical regions of code. Unlike a standard synchronized block or method, the code that is protected by an InProgress variable can be entered by multiple threads as long as all threads agree to that. One or more threads may request that no thread enter the critical section as well.

This is all controlled by a counter in the InProgress object. A counter value of 0 indicates that the critical section is quiet; the waitUntilQuiet( ) method will block until the counter is zero. A positive counter value indicates the number of threads that are presently in the critical section; the waitWhileStarted( ) method blocks until the counter is less than or equal to zero. A negative counter value indicates the number of threads that have requested that no thread enter the critical section; the waitWhileBlocked( ) method blocks until the counter is greater than or equal to zero.

A thread that wants to enter the critical section calls the start( ) method; this method blocks until the counter is greater than or equal to zero and then increments the counter to indicate that the thread has entered the critical section. When the thread leaves the critical section, it must call the stop( ) method, which decrements the counter.

A thread that wants to prevent other threads from entering the critical section must call the block( ) method; this method blocks until the counter is less than or equal to zero. It then decrements the counter to indicate that the thread wants to prevent threads from entering the critical section. When the thread wants to allow the critical section to be entered, it must call the unblock( ) method, which increments the counter.

No attempt is made to balance blocking and starting operations; a thread that calls the block( ) method may wait forever while multiple threads call the start( ) and stop( ) methods (and vice versa).

```
public class InProgress {
// Public Constructors
    public InProgress(String name);
// Public Instance Methods
    public void block() throws InterruptedException;                    synchronized
    public boolean blocked();
    public void debug(boolean debugOn);
    public boolean inProgress();
    public void start() throws InterruptedException;                    synchronized
    public void stop();                                                 synchronized
    public void unblock();                                              synchronized
    public void waitUntilQuiet() throws InterruptedException;           synchronized
    public void waitWhileBlocked() throws InterruptedException;         synchronized
    public void waitWhileStarted() throws InterruptedException;         synchronized
}
```

ReadersWriter

Jini 1.0

com.sun.jini.thread

This class implements a multiple reader, single writer lock. This type of lock is used to protect a critical section of data that changes infrequently. As long as the data isn't being changed, it's okay to allow multiple threads to read the data, but a thread that wants to write the data must have exclusive access to the data.

Writers are favored over readers; a thread waiting for the write lock blocks all other threads from obtaining the read lock.

A reader thread can temporarily release its lock by calling the readerWait( ) method; a writer thread can temporarily release its lock by calling the writerWait( ) method. These methods will attempt to regain the lock after the indicated time has passed, or after the given notification object is signalled via the waiterNotify( ) method.

```
public class ReadersWriter {
// Public Constructors
    public ReadersWriter();
// Inner Classes
    public static class ConcurrentLockException extends RuntimeException;
// Public Instance Methods
    public void readerWait(Object notifier, long time);
    public void readLock();                                        synchronized
    public void readUnlock();                                      synchronized
    public void waiterNotify(Object notifier);
    public void writeLock();                                       synchronized
    public void writerWait(Object notifier, long time);
    public void writeUnlock();                                     synchronized
}
```

ReadersWriter.ConcurrentLockException   Jini 1.0

com.sun.jini.thread   *serializable unchecked*

This exception is thrown when a thread that is blocked waiting for a ReadersWriter lock
is interrupted.

```
public static class ReadersWriter.ConcurrentLockException extends RuntimeException {
// Public Constructors
    public ConcurrentLockException();
    public ConcurrentLockException(String s);
}
```

RetryTask   Jini 1.0

com.sun.jini.thread   *runnable*

This class is used in conjunction with the TaskManager class to implement an operation
that should be attempted continually until it succeeds. This class implements the actual
operation, and the task manager is used to provide the thread in which the operation
will run. From a programmatic point of view, this task happens in the background; the
thread that creates and schedules this task will not wait for the task to complete.

In order to implement this task, you must provide three things:

• The TaskManager object that will be used to run the task. This must be passed to the
  constructor.

• An implementation of the abstract tryOnce() method. This method should perform
  the task and return true if the task succeeded and false if it failed. If the task failed,
  it will be retried in the future.

• An implementation of the runAfter() method (see the TaskManager.Task interface).

The task will not be attempted until it is explicitly scheduled into the task manager;
scheduling it is the developer's responsibility. After that, the task will be rescheduled
until the tryOnce() method returns true. The time between retries becomes successively
longer: the first retry attempt will come after one second, the next after five seconds,
then ten seconds, then one minute, then one minute again, and then every five minutes
until it succeeds. This timing sequence is defined by the retryTime() method.

```
public abstract class RetryTask implements TaskManager.Task, com.sun.jini.constants.TimeConstants {
// Public Constructors
    public RetryTask(TaskManager manager);
```

```
// Public Instance Methods
    public int attempt();                                                    synchronized
    public void cancel();                                                    synchronized
    public boolean cancelled();                                              synchronized
    public boolean complete();                                               synchronized
    public void reset();
    public long retryTime();
    public long startTime();                                                 synchronized
    public abstract boolean tryOnce();
    public boolean waitFor() throws InterruptedException;                    synchronized
// Methods Implementing Runnable
    public void run();
// Methods Implementing TaskManager.Task
    public abstract boolean runAfter(java.util.List tasks, int size);
}
```

Hierarchy: Object→ RetryTask(TaskManager.Task(Runnable), com.sun.jini.constants.TimeConstants)

StreamPlugThread   Jini 1.0
com.sun.jini.thread   *runnable*

This class defines a thread that plugs together an input stream and an output stream: data is repeatedly read from the input stream and written to the output stream. Creating an instance of this class and then calling its start( ) method is identical to calling either of the static plugTogether( ) methods—each simply writes its input stream data to its output stream.

The userProg( ) method starts a program using the Runtime.exec( ) method. It then uses the plugTogether( ) method to tie System.in, System.out, and System.err of the VM to the standard input, output, and error of the executed program.

```
public class StreamPlugThread extends Thread {
// Public Constructors
    public StreamPlugThread(java.io.InputStream in, java.io.OutputStream out);
// Public Class Methods
    public static void error(String err);
    public static void main(String[ ] args);
    public static void plugTogether(java.io.OutputStream out, java.io.InputStream in);
    public static void plugTogether(java.io.InputStream in, java.io.OutputStream out);
    public static Process userProg(String cmd) throws java.io.IOException;
// Public Methods Overriding Thread
    public void run();
}
```

Hierarchy: Object→ Thread(Runnable) → StreamPlugThread

TaskManager   Jini 1.0
com.sun.jini.thread

This class implements a thread pool that can be used to run arbitrary tasks. Tasks (which are instances of the TaskManager.Task interface) are added to the task manager, which keeps a pool of threads available to run those tasks.

The number of threads that the task manager pool will start depends upon three things: the number of tasks that are in the task manager's list, the load factor of the task manager (which defaults to 3.0), and the maximum number of threads that you specify for the task manager. Unless you've reached the maximum, this means that the number of threads will be the number of tasks divided by the load factor, or one thread for every three tasks by default. A thread that is idle for the number of milliseconds specified by the timeout in the constructor (which defaults to 15 seconds) will exit, so the number of threads remains fairly well within this range.

```
public class TaskManager {
// Public Constructors
    public TaskManager();
    public TaskManager(int maxThreads, long timeout, float loadFactor);
// Inner Classes
    public static interface Task extends Runnable;
// Public Instance Methods
    public void add(TaskManager.Task t);                                synchronized
    public void addAll(java.util.Collection c);                         synchronized
    public void addIfNew(TaskManager.Task t);                           synchronized
    public java.util.ArrayList getPending();                            synchronized
    public boolean remove(TaskManager.Task t);                          synchronized
    public boolean removeIfPending(TaskManager.Task t);                 synchronized
    public void terminate();                                            synchronized
// Protected Instance Methods
    protected boolean needThread();
// Protected Instance Fields
    protected int firstPending;
    protected final float loadFactor;
    protected final int maxThreads;
    protected final java.util.List roTasks;
    protected final java.util.ArrayList tasks;
    protected final java.util.ArrayList threads;
    protected final long timeout;
}
```

Passed To: RetryTask.RetryTask()

TaskManager.Task   Jini 1.0
com.sun.jini.thread   *runnable*

Tasks that are added to the task manager thread pool must implement this interface. The run() method of the task will be executed by one of the threads in the pool. The runAfter() method can be used to support ordering: this method should return true if the task should run after any task in the tasks array.

```
public static interface TaskManager.Task extends Runnable {
// Public Instance Methods
    public abstract boolean runAfter(java.util.List tasks, int size);
}
```

Implementations: RetryTask

Passed To: TaskManager.{add(), addIfNew(), remove(), removeIfPending()}

WakeupManager   Jini 1.0
com.sun.jini.thread

Instances of this class are used to schedule tasks to run at a particular time. Tasks are specified as objects that implement the Runnable interface.

Tasks are scheduled to run at a particular time using the schedule() method. If no Thread-Desc parameter is provided, the task will be run within the wakeup manager's own thread; the task should be short in that case. If a ThreadDesc parameter is provided, the task will be run in a new thread created with the given attributes.

A task can be cancelled using the Ticket returned from the schedule() method.

```
public class WakeupManager implements com.sun.jini.constants.TimeConstants {
// Public Constructors
    public WakeupManager();
    public WakeupManager(WakeupManager.ThreadDesc desc);
// Inner Classes
    public static class ThreadDesc;
    public static class Ticket implements Comparable;
// Public Instance Methods
    public void cancel(WakeupManager.Ticket t);
    public void cancelAll();
    public boolean isEmpty();                                                    default:true
    public WakeupManager.Ticket schedule(long when, Runnable task);
    public WakeupManager.Ticket schedule(long when, Runnable task, WakeupManager.ThreadDesc threadDesc);
    public void stop();
    public boolean stopWhenEmpty();
    public void stopWhenEmpty(boolean stop);
}
```

Hierarchy: Object→ WakeupManager(com.sun.jini.constants.TimeConstants)

WakeupManager.ThreadDesc   Jini 1.0
com.sun.jini.thread

This class controls whether tasks run by the wakeup manager run in their own thread or in the wakeup manager's thread. If an instance of this class is passed to the schedule() method, a new thread will be created based upon the parameters of this object (which default to the default thread group, a non-daemon thread, and a priority of Thread.NORM_PRIORITY). Passing an instance of this class to the constructor of the WakeupManager class affects the internal threads used to manage the task queue but does not affect whether or not tasks are run in their own thread.

```
public static class WakeupManager.ThreadDesc {
// Public Constructors
    public ThreadDesc();
    public ThreadDesc(ThreadGroup group, boolean daemon);
    public ThreadDesc(ThreadGroup group, boolean daemon, int priority);
// Public Methods Overriding Object
    public String toString();
}
```

Passed To: WakeupManager.{schedule(), WakeupManager()}

Type Of: WakeupManager.Ticket.desc

WakeupManager.Ticket   Jini 1.0
com.sun.jini.thread   *comparable*

Instances of this class are returned by the schedule() methods of the WakeupManager class. This ticket can be passed to the cancel() method to cancel an individual task. If the task is already running, it is undisturbed. Similarly, the cancelAll() method cancels all tasks but does not disturb any that are already running.

```
public static class WakeupManager.Ticket implements Comparable {
// No Constructor
// Methods Implementing Comparable
    public int compareTo(Object o);
```

```
// Public Methods Overriding Object
    public boolean equals(Object o);
    public String toString();
// Public Instance Fields
    public final WakeupManager.ThreadDesc desc;
    public final Runnable task;
    public final long when;
}
```

Passed To: WakeupManager.cancel()

Returned By: WakeupManager.schedule()

CHAPTER 15

The net.jini.core Package

The classes that are contained in the net.jini.core hierarchy correspond to the Jini Technology Core Platform (JCP). The classes form the basis of the Jini API by defining the basic interfaces of Jini. From a developers point of view, there is no difference between the these classes and those classes that are in the net.jini package and that are part of the Jini Technology Extended Platform (JXP): both are official parts of the Jini specification. The classes and interfaces contained in this hierarchy are the minimal API that all Jini services and clients must use.

The net.jini.core.discovery Package

The net.jini.core.discovery package provides support for unicast discovery. For most Jini communities, multicast discovery will be used to find lookup services, using the classes of the net.jini.discovery package. This package can be used if the hostname and network port number of the lookup service are known. Discovery of the lookup service is accomplished by trying to connect to the network location and obtaining a reference to the discovered lookup service (e.g., a net.jini.core.lookup.ServiceRegistrar object). Figure 15-1 shows the class hierarchy for this package.

Figure 15-1: The net.jini.core.discovery package

The advantage of using unicast discovery of a lookup service is that with the unicast protocol, a lookup service that is outside the range of muliticast routing can be accessed. Also, when we've discovered a lookup service using the multicast discovery protocol, a lookup locator can be obtained for that service. This locator can be used at a later time to discover directly the same lookup service.

The disadvantage of unicast discovery is that the client must have knowledge of the location of the lookup service. It cannot broadcast a request on the network for lookup services to report themselves.

LookupLocator   Jini 1.0

net.jini.core.discovery   *serializable*

This class performs the task of unicast discovery. Given a hostname and port number (or a URL that specifies a hostname and port number), this class will try to discover the lookup service at that location; it returns the discovered ServiceRegistrar object from the getRegistrar( ) method.

The URL passed to the constructor of this class has the form jini://host:port/ and follows these rules:

- The protocol must be jini:. A MalformedURLException will be thrown otherwise.

- The hostname portion of the URL defines the name of the host on which to find the lookup service. This field is mandatory.

- The network port number is optional. If it is not defined, the default port of 4160 will be used.

The last two portions of a URL—the filename and anchor—are not used and will be ignored by the LookupLocator class.

See also net.jini.lookup.LookupDiscovery.

```
public class LookupLocator implements Serializable {
// Public Constructors
    public LookupLocator(String url) throws java.net.MalformedURLException;
    public LookupLocator(String host, int port);
// Property Accessor Methods (by property name)
    public String getHost();
    public int getPort();
    public net.jini.core.lookup.ServiceRegistrar getRegistrar() throws java.io.IOException, ClassNotFoundException;
    public net.jini.core.lookup.ServiceRegistrar getRegistrar(int timeout) throws java.io.IOException,
        ClassNotFoundException;
// Public Methods Overriding Object
    public boolean equals(Object o);
    public int hashCode();
    public String toString();
// Protected Instance Fields
    protected String host;
    protected int port;
}
```

Hierarchy: Object→ LookupLocator(Serializable)

Passed To: Too many methods to list.

Returned By: com.sun.jini.discovery.LookupLocatorDiscovery.{getDiscoveredLocators(), getLocators(), getUndiscoveredLocators()}, com.sun.jini.lookup.JoinManager.getLocators(), net.jini.admin.JoinAdmin.getLookupLocators(), net.jini.core.lookup.ServiceRegistrar.getLocator(), net.jini.discovery.DiscoveryLocatorManagement.getLocators(), net.jini.discovery.IncomingMulticastAnnouncement.getLocator(), net.jini.discovery.LookupDiscoveryManager.getLocators(), net.jini.discovery.LookupDiscoveryRegistration.getLocators(), net.jini.discovery.LookupLocatorDiscovery.{getDiscoveredLocators(), getLocators(), getUndiscoveredLocators()}

The net.jini.core.entry Package

The net.jini.core.entry package is used to define Entry objects, which implement the Entry interface. This interface is simply used for type identification, since there are no methods required to implement this interface. The attributes assigned to services and the objects that are stored into the JavaSpaces service are Entry objects. Figure 15-2 shows the class hierarchy for this package.

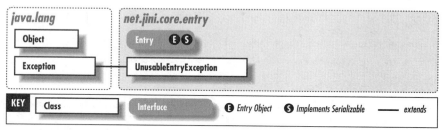

Figure 15-2: The net.jini.core.entry package

It is generally easier to use the net.jini.entry.AbstractEntry class to define entry objects. That class implements the Entry interface, and it provides some support methods—including an equals( ) method—that help the entry-matching operations work with the subclassed object. For more details on entry objects, see Chapter 4, *Basic Jini Programming.*

Entry

Jini 1.0

net.jini.core.entry

serializable entry

This interface is used to identify entry objects. No methods are required to be supported to be considered an entry object. However, the entry object must adhere to the entry specification: it must have a default, no-argument constructor, it should contain only public instance variables, and each instance variable must be a serializable object.

In most cases, it is not necessary to implement this interface directly. Instead, it is easier to extend the net.jini.entry.AbstractEntry class since that class provides comparison methods that are useful for entry objects.

```
public interface Entry extends Serializable {
}
```

Hierarchy: (Entry(Serializable))

Implementations: net.jini.entry.AbstractEntry

Passed To: Too many methods to list.

Returned By: Too many methods to list.

Type Of: UnusableEntryException.partialEntry, net.jini.core.lookup.ServiceItem.attributeSets, net.jini.core.lookup.ServiceTemplate.attributeSetTemplates

UnusableEntryException

Jini 1.0

net.jini.core.entry

serializable checked

This exception is generally thrown when an entry cannot be correctly serialized or deserialized by the service. The partialEntry variable contains the entry with the fields that were correctly deserialized; the remaining fields of that entry are null. The unusable-Fields array contains the fields that were not able to be deserialized, and the exception that caused each field to fail are found in the nestedExceptions variable.

```
public class UnusableEntryException extends Exception {
// Public Constructors
    public UnusableEntryException(Throwable e);
    public UnusableEntryException(Entry partial, String[ ] badFields, Throwable[ ] exceptions);
// Public Instance Fields
    public Throwable[ ] nestedExceptions;
    public Entry partialEntry;
    public String[ ] unusableFields;
}
```

Hierarchy: Object→ Throwable(Serializable)→ Exception→ UnusableEntryException

Thrown By: net.jini.space.JavaSpace.{read(), readIfExists(), take(), takeIfExists()}

The net.jini.core.event Package

The net.jini.core.event package provides a simple set of classes and interfaces used to support remote events. Remote events (which are either instances of or subclassed from the RemoteEvent class) are sent to listeners (which implement the RemoteEventListener interface) when the source of the event calls the notify() method of the listener. See Chapter 6, *Remote Events*, for a complete discussion of remote events. Figure 15-3 shows the class hierarchy for this package.

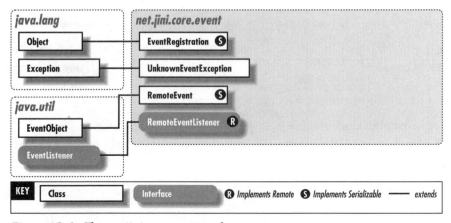

Figure 15–3: The net.jini.core.event package

The classes in this package define the interfaces between the server (which is the source of the remote event) and clients (which are the listeners for events). An instance of the EventRegistration class may be returned to clients during the registration of the listener with the service. An object of this class provides useful information to the client, including the event ID pertaining to this request, the source of the event, the current sequence number, and the lease that needs to be maintained in order to continue to receive the event.

EventRegistration

net.jini.core.event

This class is a convenient data structure that can be returned to clients who request remote events. The information returned includes the event ID pertaining to the request, the source of the events, the current sequence number, and the lease that the client must maintain.

Since it is the service that defines the registration interface, there is no requirement to use this class. The service may define an interface that returns to clients that register for events an object of this class or a subclass of this class; it may use a completely unrelated class instead.

```
public class EventRegistration implements Serializable {
// Public Constructors
    public EventRegistration(long eventID, Object source, net.jini.core.lease.Lease lease, long seqNum);
// Property Accessor Methods (by property name)
    public long getID();
    public net.jini.core.lease.Lease getLease();
    public long getSequenceNumber();
    public Object getSource();
// Protected Instance Fields
    protected long eventID;
    protected net.jini.core.lease.Lease lease;
    protected long seqNum;
    protected Object source;
}
```

Hierarchy: Object→ EventRegistration(Serializable)

Returned By: net.jini.core.lookup.ServiceRegistrar.notify(),
net.jini.discovery.LookupDiscoveryRegistration.getEventRegistration(),
net.jini.lease.LeaseRenewalSet.{setExpirationWarningListener(), setRenewalFailureListener()},
net.jini.space.JavaSpace.notify()

RemoteEvent

net.jini.core.event

This class is the superclass of all remote events in the Jini framework. The information delivered in the event includes the event ID, the source of the event, the sequence number, and the object that is to be handed back to the client. If more information is to be delivered, the service will need to subclass this class in order to provide the extra data.

Although all remote events have a sequence number, examining the sequence number itself is insufficient to determine if a remote event has been lost. Jini requires that events use increasing sequence numbers, but the sequence number may skip between events. Knowledge of the policy used by the service is necessary to understand if a skipped sequence number indicates a dropped event.

```
public class RemoteEvent extends java.util.EventObject {
// Public Constructors
    public RemoteEvent(Object source, long eventID, long seqNum, java.rmi.MarshalledObject handback);
// Property Accessor Methods (by property name)
    public long getID();
    public java.rmi.MarshalledObject getRegistrationObject();
    public long getSequenceNumber();
// Protected Instance Fields
```

net.jini.core Package

```
    protected long eventID;
    protected java.rmi.MarshalledObject handback;
    protected long seqNum;
    protected Object source;
}
```

Hierarchy: Object→ java.util.EventObject(Serializable)→ RemoteEvent

Subclasses: net.jini.core.lookup.ServiceEvent, net.jini.discovery.RemoteDiscoveryEvent, net.jini.lease.ExpirationWarningEvent, net.jini.lease.RenewalFailureEvent

Passed To: RemoteEventListener.notify()

RemoteEventListener
Jini 1.0

net.jini.core.event
remote remote event listener

This interface defines the method necessary to support remote events. When events are to be delivered to the client, the notify( ) method of the listener is called. If the event is unknown to the listener, an UnknownEventException should be thrown.

To register to receive events from a service, you must create an object that implements this interface. Since this interface extends the java.rmi.Remote interface, you will usually use a java.rmi.UnicastRemoteObject as the basis for your implementation. That object is then registered with the service in a service-specific manner.

```
public interface RemoteEventListener extends java.util.EventListener, java.rmi.Remote {
// Public Instance Methods
    public abstract void notify(RemoteEvent theEvent) throws UnknownEventException, java.rmi.RemoteException;
}
```

Hierarchy: (RemoteEventListener(java.util.EventListener, java.rmi.Remote))

Passed To: net.jini.core.lookup.ServiceRegistrar.notify(), net.jini.discovery.LookupDiscoveryService.register(), net.jini.event.MailboxRegistration.enableDelivery(), net.jini.lease.LeaseRenewalSet.{setExpirationWarningListener(), setRenewalFailureListener()}, net.jini.space.JavaSpace.notify()

Returned By: net.jini.event.MailboxRegistration.getListener()

UnknownEventException
Jini 1.0

net.jini.core.event
serializable checked

This exception should be thrown by remote event listeners when the listener does not recognize the event. The remote event should be distinguished by the source of the event and the event ID. A service that receives this exception when sending events to a listener should not send any more events of that type to that particular listener.

```
public class UnknownEventException extends Exception {
// Public Constructors
    public UnknownEventException();
    public UnknownEventException(String reason);
}
```

Hierarchy: Object→ Throwable(Serializable)→ Exception→ UnknownEventException

Thrown By: RemoteEventListener.notify()

The net.jini.core.lease Package

The net.jini.core.lease package provides the interfaces and simple support classes used to implement leasing within the Jini framework. All leases used between services and clients implement the **Lease** interface. Using this interface, the client of the lease can renew, cancel, or obtain information about a lease. Utilities may bundle leases into a lease map. A lease map may be used to renew or cancel a group of leases; it is generally used only by implementors of a leasing protocol.

This package defines how the client uses a lease. Support classes that help services implement leases are located in the com.sun.jini.lease.landlord package and support classes to help clients better manage leases are located in the net.jini.lease (com.sun.jini.lease in Jini 1.0) package. Figure 15-4 shows the class hierarchy for this package.

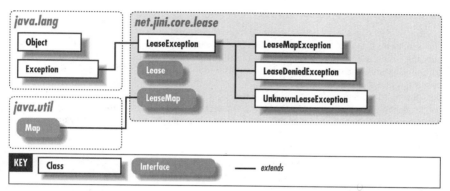

Figure 15–4: The net.jini.core.lease package

Lease

net.jini.core.lease

This interface defines the methods that must be implemented by leases in the Jini framework. To renew a lease, use the renew( ) method, passing it the amount of time that you want the lease to be valid for. That time is only a hint to the issuer of the lease, which will renew it for any amount of time less than or equal to the requested time. After renewing the lease, you can use the getExpiration( ) method to determine when the lease will actually expire. When you are finished with a lease, you can cancel it with the cancel( ) method, or you can simply let it expire.

The createLeaseMap( ) method creates a lease map with the current lease included. The canBatch( ) method allows clients to check whether a lease can be placed in the same map as the current lease.

Leases contain an expiration time. When a lease object is serialized, that expiration time will be calculated either as a duration or as an absolute time, depending on the value passed to the setSerialFormat( ) method. The default for this is Lease.DURATION, which is the better choice, since it does not require that the sender and receiver's clocks be synchronized.

```
public interface Lease {
// Public Constants
    public static final int ABSOLUTE;                                    =2
    public static final long ANY;                                        =-1
    public static final int DURATION;                                    =1
```

net.jini.core Package

```
   public static final long FOREVER;                              =9223372036854775807
// Public Instance Methods
   public abstract boolean canBatch(net.jini.core.lease.Lease lease);
   public abstract void cancel() throws UnknownLeaseException, java.rmi.RemoteException;
   public abstract LeaseMap createLeaseMap(long duration);
   public abstract long getExpiration();
   public abstract int getSerialFormat();
   public abstract void renew(long duration) throws LeaseDeniedException, UnknownLeaseException,
       java.rmi.RemoteException;
   public abstract void setSerialFormat(int format);
}
```

Implementations: com.sun.jini.lease.AbstractLease

Passed To: Too many methods to list.

Returned By: com.sun.jini.lease.LeaseRenewalEvent.getLease(),
com.sun.jini.lease.landlord.LandlordLease.Factory.newLease(),
com.sun.jini.lease.landlord.LandlordLeaseFactory.newLease(),
com.sun.jini.lease.landlord.LeaseDurationPolicy.leaseFor(),
com.sun.jini.lease.landlord.LeasePolicy.leaseFor(), net.jini.core.event.EventRegistration.getLease(),
net.jini.core.lookup.ServiceRegistration.getLease(),
net.jini.discovery.LookupDiscoveryRegistration.getLease(), net.jini.event.MailboxRegistration.getLease(),
net.jini.lease.ExpirationWarningEvent.getLease(), net.jini.lease.LeaseRenewalEvent.getLease(),
net.jini.lease.LeaseRenewalSet.{getRenewalSetLease(), remove()},
net.jini.lease.RenewalFailureEvent.getLease(), net.jini.space.JavaSpace.write()

Type Of: net.jini.core.event.EventRegistration.lease,
net.jini.core.transaction.NestableTransaction.Created.lease,
net.jini.core.transaction.Transaction.Created.lease,
net.jini.core.transaction.server.TransactionManager.Created.lease

LeaseDeniedException   Jini 1.0

net.jini.core.lease   *serializable checked*

An exception of this type is thrown when a lease request or renewal is denied by the
service.

```
public class LeaseDeniedException extends LeaseException {
// Public Constructors
   public LeaseDeniedException();
   public LeaseDeniedException(String reason);
}
```

Hierarchy: Object→ Throwable(Serializable)→ Exception→ LeaseException→
LeaseDeniedException

Thrown By: Too many methods to list.

LeaseException   Jini 1.0

net.jini.core.lease   *serializable checked*

This class is the superclass of all of the exception types in this package.

```
public class LeaseException extends Exception {
// Public Constructors
   public LeaseException();
```

```
    public LeaseException(String reason);
}
```

Hierarchy: Object→ Throwable(Serializable)→ Exception→ LeaseException

Subclasses: LeaseDeniedException, LeaseMapException, UnknownLeaseException

LeaseMap   Jini 1.0
net.jini.core.lease   *collection*

This interface defines the methods that are to be supported by lease maps. With lease maps, the client can renew or cancel leases in batches, using the renewAll( ) and cancelAll( ) methods. The canContain( ) method determines whether or not a particular lease can be added to the map; the operations of adding and removing leases from the map is accomplished with the methods of the java.util.Map interface.

Lease maps use the Lease object as their key and their duration (wrapped as a Long) as their value. They are not typically used by end-user developers, though their use is common by lease renewal managers.

```
public interface LeaseMap extends java.util.Map {
// Public Instance Methods
    public abstract void cancelAll() throws LeaseMapException, java.rmi.RemoteException;
    public abstract boolean canContainKey(Object key);
    public abstract void renewAll() throws LeaseMapException, java.rmi.RemoteException;
}
```

Hierarchy: (LeaseMap(java.util.Map))

Implementations: com.sun.jini.lease.AbstractLeaseMap

Returned By: com.sun.jini.lease.AbstractLease.createLeaseMap(),
com.sun.jini.lease.landlord.LandlordLease.createLeaseMap(),
net.jini.core.lease.Lease.createLeaseMap()

LeaseMapException   Jini 1.0
net.jini.core.lease   *serializable checked*

An exception of this type is thrown when the renewAll( ) or cancelAll( ) methods of the lease map generate an error. This exception includes a map of exceptions for all of the leases that failed to renew or be cancelled: the keys are the lease objects and the value for each key is the exception generated when the renewal or cancellation was attempted.

```
public class LeaseMapException extends LeaseException {
// Public Constructors
    public LeaseMapException(String s, java.util.Map exceptionMap);
// Public Instance Fields
    public java.util.Map exceptionMap;
}
```

Hierarchy: Object→ Throwable(Serializable)→ Exception→ LeaseException→ LeaseMapException

Thrown By: com.sun.jini.lease.AbstractLeaseMap.{cancelAll(), renewAll()},
com.sun.jini.lease.landlord.Landlord.cancelAll(),
com.sun.jini.lease.landlord.LandlordLeaseMap.{cancelAll(), renewAll()}, LeaseMap.{cancelAll(),
renewAll()}

UnknownLeaseException

Jini 1.0

net.jini.core.lease

serializable checked

An exception of this type is thrown when the lease grantor has no information about the lease, either because the lease has expired or because the lease was issued by a different service.

```
public class UnknownLeaseException extends LeaseException {
// Public Constructors
    public UnknownLeaseException();
    public UnknownLeaseException(String reason);
}
```

Hierarchy: Object→ Throwable(Serializable)→ Exception→ LeaseException→ UnknownLeaseException

Thrown By: Too many methods to list.

The net.jini.core.lookup Package

The net.jini.core.lookup package provides the interfaces and support classes used to communicate with the Jini lookup service. Figure 15-5 shows the class hierarchy for this package.

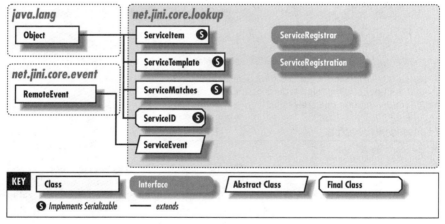

Figure 15–5: The net.jini.core.lookup package

A ServiceRegistrar object is instantiated during discovery to represent each discovered lookup service. ServiceItem objects are created to represent each registered service within the lookup service. ServiceTemplate objects are used to search for ServiceItem objects that have been registered. Whether the lookup service is found initially via multicast discovery or unicast discovery, the ServiceRegistrar can instantiate a lookup locator (net.jini.core.LookupLocator) that can be used to rediscover the service at a later point in time (e.g., after the service restarts, assuming it has saved the lookup locator).

ServiceRegistrar object are used by clients to lookup services and by services to lookup other services and to register themselves. Clients and services can also request to be notified asynchronously when changes in the lookup service occur. Looking up services is based on service attributes, which are objects that implement the net.jini.core.entry.Entry interface.

ServiceEvent

Jini 1.0

net.jini.core.lookup   *serializable remote event*

This abstract class defines the type of data that lookup service events contain. In addition to the type of data provided by remote events, the listener can obtain the service ID of the service in question, the ServiceItem object, and the type of transition that took place on the lookup service. The ServiceItem object is returned from the getServiceItem( ) method; this object will be null if the event was generated because the service was deleted. The type of transition is returned from the getTransition( ) method; its value is defined by static variables in the ServiceRegistrar class.

```
public abstract class ServiceEvent extends net.jini.core.event.RemoteEvent {
// Public Constructors
    public ServiceEvent(Object source, long eventID, long seqNo, java.rmi.MarshalledObject handback,
                    ServiceID serviceID, int transition);
// Property Accessor Methods (by property name)
    public ServiceID getServiceID();
    public abstract ServiceItem getServiceItem();
    public int getTransition();
// Protected Instance Fields
    protected ServiceID serviceID;
    protected int transition;
}
```

Hierarchy: Object→ java.util.EventObject(Serializable)→ net.jini.core.event.RemoteEvent→ ServiceEvent

ServiceID

Jini 1.0

net.jini.core.lookup   *serializable*

This class represents a universally unique ID that is assigned to the service. It should only be generated by lookup services and should not be created by the service itself, since the algorithm to guarantee uniqueness is complicated. Services should save the service ID assigned to them the first time they run and use that ID whenever they restart.

The bits of this object should not be inspected. Instead, objects of this type should be checked for equality with the equals( ) method.

```
public final class ServiceID implements Serializable {
// Public Constructors
    public ServiceID(java.io.DataInput in) throws java.io.IOException;
    public ServiceID(long mostSig, long leastSig);
// Public Instance Methods
    public long getLeastSignificantBits();
    public long getMostSignificantBits();
    public void writeBytes(java.io.DataOutput out) throws java.io.IOException;
// Public Methods Overriding Object
    public boolean equals(Object obj);
    public int hashCode();
    public String toString();
}
```

Hierarchy: Object→ ServiceID(Serializable)

Passed To: com.sun.jini.lookup.JoinManager.JoinManager(),
com.sun.jini.lookup.ServiceIDListener.serviceIDNotify(), ServiceEvent.ServiceEvent(),
ServiceItem.ServiceItem(), ServiceTemplate.ServiceTemplate(),
net.jini.discovery.OutgoingMulticastAnnouncement.marshal(),

net.jini.core Package

net.jini.discovery.OutgoingMulticastRequest.marshal(), net.jini.lookup.JoinManager.JoinManager(), net.jini.lookup.ServiceIDListener.serviceIDNotify()

Returned By: ServiceEvent.getServiceID(), ServiceRegistrar.getServiceID(), ServiceRegistration.getServiceID(), net.jini.discovery.IncomingMulticastAnnouncement.getServiceID(), net.jini.discovery.IncomingMulticastRequest.getServiceIDs()

Type Of: ServiceEvent.serviceID, ServiceItem.serviceID, ServiceTemplate.serviceID, net.jini.discovery.IncomingMulticastAnnouncement.serviceID, net.jini.discovery.IncomingMulticastRequest.serviceIDs

ServiceItem   Jini 1.0

net.jini.core.lookup   *serializable*

This class is the data type that is stored by the Jini lookup service. It includes the service ID, the proxy object used to contact the service, and the attributes of the service.

```
public class ServiceItem implements Serializable {
// Public Constructors
    public ServiceItem(ServiceID serviceID, Object service, net.jini.core.entry.Entry[ ] attrSets);
// Public Instance Fields
    public net.jini.core.entry.Entry[ ] attributeSets;
    public Object service;
    public ServiceID serviceID;
}
```

Hierarchy: Object→ ServiceItem(Serializable)

Passed To: ServiceMatches.ServiceMatches(), ServiceRegistrar.register(), net.jini.lookup.ServiceDiscoveryEvent.ServiceDiscoveryEvent(), net.jini.lookup.ServiceItemFilter.check()

Returned By: ServiceEvent.getServiceItem(), net.jini.lookup.ClientLookupManager.lookup(), net.jini.lookup.LookupCache.lookup(), net.jini.lookup.ServiceDiscoveryEvent.{getPostEventServiceItem(), getPreEventServiceItem()}

Type Of: ServiceMatches.items

ServiceMatches   Jini 1.0

net.jini.core.lookup   *serializable*

An instance of this class is returned by the lookup service when looking up multiple items using the lookup( ) method of the ServiceRegistrar class. This data structure includes the actual number of matches that the lookup service found and an array of ServiceItem objects that match the template. The maximum size of this array is provided by the maxMatches parameter to the lookup( ) method, which may be less than the total number found.

```
public class ServiceMatches implements Serializable {
// Public Constructors
    public ServiceMatches(ServiceItem[ ] items, int totalMatches);
// Public Instance Fields
    public ServiceItem[ ] items;
    public int totalMatches;
}
```

Hierarchy: Object→ ServiceMatches(Serializable)

Returned By: ServiceRegistrar.lookup()

ServiceRegistrar
net.jini.core.lookup

This interface is supported by all implementations of the Jini lookup service. Instances of the lookup service are discovered using classes in the *net.jini.discovery* package.

A service registers itself with the lookup service using the register() method of this interface. If the service does not yet have a service ID, then the serviceID field of the item parameter should be null; otherwise, it should be the previously-assigned service ID. The requested duration will be used by the lookup service to determine the initial length of the lease returned in the ServiceRegistration object; the service must obtain the lease from the ServiceRegistration object and renew the lease as long as the service wants to keep its registration valid.

Applications find services using one of the lookup() methods, providing an appropriate service template and, optionally, the maximum number of services to return. If the lookup() method that does not require a maximum number of services is used and no service matches the template, the lookup() method returns null. If a maximum number of matches is specified to the lookup() method, a ServiceMatch object is always returned. The items field of that object will be null if there are no matching services.

Applications may request to be notified when registered services change by passing a remote event listener to the notify() method. ServiceEvent objects are delivered to the listeners to inform them of changes to the lookup service database. The application specifies which events to receive by specifying a service template and the type of change that the client is interested in. The changes can be OR'ed together to request multiple types of changes. The possible changes are as follows:

TRANSITION_MATCH_NOMATCH

A service item that previously matched the requested template no longer matches the template. This is caused when the service item is removed from the lookup services (because its lease has expired) or when the service changes its attributes so that it no longer matches the template.

TRANSITION_NOMATCH_MATCH

A service item that matches the specified template was added to the lookup service, or an existing service changed its attributes so that it now matches the template. This is probably the most common usage of asynchronous lookup. This allows clients to find services when the service is registered.

TRANSITION_MATCH_MATCH

A service item that previously matched the template changed its attributes in a fashion that still matches the template. This is useful for services that use attributes to provide status data (e.g., a printer that wants to report a paper jam may simply change an attribute).

```
public interface ServiceRegistrar {
// Public Constants
    public static final int TRANSITION_MATCH_MATCH;                              =4
    public static final int TRANSITION_MATCH_NOMATCH;                            =1
    public static final int TRANSITION_NOMATCH_MATCH;                           =2
// Property Accessor Methods (by property name)
    public abstract String[ ] getGroups() throws java.rmi.RemoteException;
    public abstract net.jini.core.discovery.LookupLocator getLocator() throws java.rmi.RemoteException;
    public abstract ServiceID getServiceID();
// Public Instance Methods
```

```
    public abstract Class[ ] getEntryClasses(ServiceTemplate tmpl) throws java.rmi.RemoteException;
    public abstract Object[ ] getFieldValues(ServiceTemplate tmpl, int setIndex, String field)
        throws NoSuchFieldException, java.rmi.RemoteException;
    public abstract Class[ ] getServiceTypes(ServiceTemplate tmpl, String prefix) throws java.rmi.RemoteException;
    public abstract Object lookup(ServiceTemplate tmpl) throws java.rmi.RemoteException;
    public abstract ServiceMatches lookup(ServiceTemplate tmpl, int maxMatches) throws java.rmi.RemoteException;
    public abstract net.jini.core.event.EventRegistration notify(ServiceTemplate tmpl, int transitions,
                                            net.jini.core.event.RemoteEventListener listener,
                                            java.rmi.MarshalledObject handback, long leaseDuration)
        throws java.rmi.RemoteException;
    public abstract ServiceRegistration register(ServiceItem item, long leaseDuration) throws java.rmi.RemoteException;
}
```

Passed To: com.sun.jini.discovery.LookupLocatorDiscovery.discard(),
net.jini.discovery.DiscoveryEvent.DiscoveryEvent(), net.jini.discovery.DiscoveryManagement.discard(),
net.jini.discovery.LookupDiscovery.discard(), net.jini.discovery.LookupDiscoveryManager.{discard(),
getFrom()}, net.jini.discovery.LookupDiscoveryRegistration.discard(),
net.jini.discovery.LookupLocatorDiscovery.discard(),
net.jini.discovery.LookupUnmarshalException.LookupUnmarshalException(),
net.jini.discovery.OutgoingUnicastResponse.marshal(),
net.jini.discovery.RemoteDiscoveryEvent.{insertRegistrars(), RemoteDiscoveryEvent()}

Returned By: com.sun.jini.lookup.JoinManager.getJoinSet(),
net.jini.core.discovery.LookupLocator.getRegistrar(), net.jini.discovery.DiscoveryEvent.getRegistrars(),
net.jini.discovery.DiscoveryManagement.getRegistrars(),
net.jini.discovery.IncomingUnicastResponse.getRegistrar(),
net.jini.discovery.LookupDiscovery.getRegistrars(),
net.jini.discovery.LookupDiscoveryManager.getRegistrars(),
net.jini.discovery.LookupDiscoveryRegistration.getRegistrars(),
net.jini.discovery.LookupLocatorDiscovery.getRegistrars(),
net.jini.discovery.LookupUnmarshalException.getUnmarshalledRegs(),
net.jini.discovery.RemoteDiscoveryEvent.getRegistrars(),
net.jini.lookup.ClientLookupManager.getLookupServices(), net.jini.lookup.JoinManager.getJoinSet()

Type Of: net.jini.discovery.DiscoveryEvent.regs, net.jini.discovery.IncomingUnicastResponse.registrar,
net.jini.discovery.RemoteDiscoveryEvent.regs

ServiceRegistration   Jini 1.0

net.jini.core.lookup

When a service item is registered with the lookup service, the lookup service returns an
object that implements this interface. Using this interface, the registering service may
obtain the service ID assigned to the service and the lease of the service's registration.
The service should renew that lease as long as it wants to be registered. The service
may also add, modify, or remove attributes of the service through this interface.

```
public interface ServiceRegistration {
// Property Accessor Methods (by property name)
    public abstract net.jini.core.lease.Lease getLease();
    public abstract ServiceID getServiceID();
// Public Instance Methods
    public abstract void addAttributes(net.jini.core.entry.Entry[ ] attrSets)
        throws net.jini.core.lease.UnknownLeaseException, java.rmi.RemoteException;
    public abstract void modifyAttributes(net.jini.core.entry.Entry[ ] attrSetTemplates,
                                net.jini.core.entry.Entry[ ] attrSets)
        throws net.jini.core.lease.UnknownLeaseException, java.rmi.RemoteException;
```

```
    public abstract void setAttributes(net.jini.core.entry.Entry[ ] attrSets)
        throws net.jini.core.lease.UnknownLeaseException, java.rmi.RemoteException;
}
```

Returned By: ServiceRegistrar.register()

ServiceTemplate

net.jini.core.lookup

Jini 1.0

serializable

An instance of this class is used to match service items that are stored in the lookup service. The template data structure contains the service ID, the java.lang.Class objects of the supported interfaces, and the attributes to search for. Any of these items may be null, in which case they match all services.

```
public class ServiceTemplate implements Serializable {
// Public Constructors
    public ServiceTemplate(ServiceID serviceID, Class[ ] serviceTypes, net.jini.core.entry.Entry[ ] attrSetTemplates);
// Public Instance Fields
    public net.jini.core.entry.Entry[ ] attributeSetTemplates;
    public ServiceID serviceID;
    public Class[ ] serviceTypes;
}
```

Hierarchy: Object→ ServiceTemplate(Serializable)

Passed To: ServiceRegistrar.{getEntryClasses(), getFieldValues(), getServiceTypes(), lookup(), notify()}, net.jini.lookup.ClientLookupManager.{createLookupCache(), lookup()}

The net.jini.core.transaction Package

The net.jini.core.transaction package provides the service interface and support classes used by clients of the transaction manager. With the classes in this package, clients can obtain transaction objects that can then be used with services to group multiple requests into a single transaction. See Chapter 9, *Transactions*, for more details on transactions and the Jini transaction manager. Figure 15-6 shows the class hierarchy for this package.

In order to use a transaction, the client must first look up a Jini transaction manager on the network, using the net.jini.core.transaction.server.TransactionManager interface as the class within a net.jini.core.lookup.ServiceTemplate object. The TransactionFactory class is then used to create either a non-nestable transaction or nestable top-level transaction, depending on whether the transaction manager that is returned supports the net.jini.core.transaction.server.NestableTransactionManager interface. Nested transactions are created by calling a method of the nestable transaction object that will be the parent transaction. Sun's sample transaction manager *mahalo* does not support nested transactions.

The factory will return a Transaction.Created or NestableTransaction.Created object. This object holds the transaction object that the client should use and a lease for the transaction; the client must renew this lease until the transaction is completed. If the lease is not renewed, the transaction manager will automatically abort the transaction.

The client uses the transaction object by passing it to methods of services that require transactions. Both types of transaction objects provide methods that request that the transaction be committed or aborted. Once the transaction is finished, the client will call either of these methods to commit or roll back the group of method calls.

When the client asks that an operation be committed, the transaction manager must start the two-phase commit operation, which involves having each participant vote on the outcome of the operation, tallying the votes and determining the outcome of the

net.jini.core Package

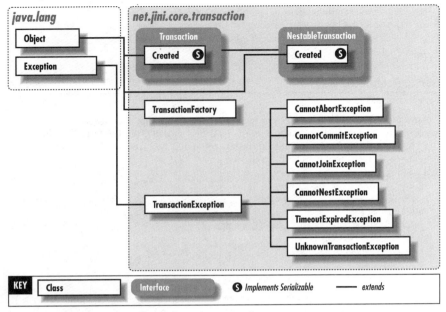

Figure 15–6: The net.jini.core.transaction package

operation, and notifying all participants of the outcome. The commit( ) and abort( ) methods may return before all participants have been notified of the outcome, but the outcome is still guaranteed.

CannotAbortException   Jini 1.0

net.jini.core.transaction   *serializable checked*

An exception of this type is thrown when the transaction cannot be aborted because a decision has already been made to commit the transaction.

```
public class CannotAbortException extends TransactionException {
// Public Constructors
    public CannotAbortException();
    public CannotAbortException(String desc);
}
```

Hierarchy: Object→ Throwable(Serializable)→ Exception→ TransactionException→ CannotAbortException

Thrown By: Transaction.abort(), net.jini.core.transaction.server.ServerTransaction.abort(), net.jini.core.transaction.server.TransactionManager.abort()

CannotCommitException   Jini 1.0

net.jini.core.transaction   *serializable checked*

An exception of this type is thrown when the transaction cannot be committed because it is already being aborted or a participant vetoed the commitment during the prepare stage of the two-phase commit.

```
public class CannotCommitException extends TransactionException {
// Public Constructors
    public CannotCommitException();
    public CannotCommitException(String desc);
}
```

Hierarchy: Object→ Throwable(Serializable)→ Exception→ TransactionException→ CannotCommitException

Thrown By: Transaction.commit(), net.jini.core.transaction.server.ServerTransaction.commit(), net.jini.core.transaction.server.TransactionManager.commit()

CannotJoinException

Jini 1.0

net.jini.core.transaction

serializable checked

An exception of this type is thrown when a participant tries to join a transaction that is no longer active.

```
public class CannotJoinException extends TransactionException {
// Public Constructors
    public CannotJoinException();
    public CannotJoinException(String desc);
}
```

Hierarchy: Object→ Throwable(Serializable)→ Exception→ TransactionException→ CannotJoinException

Thrown By: NestableTransaction.create(),
net.jini.core.transaction.server.NestableServerTransaction.{create(), promote()},
net.jini.core.transaction.server.NestableTransactionManager.{create(), promote()},
net.jini.core.transaction.server.ServerTransaction.join(),
net.jini.core.transaction.server.TransactionManager.join()

CannotNestException

Jini 1.0

net.jini.core.transaction

serializable checked

An exception of this type is thrown when a nested transaction is passed to an object that does not support nested transactions.

```
public class CannotNestException extends TransactionException {
// Public Constructors
    public CannotNestException();
    public CannotNestException(String desc);
}
```

Hierarchy: Object→ Throwable(Serializable)→ Exception→ TransactionException→ CannotNestException

NestableTransaction

Jini 1.0

net.jini.core.transaction

This interface defines the methods supported by nestable transaction objects. This interface extends the Transaction interface by adding creation methods that allow nestable transaction objects to create subtransaction objects.

The two create() methods of this interface allow the client to create a transaction that is handled either by the same transaction manager or by a transaction manager that is specified.

Instances of this class are embedded in the NestableTransaction.Created class that is obtained from the TransactionFactory class.

```
public interface NestableTransaction extends Transaction {
// Inner Classes
    public static class Created implements Serializable;
// Public Instance Methods
    public abstract NestableTransaction.Created create(long leaseTime) throws UnknownTransactionException,
        CannotJoinException, net.jini.core.lease.LeaseDeniedException, java.rmi.RemoteException;
    public abstract NestableTransaction.Created create(
                            net.jini.core.transaction.server.NestableTransactionManager mgr,
                            long leaseTime) throws UnknownTransactionException,
        CannotJoinException, net.jini.core.lease.LeaseDeniedException, java.rmi.RemoteException;
}
```

Hierarchy: (NestableTransaction(Transaction))

Implementations: net.jini.core.transaction.server.NestableServerTransaction

Passed To: NestableTransaction.Created.Created(),
net.jini.core.transaction.server.NestableServerTransaction.enclosedBy()

Type Of: NestableTransaction.Created.transaction

NestableTransaction.Created   Jini 1.0

net.jini.core.transaction   *serializable*

This is a static inner class of the NestableTransaction interface. This class is a data structure that is provided to clients when a nestable transaction is created. The data in this class includes the nestable transaction object and the lease assigned to the transaction object.

Clients obtain instances of this class from the TransactionFactory class. Clients are responsible for renewing the lease contained in this class, or the transaction will be aborted.

```
public static class NestableTransaction.Created implements Serializable {
// Public Constructors
    public Created(NestableTransaction transaction, net.jini.core.lease.Lease lease);
// Public Instance Fields
    public final net.jini.core.lease.Lease lease;
    public final NestableTransaction transaction;
}
```

Returned By: NestableTransaction.create(), TransactionFactory.create(),
net.jini.core.transaction.server.NestableServerTransaction.create()

TimeoutExpiredException   Jini 1.0

net.jini.core.transaction   *serializable checked*

An exception of this type is thrown when the time that is provided during a call to the abort( ) or commit( ) method has elapsed. This means the abort or commit has completed, but all participants have not yet been notified of the results of the two-phase commit.

```
public class TimeoutExpiredException extends TransactionException {
// Public Constructors
    public TimeoutExpiredException(boolean committed);
    public TimeoutExpiredException(String desc, boolean committed);
// Public Instance Fields
    public boolean committed;
}
```

Hierarchy: Object→ Throwable(Serializable)→ Exception→ TransactionException→
TimeoutExpiredException

Thrown By: Transaction.{abort(), commit()},
net.jini.core.transaction.server.ServerTransaction.{abort(), commit()},
net.jini.core.transaction.server.TransactionManager.{abort(), commit()}

Transaction
net.jini.core.transaction

Jini 1.0

This interface defines the methods supported by transaction objects. Transaction objects abstract the details in communicating with the transaction manager.

Clients use Transaction objects by passing them to services so that services may join the transaction. The client can abort or commit the transaction by calling the abort() or commit() methods of this interface. When a timeout is specified for these methods, these methods will wait until the transaction manager determines the outcome of the two-phase commit operation. Once that happens, these methods will wait until either the timeout has been reached or until all participants in the transaction have been notified about the outcome of the transaction. When no timeout is specified, these methods return as soon as the transaction manager has determined that the commit or abort will be successful but before all participants have been notified of the result.

Clients obtain a Transaction object from the Transaction.Created object that is returned by the TransactionFactory class.

```
public interface Transaction {
// Inner Classes
    public static class Created implements Serializable;
// Public Instance Methods
    public abstract void abort() throws UnknownTransactionException, CannotAbortException,
        java.rmi.RemoteException;
    public abstract void abort(long waitFor) throws UnknownTransactionException, CannotAbortException,
        TimeoutExpiredException, java.rmi.RemoteException;
    public abstract void commit() throws UnknownTransactionException, CannotCommitException,
        java.rmi.RemoteException;
    public abstract void commit(long waitFor) throws UnknownTransactionException, CannotCommitException,
        TimeoutExpiredException, java.rmi.RemoteException;
}
```

Implementations: NestableTransaction, net.jini.core.transaction.server.ServerTransaction

Passed To: Transaction.Created.Created(), net.jini.space.JavaSpace.{notify(), read(), readIfExists(), take(), takeIfExists(), write()}

Type Of: Transaction.Created.transaction

Transaction.Created
net.jini.core.transaction

Jini 1.0
serializable

This is a static inner class of the Transaction interface. Objects of this class are used as a data structure that is provided to clients when a transaction is created. The data in this class includes the transaction object and the lease assigned to the transaction object.

Instances of this class are created by the TransactionFactory class. Clients are responsible for renewing the lease contained in this class.

```
public static class Transaction.Created implements Serializable {
// Public Constructors
    public Created(Transaction transaction, net.jini.core.lease.Lease lease);
```

```
// Public Instance Fields
    public final net.jini.core.lease.Lease lease;
    public final Transaction transaction;
}
```

Returned By: TransactionFactory.create()

TransactionException   Jini 1.0

net.jini.core.transaction   *serializable checked*

This class is the superclass of all of the exception types in this package and the
net.jini.core.transaction.server package.

```
public class TransactionException extends Exception {
// Public Constructors
    public TransactionException();
    public TransactionException(String desc);
}
```

Hierarchy: Object→ Throwable(Serializable)→ Exception→ TransactionException

Subclasses: CannotAbortException, CannotCommitException, CannotJoinException,
CannotNestException, TimeoutExpiredException, UnknownTransactionException,
net.jini.core.transaction.server.CrashCountException

Thrown By: net.jini.space.JavaSpace.{notify(), read(), readIfExists(), take(), takeIfExists(), write()}

TransactionFactory   Jini 1.0

net.jini.core.transaction

This class is the factory used to create transaction objects. Clients call the static create( )
methods of this class to obtain non-nestable transaction and nestable top-level transaction objects.

```
public class TransactionFactory {
// No Constructor
// Public Class Methods
    public static NestableTransaction.Created create(net.jini.core.transaction.server.NestableTransactionManager mgr,
                        long leaseTime) throws net.jini.core.lease.LeaseDeniedException,
        java.rmi.RemoteException;
    public static Transaction.Created create(net.jini.core.transaction.server.TransactionManager mgr, long leaseTime)
        throws net.jini.core.lease.LeaseDeniedException, java.rmi.RemoteException;
}
```

UnknownTransactionException   Jini 1.0

net.jini.core.transaction   *serializable checked*

An exception of this type is thrown when the transaction is unknown to the transaction
manager. This is usually caused because the transaction has been previously aborted or
committed.

```
public class UnknownTransactionException extends TransactionException {
// Public Constructors
    public UnknownTransactionException();
    public UnknownTransactionException(String desc);
}
```

Hierarchy: Object→ Throwable(Serializable)→ Exception→ TransactionException→ UnknownTransactionException

Thrown By: Too many methods to list.

The *net.jini.core.transaction.server* Package

The net.jini.core.transaction.server package provides interfaces and support classes used by services that want to become participants of a transaction, as well as the service interface of the transaction manager itself. Figure 15-7 shows the class hierarchy for this package.

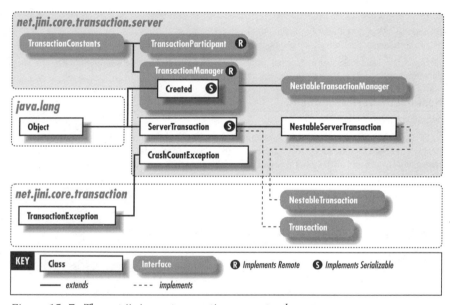

Figure 15–7: The net.jini.core.transaction.server package

The interface that is supported by the Jini transaction manager is either the Transaction-Manager or NestableTransactionManager interface. In order to use a transaction, you use one of these interfaces as the class within a net.jini.core.lookup.ServiceTemplate object. The NestableTransactionManager interface is a subclass of the TransactionManager interface; this allows clients to search in the lookup service for something that implements just for the TransactionManager interface.

Instances of the ServerTransaction class and the NestableServerTransaction class are returned from the net.jini.core.transaction.TransactionFactory class. Since the net.jini.core.transaction.Transaction interface does not provide the ability to obtain the status of the transaction or the ability to join a transaction, you must cast the object that is returned from the Transaction-Factory to a ServerTransaction or NestableServerTransaction object in order to perform those operations.

To join a transaction, the participant must support the TransactionParticipant interface.

CrashCountException   Jini 1.0

net.jini.core.transaction.server   *serializable checked*

An exception of this type is thrown when the participant tries to rejoin a transaction with a different crash count. This can be caused when the participant crashes and is unable to restore the correct state after the crash. The transaction manager will abort the offending transaction, since this participant cannot continue with the transaction.

```
public class CrashCountException extends net.jini.core.transaction.TransactionException {
// Public Constructors
    public CrashCountException();
    public CrashCountException(String reason);
}
```

Hierarchy: Object→ Throwable(Serializable)→ Exception→
net.jini.core.transaction.TransactionException→ CrashCountException

Thrown By: NestableServerTransaction.promote(), NestableTransactionManager.promote(), ServerTransaction.join(), TransactionManager.join()

NestableServerTransaction   Jini 1.0

net.jini.core.transaction.server   *serializable*

This class is a subclass of the ServerTransaction class and is an implementation of the NestableTransaction interface. It implements the extra methods required by the Nestable-Transaction interface and also provides the ability to promote a transaction to its parent transaction.

```
public class NestableServerTransaction extends ServerTransaction
        implements net.jini.core.transaction.NestableTransaction {
// Public Constructors
    public NestableServerTransaction(NestableTransactionManager mgr, long id,
                                     NestableServerTransaction parent);
// Public Instance Methods
    public boolean enclosedBy(net.jini.core.transaction.NestableTransaction enclosing);
    public void promote(TransactionParticipant[ ] parts, long[ ] crashCounts, TransactionParticipant drop)
        throws net.jini.core.transaction.UnknownTransactionException, net.jini.core.transaction.CannotJoinException,
        CrashCountException, java.rmi.RemoteException;
// Methods Implementing NestableTransaction
    public net.jini.core.transaction.NestableTransaction.Created create(long leaseTime)
        throws net.jini.core.transaction.UnknownTransactionException, net.jini.core.transaction.CannotJoinException,
        net.jini.core.lease.LeaseDeniedException, java.rmi.RemoteException;
    public net.jini.core.transaction.NestableTransaction.Created create(NestableTransactionManager mgr,
                                     long leaseTime)
        throws net.jini.core.transaction.UnknownTransactionException, net.jini.core.transaction.CannotJoinException,
        net.jini.core.lease.LeaseDeniedException, java.rmi.RemoteException;
// Public Methods Overriding ServerTransaction
    public boolean isNested();
// Public Instance Fields
    public final NestableServerTransaction parent;
}
```

Hierarchy: Object→ ServerTransaction(Serializable, net.jini.core.transaction.Transaction)→
NestableServerTransaction(net.jini.core.transaction.NestableTransaction(net.jini.core.transaction.Transaction))

Passed To: NestableServerTransaction.NestableServerTransaction()

Type Of: NestableServerTransaction.parent

NestableTransactionManager
Jini 1.0

net.jini.core.transaction.server
remote

This interface is implemented by the nestable transaction manager and is used by the NestableServerTransaction object that is returned by the transaction factory.

This interface extends the TransactionManager interface and also adds the ability to promote a subtransaction to its parent. The promotion process should be used by the subtransaction's transaction manager to pass its participants to its parents. This is a transaction manager to transaction manager request; clients and participants should not be involved in the promotion process.

```
public interface NestableTransactionManager extends TransactionManager {
// Public Instance Methods
    public abstract TransactionManager.Created create(NestableTransactionManager parentMgr, long parentID,
                        long lease)
        throws net.jini.core.transaction.UnknownTransactionException, net.jini.core.transaction.CannotJoinException,
        net.jini.core.lease.LeaseDeniedException, java.rmi.RemoteException;
    public abstract void promote(long id, TransactionParticipant[ ] parts, long[ ] crashCounts,
                        TransactionParticipant drop)
        throws net.jini.core.transaction.UnknownTransactionException, net.jini.core.transaction.CannotJoinException,
        CrashCountException, java.rmi.RemoteException;
}
```

Hierarchy: (NestableTransactionManager(TransactionManager(java.rmi.Remote, TransactionConstants)))

Passed To: net.jini.core.transaction.NestableTransaction.create(), net.jini.core.transaction.TransactionFactory.create(), NestableServerTransaction.{create(), NestableServerTransaction()}, NestableTransactionManager.create()

ServerTransaction
Jini 1.0

net.jini.core.transaction.server
serializable

This class is an implementation of the Transaction interface and is instantiated by the TransactionFactory if the transaction manager is not nestable. A service that wants to join a transaction receives a Transaction object from the client, casts it to a ServerTransaction object, and calls that object's join() method, providing it a TransactionParticipant object. The transaction manager will contact the transaction participant to ask it to commit or rollback the transaction when necessary.

```
public class ServerTransaction implements Serializable, net.jini.core.transaction.Transaction {
// Public Constructors
    public ServerTransaction(TransactionManager mgr, long id);
// Public Instance Methods
    public int getState() throws net.jini.core.transaction.UnknownTransactionException, java.rmi.RemoteException;
    public boolean isNested();                                                                    constant
    public void join(TransactionParticipant part, long crashCount)
        throws net.jini.core.transaction.UnknownTransactionException, net.jini.core.transaction.CannotJoinException,
        CrashCountException, java.rmi.RemoteException;
// Methods Implementing Transaction
    public void abort() throws net.jini.core.transaction.UnknownTransactionException,
        net.jini.core.transaction.CannotAbortException, java.rmi.RemoteException;
    public void abort(long waitFor) throws net.jini.core.transaction.UnknownTransactionException,
        net.jini.core.transaction.CannotAbortException, net.jini.core.transaction.TimeoutExpiredException,
        java.rmi.RemoteException;
    public void commit() throws net.jini.core.transaction.UnknownTransactionException,
        net.jini.core.transaction.CannotCommitException, java.rmi.RemoteException;
```

net.jini.core Package

```
     public void commit(long waitFor) throws net.jini.core.transaction.UnknownTransactionException,
          net.jini.core.transaction.CannotCommitException, net.jini.core.transaction.TimeoutExpiredException,
          java.rmi.RemoteException;
// Public Methods Overriding Object
     public boolean equals(Object other);
     public int hashCode( );
// Public Instance Fields
     public final long id;
     public final TransactionManager mgr;
}
```

Hierarchy: Object→ ServerTransaction(Serializable, net.jini.core.transaction.Transaction)

Subclasses: NestableServerTransaction

TransactionConstants   Jini 1.0

net.jini.core.transaction.server

This interface defines the constants used to represent the different states of a transaction. The interfaces of the transaction managers and participants extend this interface so that they may use the constants directly without referring to this interface.

```
public interface TransactionConstants {
// Public Constants
     public static final int ABORTED;                                    =6
     public static final int ACTIVE;                                     =1
     public static final int COMMITTED;                                  =5
     public static final int NOTCHANGED;                                 =4
     public static final int PREPARED;                                   =3
     public static final int VOTING;                                     =2
}
```

Implementations: com.sun.jini.constants.TxnConstants, TransactionManager, TransactionParticipant

TransactionManager   Jini 1.0

net.jini.core.transaction.server   *remote*

This interface is implemented by the transaction manager and is used by the ServerTransaction object that is returned by the transaction factory. The operations of this class are opaque to the developer. This interface provides the ability to create, join, abort, commit, and obtain the status of a transaction.

```
public interface TransactionManager extends java.rmi.Remote, TransactionConstants {
// Inner Classes
     public static class Created implements Serializable;
// Public Instance Methods
     public abstract void abort(long id) throws net.jini.core.transaction.UnknownTransactionException,
          net.jini.core.transaction.CannotAbortException, java.rmi.RemoteException;
     public abstract void abort(long id, long waitFor) throws net.jini.core.transaction.UnknownTransactionException,
          net.jini.core.transaction.CannotAbortException, net.jini.core.transaction.TimeoutExpiredException,
          java.rmi.RemoteException;
     public abstract void commit(long id) throws net.jini.core.transaction.UnknownTransactionException,
          net.jini.core.transaction.CannotCommitException, java.rmi.RemoteException;
     public abstract void commit(long id, long waitFor) throws net.jini.core.transaction.UnknownTransactionException,
          net.jini.core.transaction.CannotCommitException, net.jini.core.transaction.TimeoutExpiredException,
          java.rmi.RemoteException;
     public abstract TransactionManager.Created create(long lease) throws net.jini.core.lease.LeaseDeniedException,
          java.rmi.RemoteException;
```

```
    public abstract int getState(long id) throws net.jini.core.transaction.UnknownTransactionException,
        java.rmi.RemoteException;
    public abstract void join(long id, TransactionParticipant part, long crashCount)
        throws net.jini.core.transaction.UnknownTransactionException, net.jini.core.transaction.CannotJoinException,
        CrashCountException, java.rmi.RemoteException;
}
```

Hierarchy: (TransactionManager(java.rmi.Remote, TransactionConstants))

Implementations: NestableTransactionManager

Passed To: net.jini.core.transaction.TransactionFactory.create(), ServerTransaction.ServerTransaction(), TransactionParticipant.{abort(), commit(), prepare(), prepareAndCommit()}

Type Of: ServerTransaction.mgr

TransactionManager.Created   Jini 1.0
net.jini.core.transaction.server   *serializable*

This is a static inner class of the TransactionManager interface. Objects of this class are used as data structures that are provided to clients when a transaction is created. The data in this class includes the ID of the transaction and the lease assigned to the transaction. This class is never used by the developer.

```
public static class TransactionManager.Created implements Serializable {
// Public Constructors
    public Created(long id, net.jini.core.lease.Lease lease);
// Public Instance Fields
    public final long id;
    public final net.jini.core.lease.Lease lease;
}
```

Returned By: NestableTransactionManager.create(), TransactionManager.create()

TransactionParticipant   Jini 1.0
net.jini.core.transaction.server   *remote*

This remote interface is implemented by objects that want to join a transaction. The methods of this interface allows the transaction manager to inform the participant either to abort or to commit its operations. The commit operation is a two-phase operation: the transaction manager will first call the prepare( ) method of the transaction participant, asking it to vote on the outcome of the transaction. The participant must return either TransactionConstants.PREPARED, which indicates that it wants the transaction to succeed and is prepared to commit it; TransactionConstants.ABORT, which indicates that the transaction must be aborted; or TransactionConstants.NOTCHANGED, which indicates that the service did not change any data in the transaction.

If the participant voted to prepare the transaction, then at a later time the transaction manager will call an additional methods of the participant interface. The commit( ) method will be called if all participants voted to prepare the data, in which case the service must roll forward its changes. The abort( ) method will be called otherwise, in which case the service must roll back its data.

The transaction manager may choose to call the prepareAndCommit( ) method rather than the prepare( ) method; this indicates that this participant is the only participant in the transaction. The participant must either roll forward its data and return TransactionConstants.COMMITTED, or it must roll back the data and return ABORT.

net.jini.core Package

```
public interface TransactionParticipant extends java.rmi.Remote, TransactionConstants {
// Public Instance Methods
    public abstract void abort(TransactionManager mgr, long id)
        throws net.jini.core.transaction.UnknownTransactionException, java.rmi.RemoteException;
    public abstract void commit(TransactionManager mgr, long id)
        throws net.jini.core.transaction.UnknownTransactionException, java.rmi.RemoteException;
    public abstract int prepare(TransactionManager mgr, long id)
        throws net.jini.core.transaction.UnknownTransactionException, java.rmi.RemoteException;
    public abstract int prepareAndCommit(TransactionManager mgr, long id)
        throws net.jini.core.transaction.UnknownTransactionException, java.rmi.RemoteException;
}
```

Hierarchy: (TransactionParticipant(java.rmi.Remote, TransactionConstants))

Passed To: NestableServerTransaction.promote(), NestableTransactionManager.promote(), ServerTransaction.join(), TransactionManager.join()

CHAPTER 16

The net.jini Packages

The net.jini package hierarchy contains the packages that make up the Jini Technology Extended Platform (JXP). This includes utility classes to handle lookup and discovery, joining lookup services, leasing, administration, and event processing. This package also includes the service interface for the JavaSpaces service. The net.jini.core package hierarchy is not part of this component; it is documented separately. However, from a developer's perspective, there is no difference between the two sets of APIs; both are official parts of the Jini specification.

In 1.1, many new classes were added to this package. Some of these moved into this category from the Jini Software Kit (JSK) where they were in various com.sun packages. In 1.1, you can use either class definition by specifying the full package name (or changing the import statement), but you should migrate to the classes in this package as soon as possible. Some of the classes changed their API when they moved between packages, and the com.sun classes may not be carried through future releases.

The net.jini.admin Package

The net.jini.admin package contains the interfaces that Jini services are encouraged to implement in order for clients to be able to administer the service. In order for a service to be administrable, it must support the Administrable interface. This interface provides one method that returns the administration object for the service.

This package also contains the JoinAdmin interface. This interface should be implemented by services that want to allow clients to control the parameters used in the join protocol. With this interface, clients can control what groups, attributes, etc. the service will use to join the Jini community.

See Chapter 7, *Service Administration*, for more information on administration. Figure 16-1 shows the class hierarchy for this package.

Administrable   Jini 1.0

net.jini.admin

This interface is implemented by services that are administrable. To see if a service is administrable, use the **instanceof** operator to see if it implements this interface; if it does, cast the object and use the **getAdmin()** method to obtain the object that can be

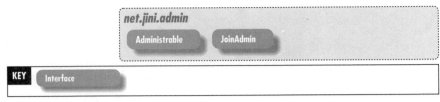

Figure 16–1: The net.jini.admin package

used to perform administration tasks on the service.

See also com.sun.jini.admin.DestroyAdmin, com.sun.jini.admin.StorageLocationAdmin, and net.jini.lookup.DiscoveryAdmin.

```
public interface Administrable {
// Public Instance Methods
    public abstract Object getAdmin() throws java.rmi.RemoteException;
}
```

JoinAdmin   Jini 1.0

net.jini.admin

This interface is implemented by the administration object of a service if the service wants to allow clients to control how the service will join the Jini network. This interface allows you to get and modify the service attributes, the groups the service will join, and the lookup locators the service should use for unicast discovery.

```
public interface JoinAdmin {
// Property Accessor Methods (by property name)
    public abstract net.jini.core.entry.Entry[ ] getLookupAttributes() throws java.rmi.RemoteException;
    public abstract String[ ] getLookupGroups() throws java.rmi.RemoteException;
    public abstract void setLookupGroups(String[ ] groups) throws java.rmi.RemoteException;
    public abstract net.jini.core.discovery.LookupLocator[ ] getLookupLocators() throws java.rmi.RemoteException;
    public abstract void setLookupLocators(net.jini.core.discovery.LookupLocator[ ] locators)
        throws java.rmi.RemoteException;
// Public Instance Methods
    public abstract void addLookupAttributes(net.jini.core.entry.Entry[ ] attrSets) throws java.rmi.RemoteException;
    public abstract void addLookupGroups(String[ ] groups) throws java.rmi.RemoteException;
    public abstract void addLookupLocators(net.jini.core.discovery.LookupLocator[ ] locators)
        throws java.rmi.RemoteException;
    public abstract void modifyLookupAttributes(net.jini.core.entry.Entry[ ] attrSetTemplates,
                                                net.jini.core.entry.Entry[ ] attrSets)
        throws java.rmi.RemoteException;
    public abstract void removeLookupGroups(String[ ] groups) throws java.rmi.RemoteException;
    public abstract void removeLookupLocators(net.jini.core.discovery.LookupLocator[ ] locators)
        throws java.rmi.RemoteException;
}
```

The net.jini.discovery Package

This package contains classes that assist Jini clients to participate in the lookup service discovery protocols (both unicast and multicast). Jini services can use these classes, but they generally use the com.sun.jini.lookup.JoinManager class (net.jini.lookup.JoinManager in 1.1) instead. However, Jini services may delegate management of the lookup and discovery protocols to a lookup discovery service; the interface to that service is also defined in this package.

The LookupDiscovery class is used for multicast discovery. An instance of this class will initiate multicast discovery, passing all lookup services that it finds to an object that implements the DiscoveryListener interface. To discover lookup services, create a class that implements the DiscoveryListener interface, then instantiate a LookupDiscovery object, passing it a reference to the discovery listener. The LookupDiscovery object will pass all lookup services it finds to the listener. The lookup services sent to the listener will be included as part of the DiscoveryEvent objects. See Chapter 4, *Basic Jini Programming*, for more information on discovery of lookup services.

In 1.1, there are additional classes that can be used in place of the LookupDiscovery class. The LookupDiscoveryManager is used to perform both multicast discovery and unicast discovery to a set of known lookup services. The LookupLocatorDiscovery class is used to perform only unicast discovery. These classes all implement the DiscoveryManagement interface, also new in 1.1, which provides a generalized interface for lookup discovery.

Unicast discovery in 1.0 is performed with the net.jini.core.discovery.LookupLocator class, which is used heavily by the classes in this package. The class hierarchy for the net.jini.discovery package is shown in Figure 16-2.

When you use the most common classes of this package, the details of the discovery protocol are hidden from you. You create objects that perform discovery, and you're notified when they discover lookup services. If you're curious about the details of what goes on, here's a brief explanation.

There are two parts of the discovery protocol that use multicasting. A service may use multicasting to discover lookup services, and lookup services will use multicasting to announce their existence to services and clients already on the network.

Multicast discovery of lookup services:

In order to discover lookup services, the requesting client must send a multicast packet onto the network. While the requestor may send more than one packet, there is no ordering to the packets, nor does it matter if all the packets are heard. The multicast packets are created with the OutgoingMulticastRequest class and unmarshalled with the IncomingMulticastRequest class.

There are three pieces of information included in the packets. First is the network port on which the requestor is listening to continue discovery. Second are the groups the requestor is trying to discover. The groups may be separated into different multicast packets if there is not enough room in a single packet to store the groups. However, there is no ordering of the packets. Each packet is self-contained with the same header information (such as the port) and specifies different groups as if they were separate requests.

The last piece of the multicast packet is the lookup services that the requestor has already heard from; lookup services will not re-respond if they are in this list. If there is not enough room in the multicast packet, this list is truncated. This can cause lookup services that have already been discovered to re-report their existence. This is inefficient but is not a problem. The requestor can simply ignore the lookup services that it has already discovered.

The lookup services will connect to the network address specified in the multicast packets. This causes the requestor to continue the discovery process with that lookup service by using unicast discovery.

Lost packets may be handled by retrying the request. Since it is not possible to determine if a packet has been lost, the solution is to retry the packet a few times and only for a short period of time. Once it is decided that all lookup services on the network have replied, there is no reason to retry (whether this is correct or not). Retrying the

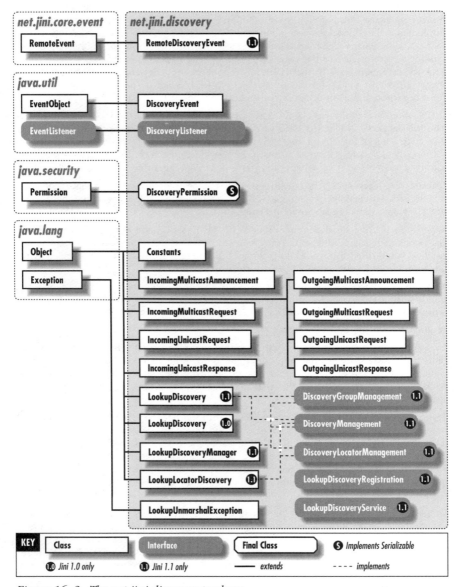

Figure 16–2: The net.jini.discovery package

request protocol is not necessary to discover new lookup services since new lookup services will use the announcement protocol.

Multicast announcement of lookup services:

The multicast announcement protocol is used by lookup services to announce their existence to the Jini community. While the announcer may send more than one packet, there is no ordering to the packets, nor does it matter if all the packets are heard. The multicast packets are created with the OutgoingMulticastAnnouncement class and unmarshalled with the IncomingMulticastAnnouncement class.

There are three pieces of information included in these packets. The first two are the service ID of the lookup service and the lookup locator that can be used to discover the lookup service. As with the request protocol, there is no ordering with multicast packets—all packets have the same header, which includes these two bits of information.

The last piece of the multicast packet is the set of groups that the lookup service supports. If the groups do not fit in one multicast packet, then the groups will be split onto many multicast packets.

Once the announcement is received by the Jini services, they can use the lookup locator that was provided (which uses the unicast discovery protocol) to obtain a reference to the lookup service.

Lost packets are handled by retrying the announcement from time to time.

Unicast discovery of lookup services:

There are three ways to participate in unicast discovery. If a lookup locator is used, the discovering entity will initiate a unicast connection to the lookup service. If the multicast request protocol is used, the lookup service will initiate a unicast connection to the discovering entity. And finally, if the multicast announcement protocol is used, the discovering entity will use the lookup locator that it received to initiate a unicast connection to the lookup service.

It does not matter which entity initiates the unicast connection. The discovering entity must send a unicast discover request and the lookup service must send the response. The request is placed onto the stream with the OutgoingUnicastRequest class and marshalled with the IncomingUnicastRequest class. The response is placed onto the stream with the OutgoingUnicastResponse class and marshalled with the IncomingUnicastResponse class.

The format of the request is simply the protocol version of the request. No other information is passed to the lookup service. The lookup service simply confirms that it supports the protocol and responds. The format of the response currently includes the ServiceRegistrar of the lookup service and all the groups that it supports.

Packet ordering and lost packets are handled by the underlying TCP protocol.

Constants   Jini 1.0

net.jini.discovery

This class contains the IP addresses for the multicast request and announcement protocol. The static methods in this class return java.net.InetAddress objects that represent the multicast addresses. Developers do not use this class directly.

```
public class Constants {
// No Constructor
// Public Constants
    public static final short discoveryPort;                                =4160
// Public Class Methods
    public static final java.net.InetAddress getAnnouncementAddress() throws java.net.UnknownHostException;
    public static final java.net.InetAddress getRequestAddress() throws java.net.UnknownHostException;
}
```

net.jini
Packages

DiscoveryEvent

Jini 1.0

net.jini.discovery

serializable event

An event of this type is passed to the DiscoveryListener by the LookupDiscovery object when it discovers or discards one or more lookup services. The getRegistrars() method returns an array containing the ServiceRegistrar for each newly discovered or discarded lookup service. The listener knows whether those services were discovered or discarded based on the method that the event was passed to: the discovered() method or the discarded() method of the DiscoveryListener interface.

```
public class DiscoveryEvent extends java.util.EventObject {
// Public Constructors
    public DiscoveryEvent(Object source, net.jini.core.lookup.ServiceRegistrar[ ] regs);
// Public Instance Methods
    public net.jini.core.lookup.ServiceRegistrar[ ] getRegistrars();
// Protected Instance Fields
    protected net.jini.core.lookup.ServiceRegistrar[ ] regs;
}
```

Hierarchy: Object→ java.util.EventObject(Serializable)→ DiscoveryEvent

Passed To: DiscoveryListener.{discarded(), discovered()}

DiscoveryGroupManagement

Jini 1.1 Alpha

net.jini.discovery

This interface defines methods and constants related to multicast discovery. The methods of this interface define how the groups of a lookup services may be set or retrieved.

The ALL_GROUPS constant is useful when you want discovery to find all groups in the multicast network. If you want to instantiate an object that implements this interface (e.g., a LookupDiscovery object) but not have that object actually start participating in discovery, you can use the NO_GROUPS constant. Later, you can use the setGroups() method to pass in a set of groups for which discovery should be started.

```
public interface DiscoveryGroupManagement {
// Public Constants
    public static final String[ ] ALL_GROUPS;
    public static final String[ ] NO_GROUPS;
// Public Instance Methods
    public abstract void addGroups(String[ ] groups) throws java.io.IOException;
    public abstract String[ ] getGroups();
    public abstract void removeGroups(String[ ] groups);
    public abstract void setGroups(String[ ] groups) throws java.io.IOException;
}
```

Implementations: LookupDiscovery, LookupDiscoveryManager

DiscoveryListener

Jini 1.0

net.jini.discovery

event listener

This interface must be implemented by a listener in order to be registered with the LookupDiscovery class. The discovered() method is called when new lookup services are found. The discarded() method is called when previous lookup services are discarded or no longer support the groups requested.

```
public interface DiscoveryListener extends java.util.EventListener {
// Public Instance Methods
```

```
    public abstract void discarded(DiscoveryEvent e);
    public abstract void discovered(DiscoveryEvent e);
}
```

Hierarchy: (DiscoveryListener(java.util.EventListener))

Passed To: com.sun.jini.discovery.LookupLocatorDiscovery.{addDiscoveryListener(), removeDiscoveryListener()}, DiscoveryManagement.{addDiscoveryListener(), removeDiscoveryListener()}, LookupDiscovery.{addDiscoveryListener(), removeDiscoveryListener()}, LookupDiscoveryManager.{addDiscoveryListener(), LookupDiscoveryManager(), removeDiscoveryListener()}, net.jini.discovery.LookupLocatorDiscovery.{addDiscoveryListener(), removeDiscoveryListener()}

DiscoveryLocatorManagement   Jini 1.1 Alpha

net.jini.discovery

This interface defines methods related to unicast discovery. The methods of this interface define how lookup locators used to find lookup services may be retrieved, set, or modified.

```
public interface DiscoveryLocatorManagement {
    // Public Instance Methods
    public abstract void addLocators(net.jini.core.discovery.LookupLocator[ ] locators);
    public abstract net.jini.core.discovery.LookupLocator[ ] getLocators();
    public abstract void removeLocators(net.jini.core.discovery.LookupLocator[ ] locators);
    public abstract void setLocators(net.jini.core.discovery.LookupLocator[ ] locators);
}
```

Implementations: LookupDiscoveryManager, net.jini.discovery.LookupLocatorDiscovery

DiscoveryManagement   Jini 1.1 Alpha

net.jini.discovery

This interface defines methods related to discovery. Through this interface you register for discovery events, discard a lookup service, or terminate the discovery process. The LookupDiscovery class implements this interface in 1.1.

```
public interface DiscoveryManagement {
    // Event Registration Methods (by event name)
    public abstract void addDiscoveryListener(DiscoveryListener l);
    public abstract void removeDiscoveryListener(DiscoveryListener l);
    // Public Instance Methods
    public abstract void discard(net.jini.core.lookup.ServiceRegistrar proxy);
    public abstract net.jini.core.lookup.ServiceRegistrar[ ] getRegistrars();
    public abstract void terminate();
}
```

Implementations: LookupDiscovery, LookupDiscoveryManager, net.jini.discovery.LookupLocatorDiscovery

Passed To: net.jini.lookup.ClientLookupManager.ClientLookupManager(), net.jini.lookup.JoinManager.JoinManager()

Returned By: net.jini.lookup.ClientLookupManager.getDiscoveryManager(), net.jini.lookup.JoinManager.getDiscoveryManager()

DiscoveryPermission   Jini 1.0

net.jini.discovery   *serializable permission*

In order to participate in the multicast discovery protocol, services and clients must have this permission with a name that includes the groups that the requested lookup service must support. For the default (public) group, that name is the empty string. Developers do not use this class, but administrators may need to add this class name and the group name(s) to the appropriate *java.policy* file.

```
public final class DiscoveryPermission extends java.security.Permission implements Serializable {
// Public Constructors
   public DiscoveryPermission(String group);
   public DiscoveryPermission(String group, String action);
// Public Methods Overriding Permission
   public boolean equals(Object obj);
   public String getActions();
   public int hashCode();
   public boolean implies(java.security.Permission p);
   public java.security.PermissionCollection newPermissionCollection();
}
```

Hierarchy: Object→ java.security.Permission(java.security.Guard, Serializable)→ DiscoveryPermission(Serializable)

IncomingMulticastAnnouncement   Jini 1.0

net.jini.discovery

This class is used to unmarshal the multicast datagram packets that are sent by the lookup service to announce its existence. The data obtained includes the service ID of the lookup service, a lookup locator used to unicast discover the lookup service, and the groups that the lookup service supports. Developers do not use this class directly.

```
public class IncomingMulticastAnnouncement {
// Public Constructors
   public IncomingMulticastAnnouncement(java.net.DatagramPacket p) throws java.io.IOException;
// Property Accessor Methods (by property name)
   public String[ ] getGroups();
   public net.jini.core.discovery.LookupLocator getLocator();
   public net.jini.core.lookup.ServiceID getServiceID();
// Public Methods Overriding Object
   public boolean equals(Object o);
   public int hashCode();
// Protected Instance Fields
   protected String[ ] groups;
   protected net.jini.core.discovery.LookupLocator locator;
   protected final int protoVersion;                                    =1
   protected net.jini.core.lookup.ServiceID serviceID;
}
```

IncomingMulticastRequest   Jini 1.0

net.jini.discovery

This class is used to unmarshal the multicast datagram packets that are sent by the discovering entities to request lookup services. The data contains the network address of the service, the groups that the service needs the lookup service to support, and the service IDs of the lookup services that have already responded. Developers do not use this class directly.

```
public class IncomingMulticastRequest {
// Public Constructors
    public IncomingMulticastRequest(java.net.DatagramPacket dgram) throws java.io.IOException;
// Property Accessor Methods (by property name)
    public java.net.InetAddress getAddress();
    public String[ ] getGroups();
    public int getPort();
    public net.jini.core.lookup.ServiceID[ ] getServiceIDs();
// Public Methods Overriding Object
    public boolean equals(Object o);
    public int hashCode();
// Protected Instance Fields
    protected java.net.InetAddress addr;
    protected String[ ] groups;
    protected int port;
    protected final int protoVersion;                                              =1
    protected net.jini.core.lookup.ServiceID[ ] serviceIDs;
}
```

IncomingUnicastRequest   Jini 1.0

net.jini.discovery

This class is used to unmarshal the incoming request from a network data stream. Data is read from the stream and checked to see that it is a valid incoming unicast request. Developers do not use this class directly.

```
public class IncomingUnicastRequest {
// Public Constructors
    public IncomingUnicastRequest(java.io.InputStream str) throws java.io.IOException;
// Protected Instance Fields
    protected int protoVersion;
}
```

IncomingUnicastResponse   Jini 1.0

net.jini.discovery

This class is used to unmarshal the incoming response from a network data stream. The response is sent in answer to a unicast discovery request. The ServiceRegistrar object that represents the lookup service and all the groups that the lookup service supports are included in the data stream. Developers do not use this class directly.

```
public class IncomingUnicastResponse {
// Public Constructors
    public IncomingUnicastResponse(java.io.InputStream str) throws java.io.IOException, ClassNotFoundException;
// Public Instance Methods
    public String[ ] getGroups();
    public net.jini.core.lookup.ServiceRegistrar getRegistrar();
// Public Methods Overriding Object
    public boolean equals(Object o);
    public int hashCode();
// Protected Instance Fields
    protected String[ ] groups;
    protected net.jini.core.lookup.ServiceRegistrar registrar;
}
```

LookupDiscovery
Jini 1.0

net.jini.discovery

This class is the main class that handles the multicast discovery protocol. To use multicast discovery, construct an instance of this class, passing it the array of groups that you want the discovered lookup services to support.

In 1.1, this class implements the DiscoveryManagement interface. In 1.0, this class implements the same methods, even though that interface does not exist in 1.0.

The addDiscoveryListener( ) method associates a DiscoveryListener object with the lookup discovery object. If the lookup discovery object has already discovered some instances of the lookup service, the discovery listener is immediately notified that those services exist. Other notifications follow when new lookup services are discovered and when lookup services are discarded.

When you receive an error while accessing a lookup service, you should call the discard( ) method. This sends the notification to all listeners that the lookup service is no longer valid (though it will be rediscovered if the lookup service comes back up). If you use the setGroups( ), addGroups( ), or removeGroups( ) methods to change the groups that you are interested in discovering, lookup services which don't support the new groups will be also discarded.

This class creates a number of daemon threads to perform its operations. To kill those threads and stop participating in discovery, call the terminate( ) method.

```
public class LookupDiscovery implements DiscoveryGroupManagement, DiscoveryManagement {
// Public Constructors
    public LookupDiscovery(String[ ] groups) throws java.io.IOException;
// Public Constants
    public static final String[ ] ALL_GROUPS;
    public static final String[ ] NO_GROUPS;
// Event Registration Methods (by event name)
    public void addDiscoveryListener(DiscoveryListener l);                 Implements:DiscoveryManagement
    public void removeDiscoveryListener(DiscoveryListener l);              Implements:DiscoveryManagement
// Methods Implementing DiscoveryGroupManagement
    public void addGroups(String[ ] newGroups) throws java.io.IOException;
    public String[ ] getGroups();
    public void removeGroups(String[ ] oldGroups);
    public void setGroups(String[ ] newGroups) throws java.io.IOException;
// Methods Implementing DiscoveryManagement
    public void addDiscoveryListener(DiscoveryListener l);
    public void discard(net.jini.core.lookup.ServiceRegistrar reg);
1.1 public net.jini.core.lookup.ServiceRegistrar[ ] getRegistrars();
    public void removeDiscoveryListener(DiscoveryListener l);
    public void terminate();
// Public Methods Overriding Object
    public void finalize();
}
```

Hierarchy: Object→ LookupDiscovery(DiscoveryGroupManagement, DiscoveryManagement)

LookupDiscoveryManager
Jini 1.1 Alpha

net.jini.discovery

This class is used to handle both multicast and unicast discovery; it allows a client or service to participate in multicast discovery with the network's multicast radius and to discover specific lookup services (using unicast discovery) that exist at known locations. It is available in 1.1 only.

●

This class handles multicast discovery in the same way as the LookupDiscovery class. It handles unicast discovery in the same way as the LookupLocatorDiscovery class.

```
public class LookupDiscoveryManager implements DiscoveryGroupManagement, DiscoveryLocatorManagement,
        DiscoveryManagement {
// Public Constructors
    public LookupDiscoveryManager(String[ ] groups, net.jini.core.discovery.LookupLocator[ ] locators,
                        DiscoveryListener listener) throws java.io.IOException;
// Public Constants
    public static final int FROM_GROUP;                                                =1
    public static final int FROM_LOCATOR;                                              =2
// Event Registration Methods (by event name)
    public void addDiscoveryListener(DiscoveryListener l);              Implements:DiscoveryManagement
    public void removeDiscoveryListener(DiscoveryListener l);           Implements:DiscoveryManagement
// Public Instance Methods
    public int getFrom(net.jini.core.lookup.ServiceRegistrar proxy);
// Methods Implementing DiscoveryGroupManagement
    public void addGroups(String[ ] groups) throws java.io.IOException;
    public String[ ] getGroups();
    public void removeGroups(String[ ] groups);
    public void setGroups(String[ ] groups) throws java.io.IOException;
// Methods Implementing DiscoveryLocatorManagement
    public void addLocators(net.jini.core.discovery.LookupLocator[ ] locators);
    public net.jini.core.discovery.LookupLocator[ ] getLocators();
    public void removeLocators(net.jini.core.discovery.LookupLocator[ ] locators);
    public void setLocators(net.jini.core.discovery.LookupLocator[ ] locators);
// Methods Implementing DiscoveryManagement
    public void addDiscoveryListener(DiscoveryListener l);
    public void discard(net.jini.core.lookup.ServiceRegistrar proxy);
    public net.jini.core.lookup.ServiceRegistrar[ ] getRegistrars();
    public void removeDiscoveryListener(DiscoveryListener l);
    public void terminate();
}
```

Hierarchy: Object→ LookupDiscoveryManager(DiscoveryGroupManagement, DiscoveryLocatorManagement, DiscoveryManagement)

LookupDiscoveryRegistration
Jini 1.1 Alpha

net.jini.discovery

This is the interface that is implemented by the object returned by a lookup discovery service, such as Sun's *fiddler* service, when a client registers with the service. A class that implements this interface is returned from the register( ) method of the LookupDiscoveryService class.

Clients that register with a lookup discovery service must renew the lease returned from the getLease( ) method as long as they want the registration to remain current. They use the other methods of this interface to configure lookup discovery in the same way as they would use the LookupDiscoveryManager class.

```
public interface LookupDiscoveryRegistration {
// Property Accessor Methods (by property name)
    public abstract net.jini.core.event.EventRegistration getEventRegistration();
    public abstract String[ ] getGroups() throws java.rmi.RemoteException;
    public abstract void setGroups(String[ ] groups) throws java.rmi.RemoteException;
    public abstract net.jini.core.lease.Lease getLease();
    public abstract net.jini.core.discovery.LookupLocator[ ] getLocators() throws java.rmi.RemoteException;
    public abstract void setLocators(net.jini.core.discovery.LookupLocator[ ] locators)
        throws java.rmi.RemoteException;
```

net.jini Packages

```
    public abstract net.jini.core.lookup.ServiceRegistrar[ ] getRegistrars( ) throws LookupUnmarshalException,
        java.rmi.RemoteException;
// Public Instance Methods
    public abstract void addGroups(String[ ] groups) throws java.rmi.RemoteException;
    public abstract void addLocators(net.jini.core.discovery.LookupLocator[ ] locators)
        throws java.rmi.RemoteException;
    public abstract void discard(net.jini.core.lookup.ServiceRegistrar registrar) throws java.rmi.RemoteException;
    public abstract void removeGroups(String[ ] groups) throws java.rmi.RemoteException;
    public abstract void removeLocators(net.jini.core.discovery.LookupLocator[ ] locators)
        throws java.rmi.RemoteException;
}
```

Returned By: LookupDiscoveryService.register()

LookupDiscoveryService   Jini 1.1 Alpha

net.jini.discovery

This interface is the service interface of the lookup discovery service. Clients that want
to delegate the management of the lookup and discovery operations find a lookup discovery service by specifying this interface in a net.jini.core.lookup.ServiceTemplate object
and then use that object to find the service in an already discovered lookup service.
Once a lookup discovery service is found, the client must register with it using the
register( ) method; the client can then configure the service using the methods of the
LookupDiscoveryRegistration interface.

```
public interface LookupDiscoveryService {
// Public Instance Methods
    public abstract LookupDiscoveryRegistration register(String[ ] groups,
                               net.jini.core.discovery.LookupLocator[ ] locators,
                               net.jini.core.event.RemoteEventListener listener,
                               java.rmi.MarshalledObject handback, long leaseDuration)
        throws java.rmi.RemoteException;
}
```

LookupLocatorDiscovery   Jini 1.1 Alpha

net.jini.discovery

Instances of this class are used to participate in unicast discovery. This class attempts to
discover a lookup service at the location specified by each net.jini.core.lookup.LookupLoca-
tor object that is passed to the constructor of this class and by any lookup locators that
are passed to the addLocators( ) or setLocators( ) methods.

When this class locates a lookup service, it notifies all registered listeners. When a listener is first added via the addDiscoveryListener( ) method, the listener will be notified
immediately with all previously discovered services.

If an error occurs while you are communicating with a lookup service, you should pass
that lookup service to the discard( ) method. All listeners will be notified that the given
service has been discarded. Services may also be discarded as a result of changes made
to the set of lookup locators.

This class starts a number of daemon threads, which are killed when you call the
terminate( ) method. This method is also called when the object is garbage collected.

```
public class LookupLocatorDiscovery implements DiscoveryLocatorManagement, DiscoveryManagement {
// Public Constructors
    public LookupLocatorDiscovery(net.jini.core.discovery.LookupLocator[ ] locators);
```

```
// Event Registration Methods (by event name)
    public void addDiscoveryListener(DiscoveryListener l);                Implements:DiscoveryManagement
    public void removeDiscoveryListener(DiscoveryListener l);        Implements:DiscoveryManagement synchronized
// Public Instance Methods
    public net.jini.core.discovery.LookupLocator[ ] getDiscoveredLocators();                        synchronized
    public net.jini.core.discovery.LookupLocator[ ] getUndiscoveredLocators();                      synchronized
// Methods Implementing DiscoveryLocatorManagement
    public void addLocators(net.jini.core.discovery.LookupLocator[ ] locators);                      synchronized
    public net.jini.core.discovery.LookupLocator[ ] getLocators();                                  synchronized
    public void removeLocators(net.jini.core.discovery.LookupLocator[ ] locators);
    public void setLocators(net.jini.core.discovery.LookupLocator[ ] locators);
// Methods Implementing DiscoveryManagement
    public void addDiscoveryListener(DiscoveryListener l);
    public void discard(net.jini.core.lookup.ServiceRegistrar proxy);
    public net.jini.core.lookup.ServiceRegistrar[ ] getRegistrars();
    public void removeDiscoveryListener(DiscoveryListener l);                                        synchronized
    public void terminate();                                                                        synchronized
}
```

Hierarchy: Object→ net.jini.discovery.LookupLocatorDiscovery(DiscoveryLocatorManagement, DiscoveryManagement)

LookupUnmarshalException

Jini 1.1 Alpha

net.jini.discovery

serializable checked

There are many instances when the lookup discovery service returns to the client an array of service registrars. When the lookup discovery service unmarshals the service registrars to deliver them to the client, it may get an IOException or ClassNotFoundException. When that happens, it will throw this exception instead of returning an array of service registrars.

Instances of this class hold two arrays: an array of successfully unmarshalled service registrars, and an array of those that could not be unmarshalled. You retrieve these arrays with the getUnmarshalledRegs( ) and getStillMarshalledRegs( ) methods, respectively. You can also retrieve the exceptions that were thrown when attempting to unmarshal via the getExceptions( ) methods. There is a one-to-one correspondence between the elements of this array and the elements of the array returned by the getStillMarshalledRegs( ) method.

```
public class LookupUnmarshalException extends Exception {
// Public Constructors
    public LookupUnmarshalException(net.jini.core.lookup.ServiceRegistrar[ ] unmarshalledRegs,
                            java.rmi.MarshalledObject[ ] stillMarshalledRegs, Throwable[ ] exceptions);
// Property Accessor Methods (by property name)
    public Throwable[ ] getExceptions();
    public String getMessage();                                                            Overrides:Throwable
    public java.rmi.MarshalledObject[ ] getStillMarshalledRegs();
    public net.jini.core.lookup.ServiceRegistrar[ ] getUnmarshalledRegs();
}
```

Hierarchy: Object→ Throwable(Serializable)→ Exception→ LookupUnmarshalException

Thrown By: LookupDiscoveryRegistration.getRegistrars(), RemoteDiscoveryEvent.getRegistrars()

OutgoingMulticastAnnouncement

Jini 1.0

net.jini.discovery

This class is used to create the data packets that are sent by lookup services that use the multicast announcement protocol. The packets created represent the service ID of the lookup service, a lookup locator to discover the lookup service, and the groups that are supported by the lookup service. Developers do not use this class directly.

```
public class OutgoingMulticastAnnouncement {
// Public Constructors
    public OutgoingMulticastAnnouncement();
// Protected Constants
    protected static final int maxPacketSize;
    protected static final int minMaxPacketSize;                              =512
    protected static final int protocolVersion;                                =1
// Public Class Methods
    public static java.net.DatagramPacket[ ] marshal(net.jini.core.lookup.ServiceID id,
                                        net.jini.core.discovery.LookupLocator loc, String[ ] groups)
        throws java.io.IOException;
}
```

OutgoingMulticastRequest

Jini 1.0

net.jini.discovery

This class is used to create the data packets that are to be sent by the discovering entities to discover lookup services. The packets created represent the network port number for lookup services to establish a unicast connection to, the groups that need to be supported, and the service IDs that have been already heard from. The list of service IDs may be truncated. The network address for the sender is also encoded as part of the datagram packets.

Developers do not use this class directly.

```
public class OutgoingMulticastRequest {
// Public Constructors
    public OutgoingMulticastRequest();
// Protected Constants
    protected static final int maxPacketSize;
    protected static final int minMaxPacketSize;                              =512
    protected static final int protocolVersion;                                =1
// Public Class Methods
    public static java.net.DatagramPacket[ ] marshal(int responsePort, String[ ] groups,
                                        net.jini.core.lookup.ServiceID[ ] heard)
        throws java.io.IOException;
}
```

OutgoingUnicastRequest

Jini 1.0

net.jini.discovery

This class is used to write the outgoing request for unicast discovery to a network data stream. At present, only the protocol version is sent. This class is only used by the discovering entity; developers do not use this class directly.

```
public class OutgoingUnicastRequest {
// Public Constructors
    public OutgoingUnicastRequest();
// Protected Constants
```

```
    protected static final int protoVersion;                                    =1
// Public Class Methods
    public static void marshal(java.io.OutputStream str) throws java.io.IOException;
}
```

OutgoingUnicastResponse

net.jini.discovery

This class is used to write the outgoing response to a unicast discovery request to a network data stream. The ServiceRegistrar object that represents the lookup service and all the groups that the lookup service supports are written to the data stream. This class is only used by the lookup service, not directly by developers.

```
public class OutgoingUnicastResponse {
// Public Constructors
    public OutgoingUnicastResponse();
// Public Class Methods
    public static void marshal(java.io.OutputStream str, net.jini.core.lookup.ServiceRegistrar reg, String[ ] groups)
        throws java.io.IOException;
// Protected Instance Fields
    protected int protoVersion;
}
```

RemoteDiscoveryEvent

net.jini.discovery   *serializable remote event*

Instances of this class are delivered by the lookup discovery service whenever it discovers or discards a lookup service. If this event is being used to notify clients that lookup services have been discarded, the isDiscarded( ) method returns true; otherwise, this event is being used to notify clients that lookup services have been discovered. In either case, the set of lookup services in question is returned via the getRegistrars( ) method.

This is a remote event and follows Jini's remote event specification. There is no guarantee that sequence numbers of this class will not skip, so a client that receives an event with a sequence number that is more than one greater than the previous event may or may not have missed an event. When this happens, a client should call the getRegistrars( ) method on the lookup service registration object to make sure that the set of discovered lookup services returned by that method is consistent with the set that that client is using locally. The getRegistrars( ) method is expensive, so it should be used only when an event may have been dropped.

```
public class RemoteDiscoveryEvent extends net.jini.core.event.RemoteEvent {
// Public Constructors
    public RemoteDiscoveryEvent(Object source, long eventID, long seqNum, java.rmi.MarshalledObject handback,
                    boolean discarded, net.jini.core.lookup.ServiceRegistrar[ ] registrars)
        throws java.io.IOException;
// Public Class Methods
    public static int indexFirstNull(Object[ ] arr);
    public static void insertRegistrars(net.jini.core.lookup.ServiceRegistrar[ ] regsArray, java.util.ArrayList regsList);
    public static java.util.ArrayList unmarshalRegistrars(java.util.ArrayList marshalledRegs,
                    java.util.ArrayList unmarshalledRegs);
// Public Instance Methods
    public net.jini.core.lookup.ServiceRegistrar[ ] getRegistrars() throws LookupUnmarshalException;
    public boolean isDiscarded();
// Protected Instance Fields
```

```
    protected boolean discarded;
    protected java.util.ArrayList marshalledRegs;
    protected net.jini.core.lookup.ServiceRegistrar[ ] regs;
}
```

Hierarchy: Object→ java.util.EventObject(Serializable)→ net.jini.core.event.RemoteEvent→
RemoteDiscoveryEvent

The net.jini.entry Package

The net.jini.entry package provides utilities for entry objects. Currently, there is only one
class that is used to support the creation of entry objects. The AbstractEntry object implements the net.jini.core.entry.Entry interface and provides a few methods that can be used
to compare entry objects. See Chapter 4, for more information on entry objects. Figure
16-3 shows the class hierarchy for this package.

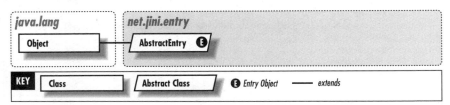

Figure 16–3: The net.jini.entry package

AbstractEntry   Jini 1.0

net.jini.entry   *serializable entry*

A basic implementation of the Entry interface. This class should be used to ease implementation of new entry classes. This class provides a definition of the standard equals( )
method that is correct according to the entry specification: each field is checked indi-
vidually to see if it is the same between the two objects. The logic also applies to the
static equals( ) method of this class.

```
public abstract class AbstractEntry implements net.jini.core.entry.Entry {
// Public Constructors
    public AbstractEntry();
// Public Class Methods
    public static boolean equals(net.jini.core.entry.Entry e1, net.jini.core.entry.Entry e2);
    public static int hashCode(net.jini.core.entry.Entry entry);
    public static String toString(net.jini.core.entry.Entry entry);
// Public Methods Overriding Object
    public boolean equals(Object other);
    public int hashCode();
    public String toString();
}
```

Hierarchy: Object→ AbstractEntry(net.jini.core.entry.Entry(Serializable))

Subclasses: net.jini.lookup.entry.Address, net.jini.lookup.entry.Comment,
net.jini.lookup.entry.Location, net.jini.lookup.entry.Name, net.jini.lookup.entry.ServiceInfo,
net.jini.lookup.entry.ServiceType, net.jini.lookup.entry.Status

The net.jini.event Package

The net.jini.event package defines classes related to the event mailbox service. These classes are available only in Jini 1.1, when this service became part of the Jini specification. This package defines only the service interface for the event mailbox service. The class hierarchy for this package is shown in Figure 16-4.

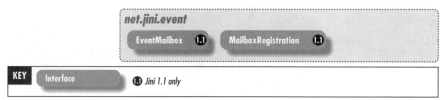

Figure 16-4: The net.jini.event package

EventMailbox   Jini 1.1 Alpha
net.jini.event

This is the service interface for the event mailbox service. Clients that want to use the event mailbox specify this class in a net.jini.core.lookup.ServiceTemplate object and locate the service in the Jini lookup service. They then use the register( ) method to register with the event mailbox service.

```
public interface EventMailbox {
// Public Instance Methods
    public abstract MailboxRegistration register(long lease) throws java.rmi.RemoteException;
}
```

MailboxRegistration   Jini 1.1 Alpha
net.jini.event

An object that implements this interface is returned when a client registers with the event mailbox service. The client must retrieve the registration lease (with the getLease( ) method) and is responsible for ensuring that the lease is renewed.

The client retrieves a net.jini.core.event.RemoteEventListener object from the registration object and uses this anywhere a remote event listener is required. Services send events to the listener; events are held in the mailbox until the client calls the enableDelivery( ) method of the mailbox service. The mailbox then sends the held events to the listener passed to the enableDelivery( ) method; it continues to send any new events until the disableDelivery( ) method is called, at which point it holds the events again. This cycle continues until the client cancels (or allows to expire) the lease in this object.

```
public interface MailboxRegistration {
// Public Instance Methods
    public abstract void disableDelivery() throws java.rmi.RemoteException;
    public abstract void enableDelivery(net.jini.core.event.RemoteEventListener target)
        throws java.rmi.RemoteException;
    public abstract net.jini.core.lease.Lease getLease();
    public abstract net.jini.core.event.RemoteEventListener getListener();
}
```

Returned By: EventMailbox.register()

The net.jini.lease Package

The net.jini.lease package defines classes related to the renewal of leases. These classes are available only in Jini 1.1, although some of these classes were available in Jini 1.0 in the com.sun.jini.lease package. The class hierarchy for this package is shown in Figure 16-5.

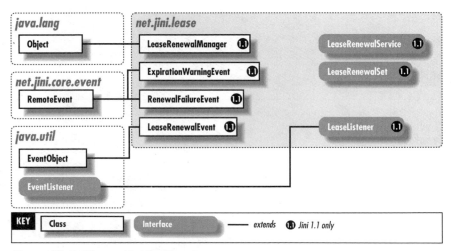

Figure 16–5: The net.jini.lease package

There are two types of lease renewal classes in this package. A lease renewal manager executes locally, within the VM of the application that creates it. It makes remote calls to the issuer of each lease to renew the lease. A lease renewal service is a remote service, executing in its own VM. You make a remote call to register leases with it, and then it makes the calls to the lease issuer to renew the lease. Programatically, this means that lease renewal managers issue local events, and lease renewal services issue remote events.

ExpirationWarningEvent   Jini 1.1 Alpha
net.jini.lease   *serializable remote event*

Events of this type are sent to holders of a lease renewal set managed by a lease renewal service when the lease renewal set is about to expire. The lease in question is returned from the getLease() method and is the lease that the client holds on the lease renewal set; this method does not warn you if a lease in the lease renewal set is about to expire.

```
public class ExpirationWarningEvent extends net.jini.core.event.RemoteEvent {
// Public Constructors
    public ExpirationWarningEvent(Object source, long eventID, long seqNum, java.rmi.MarshalledObject handback,
                      net.jini.core.lease.Lease lease);
// Public Instance Methods
    public net.jini.core.lease.Lease getLease();
}
```

Hierarchy: Object→ java.util.EventObject(Serializable)→ net.jini.core.event.RemoteEvent→ ExpirationWarningEvent

LeaseListener

net.jini.lease

event listener

This interface is used in conjunction with a lease renewal manager. Objects that implement this interface can be registered with the lease renewal manager and they will be notified when the lease renewal manager is unable to renew a particular lease. Information about the lease and why it failed to renew are encapsulated in the lease event object passed to the notify( ) method of this interface. This class is available in Jini 1.0 as com.sun.jini.lease.LeaseListener.

```
public interface LeaseListener extends java.util.EventListener {
// Public Instance Methods
    public abstract void notify(net.jini.lease.LeaseRenewalEvent e);
}
```

Hierarchy: (net.jini.lease.LeaseListener(java.util.EventListener))

Passed To: net.jini.lease.LeaseRenewalManager.{LeaseRenewalManager(), renewFor(), renewUntil()}

LeaseRenewalEvent

net.jini.lease

serializable event

Objects of this type are sent to lease listeners by a lease renewal manager when the manager is unable to renew a particular lease. The lease that failed to be renewed is returned from the getLease( ) method, and the getException( ) method returns the exception that the lease renewal manager received when attempting to renew the lease. This class is available in Jini 1.0 as com.sun.jini.lease.LeaseRenewalEvent.

```
public class LeaseRenewalEvent extends java.util.EventObject {
// Public Constructors
    public LeaseRenewalEvent(net.jini.lease.LeaseRenewalManager source, net.jini.core.lease.Lease lease,
                            long expiration, Exception ex);
// Property Accessor Methods (by property name)
    public Exception getException();
    public long getExpiration();
    public net.jini.core.lease.Lease getLease();
}
```

Hierarchy: Object→ java.util.EventObject(Serializable)→ net.jini.lease.LeaseRenewalEvent

Passed To: net.jini.lease.LeaseListener.notify()

LeaseRenewalManager

net.jini.lease

This class implements a utility that can be used to renew leases. This class creates an internal thread that wakes up when necessary to renew a lease under its management. The renewals happen in the same process that created the lease renewal manager; this is different than the lease renewal service, which is a separate remote service in the Jini community.

Leases may be renewed for a particular amount of time via the renewFor( ) method; they may be renewed until a particular point in time with the renewUntil( ) method. Typically, you use the renewFor( ) method specifying a duration of Lease.FOREVER and then explicitly cancel the lease when you are done with it.

The getExpiration( ) and setExpiration( ) methods operate on the desired expiration time of the lease; this expiration is calculated based on the argument to the renewUntil( ) or renewFor( ) method. The lease renewal manager will continually renew the lease as needed until the desired expiration time passes.

net.jini Packages

This class is available with a slightly different interface in Jini 1.0 as com.sun.jini.lease.LeaseRenewalManager.

```
public class LeaseRenewalManager {
// Public Constructors
    public LeaseRenewalManager();
    public LeaseRenewalManager(net.jini.core.lease.Lease lease, long expiration,
                               net.jini.lease.LeaseListener listener);
// Public Instance Methods
    public void cancel(net.jini.core.lease.Lease lease) throws net.jini.core.lease.UnknownLeaseException,
        java.rmi.RemoteException;
    public void clear();                                                                synchronized
    public long getExpiration(net.jini.core.lease.Lease lease)                          synchronized
        throws net.jini.core.lease.UnknownLeaseException;
    public void remove(net.jini.core.lease.Lease lease)                                 synchronized
        throws net.jini.core.lease.UnknownLeaseException;
    public void renewFor(net.jini.core.lease.Lease lease, long duration, net.jini.lease.LeaseListener listener);
    public void renewUntil(net.jini.core.lease.Lease lease, long expiration, net.jini.lease.LeaseListener listener);
    public void setExpiration(net.jini.core.lease.Lease lease, long expiration)         synchronized
        throws net.jini.core.lease.UnknownLeaseException;
}
```

Passed To: net.jini.lease.LeaseRenewalEvent.LeaseRenewalEvent(),
net.jini.lookup.ClientLookupManager.ClientLookupManager(), net.jini.lookup.JoinManager.JoinManager()

Returned By: net.jini.lookup.ClientLookupManager.getLeaseRenewalManager(),
net.jini.lookup.JoinManager.getLeaseRenewalManager()

LeaseRenewalService   Jini 1.1 Alpha

net.jini.lease

This is the service interface to a remote lease renewal service. You can find such a service on your network by using this interface to construct the service template passed to the lookup( ) method of the net.jini.core.lookup.ServiceRegistrar. Once you've found such a service, you use the createLeaseRenewalSet( ) method to create a set to which you add leases that the renewal service should renew.

```
public interface LeaseRenewalService {
// Public Instance Methods
    public abstract LeaseRenewalSet createLeaseRenewalSet(long leaseDuration) throws java.rmi.RemoteException;
}
```

LeaseRenewalSet   Jini 1.1 Alpha

net.jini.lease

This interface is implemented by the object returned from the lease renewal service. You can add a lease to this set with the renewFor( ) method, and the lease renewal service will renew the lease until the specified amount of time has elapsed.

The lease renewal set is itself a leased resource; its lease is returned by the getRenewalSetLease( ) method. However, the point of the lease renewal service is to delegate lease renewals, so this lease is not typically used. Instead, the client creates the lease renewal set with a particular duration, which the lease renewal service agrees to honor (unlike a regular lease, where the lease issuer will adjust the requested duration). Then the client asks to be notified sometime before the lease renewal set expires; registration for this notification happens by calling the setExpirationWarningListener( ) method. The listener passed to this method will be notified minWarning milliseconds before the lease renewal set expires. The listener then obtains the lease contained in the

ExpirationWarningEvent and renews that lease, which extends the expiration of the lease renewal set. You may register only one listener for the expiration warning; each call to the setExpirationWarningListener( ) method replaces the previously registered listener (if any).

If you want to be notified when a lease could not be renewed, create a remote event listener and pass it to the setRenewalFailureListener( ) method. The listener will receive a RenewalFailureEvent whenever a particular lease could not be renewed. You may register only one listener for renewal failures; each call to the setRenewalFailureListener( ) method replaces the previously registered listener (if any).

```
public interface LeaseRenewalSet {
// Public Instance Methods
    public abstract void clearExpirationWarningListener() throws java.rmi.RemoteException;
    public abstract void clearRenewalFailureListener() throws java.rmi.RemoteException;
    public abstract net.jini.core.lease.Lease getRenewalSetLease();
    public abstract net.jini.core.lease.Lease remove(net.jini.core.lease.Lease leaseToRemove)
        throws java.rmi.RemoteException;
    public abstract void renewFor(net.jini.core.lease.Lease leaseToRenew, long membershipDuration)
        throws java.rmi.RemoteException;
    public abstract net.jini.core.event.EventRegistration setExpirationWarningListener(
                                    net.jini.core.event.RemoteEventListener listener,
                                    long minWarning,
                                    java.rmi.MarshalledObject handback)
        throws java.rmi.RemoteException;
    public abstract net.jini.core.event.EventRegistration setRenewalFailureListener(
                                    net.jini.core.event.RemoteEventListener listener,
                                    java.rmi.MarshalledObject handback)
        throws java.rmi.RemoteException;
}
```

Returned By: LeaseRenewalService.createLeaseRenewalSet()

RenewalFailureEvent

Jini 1.1 Alpha

net.jini.lease

serializable remote event

Events of this type are sent by the lease renewal service whenever the service is unable to renew a particular lease. The lease in question can be retrieved from the getLease( ) method, and the error that the lease renewal service received while attempting to renew the lease can be retrieved from the getThrowable( ) method.

```
public class RenewalFailureEvent extends net.jini.core.event.RemoteEvent {
// Public Constructors
    public RenewalFailureEvent(Object source, long eventID, long seqNum, java.rmi.MarshalledObject handback,
                        java.rmi.MarshalledObject marshaledLease, Throwable throwable);
// Public Instance Methods
    public net.jini.core.lease.Lease getLease() throws java.io.IOException, ClassNotFoundException;
    public Throwable getThrowable();
}
```

Hierarchy: Object → java.util.EventObject(Serializable) → net.jini.core.event.RemoteEvent → RenewalFailureEvent

The net.jini.lookup Package

The net.jini.lookup package provides classes and interfaces that assist clients and services that work with the lookup service. Clients can use the ClientLookupManager class to locate particular services in the Jini community, and services can use the JoinManager class to register with a set of lookup services. Except for the DiscoveryAdmin interface, which allows clients to configure the parameters of a lookup service, the items in this package are available only in Jini 1.1, though the JoinManager is based on a Sun-specific utility class that ships with Jini 1.0. Figure 16-6 shows the class hierarchy for this package.

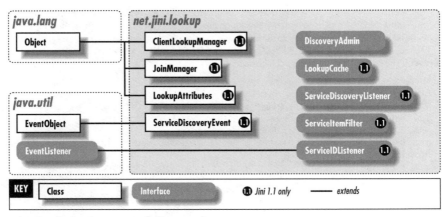

Figure 16–6: The net.jini.lookup package

ClientLookupManager   Jini 1.1 Alpha
net.jini.lookup

This class is used by clients to find specific services in the Jini community. Instances of this class use the given net.jini.discovery.DiscoveryManagement object to manage the discovery of the lookup services; the client can then use the methods of this class to find services within those discovered lookup services. There are three primary ways in which this class is used.

A client that needs to locate new services frequently should use the createLookupCache() method. This method returns a LookupCache object, which will manage the discovery of lookup services that have a registration of the requested service. The lookup cache will find these services as they are registered in the Jini community and download the service objects. The client can then query the cache to find services; since the cache is local, this is much faster than making repeated calls to the lookup() method of the net.jini.core.lookup.ServiceRegistrar interface.

A client that needs notification of when new services are located or when existing services change (e.g., the service attributes change) should use the createLookupCache() method and then register a ServiceDiscoveryListener object with the cache.

Clients that need to find new services infrequently should use the lookup() methods of this class. Those methods will query all discovered lookup services to find a service that matches the given template. This operation is very similar to how clients find a service using the lookup() method of a service registrar, though the lookup() methods of this class have richer semantics: in addition to gathering services from multiple lookup services, the lookup() method of this class can use a ServiceItemFilter object to restrict the returned services.

The daemon threads created by this class and its discovery management object are stopped when the terminate() method is called.

```
public class ClientLookupManager {
// Public Constructors
```

```
          public ClientLookupManager(net.jini.discovery.DiscoveryManagement discoveryMgr,
                             net.jini.lease.LeaseRenewalManager leaseMgr) throws java.io.IOException;
// Property Accessor Methods (by property name)
          public net.jini.discovery.DiscoveryManagement getDiscoveryManager();
          public net.jini.lease.LeaseRenewalManager getLeaseRenewalManager();
          public net.jini.core.lookup.ServiceRegistrar[ ] getLookupServices();
// Public Instance Methods
          public LookupCache createLookupCache(net.jini.core.lookup.ServiceTemplate tmpl, ServiceItemFilter filter,
                             ServiceDiscoveryListener listener) throws java.rmi.RemoteException;
          public net.jini.core.lookup.ServiceItem lookup(net.jini.core.lookup.ServiceTemplate tmpl, ServiceItemFilter filter);
          public net.jini.core.lookup.ServiceItem lookup(net.jini.core.lookup.ServiceTemplate tmpl, ServiceItemFilter filter,
                             long wait) throws InterruptedException, java.rmi.RemoteException;
          public net.jini.core.lookup.ServiceItem[ ] lookup(net.jini.core.lookup.ServiceTemplate tmpl, int maxMatches,
                             ServiceItemFilter filter);
          public net.jini.core.lookup.ServiceItem[ ] lookup(net.jini.core.lookup.ServiceTemplate tmpl, int minMaxMatch,
                             int maxMatches, ServiceItemFilter filter, long wait)
          throws InterruptedException, java.rmi.RemoteException;
          public void terminate();
}
```

DiscoveryAdmin   Jini 1.0

net.jini.lookup

This interface is provided to allow clients to administer the discovery parameters of a
lookup service. The client may adjust the groups that the lookup service will support
and the network port number the lookup service will listen to for unicast discovery.

```
public interface DiscoveryAdmin {
// Public Instance Methods
          public abstract void addMemberGroups(String[ ] groups) throws java.rmi.RemoteException;
          public abstract String[ ] getMemberGroups() throws java.rmi.RemoteException;
          public abstract int getUnicastPort() throws java.rmi.RemoteException;
          public abstract void removeMemberGroups(String[ ] groups) throws java.rmi.RemoteException;
          public abstract void setMemberGroups(String[ ] groups) throws java.rmi.RemoteException;
          public abstract void setUnicastPort(int port) throws java.io.IOException, java.rmi.RemoteException;
}
```

JoinManager   Jini 1.1 Alpha

net.jini.lookup

This class is used by services to discover and register with lookup services. Discovery
of lookup services is accomplished with the DiscoveryManagement object passed to the
constructor of this class; if that parameter is null then a new LookupDiscoveryManager
object will be used. The lease to the lookup services will be managed by the given
LeaseRenewalManager object; if that parameter is null then a new manager will be created.
Whenever a lookup service is discovered, this class will register the service object (the
first parameter of the constructor) with the lookup service.

If the service has previously registered with a lookup service and has saved its assigned
service ID, that ID should be passed as the third parameter to the constructor of this
object. Otherwise, the third parameter should be an object that implements the ServiceI-
DListener interface. When the service is assigned an ID, that listener will be notified and
can save the service ID so that the next time the service starts, it reuses the service ID.

Whenever the attributes of the service change, the service is responsible for updating
the lookup service using the addAttributes( ), modifyAttributes( ), or setAttributes( ) methods.

The terminate( ) method stops all daemon threads of this class as well as terminating the discovery manager.

This class is available with a slightly different interface in Jini 1.0 as com.sun.jini.lookup.JoinManager.

```
public class JoinManager {
// Public Constructors
    public JoinManager(Object obj, net.jini.core.entry.Entry[ ] attrSets, net.jini.lookup.ServiceIDListener callback,
                       net.jini.discovery.DiscoveryManagement discoverMgr,
                       net.jini.lease.LeaseRenewalManager leaseMgr) throws java.io.IOException;
    public JoinManager(Object obj, net.jini.core.entry.Entry[ ] attrSets, net.jini.core.lookup.ServiceID serviceID,
                       net.jini.discovery.DiscoveryManagement discoverMgr,
                       net.jini.lease.LeaseRenewalManager leaseMgr) throws java.io.IOException;
// Property Accessor Methods (by property name)
    public net.jini.core.entry.Entry[ ] getAttributes();
    public void setAttributes(net.jini.core.entry.Entry[ ] attrSets);
    public net.jini.discovery.DiscoveryManagement getDiscoveryManager();
    public net.jini.core.lookup.ServiceRegistrar[ ] getJoinSet();
    public net.jini.lease.LeaseRenewalManager getLeaseRenewalManager();
// Public Instance Methods
    public void addAttributes(net.jini.core.entry.Entry[ ] attrSets);
    public void addAttributes(net.jini.core.entry.Entry[ ] attrSets, boolean checkSC);
    public void modifyAttributes(net.jini.core.entry.Entry[ ] attrSetTemplates, net.jini.core.entry.Entry[ ] attrSets);
    public void modifyAttributes(net.jini.core.entry.Entry[ ] attrSetTemplates, net.jini.core.entry.Entry[ ] attrSets,
                       boolean checkSC);
    public void terminate();
}
```

LookupCache   Jini 1.1 Alpha

net.jini.lookup

A class that implements this interface is created by the ClientLookupManager class. The client lookup manager will discover lookup services and find registered services within those lookup services; registered services that match the clients interest can be downloaded immediately and cached in the lookup cache. When the client needs to find a service, it looks it up locally in the cache (using one of the lookup( ) methods) rather than making remote calls to each lookup service.

If the client needs immediate notification when a new matching service is available or when an existing service becomes unavailable, it must register a service discovery listener with the cache.

```
public interface LookupCache {
// Event Registration Methods (by event name)
    public abstract void addListener(ServiceDiscoveryListener l);
    public abstract void removeListener(ServiceDiscoveryListener l);
// Public Instance Methods
    public abstract void discard(Object serviceReference);
    public abstract net.jini.core.lookup.ServiceItem lookup(ServiceItemFilter filter);
    public abstract net.jini.core.lookup.ServiceItem[ ] lookup(ServiceItemFilter filter, int maxMatches);
    public abstract void terminate();
}
```

Returned By: ClientLookupManager.createLookupCache()

ServiceDiscoveryEvent

Jini 1.1 Alpha

net.jini.lookup

serializable event

Instances of this class are passed to service discovery listeners by the lookup cache. The event contains two service items: one that reflects the state of the service before the event and one that reflects the state of the service after the event. Note that this is not a remote event.

There are three types of events that can occur. The lookup cache may have discovered a new service, in which case the getPreEventServiceItem( ) method will return null. The lookup cache may have discarded an existing service, in which case the getPostEventServiceItem( ) method will return null. Otherwise, the attributes of the service have changed, and both of these items will return a valid service item.

You must not modify the service items returned by the methods of this class, or the lookup cache will end up corrupted.

```
public class ServiceDiscoveryEvent extends java.util.EventObject {
// Public Constructors
    public ServiceDiscoveryEvent(Object source, net.jini.core.lookup.ServiceItem preEventItem,
                            net.jini.core.lookup.ServiceItem postEventItem);
// Public Instance Methods
    public net.jini.core.lookup.ServiceItem getPostEventServiceItem();
    public net.jini.core.lookup.ServiceItem getPreEventServiceItem();
}
```

Hierarchy: Object→ java.util.EventObject(Serializable)→ ServiceDiscoveryEvent

Passed To: ServiceDiscoveryListener.{serviceAdded(), serviceChanged(), serviceRemoved()}

ServiceDiscoveryListener

Jini 1.1 Alpha

net.jini.lookup

The lookup cache keeps a list of service discovery listeners and notifies each of them when it discovers a new service, when an existing service changes its attributes, or when an existing service is discarded. Implementors of this interface can determine the type of event by the method that is called, although the service discovery event also encapsulates the event type.

```
public interface ServiceDiscoveryListener {
// Public Instance Methods
    public abstract void serviceAdded(ServiceDiscoveryEvent event);
    public abstract void serviceChanged(ServiceDiscoveryEvent event);
    public abstract void serviceRemoved(ServiceDiscoveryEvent event);
}
```

Passed To: ClientLookupManager.createLookupCache(), LookupCache.{addListener(), removeListener()}

ServiceIDListener

Jini 1.1 Alpha

net.jini.lookup

event listener

This interface is used by the JoinManager class. When the join manager registers its service object with its first lookup service, that lookup service assigns a service ID. The join manager retrieves that ID and passes it to all registered service ID listeners. The listener should save the ID to persistent storage; the next time the service registers, it should use that service ID when it instantiates the join manager. This class is available in Jini 1.0 as com.sun.jini.lookup.ServiceIDListener.

```
public interface ServiceIDListener extends java.util.EventListener {
// Public Instance Methods
    public abstract void serviceIDNotify(net.jini.core.lookup.ServiceID serviceID);
}
```

Hierarchy: (net.jini.lookup.ServiceIDListener(java.util.EventListener))

Passed To: net.jini.lookup.JoinManager.JoinManager()

ServiceItemFilter   Jini 1.1 Alpha
net.jini.lookup

When you search for services in the lookup service, you can specify that the service must have a particular type and match a given set of attributes. If you want more control, you can use an object that implements this interface in conjunction with the Client-LookupManager class. The lookup( ) methods of that class call the check( ) method of the service item filter to determine if the service should be included in the return list; this allows you to provide any kind of service filtering that you need.

```
public interface ServiceItemFilter {
// Public Instance Methods
    public abstract boolean check(net.jini.core.lookup.ServiceItem item);
}
```

Passed To: ClientLookupManager.{createLookupCache(), lookup()}, LookupCache.lookup()

The net.jini.lookup.entry Package

The net.jini.lookup.entry package provides some attribute types that services can use when they register with the lookup service. Since the lookup service can support any Entry object for attributes, attributes are not restricted to this list. However, this list may be complete enough for generic cases so that services will not need to implement their own entry types. See Chapter 4 for more information on entry objects and attributes.

In addition, this package provides a matching *JavaBean* for each entry type so that tools can access and manipulate the attributes. The bean for each object contains an embedded instance of the entry object and a number of methods to operate on that entry's fields. Entry objects contain fields of information, and their corresponding JavaBean object has a get and set method for each field. For example, an Address object contains a country field so its JavaBean object has setCountry( ) and getCountry( ) methods. The definition of these methods follows standard JavaBean conventions.

The JavaBean classes must also implement the makeLink( ) and followLink( ) methods; these methods are used to set or retrieve the entry object that is contained within the JavaBean object. These methods are specified as part of the EntryBean interface. Furthermore, the name of the JavaBean is very specific, since a class (the EntryBeans class) is provided to obtain the supporting JavaBeans from any entry object. That name must be the class name followed by Bean (e.g., AddressBean for the Address class).

Figure 16-7 shows the class hierarchy for this package.

Address   Jini 1.0
net.jini.lookup.entry   *serializable entry*

An Entry object of this class type is used to represent an address. The address attribute can be used to assign a mailable location to a service (see also the Location attribute). With this attribute, you can assign to the service a street address, city, state, zip code, country, and organization name.

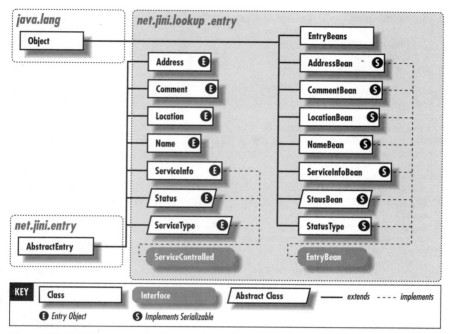

Figure 16–7: The net.jini.lookup.entry package

```
public class Address extends net.jini.entry.AbstractEntry {
// Public Constructors
    public Address();
    public Address(String street, String organization, String organizationalUnit, String locality, String stateOrProvince,
                   String postalCode, String country);
// Public Instance Fields
    public String country;
    public String locality;
    public String organization;
    public String organizationalUnit;
    public String postalCode;
    public String stateOrProvince;
    public String street;
}
```

Hierarchy: Object→ net.jini.entry.AbstractEntry(net.jini.core.entry.Entry(Serializable))→ Address

Type Of: AddressBean.assoc

AddressBean   Jini 1.0

net.jini.lookup.entry   *serializable*

A JavaBean class that is used to handle an Address attribute. There is a JavaBean property for every field of the attribute.

```
public class AddressBean implements EntryBean, Serializable {
// Public Constructors
```

```
     public AddressBean();
// Property Accessor Methods (by property name)
     public String getCountry();                                    default:null
     public void setCountry(String x);
     public String getLocality();                                   default:null
     public void setLocality(String x);
     public String getOrganization();                               default:null
     public void setOrganization(String x);
     public String getOrganizationalUnit();                         default:null
     public void setOrganizationalUnit(String x);
     public String getPostalCode();                                 default:null
     public void setPostalCode(String x);
     public String getStateOrProvince();                            default:null
     public void setStateOrProvince(String x);
     public String getStreet();                                     default:null
     public void setStreet(String x);
// Methods Implementing EntryBean
     public net.jini.core.entry.Entry followLink();
     public void makeLink(net.jini.core.entry.Entry e);
// Protected Instance Fields
     protected Address assoc;
}
```

Hierarchy: Object→ AddressBean(EntryBean, Serializable)

Comment   Jini 1.0

net.jini.lookup.entry   *serializable entry*

An Entry object of this class type is used to represent a single string. The Comment attribute can be used to attach a comment string to a service.

```
public class Comment extends net.jini.entry.AbstractEntry {
// Public Constructors
     public Comment();
     public Comment(String comment);
// Public Instance Fields
     public String comment;
}
```

Hierarchy: Object→ net.jini.entry.AbstractEntry(net.jini.core.entry.Entry(Serializable))→ Comment

Type Of: CommentBean.assoc

CommentBean   Jini 1.0

net.jini.lookup.entry   *serializable*

A JavaBean class that is used to handle a Comment attribute. There is only a single property that represents the single field of the attribute.

```
public class CommentBean implements EntryBean, Serializable {
// Public Constructors
     public CommentBean();
// Public Instance Methods
     public String getComment();                                    default:null
     public void setComment(String x);
// Methods Implementing EntryBean
     public net.jini.core.entry.Entry followLink();
```

```
    public void makeLink(net.jini.core.entry.Entry e);
// Protected Instance Fields
    protected Comment assoc;
}
```

Hierarchy: Object→ CommentBean(EntryBean, Serializable)

EntryBean   Jini 1.0
net.jini.lookup.entry

The interface that defines the makeLink( ) and followLink( ) methods that the entry Java-aBean must support. Those methods are used to set and retrieve the Entry object embedded within the entry bean.

```
public interface EntryBean {
// Public Instance Methods
    public abstract net.jini.core.entry.Entry followLink();
    public abstract void makeLink(net.jini.core.entry.Entry e);
}
```

Implementations: AddressBean, CommentBean, LocationBean, NameBean, ServiceInfoBean, StatusBean

Returned By: EntryBeans.createBean()

EntryBeans   Jini 1.0
net.jini.lookup.entry

A class that is used to obtain an entry JavaBean. This class can be used to find the JavaBean class given any entry class. To do so, it assumes that the JavaBean class follows the naming convention of the JavaBean classes in this package (the class name followed by Bean).

```
public class EntryBeans {
// Public Constructors
    public EntryBeans();
// Public Class Methods
    public static EntryBean createBean(net.jini.core.entry.Entry ent) throws ClassNotFoundException,
        java.io.IOException;
    public static Class getBeanClass(Class c) throws ClassNotFoundException;
}
```

Location   Jini 1.0
net.jini.lookup.entry   *serializable entry*

An entry object of this class type is used to define the location of the service (see also the Address attribute).

With this attribute, you can assign the floor, the room, or the building name to the service. Unlike the address attribute, this location defined cannot be used as a mailing address.

```
public class Location extends net.jini.entry.AbstractEntry {
// Public Constructors
    public Location();
    public Location(String floor, String room, String building);
// Public Instance Fields
    public String building;
```

net.jini Packages

```
    public String floor;
    public String room;
}
```

Hierarchy: Object→ net.jini.entry.AbstractEntry(net.jini.core.entry.Entry(Serializable))→ Location

Type Of: LocationBean.assoc

LocationBean   Jini 1.0

net.jini.lookup.entry   *serializable*

A JavaBean class that is used to handle a Location attribute. There is a JavaBean property for every field of the attribute.

```
public class LocationBean implements EntryBean, Serializable {
// Public Constructors
    public LocationBean();
// Property Accessor Methods (by property name)
    public String getBuilding();                                         default:null
    public void setBuilding(String x);
    public String getFloor();                                            default:null
    public void setFloor(String x);
    public String getRoom();                                             default:null
    public void setRoom(String x);
// Methods Implementing EntryBean
    public net.jini.core.entry.Entry followLink();
    public void makeLink(net.jini.core.entry.Entry e);
// Protected Instance Fields
    protected Location assoc;
}
```

Hierarchy: Object→ LocationBean(EntryBean, Serializable)

Name   Jini 1.0

net.jini.lookup.entry   *serializable entry*

An Entry object of this class type is used to represent the name of the service. With this attribute, you can assign any string as the name of the service.

```
public class Name extends net.jini.entry.AbstractEntry {
// Public Constructors
    public Name();
    public Name(String name);
// Public Instance Fields
    public String name;
}
```

Hierarchy: Object→ net.jini.entry.AbstractEntry(net.jini.core.entry.Entry(Serializable))→ Name

Type Of: NameBean.assoc

NameBean   Jini 1.0

net.jini.lookup.entry   *serializable*

A JavaBean class that is used to handle a Name attribute. There is only a single property that represents the single field of the attribute.

```
public class NameBean implements EntryBean, Serializable {
// Public Constructors
```

```
  public NameBean();
// Public Instance Methods
  public String getName();                                                       default:null
  public void setName(String x);
// Methods Implementing EntryBean
  public net.jini.core.entry.Entry followLink();
  public void makeLink(net.jini.core.entry.Entry e);
// Protected Instance Fields
  protected Name assoc;
}
```

Hierarchy: Object→ NameBean(EntryBean, Serializable)

ServiceControlled   Jini 1.0

net.jini.lookup.entry

This interface should be implemented by an attribute if clients of the service are not allowed to modify the attribute. This interface is simply used for type identification since there are no methods that need to be implemented; a service that implements an administrative interface to change attributes should not allow an attribute that implements the ServiceControlled interface to be changed.

```
public interface ServiceControlled {
}
```

Implementations: ServiceInfo, ServiceType, Status

ServiceInfo   Jini 1.0

net.jini.lookup.entry   *serializable entry*

An Entry object of this class type represents the information that can be used to determine the implementation of the service. With this attribute, you can assign a name, manufacturer, vendor, version, model, and serial number to a service. This information can be used to determine what version of the service is running.

```
public class ServiceInfo extends net.jini.entry.AbstractEntry implements ServiceControlled {
// Public Constructors
  public ServiceInfo();
  public ServiceInfo(String name, String manufacturer, String vendor, String version, String model,
              String serialNumber);
// Public Instance Fields
  public String manufacturer;
  public String model;
  public String name;
  public String serialNumber;
  public String vendor;
  public String version;
}
```

Hierarchy: Object→ net.jini.entry.AbstractEntry(net.jini.core.entry.Entry(Serializable))→ ServiceInfo(ServiceControlled)

Type Of: ServiceInfoBean.assoc

ServiceInfoBean

Jini 1.0

net.jini.lookup.entry

serializable

A JavaBean class that is used to handle a ServiceInfo attribute. There is a JavaBean property for every field of the attribute.

```
public class ServiceInfoBean implements EntryBean, Serializable {
// Public Constructors
    public ServiceInfoBean();
// Property Accessor Methods (by property name)
    public String getManufacturer();                                    default:null
    public void setManufacturer(String x);
    public String getModel();                                           default:null
    public void setModel(String x);
    public String getName();                                            default:null
    public void setName(String x);
    public String getSerialNumber();                                    default:null
    public void setSerialNumber(String x);
    public String getVendor();                                          default:null
    public void setVendor(String x);
    public String getVersion();                                         default:null
    public void setVersion(String x);
// Methods Implementing EntryBean
    public net.jini.core.entry.Entry followLink();
    public void makeLink(net.jini.core.entry.Entry e);
// Protected Instance Fields
    protected ServiceInfo assoc;
}
```

Hierarchy: Object → ServiceInfoBean(EntryBean, Serializable)

ServiceType

Jini 1.0

net.jini.lookup.entry

serializable entry

An entry object of this type is used to provide information for a human that uses or maintains the service. Such information includes an icon for the service, the display name of the service, and a short description about the service.

This class is abstract; hence, you will need to implement the fields and methods needed for this object. Since the fields of this entry class are not defined, there is no matching ServiceTypeBean class. See also the com.sun.jini.lookup.entry.BasicServiceType class.

```
public abstract class ServiceType extends net.jini.entry.AbstractEntry implements ServiceControlled {
// Public Constructors
    public ServiceType();
// Public Instance Methods
    public String getDisplayName();                                     constant
    public java.awt.Image getIcon(int iconKind);                        constant
    public String getShortDescription();                                constant
}
```

Hierarchy: Object → net.jini.entry.AbstractEntry(net.jini.core.entry.Entry(Serializable)) → ServiceType(ServiceControlled)

Subclasses: com.sun.jini.lookup.entry.BasicServiceType

Status

net.jini.lookup.entry   *serializable entry*

An Entry object of this abstract class type is used to represent the status of the service. This class is abstract and will need to be subclassed to add other fields that may be needed for the status.

The single field is of StatusType and represents the severity of the status condition.

```
public abstract class Status extends net.jini.entry.AbstractEntry implements ServiceControlled {
// Protected Constructors
    protected Status( );
    protected Status(StatusType severity);
// Public Instance Fields
    public StatusType severity;
}
```

Hierarchy: Object→ net.jini.entry.AbstractEntry(net.jini.core.entry.Entry(Serializable))→ Status(ServiceControlled)

Type Of: StatusBean.assoc

StatusBean

net.jini.lookup.entry   *serializable*

A JavaBean class that is used to handle a status attribute. There is only a single property that represents the single field of the attribute.

Since the Entry type is abstract, this class is also abstract.

```
public abstract class StatusBean implements EntryBean, Serializable {
// Protected Constructors
    protected StatusBean( );
// Public Instance Methods
    public StatusType getSeverity( );
    public void setSeverity(StatusType x);
// Methods Implementing EntryBean
    public net.jini.core.entry.Entry followLink( );
    public void makeLink(net.jini.core.entry.Entry e);
// Protected Instance Fields
    protected Status assoc;
}
```

Hierarchy: Object→ StatusBean(EntryBean, Serializable)

StatusType

net.jini.lookup.entry   *serializable*

An object of this class is used by the Status entry class to represent the severity of the status condition. Currently, only four severity levels are defined.

```
public class StatusType implements Serializable {
// No Constructor
// Public Constants
    public static final StatusType ERROR;
    public static final StatusType NORMAL;
    public static final StatusType NOTICE;
    public static final StatusType WARNING;
}
```

Hierarchy: Object→ StatusType(Serializable)

Passed To: Status.Status(), StatusBean.setSeverity()

Returned By: StatusBean.getSeverity()

Type Of: Status.severity, StatusType.{ERROR, NORMAL, NOTICE, WARNING}

The net.jini.space Package

The net.jini.space package provides the service interface and related classes of the JavaSpaces service. A reference to a JavaSpaces service may be obtained by looking up the JavaSpace interface in the Jini lookup service. See Chapter 10, *The JavaSpaces Service*, for more information on the JavaSpaces service. Figure 16-8 shows the class hierarchy for this package.

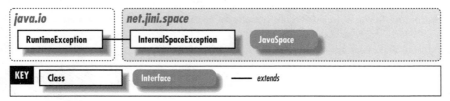

Figure 16–8: The net.jini.space package

InternalSpaceException   Jini 1.0
net.jini.space   *serializable unchecked*

An exception of this type is thrown when the JavaSpaces service encounters an internal error.

```
public class InternalSpaceException extends RuntimeException {
// Public Constructors
    public InternalSpaceException(String str);
    public InternalSpaceException(String str, Throwable ex);
// Public Methods Overriding Throwable
    public void printStackTrace();
    public void printStackTrace(java.io.PrintWriter out);
    public void printStackTrace(java.io.PrintStream out);
// Public Instance Fields
    public final Throwable nestedException;
}
```

Hierarchy: Object→ Throwable(Serializable)→ Exception→ RuntimeException→ InternalSpaceException

JavaSpace   Jini 1.0
net.jini.space

This interface is implemented by all JavaSpaces services. It provides seven methods that support the four operations of the JavaSpaces service: you can read, write, or take entries out of a JavaSpace, and you can register to be notified when entries in the JavaSpace change.

Reading, writing, or taking entries in a JavaSpace may occur within a transaction. To accomplish that, you must create a transaction object using the transaction service and pass that object to all read, write, or take operations that should be involved in the transaction. When you have completed the operations, you must then commit or abort the transaction. Entries that are written or taken during a transaction will not be seen by other clients of the service until the transaction is completed. If you do not need to group operations in the JavaSpace within a transaction, you may specify null for the transaction parameter.

```
public interface JavaSpace {
// Public Constants
    public static final long NO_WAIT;                                              =0
// Public Instance Methods
    public abstract net.jini.core.event.EventRegistration notify(net.jini.core.entry.Entry tmpl,
                            net.jini.core.transaction.Transaction txn,
                            net.jini.core.event.RemoteEventListener listener,
                            long lease, java.rmi.MarshalledObject handback)
        throws net.jini.core.transaction.TransactionException, SecurityException, java.rmi.RemoteException;
    public abstract net.jini.core.entry.Entry read(net.jini.core.entry.Entry tmpl, net.jini.core.transaction.Transaction txn,
                            long timeout) throws net.jini.core.entry.UnusableEntryException,
        net.jini.core.transaction.TransactionException, SecurityException, InterruptedException,
        java.rmi.RemoteException;
    public abstract net.jini.core.entry.Entry readIfExists(net.jini.core.entry.Entry tmpl,
                            net.jini.core.transaction.Transaction txn, long timeout)
        throws net.jini.core.entry.UnusableEntryException, net.jini.core.transaction.TransactionException,
        SecurityException, InterruptedException, java.rmi.RemoteException;
    public abstract net.jini.core.entry.Entry snapshot(net.jini.core.entry.Entry e) throws java.rmi.RemoteException;
    public abstract net.jini.core.entry.Entry take(net.jini.core.entry.Entry tmpl, net.jini.core.transaction.Transaction txn,
                            long timeout) throws net.jini.core.entry.UnusableEntryException,
        net.jini.core.transaction.TransactionException, SecurityException, InterruptedException,
        java.rmi.RemoteException;
    public abstract net.jini.core.entry.Entry takeIfExists(net.jini.core.entry.Entry tmpl,
                            net.jini.core.transaction.Transaction txn, long timeout)
        throws net.jini.core.entry.UnusableEntryException, net.jini.core.transaction.TransactionException,
        SecurityException, InterruptedException, java.rmi.RemoteException;
    public abstract net.jini.core.lease.Lease write(net.jini.core.entry.Entry entry, net.jini.core.transaction.Transaction txn,
                            long lease) throws net.jini.core.transaction.TransactionException,
        SecurityException, java.rmi.RemoteException;
}
```

CHAPTER 17

The java Packages

In this chapter, we'll discuss classes in the Java SDK that are important to Jini. We do not intend to present a discussion of all classes in the Java SDK; those classes are documented in *Java in a Nutshell, 3rd Edition*, and *Java Enterprise in a Nutshell*. Both are excellent reference sources for the classes that make up the core API of Java and Java's extension APIs that are very useful in a distributed computing environment.

The java.io Package

The java.io package contains several classes that relate to I/O. In this section, we provide a reference only to those classes that deal with object serialization, which we frequently use in a Jini environment. Figure 17-1 shows the class hierarchy for this subset of the package.

Object serialization is possible only on objects that implement the Serializable or Externalizable interface. A Serializable class can automatically save and reconstitute all nontransient instance variables of the class. Instance variables that are not serializable or that need to be handled in a special manner must be marked as transient, and the implementor of the class must treat those variables specifically in the readObject( ) and writeObject( ) methods.

An Externalizable class will not automatically save or reconstitute any variables; the developer is able to have full control over what data is written to and read from the streams in this case. The developer must also handle the superclass of the Externalizable class and must provide any version control functionality that is desired.

See Chapter 3, *Remote Method Invocation*, for examples and more details on object serialization.

Externalizable
<div style="display:flex;justify-content:space-between"><span></span><span>**Java 1.1**</span></div>

java.io   *serializable*

This interface indicates that a class wishes to participate in object serialization, and wants full control over that serialization. Externalizable classes are saved and reconstituted using the writeExternal( ) and readExternal( ) methods, respectively. These methods are responsible for writing and reading all data that the object wants to save or restore.

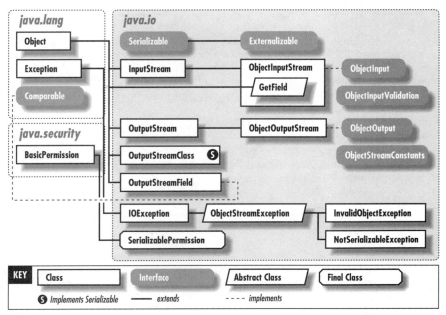

Figure 17–1: A subset of the java.io package

```
public interface Externalizable extends Serializable {
// Public Instance Methods
    public abstract void readExternal(ObjectInput in) throws IOException, ClassNotFoundException;
    public abstract void writeExternal(ObjectOutput out) throws IOException;
}
```

Hierarchy: (Externalizable(Serializable))

Implementations: java.rmi.server.RemoteRef

InvalidObjectException
java.io

Java 1.1

serializable checked

This exception is thrown when the requested validation of a deserialized object fails. It is not thrown unless you register a validator with the ObjectInputStream used for serialization.

```
public class InvalidObjectException extends ObjectStreamException {
// Public Constructors
    public InvalidObjectException(String reason);
}
```

Hierarchy: Object→ Throwable(Serializable)→ Exception→ IOException→ ObjectStreamException→ InvalidObjectException

Thrown By: ObjectInputStream.registerValidation(), ObjectInputValidation.validateObject()

NotSerializableException

java.io

This exception indicates that an attempt was made to write a nonserializable class to an ObjectOutputStream. This exception is thrown when a nonserializable class is serialized directly, or when you attempt to serialize a serializable object containing a nontransient, nonserializable instance variable.

```
public class NotSerializableException extends ObjectStreamException {
// Public Constructors
    public NotSerializableException();
    public NotSerializableException(String classname);
}
```

Hierarchy: Object→ Throwable(Serializable)→ Exception→ IOException→ ObjectStreamException→ NotSerializableException

ObjectInput

java.io

This interface is used by streams that can read Serializable or Externalizable objects. In addition to the methods provided by the DataInput interface, this interface defines the readObject( ) method, which is used to read the state of an entire object.

```
public interface ObjectInput extends DataInput {
// Public Instance Methods
    public abstract int available() throws IOException;
    public abstract void close() throws IOException;
    public abstract int read() throws IOException;
    public abstract int read(byte[ ] b) throws IOException;
    public abstract int read(byte[ ] b, int off, int len) throws IOException;
    public abstract Object readObject() throws ClassNotFoundException, IOException;
    public abstract long skip(long n) throws IOException;
}
```

Hierarchy: (ObjectInput(DataInput))

Implementations: ObjectInputStream

Passed To: Externalizable.readExternal(), java.rmi.server.ObjID.read()

Returned By: java.rmi.server.RemoteCall.getInputStream()

ObjectInputStream

java.io

This input stream filter is used to deserialize objects from the input stream source. Objects are read using the readObject( ) method; primitive data types can be read using any of the methods of the DataInputStream class.

```
public class ObjectInputStream extends InputStream implements ObjectInput, ObjectStreamConstants {
// Public Constructors
    public ObjectInputStream(InputStream in) throws IOException, StreamCorruptedException;
// Protected Constructors
1.2 protected ObjectInputStream() throws IOException, SecurityException;
// Inner Classes
1.2 public abstract static class GetField;
// Public Instance Methods
    public void defaultReadObject() throws IOException, ClassNotFoundException, NotActiveException;
1.2 public ObjectInputStream.GetField readFields() throws IOException, ClassNotFoundException, NotActiveException;
```

```
    public void registerValidation(ObjectInputValidation obj, int prio) throws NotActiveException,          synchronized
        InvalidObjectException;
// Methods Implementing DataInput
    public boolean readBoolean() throws IOException;
    public byte readByte() throws IOException;
    public char readChar() throws IOException;
    public double readDouble() throws IOException;
    public float readFloat() throws IOException;
    public void readFully(byte[ ] data) throws IOException;
    public void readFully(byte[ ] data, int offset, int size) throws IOException;
    public int readInt() throws IOException;
    public long readLong() throws IOException;
    public short readShort() throws IOException;
    public int readUnsignedByte() throws IOException;
    public int readUnsignedShort() throws IOException;
    public String readUTF() throws IOException;
    public int skipBytes(int len) throws IOException;
// Methods Implementing ObjectInput
    public int available() throws IOException;
    public void close() throws IOException;
    public int read() throws IOException;
    public int read(byte[ ] b, int off, int len) throws IOException;
    public final Object readObject() throws OptionalDataException, ClassNotFoundException, IOException;
// Protected Instance Methods
    protected boolean enableResolveObject(boolean enable) throws SecurityException;
1.2 protected Object readObjectOverride() throws OptionalDataException, ClassNotFoundException,          constant
        IOException;
    protected void readStreamHeader() throws IOException, StreamCorruptedException;
    protected Class resolveClass(ObjectStreamClass v) throws IOException, ClassNotFoundException;
    protected Object resolveObject(Object obj) throws IOException;
// Deprecated Public Methods
#   public String readLine() throws IOException;                                                   Implements:DataInput
}
```

Hierarchy: Object→ InputStream→ ObjectInputStream(ObjectInput(DataInput),
ObjectStreamConstants)

ObjectInputStream.GetField   Java 1.2

java.io

This class (returned from the readFields( ) method of the ObjectInputStream class) lets you
examine the values of nontransient fields of the object currently being processed by the
ObjectInputStream. You must know the name of the field to request it from this object.

```
public abstract static class ObjectInputStream.GetField {
// Public Constructors
    public GetField();
// Public Instance Methods
    public abstract boolean defaulted(String name) throws IOException, IllegalArgumentException;
    public abstract boolean get(String name, boolean defvalue) throws IOException, IllegalArgumentException;
    public abstract byte get(String name, byte defvalue) throws IOException, IllegalArgumentException;
    public abstract char get(String name, char defvalue) throws IOException, IllegalArgumentException;
    public abstract short get(String name, short defvalue) throws IOException, IllegalArgumentException;
    public abstract int get(String name, int defvalue) throws IOException, IllegalArgumentException;
    public abstract long get(String name, long defvalue) throws IOException, IllegalArgumentException;
    public abstract float get(String name, float defvalue) throws IOException, IllegalArgumentException;
```

```
    public abstract double get(String name, double defvalue) throws IOException, IllegalArgumentException;
    public abstract Object get(String name, Object defvalue) throws IOException, IllegalArgumentException;
    public abstract ObjectStreamClass getObjectStreamClass();
}
```

Returned By: ObjectInputStream.readFields()

ObjectInputValidation   Java 1.1

java.io

This interface provides a callback mechanism for developers to validate objects that are read from an ObjectInputStream. You register an object of this type in the readObject( ) method of the serializable object; after the object has been read, its validateObject( ) method will be called.

```
public interface ObjectInputValidation {
// Public Instance Methods
    public abstract void validateObject() throws InvalidObjectException;
}
```

Passed To: ObjectInputStream.registerValidation()

ObjectOutput   Java 1.1

java.io

This interface is used by streams that can write Serializable or Externalizable objects.

```
public interface ObjectOutput extends DataOutput {
// Public Instance Methods
    public abstract void close() throws IOException;
    public abstract void flush() throws IOException;
    public abstract void write(byte[ ] b) throws IOException;
    public abstract void write(int b) throws IOException;
    public abstract void write(byte[ ] b, int off, int len) throws IOException;
    public abstract void writeObject(Object obj) throws IOException;
}
```

Hierarchy: (ObjectOutput(DataOutput))

Implementations: ObjectOutputStream

Passed To: Externalizable.writeExternal(), ObjectOutputStream.PutField.write(), java.rmi.server.ObjID.write(), java.rmi.server.RemoteRef.getRefClass()

Returned By: java.rmi.server.RemoteCall.{getOutputStream(), getResultStream()}

ObjectOutputStream   Java 1.1

java.io

This output stream filter is used to serialize objects to the output stream destination. Objects are written using the writeObject( ) method; primitive data can be written using any method of the DataOutputStream class.

```
public class ObjectOutputStream extends OutputStream implements ObjectOutput, ObjectStreamConstants {
// Public Constructors
    public ObjectOutputStream(OutputStream out) throws IOException;
// Protected Constructors
1.2 protected ObjectOutputStream() throws IOException, SecurityException;
// Inner Classes
```

```
1.2 public abstract static class PutField;
// Public Instance Methods
    public void defaultWriteObject() throws IOException;
1.2 public ObjectOutputStream.PutField putFields() throws IOException;
    public void reset() throws IOException;
1.2 public void useProtocolVersion(int version) throws IOException;
1.2 public void writeFields() throws IOException;
// Methods Implementing DataOutput
    public void writeBoolean(boolean data) throws IOException;
    public void writeByte(int data) throws IOException;
    public void writeBytes(String data) throws IOException;
    public void writeChar(int data) throws IOException;
    public void writeChars(String data) throws IOException;
    public void writeDouble(double data) throws IOException;
    public void writeFloat(float data) throws IOException;
    public void writeInt(int data) throws IOException;
    public void writeLong(long data) throws IOException;
    public void writeShort(int data) throws IOException;
    public void writeUTF(String data) throws IOException;
// Methods Implementing ObjectOutput
    public void close() throws IOException;
    public void flush() throws IOException;
    public void write(byte[ ] b) throws IOException;
    public void write(int data) throws IOException;
    public void write(byte[ ] b, int off, int len) throws IOException;
    public final void writeObject(Object obj) throws IOException;
// Protected Instance Methods
    protected void annotateClass(Class cl) throws IOException;                    empty
    protected void drain() throws IOException;
    protected boolean enableReplaceObject(boolean enable) throws SecurityException;
    protected Object replaceObject(Object obj) throws IOException;
1.2 protected void writeObjectOverride(Object obj) throws IOException;            empty
    protected void writeStreamHeader() throws IOException;
}
```

Hierarchy: Object→ OutputStream→ ObjectOutputStream(ObjectOutput(DataOutput), ObjectStreamConstants)

ObjectOutputStream.PutField   Java 1.2

java.io

An object with this interface is returned by the putFields( ) method of the ObjectOutput-Stream class; you cannot directly construct a useful object that uses this class.

Use this object to enable complete control over the data that is written to a serialized stream, particularly when the fields have changed from one version of the object to another. Begin by defining a private static variable called serialPersistentFields in the object; that variable must contain an array of ObjectStreamField objects, each of which represents a field that you want to be included when the object is serialized. Then in the writeObject( ) method, obtain the PutField object and call its put( ) methods to write out the actual data for the fields listed in the order specified by the serialPersistentFields array. Then call the write( ) method of the PutField object to complete serialization.

Data written in this manner must be deserialized in the readObject() method using an ObjectInputStream.GetField object.

```
public abstract static class ObjectOutputStream.PutField {
// Public Constructors
    public PutField();
// Public Instance Methods
    public abstract void put(String name, long value);
    public abstract void put(String name, int value);
    public abstract void put(String name, Object value);
    public abstract void put(String name, boolean value);
    public abstract void put(String name, short value);
    public abstract void put(String name, char value);
    public abstract void put(String name, byte value);
    public abstract void put(String name, float value);
    public abstract void put(String name, double value);
    public abstract void write(ObjectOutput out) throws IOException;
}
```

Returned By: ObjectOutputStream.putFields()

ObjectStreamClass   Java 1.1

java.io   *serializable*

This class provides the internal description of a Serializable object. Developers do not use this class.

```
public class ObjectStreamClass implements Serializable {
// No Constructor
// Public Constants
1.2 public static final ObjectStreamField[ ] NO_FIELDS;
// Public Class Methods
    public static ObjectStreamClass lookup(Class cl);
// Property Accessor Methods (by property name)
1.2 public ObjectStreamField[ ] getFields();
    public String getName();
    public long getSerialVersionUID();
// Public Instance Methods
    public Class forClass();
1.2 public ObjectStreamField getField(String name);
// Public Methods Overriding Object
    public String toString();
}
```

Hierarchy: Object→ ObjectStreamClass(Serializable)

Passed To: ObjectInputStream.resolveClass()

Returned By: ObjectInputStream.GetField.getObjectStreamClass(), ObjectStreamClass.lookup()

ObjectStreamConstants   Java 1.2

java.io

This interface defines constants that are used to define header and other non-object data in an object stream. Developers do not use this class.

```
public interface ObjectStreamConstants {
// Public Constants
    public static final int baseWireHandle;                      =8257536
    public static final int PROTOCOL_VERSION_1;                        =1
    public static final int PROTOCOL_VERSION_2;                        =2
```

```
    public static final byte SC_BLOCK_DATA;                                              =8
    public static final byte SC_EXTERNALIZABLE;                                          =4
    public static final byte SC_SERIALIZABLE;                                            =2
    public static final byte SC_WRITE_METHOD;                                            =1
    public static final short STREAM_MAGIC;                                          =-21267
    public static final short STREAM_VERSION;                                            =5
    public static final SerializablePermission SUBCLASS_IMPLEMENTATION_PERMISSION;
    public static final SerializablePermission SUBSTITUTION_PERMISSION;
    public static final byte TC_ARRAY;                                                 =117
    public static final byte TC_BASE;                                                  =112
    public static final byte TC_BLOCKDATA;                                             =119
    public static final byte TC_BLOCKDATALONG;                                         =122
    public static final byte TC_CLASS;                                                 =118
    public static final byte TC_CLASSDESC;                                             =114
    public static final byte TC_ENDBLOCKDATA;                                          =120
    public static final byte TC_EXCEPTION;                                             =123
    public static final byte TC_MAX;                                                   =123
    public static final byte TC_NULL;                                                  =112
    public static final byte TC_OBJECT;                                                =115
    public static final byte TC_REFERENCE;                                             =113
    public static final byte TC_RESET;                                                 =121
    public static final byte TC_STRING;                                                =116
}
```

Implementations: ObjectInputStream, ObjectOutputStream

ObjectStreamException   Java 1.1

java.io   *serializable checked*

This is the superclass of all object stream exceptions.

```
public abstract class ObjectStreamException extends IOException {
// Protected Constructors
    protected ObjectStreamException();
    protected ObjectStreamException(String classname);
}
```

Hierarchy: Object→ Throwable(Serializable)→ Exception→ IOException→ ObjectStreamException

Subclasses: InvalidObjectException, NotSerializableException

ObjectStreamField   Java 1.2

java.io   *comparable*

This class is the definition of a particular field within the serialized stream. It is not used by developers.

```
public class ObjectStreamField implements Comparable {
// Public Constructors
    public ObjectStreamField(String n, Class clazz);
// Property Accessor Methods (by property name)
    public String getName();
    public int getOffset();
    public boolean isPrimitive();
    public Class getType();
    public char getTypeCode();
    public String getTypeString();
```

```
// Methods Implementing Comparable
    public int compareTo(Object o);
// Public Methods Overriding Object
    public String toString();
// Protected Instance Methods
    protected void setOffset(int offset);
}
```

Hierarchy: Object→ ObjectStreamField(Comparable)

Returned By: ObjectStreamClass.{getField(), getFields()}

Type Of: ObjectStreamClass.NO_FIELDS

Serializable   Java 1.1
java.io   *serializable*

This interface marks a class as serializable. It is used for type identification only, since it has no methods. However, defining a class as Serializable enables its private readObject( ) and writeObject( ) methods. The writeObject( ) method should call the defaultWriteObject( ) method of the given ObjectOutputStream, which will write all data of the object except for its transient instance variables. This method should then write all transient data in whatever format it feels is appropriate.

The readObject( ) method should call the defaultReadObject( ) method of the given ObjectInputStream, which restore all data of the object except for transient data. This method should then read in the transient data in the format that it was written by the writeObject( ) method.

```
public interface Serializable {
}
```

Implementations: Too many classes to list.

SerializablePermission   Java 1.2
java.io   *serializable permission*

This class is used by the object stream classes to require that applications have certain permissions to perform certain serialization operations. In particular, a program must have the serializable permission named enableSubclassImplementation to subclass the ObjectInputStream or ObjectOutputStream classes or the permission named enableSubstitution to use the enableReplaceObject( ) method of the ObjectOutputStream class. Developers do not use this class, though administrators may need to list this class name and targets in the appropriate *java.policy* file.

```
public final class SerializablePermission extends java.security.BasicPermission {
// Public Constructors
    public SerializablePermission(String name);
    public SerializablePermission(String name, String actions);
}
```

Hierarchy: Object→ java.security.Permission(java.security.Guard, Serializable)→
java.security.BasicPermission(Serializable)→ SerializablePermission

Type Of: ObjectStreamConstants.{SUBCLASS_IMPLEMENTATION_PERMISSION,
SUBSTITUTION_PERMISSION}

The java.rmi Package

The java.rmi package contains the set of RMI code that is common to both clients and servers. Subpackages of this package define the server interfaces (as well as some administrative interfaces). Figure 17-2 shows the class hierarchy for this package.

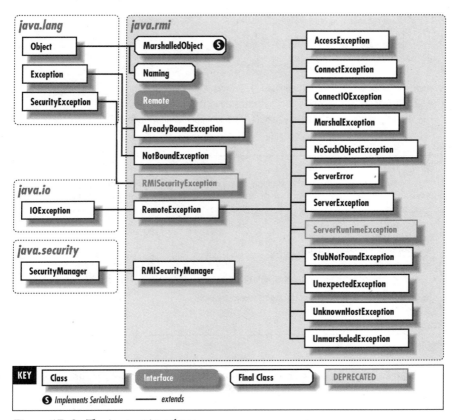

Figure 17-2: The java.rmi package

For the most part, this package defines exceptions that can occur in the communications between client and server. The most interesting class in this package for developers is the MarshalledObject class. Jini services use the MarshalledObject to store serialized objects because that class includes the location from which the class was loaded; when a marshalled object is reconstituted, the service is able to reload the class definition if necessary. Marshalled objects appear in a number of Jini interfaces and this class is used to define the serialization semantics of net.jini.core.entry.Entry objects.

This package also contains client-side facilities of the RMI registry (the Naming class). This class is not usually used in a Jini environment, though it may be useful for testing purposes (see the java.rmi.registry package).

Examples of RMI servers and clients are shown in Chapter 3.

AccessException

java.rmi

Java 1.1

serializable checked

This exception is thrown by *rmiregistry* and its associated classes. It is used to indicate that a particular host does not have permission to perform the attempted operation in the registry.

```
public class AccessException extends RemoteException {
// Public Constructors
    public AccessException(String s);
    public AccessException(String s, Exception ex);
}
```

Hierarchy: Object→ Throwable(Serializable)→ Exception→ java.io.IOException→ RemoteException→ AccessException

Thrown By: java.rmi.registry.Registry.{bind(), list(), lookup(), rebind(), unbind()}

AlreadyBoundException

java.rmi

Java 1.1

serializable checked

This exception is thrown by the Naming class when an RMI server attempts to register a name that is already registered. Jini programs do not typically use the Naming class.

```
public class AlreadyBoundException extends Exception {
// Public Constructors
    public AlreadyBoundException();
    public AlreadyBoundException(String s);
}
```

Hierarchy: Object→ Throwable(Serializable)→ Exception→ AlreadyBoundException

Thrown By: Naming.bind(), java.rmi.registry.Registry.bind()

ConnectException

java.rmi

Java 1.1

serializable checked

This exception is thrown when an RMI call fails because an initial connection to the remote host cannot be made. It indicates that the service is no longer running on the machine or the machine cannot be contacted.

```
public class ConnectException extends RemoteException {
// Public Constructors
    public ConnectException(String s);
    public ConnectException(String s, Exception ex);
}
```

Hierarchy: Object→ Throwable(Serializable)→ Exception→ java.io.IOException→ RemoteException→ java.rmi.ConnectException

ConnectIOException

java.rmi

Java 1.1

serializable checked

This exception is thrown when the client receives an I/O exception while attempting an initial connection to the service.

```
public class ConnectIOException extends RemoteException {
// Public Constructors
    public ConnectIOException(String s);
```

```
    public ConnectIOException(String s, Exception ex);
}
```

Hierarchy: Object→ Throwable(Serializable)→ Exception→ java.io.IOException→
RemoteException→ ConnectIOException

MarshalException   Java 1.1
java.rmi   *serializable checked*

This exception is thrown when the attempt to marshal (i.e. serialize) parameters or
return values during a remote method invocation fails. It usually means that a non-serializable class was encountered, though it could mean that another I/O exception
occurred (which usually means the server has crashed). This exception can be thrown
as the server passes its return value, which means that the call may have completed
successfully on the server.

```
public class MarshalException extends RemoteException {
// Public Constructors
    public MarshalException(String s);
    public MarshalException(String s, Exception ex);
}
```

Hierarchy: Object→ Throwable(Serializable)→ Exception→ java.io.IOException→
RemoteException→ MarshalException

MarshalledObject   Java 1.2
java.rmi   *serializable*

This class provides a wrapper around a serialized object. The Serializable object that is
passed to the constructor of this class is serialized into a byte array. The get( ) method
deserializes the object and returns it.

Remote objects within a marshalled object are serialized as their stubs. Deserializing
them will cause them to attempt to reconnect to their server.

The equals( ) method of a marshalled object compares its internal byte array with its target's internal byte array. They compare as equal only if every byte matches. This is
more efficient than deserializing the objects and using their equals( ) definition, but it is
not as precise. If an object has special semantics for its equals( ) method, those semantics are lost when a comparison of the marshalled object is performed: a URL constructed from the string *http://piccolo.East.Sun.COM/* and one constructed from the
string *http://129.151.119.8/* will compare as equal, but marshalled objects of those
URLs will not compare as equal. This is an important consideration in dealing with
net.jini.core.entry.Entry objects, since tools to compare entry objects often compare their
marshalled data.

Comparison of marshalled objects does not include their codebase annotations.

```
public final class MarshalledObject implements Serializable {
// Public Constructors
    public MarshalledObject(Object obj) throws java.io.IOException;
// Public Instance Methods
    public Object get( ) throws java.io.IOException, ClassNotFoundException;
// Public Methods Overriding Object
    public boolean equals(Object obj);
    public int hashCode( );
}
```

Hierarchy: Object→ MarshalledObject(Serializable)

Passed To: Too many methods to list.

Returned By: java.rmi.activation.ActivationDesc.getData(),
java.rmi.activation.ActivationGroup.newInstance(), java.rmi.activation.ActivationGroupDesc.getData(),
java.rmi.activation.ActivationInstantiator.newInstance(), java.rmi.activation.Activator.activate(),
net.jini.core.event.RemoteEvent.getRegistrationObject(),
net.jini.discovery.LookupUnmarshalException.getStillMarshalledRegs()

Type Of: net.jini.core.event.RemoteEvent.handback

Naming   Java 1.1
java.rmi

This class allows RMI clients and servers to interact with instances of the RMI registry. It
is not used in Jini environments, where registry information is retrieved instead from
the Jini lookup service.

```
public final class Naming {
// No Constructor
// Public Class Methods
    public static void bind(String name, Remote obj) throws AlreadyBoundException, java.net.MalformedURLException,
        RemoteException;
    public static String[ ] list(String name) throws RemoteException, java.net.MalformedURLException;
    public static Remote lookup(String name) throws NotBoundException, java.net.MalformedURLException,
        RemoteException;
    public static void rebind(String name, Remote obj) throws RemoteException, java.net.MalformedURLException;
    public static void unbind(String name) throws RemoteException, NotBoundException,
        java.net.MalformedURLException;
}
```

NoSuchObjectException   Java 1.1
java.rmi   *serializable checked*

This exception is thrown when an operation is attempted on an RMI stub where the
server has already garbage collected the object. This situation occurs because a network interruption between client and server has prevented the RMI client-side code
from renewing its lease to the server object. If this exception occurs, no other communication to the server is possible.

```
public class NoSuchObjectException extends RemoteException {
// Public Constructors
    public NoSuchObjectException(String s);
}
```

Hierarchy: Object→ Throwable(Serializable)→ Exception→ java.io.IOException→
RemoteException→ NoSuchObjectException

Thrown By: java.rmi.activation.Activatable.unexportObject(), java.rmi.server.RemoteObject.toStub(),
java.rmi.server.UnicastRemoteObject.unexportObject()

NotBoundException   Java 1.1
java.rmi   *serializable checked*

This exception is thrown by the Registry class when a lookup( ) or unbind( ) method is
attempted on a service name for which nothing is registered.

```
public class NotBoundException extends Exception {
// Public Constructors
    public NotBoundException();
    public NotBoundException(String s);
}
```

Hierarchy: Object→ Throwable(Serializable)→ Exception→ NotBoundException

Thrown By: Naming.{lookup(), unbind()}, java.rmi.registry.Registry.{lookup(), unbind()}

Remote

java.rmi

This interface is used for type identification; it identifies classes that are intended for use in a remote method invocation. Classes that implement this interface are treated differently by the underlying RMI classes: when a Remote class is serialized, a stub class (which also implements this interface) is sent to the receiving class. Upon deserialization, the stub class makes all the necessary network connections back to the original server.

Methods in a Remote interface are required to throw RemoteException; this requirement is enforced by *rmic*.

```
public interface Remote {
}
```

Implementations: com.sun.jini.lease.landlord.Landlord, java.rmi.activation.ActivationInstantiator, java.rmi.activation.ActivationMonitor, java.rmi.activation.ActivationSystem, java.rmi.activation.Activator, java.rmi.dgc.DGC, java.rmi.registry.Registry, java.rmi.server.RemoteObject, net.jini.core.event.RemoteEventListener, net.jini.core.transaction.server.TransactionManager, net.jini.core.transaction.server.TransactionParticipant

Passed To: Too many methods to list.

Returned By: Naming.lookup(), java.rmi.activation.Activatable.{exportObject(), register()}, java.rmi.activation.ActivationID.activate(), java.rmi.registry.Registry.lookup(), java.rmi.server.RemoteObject.toStub(), java.rmi.server.UnicastRemoteObject.exportObject()

RemoteException

java.rmi

This is the superclass for virtually all exceptions thrown by the RMI packages. This exception indicates that something has gone wrong in the method invocation; the cause of the exception is held in the instance variable detail. That usage is not required, however; there are cases when the detail instance variable is null, which indicate a generic exception.

Although this exception is a subclass of the IOException class, strictly speaking a RemoteException may not be related to I/O: if the code executing on the server throws a runtime exception (e.g., a NullPointerException), that runtime exception is bundled into an RemoteException and passed back to the client. In that case, the remote exception is a ServerRuntimeException, which contains the NullPointerException.

```
public class RemoteException extends java.io.IOException {
// Public Constructors
    public RemoteException();
    public RemoteException(String s);
    public RemoteException(String s, Throwable ex);
```

```
// Public Methods Overriding Throwable
    public String getMessage();                                            default:null
1.2 public void printStackTrace();
1.2 public void printStackTrace(java.io.PrintStream ps);
1.2 public void printStackTrace(java.io.PrintWriter pw);
// Public Instance Fields
    public Throwable detail;
}
```

Hierarchy: Object→ Throwable(Serializable)→ Exception→ java.io.IOException→
RemoteException

Subclasses: AccessException, java.rmi.ConnectException, ConnectIOException, MarshalException,
NoSuchObjectException, ServerError, ServerException, ServerRuntimeException,
StubNotFoundException, UnexpectedException, java.rmi.UnknownHostException, UnmarshalException,
java.rmi.activation.ActivateFailedException, java.rmi.server.ExportException,
java.rmi.server.SkeletonMismatchException, java.rmi.server.SkeletonNotFoundException

Passed To: com.sun.jini.proxy.ThrowThis.ThrowThis()

Thrown By: Too many methods to list.

RMISecurityException   Java 1.1; Deprecated in Java 1.2

java.rmi   *serializable unchecked*

This class is deprecated in Java 2 and has no replacement. The Java 1.1 implementation
of the RMISecurityManager class threw this exception.

```
public class RMISecurityException extends SecurityException {
// Public Constructors
#   public RMISecurityException(String name);
#   public RMISecurityException(String name, String arg);
}
```

Hierarchy: Object→ Throwable(Serializable)→ Exception→ RuntimeException→
SecurityException→ RMISecurityException

RMISecurityManager   Java 1.1

java.rmi

The RMI specification requires that any participant in an RMI call that involves the
transfer of code must have a security manager installed. This helps to protect the
integrity of the system, analogous to when an applet downloads code from an HTTP
server. In a Jini environment, services are clients of the Jini lookup service, so they
must have a security manager; clients obviously need one as well.

This class exists for historical reasons; it had a specific implementation in Java 1.1. In
Java 2, this class is empty; it inherits its entire behavior from the SecurityManager class.

```
public class RMISecurityManager extends SecurityManager {
// Public Constructors
    public RMISecurityManager();
}
```

Hierarchy: Object→ SecurityManager→ RMISecurityManager

ServerError

java.rmi

This error indicates that the method running on the server threw an error; the detail variable in this case will be an instance of the Error class.

```
public class ServerError extends RemoteException {
// Public Constructors
    public ServerError(String s, Error err);
}
```

Hierarchy: Object→ Throwable(Serializable)→ Exception→ java.io.IOException→ RemoteException→ ServerError

ServerException

java.rmi

This exception indicates that the method running on the server threw a checked exception; the detail variable in this case will be an instance of the Exception class.

```
public class ServerException extends RemoteException {
// Public Constructors
    public ServerException(String s);
    public ServerException(String s, Exception ex);
}
```

Hierarchy: Object→ Throwable(Serializable)→ Exception→ java.io.IOException→ RemoteException→ ServerException

ServerRuntimeException

java.rmi

This exception indicates that the method running on the server threw an unchecked (i.e, runtime) exception; the detail variable in this case will be an instance of the Exception class. This class is deprecated in 1.2.

```
public class ServerRuntimeException extends RemoteException {
// Public Constructors
#   public ServerRuntimeException(String s, Exception ex);
}
```

Hierarchy: Object→ Throwable(Serializable)→ Exception→ java.io.IOException→ RemoteException→ ServerRuntimeException

StubNotFoundException

java.rmi

This exception is thrown when a Remote object is serialized or deserialized and the class that defines the stub for that object cannot be found. It typically occurs in the client if you haven't set the server's java.rmi.server.codebase correctly, or if the client does not have a security manager and hence is prevented from downloading code.

```
public class StubNotFoundException extends RemoteException {
// Public Constructors
    public StubNotFoundException(String s);
    public StubNotFoundException(String s, Exception ex);
}
```

Hierarchy: Object→ Throwable(Serializable)→ Exception→ java.io.IOException→ RemoteException→ StubNotFoundException

UnexpectedException   Java 1.1

java.rmi   *serializable checked*

This exception is thrown when the server throws an exception that the client is not expecting (because it was not in the method's signature). That can happen only if the interface definition between the client and server is inconsistent.

```
public class UnexpectedException extends RemoteException {
// Public Constructors
    public UnexpectedException(String s);
    public UnexpectedException(String s, Exception ex);
}
```

Hierarchy: Object→ Throwable(Serializable)→ Exception→ java.io.IOException→ RemoteException→ UnexpectedException

UnknownHostException   Java 1.1

java.rmi   *serializable checked*

This exception indicates that the connection to a Remote server could not be made because the underlying network code threw a java.net.UnknownHostException.

```
public class UnknownHostException extends RemoteException {
// Public Constructors
    public UnknownHostException(String s);
    public UnknownHostException(String s, Exception ex);
}
```

Hierarchy: Object→ Throwable(Serializable)→ Exception→ java.io.IOException→ RemoteException→ java.rmi.UnknownHostException

Thrown By: java.rmi.registry.RegistryHandler.registryStub()

UnmarshalException   Java 1.1

java.rmi   *serializable checked*

This exception is thrown in many instances to indicate that the server was unable to unmarshal (i.e., deserialize) the parameters to the method, or that the client was unable to unmarshal the return value of the method. It most often occurs because one side is unable to find the class definition for the object it is deserializing.

```
public class UnmarshalException extends RemoteException {
// Public Constructors
    public UnmarshalException(String s);
    public UnmarshalException(String s, Exception ex);
}
```

Hierarchy: Object→ Throwable(Serializable)→ Exception→ java.io.IOException→ RemoteException→ UnmarshalException

The java.rmi.activation Package

The java.rmi.activation package defines the classes necessary to write an activatable RMI server. This is a server-side only package; clients do not know and cannot tell if an RMI server is activatable or not. Figure 17-3 shows the class hierarchy for this package.

Server activation allows servers to terminate when they are idle and be automatically restarted when they are required. There is a central process, the Remote Method Invocation Daemon (*rmid*), that is responsible for spawning the servers whenever there is a request for the corresponding service. There are two prime benefits to using server activation:

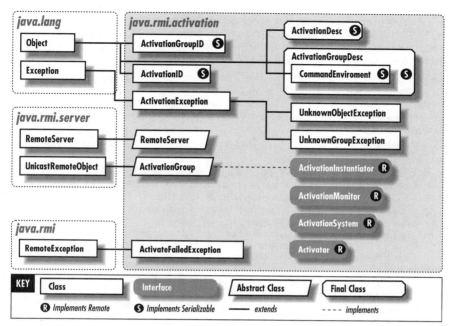

Figure 17–3: The java.rmi.activation package

- It reduces the resources required for a machine to support many servers, since the servers can exit when they are idle.

- It simplifies startup for a group of servers. *rmid* preserves its state between invocations, so that once a server is registered with *rmid*, that's all that needs to happen. If the machine (or *rmid*) crashes and *rmid* is restarted, it still knows about all the services and can restart them as needed.

In a Jini community, an activatable service must find a lease renewal service to be effective. Otherwise, the Jini service must always be active to maintain its lease. If no lease renewal service is available, the activatable Jini service must arrange for *rmid* to restart it immediately (without waiting for a request) so that the service may reregister itself with the Jini lookup service.

The process of spawning a server requires creating a new VM in which the server runs; it does not run in the same VM as *rmid*. Servers may be grouped into the same VM by using activation groups.

Activatable services are explained in more detail in Chapter 3, and a full activatable Jini implementation is shown in Chapter 11, *Helper Services*.

Activatable

java.rmi.activation

Java 1.2

serializable remote

This is the superclass for most activatable services. An activatable service is created by implementing a Remote interface and by either subclassing this class or by using the static exportObject( ) method of this class. Those two techniques are identical; the constructors of this class simply call the exportObject( ) method for you.

In either case, the constructor for an activatable service must be public and must take exactly two parameters: an ActivationID object and a MarshalledObject. If you fail to provide the appropriate constructor, an ActivateFailedException will be thrown to the client when *rmid* attempts to activate the service. The two-argument constructor must call one of the constructors of this class.

For Jini services that have not found a lease-renewal service, you should provide a value of true for the restart parameter of the constructor (when it calls the super( ) constructor) or the exportObject( ) method—that tells *rmid* to restart the service automatically when *rmid* restarts, which allows the service to register itself with the Jini lookup service and maintain its leases with the lookup service.

```
public abstract class Activatable extends java.rmi.server.RemoteServer {
// Protected Constructors
    protected Activatable(ActivationID id, int port) throws java.rmi.RemoteException;
    protected Activatable(ActivationID id, int port, java.rmi.server.RMIClientSocketFactory csf,
                    java.rmi.server.RMIServerSocketFactory ssf) throws java.rmi.RemoteException;
    protected Activatable(String location, java.rmi.MarshalledObject data, boolean restart, int port)
        throws ActivationException, java.rmi.RemoteException;
    protected Activatable(String location, java.rmi.MarshalledObject data, boolean restart, int port,
                    java.rmi.server.RMIClientSocketFactory csf, java.rmi.server.RMIServerSocketFactory ssf)
        throws ActivationException, java.rmi.RemoteException;
// Public Class Methods
    public static java.rmi.Remote exportObject(java.rmi.Remote obj, ActivationID id, int port)
        throws java.rmi.RemoteException;
    public static ActivationID exportObject(java.rmi.Remote obj, String location, java.rmi.MarshalledObject data,
                    boolean restart, int port) throws ActivationException,
        java.rmi.RemoteException;
    public static java.rmi.Remote exportObject(java.rmi.Remote obj, ActivationID id, int port,
                    java.rmi.server.RMIClientSocketFactory csf,
                    java.rmi.server.RMIServerSocketFactory ssf)
        throws java.rmi.RemoteException;
    public static ActivationID exportObject(java.rmi.Remote obj, String location, java.rmi.MarshalledObject data,
                    boolean restart, int port, java.rmi.server.RMIClientSocketFactory csf,
                    java.rmi.server.RMIServerSocketFactory ssf) throws ActivationException,
        java.rmi.RemoteException;
    public static boolean inactive(ActivationID id) throws UnknownObjectException, ActivationException,
        java.rmi.RemoteException;
    public static java.rmi.Remote register(ActivationDesc desc) throws UnknownGroupException, ActivationException,
        java.rmi.RemoteException;
    public static boolean unexportObject(java.rmi.Remote obj, boolean force)
        throws java.rmi.NoSuchObjectException;
    public static void unregister(ActivationID id) throws UnknownObjectException, ActivationException,
        java.rmi.RemoteException;
// Protected Instance Methods
    protected ActivationID getID();
}
```

Hierarchy: Object→ java.rmi.server.RemoteObject(java.rmi.Remote, Serializable)→ java.rmi.server.RemoteServer→ Activatable

ActivateFailedException   Java 1.2

java.rmi.activation   *serializable checked*

This exception indicates that *rmid* was unable to create the activatable service. This can happen if the constructor for the service does not have the correct signature, or for other internal failures to *rmid*.

```
public class ActivateFailedException extends java.rmi.RemoteException {
// Public Constructors
    public ActivateFailedException(String s);
    public ActivateFailedException(String s, Exception ex);
}
```

Hierarchy: Object→ Throwable(Serializable)→ Exception→ java.io.IOException→ java.rmi.RemoteException→ ActivateFailedException

ActivationDesc

java.rmi.activation

Java 1.2

serializable

This class encapsulates the information that rmid needs in order to start a service:

- The activation group ID that specifies the activation group to which this service should belong.

- The class name of the service (i.e., the class *rmid* constructs to run the service).

- The location from which *rmid* (and clients) can download the code that defines the service (i.e., the value to use for the java.rmi.server.codebase property).

- The marshalled object that *rmid* should pass to the constructor of the service.

- A boolean that indicates whether or not *rmid* should restart the service automatically after a failure. For Jini services that are not using a lease renewal service, this should be true.

```
public final class ActivationDesc implements Serializable {
// Public Constructors
    public ActivationDesc(String className, String location, java.rmi.MarshalledObject data)
        throws ActivationException;
    public ActivationDesc(ActivationGroupID groupID, String className, String location,
                          java.rmi.MarshalledObject data);
    public ActivationDesc(String className, String location, java.rmi.MarshalledObject data, boolean restart)
        throws ActivationException;
    public ActivationDesc(ActivationGroupID groupID, String className, String location,
                          java.rmi.MarshalledObject data, boolean restart);
// Property Accessor Methods (by property name)
    public String getClassName();
    public java.rmi.MarshalledObject getData();
    public ActivationGroupID getGroupID();
    public String getLocation();
    public boolean getRestartMode();
// Public Methods Overriding Object
    public boolean equals(Object obj);
    public int hashCode();
}
```

Hierarchy: Object→ ActivationDesc(Serializable)

Passed To: Activatable.register(), ActivationGroup.newInstance(), ActivationInstantiator.newInstance(), ActivationSystem.{registerObject(), setActivationDesc()}

Returned By: ActivationSystem.{getActivationDesc(), setActivationDesc()}

ActivationException
Java 1.2

java.rmi.activation
serializable checked

This is a generic exception used by the activation package.

```
public class ActivationException extends Exception {
// Public Constructors
      public ActivationException();
      public ActivationException(String s);
      public ActivationException(String s, Throwable ex);
// Public Methods Overriding Throwable
      public String getMessage();                                              default:null
      public void printStackTrace();
      public void printStackTrace(java.io.PrintWriter pw);
      public void printStackTrace(java.io.PrintStream ps);
// Public Instance Fields
      public Throwable detail;
}
```

Hierarchy: Object→ Throwable(Serializable)→ Exception→ ActivationException

Subclasses: UnknownGroupException, UnknownObjectException

Thrown By: Too many methods to list.

ActivationGroup
Java 1.2

java.rmi.activation
serializable remote

Each activatable service belongs to an activation group, which is modeled by this class. Each VM that is started by rmid runs all the services that were registered in the same activation group, which means that there is a one-to-one correspondence between activation groups and VMs started by *rmid.*

An activation group is created by instantiating an ActivationGroupDesc object and using that object to obtain the activation group ID from the registerGroup( ) method. Both the group description and ID are then passed to the createGroup( ) method to create the group.

Once the group has been created, it is used implicitly by the ActivationDesc class when activation descriptions are created (although that class allows you to specify a particular group ID as well). The remaining public methods of this class are called by the Activatable class; as a developer, you should not call those methods.

```
public abstract class ActivationGroup extends java.rmi.server.UnicastRemoteObject
        implements ActivationInstantiator {
// Protected Constructors
      protected ActivationGroup(ActivationGroupID groupID) throws java.rmi.RemoteException;
// Public Class Methods
      public static ActivationGroup createGroup(ActivationGroupID id, ActivationGroupDesc desc,    synchronized
                     long incarnation) throws ActivationException;
      public static ActivationGroupID currentGroupID();                                           synchronized
      public static ActivationSystem getSystem() throws ActivationException;                      synchronized
      public static void setSystem(ActivationSystem system) throws ActivationException;            synchronized
// Public Instance Methods
      public abstract void activeObject(ActivationID id, java.rmi.Remote obj) throws ActivationException,
                     UnknownObjectException, java.rmi.RemoteException;
      public boolean inactiveObject(ActivationID id) throws ActivationException, UnknownObjectException,
                     java.rmi.RemoteException;
// Methods Implementing ActivationInstantiator
```

```
    public abstract java.rmi.MarshalledObject newInstance(ActivationID id, ActivationDesc desc)
        throws ActivationException, java.rmi.RemoteException;
// Protected Instance Methods
    protected void activeObject(ActivationID id, java.rmi.MarshalledObject mobj) throws ActivationException,
        UnknownObjectException, java.rmi.RemoteException;
    protected void inactiveGroup() throws UnknownGroupException, java.rmi.RemoteException;
}
```

Hierarchy: Object→ java.rmi.server.RemoteObject(java.rmi.Remote, Serializable)→
java.rmi.server.RemoteServer→ java.rmi.server.UnicastRemoteObject→
ActivationGroup(ActivationInstantiator(java.rmi.Remote))

Returned By: ActivationGroup.createGroup()

ActivationGroupDesc

Java 1.2

java.rmi.activation

serializable

This class encapsulates the information that is used to spawn the virtual machine for an activatable group: the path and command-line arguments that should be used to spawn the new VM.

Properties that would otherwise be passed as command-line arguments should be encapsulated into the **properties** parameter of the constructor of this class. This usually always includes the *policy* file that the process should use.

```
public final class ActivationGroupDesc implements Serializable {
// Public Constructors
    public ActivationGroupDesc(java.util.Properties overrides, ActivationGroupDesc.CommandEnvironment cmd);
    public ActivationGroupDesc(String className, String location, java.rmi.MarshalledObject data,
                    java.util.Properties overrides, ActivationGroupDesc.CommandEnvironment cmd);
// Inner Classes
    public static class CommandEnvironment implements Serializable;
// Property Accessor Methods (by property name)
    public String getClassName();
    public ActivationGroupDesc.CommandEnvironment getCommandEnvironment();
    public java.rmi.MarshalledObject getData();
    public String getLocation();
    public java.util.Properties getPropertyOverrides();
// Public Methods Overriding Object
    public boolean equals(Object obj);
    public int hashCode();
}
```

Hierarchy: Object→ ActivationGroupDesc(Serializable)

Passed To: ActivationGroup.createGroup(), ActivationSystem.{registerGroup(), setActivationGroupDesc()}

Returned By: ActivationSystem.{getActivationGroupDesc(), setActivationGroupDesc()}

ActivationGroupDesc.CommandEnvironment

Java 1.2

java.rmi.activation

serializable

When you create an ActivationGroupDesc object and want to specify the path used to start the VM or to specify command-line arguments (other than properties), you pass a non-null instance of this class.

```
public static class ActivationGroupDesc.CommandEnvironment implements Serializable {
// Public Constructors
```

```
    public CommandEnvironment(String cmdpath, String[ ] argv);
// Public Instance Methods
    public String[ ] getCommandOptions();
    public String getCommandPath();
// Public Methods Overriding Object
    public boolean equals(Object obj);
    public int hashCode();
}
```

Passed To: ActivationGroupDesc.ActivationGroupDesc()

Returned By: ActivationGroupDesc.getCommandEnvironment()

ActivationGroupID
Java 1.2

java.rmi.activation
serializable

This class uniquely defines the activation group to which a particular VM belongs. You typically obtain an instance of this class by calling the registerGroup() method of the ActivationGroup class. Developers should treat this as an opaque class.

```
public class ActivationGroupID implements Serializable {
// Public Constructors
    public ActivationGroupID(ActivationSystem system);
// Public Instance Methods
    public ActivationSystem getSystem();
// Public Methods Overriding Object
    public boolean equals(Object obj);
    public int hashCode();
}
```

Hierarchy: Object→ ActivationGroupID(Serializable)

Passed To: ActivationDesc.ActivationDesc(), ActivationGroup.{ActivationGroup(), createGroup()}, ActivationMonitor.inactiveGroup(), ActivationSystem.{activeGroup(), getActivationGroupDesc(), setActivationGroupDesc(), unregisterGroup()}

Returned By: ActivationDesc.getGroupID(), ActivationGroup.currentGroupID(), ActivationSystem.registerGroup()

ActivationID
Java 1.2

java.rmi.activation
serializable

This class uniquely identifies an activatable service within a VM. It is normally opaque to the developer. Instances of this class are passed to the service via its constructor; the service typically saves the ID so that it may use it in other calls of the activation system.

```
public class ActivationID implements Serializable {
// Public Constructors
    public ActivationID(Activator activator);
// Public Instance Methods
    public java.rmi.Remote activate(boolean force) throws ActivationException, UnknownObjectException,
        java.rmi.RemoteException;
// Public Methods Overriding Object
    public boolean equals(Object obj);
    public int hashCode();
}
```

Hierarchy: Object→ ActivationID(Serializable)

Passed To: Too many methods to list.

Returned By: Activatable.{exportObject(), getID()}, ActivationSystem.registerObject()

ActivationInstantiator

java.rmi.activation

Java 1.2

remote

This interface defines the mechanism for *rmid* to create new instances of activatable services within a particular group. Developers do not call the methods of this interface directly.

```
public interface ActivationInstantiator extends java.rmi.Remote {
// Public Instance Methods
    public abstract java.rmi.MarshalledObject newInstance(ActivationID id, ActivationDesc desc)
        throws ActivationException, java.rmi.RemoteException;
}
```

Hierarchy: (ActivationInstantiator(java.rmi.Remote))

Implementations: ActivationGroup

Passed To: ActivationSystem.activeGroup()

ActivationMonitor

java.rmi.activation

Java 1.2

remote

An activation monitor is associated with each activation group; the group is responsible for notifying its monitor that objects within the group are becoming active or inactive. Developers do not use this class directly.

```
public interface ActivationMonitor extends java.rmi.Remote {
// Public Instance Methods
    public abstract void activeObject(ActivationID id, java.rmi.MarshalledObject obj) throws UnknownObjectException,
        java.rmi.RemoteException;
    public abstract void inactiveGroup(ActivationGroupID id, long incarnation) throws UnknownGroupException,
        java.rmi.RemoteException;
    public abstract void inactiveObject(ActivationID id) throws UnknownObjectException, java.rmi.RemoteException;
}
```

Hierarchy: (ActivationMonitor(java.rmi.Remote))

Returned By: ActivationSystem.activeGroup()

ActivationSystem

java.rmi.activation

Java 1.2

remote

This interface defines the operations of the activation system. From a developer's perspective, the activation system (there is only one in each VM) is responsible for assigning activation group IDs via the registerGroup() method. The activation system in use is returned from the ActivationGroup.getSystem() method.

Developers should not call the other methods of this class.

```
public interface ActivationSystem extends java.rmi.Remote {
// Public Constants
    public static final int SYSTEM_PORT;                                          =1098
// Public Instance Methods
    public abstract ActivationMonitor activeGroup(ActivationGroupID id, ActivationInstantiator group, long incarnation)
        throws UnknownGroupException, ActivationException, java.rmi.RemoteException;
    public abstract ActivationDesc getActivationDesc(ActivationID id) throws ActivationException,
        UnknownObjectException, java.rmi.RemoteException;
```

```
    public abstract ActivationGroupDesc getActivationGroupDesc(ActivationGroupID id) throws ActivationException,
        UnknownGroupException, java.rmi.RemoteException;
    public abstract ActivationGroupID registerGroup(ActivationGroupDesc desc) throws ActivationException,
        java.rmi.RemoteException;
    public abstract ActivationID registerObject(ActivationDesc desc) throws ActivationException,
        UnknownGroupException, java.rmi.RemoteException;
    public abstract ActivationDesc setActivationDesc(ActivationID id, ActivationDesc desc) throws ActivationException,
        UnknownObjectException, UnknownGroupException, java.rmi.RemoteException;
    public abstract ActivationGroupDesc setActivationGroupDesc(ActivationGroupID id, ActivationGroupDesc desc)
        throws ActivationException, UnknownGroupException, java.rmi.RemoteException;
    public abstract void shutdown() throws java.rmi.RemoteException;
    public abstract void unregisterGroup(ActivationGroupID id) throws ActivationException, UnknownGroupException,
        java.rmi.RemoteException;
    public abstract void unregisterObject(ActivationID id) throws ActivationException, UnknownObjectException,
        java.rmi.RemoteException;
}
```

Hierarchy: (ActivationSystem(java.rmi.Remote))

Passed To: ActivationGroup.setSystem(), ActivationGroupID.ActivationGroupID()

Returned By: ActivationGroup.getSystem(), ActivationGroupID.getSystem()

Activator
Java 1.2

java.rmi.activation
remote

A class that implements this interface must work with the ActivationSystem class to provide the basic functionality of activation; the Activator object actually spawns VMs to activate the given object. Developers do not interact with this interface directly.

```
public interface Activator extends java.rmi.Remote {
// Public Instance Methods
    public abstract java.rmi.MarshalledObject activate(ActivationID id, boolean force) throws ActivationException,
        UnknownObjectException, java.rmi.RemoteException;
}
```

Hierarchy: (Activator(java.rmi.Remote))

Passed To: ActivationID.ActivationID()

UnknownGroupException
Java 1.2

java.rmi.activation
serializable checked

This exception indicates that an operation encountered an invalid ActivationGroupID object—an ID that was not provided by the ActivationSystem class.

```
public class UnknownGroupException extends ActivationException {
// Public Constructors
    public UnknownGroupException(String s);
}
```

Hierarchy: Object→ Throwable(Serializable)→ Exception→ ActivationException→ UnknownGroupException

Thrown By: Activatable.register(), ActivationGroup.inactiveGroup(), ActivationMonitor.inactiveGroup(), ActivationSystem.{activeGroup(), getActivationGroupDesc(), registerObject(), setActivationDesc(), setActivationGroupDesc(), unregisterGroup()}

UnknownObjectException

Java 1.2

java.rmi.activation

serializable checked

This exception indicates that an operation encountered an invalid ActivationID object—an ID that was not provided by the ActivationSystem class (and which would have eventually been provided to the constructor of an activatable service).

```
public class UnknownObjectException extends ActivationException {
// Public Constructors
    public UnknownObjectException(String s);
}
```

Hierarchy: Object→ Throwable(Serializable)→ Exception→ ActivationException→ UnknownObjectException

Thrown By: Activatable.{inactive(), unregister()}, ActivationGroup.{activeObject(), inactiveObject()}, ActivationID.activate(), ActivationMonitor.{activeObject(), inactiveObject()}, ActivationSystem.{getActivationDesc(), setActivationDesc(), unregisterObject()}, Activator.activate()

The java.rmi.dgc Package

The java.rmi.dgc package defines some classes and interfaces that are used by RMI's distributed garbage collector. The distributed garbage collector uses a variant of the leasing paradigm that Jini uses, although its implementation is completely different. Figure 17-4 shows the class hierarchy for this package.

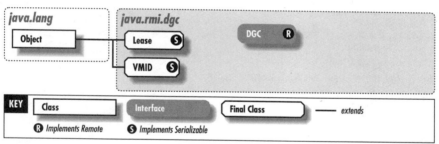

Figure 17-4: The java.rmi.dgc package

When a stub object is delivered to the client, the stub takes out a lease on the service object. This lease will be continually renewed until the stub on the client is garbage collected, at which time the lease will be explicitly cancelled. If the client exits or is otherwise unable to renew the lease, it will expire. When the lease is cancelled or expires, the service object will become eligible for garbage collection (assuming, of course, that the server doesn't have another reference to it).

This all happens transparently to developers. The only control a developer has over this process is the values used to control when the lease is renewed or when it expires. These values are set on the command line via the following properties:

```
piccolo% java -Djava.rmi.dgc.leaseValue=600000 -Dsun.rmi.dgc.checkInterval=300000 ...
```

The *leaseValue* property specifies the duration in milliseconds of the lease; the *checkInterval* property specifies the duration after which the client will attempt to renew the lease.

Developers will not use these classes directly.

DGC   Java 1.1
java.rmi.dgc   *remote*

This interface defines the implementation of the distributed garbage collector: clients call the dirty( ) method to renew leases and the clean( ) method to cancel the lease. There are no public implementations of this class.

```
public interface DGC extends java.rmi.Remote {
// Public Instance Methods
    public abstract void clean(java.rmi.server.ObjID[ ] ids, long sequenceNum, VMID vmid, boolean strong)
        throws java.rmi.RemoteException;
    public abstract java.rmi.dgc.Lease dirty(java.rmi.server.ObjID[ ] ids, long sequenceNum, java.rmi.dgc.Lease lease)
        throws java.rmi.RemoteException;
}
```

Hierarchy: (DGC(java.rmi.Remote))

Lease   Java 1.1
java.rmi.dgc   *serializable*

This class defines the lease used by the distributed garbage collector. It is very different from, and in no way related to, the net.jini.core.lease.Lease interface. There is no way to obtain the instances of this class that are used by the distributed garbage collector.

```
public final class Lease implements Serializable {
// Public Constructors
    public Lease(VMID id, long duration);
// Public Instance Methods
    public long getValue();
    public VMID getVMID();
}
```

Hierarchy: Object→ java.rmi.dgc.Lease(Serializable)

Passed To: DGC.dirty()

Returned By: DGC.dirty()

VMID   Java 1.1
java.rmi.dgc   *serializable*

This class defines what is essentially a universal unique ID (UUID): instances of this class are unique across VMs, which allows the distributed garbage collector to identify client VMs. There is no way to interact with this class in the distributed garbage collector.

```
public final class VMID implements Serializable {
// Public Constructors
    public VMID();
// Public Class Methods
    public static boolean isUnique();                                       constant
// Public Methods Overriding Object
    public boolean equals(Object obj);
    public int hashCode();
    public String toString();
}
```

Hierarchy: Object→ VMID(Serializable)

Passed To: DGC.clean(), java.rmi.dgc.Lease.Lease()

Returned By: java.rmi.dgc.Lease.getVMID()

The java.rmi.registry Package

The java.rmi.registry package contains the classes necessary to create and interact with instances of the RMI registry. The RMI registry is the way that RMI clients can find RMI servers, but in a Jini environment it is not used: Jini clients find Jini services using the Jini lookup service. Still, the RMI registry may be useful for testing your RMI-based Jini services since it requires less code to deal with the RMI registry than with the Jini lookup service. For examples of using the RMI registry, see Chapter 3.

Each instance of the RMI registry listens to a specific port (by default, 1099). Services register themselves by connecting to a registry on a specific host on a specific port; clients must look up services with the same host/port combination. Clients use a URL to look up particular services; this URL is of the form *rmi://hostname:port/ServiceName*.

Instances of the RMI registry can be created with the *rmiregistry* executable or by using the LocateRegistry class of this package. Figure 17-5 shows the class hierarchy for this package.

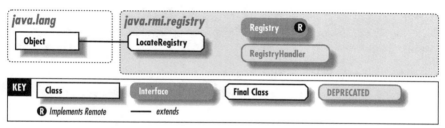

Figure 17-5: The java.rmi.registry package

LocateRegistry   Java 1.1

java.rmi.registry

This class provides two different operations:

*   It creates an instance of the RMI registry that listens on the specified port and returns a reference to that registry.

*   It returns a references to an existing RMI registry that is running at the given host (or on the local host if no host is specified) and is listening on the specified port (or 1099 if no port is specified). Creating this references always succeeds; you won't know if the registry is actually running until you invoke a method on the returned reference.

```
public final class LocateRegistry {
// No Constructor
// Public Class Methods
    public static Registry createRegistry(int port) throws java.rmi.RemoteException;
1.2 public static Registry createRegistry(int port, java.rmi.server.RMIClientSocketFactory csf,
                            java.rmi.server.RMIServerSocketFactory ssf) throws java.rmi.RemoteException;
    public static Registry getRegistry() throws java.rmi.RemoteException;
    public static Registry getRegistry(String host) throws java.rmi.RemoteException;
    public static Registry getRegistry(int port) throws java.rmi.RemoteException;
```

```
    public static Registry getRegistry(String host, int port) throws java.rmi.RemoteException;
1.2 public static Registry getRegistry(String host, int port, java.rmi.server.RMIClientSocketFactory csf)
        throws java.rmi.RemoteException;
}
```

Registry

java.rmi.registry

Java 1.1

remote

This class defines the interface provided by an RMI registry. The registry associates service names with service objects.

```
public interface Registry extends java.rmi.Remote {
// Public Constants
    public static final int REGISTRY_PORT;                                         =1099
// Public Instance Methods
    public abstract void bind(String name, java.rmi.Remote obj) throws java.rmi.RemoteException,
        java.rmi.AlreadyBoundException, java.rmi.AccessException;
    public abstract String[ ] list() throws java.rmi.RemoteException, java.rmi.AccessException;
    public abstract java.rmi.Remote lookup(String name) throws java.rmi.RemoteException, java.rmi.NotBoundException
        , java.rmi.AccessException;
    public abstract void rebind(String name, java.rmi.Remote obj) throws java.rmi.RemoteException,
        java.rmi.AccessException;
    public abstract void unbind(String name) throws java.rmi.RemoteException, java.rmi.NotBoundException,
        java.rmi.AccessException;
}
```

Hierarchy: (Registry(java.rmi.Remote))

Returned By: LocateRegistry.{createRegistry(), getRegistry()}, RegistryHandler.{registryImpl(),
registryStub()}

RegistryHandler

Java 1.1; Deprecated in Java 1.2

java.rmi.registry

This interface is deprecated in Java 2 and has no replacement. No class implements this
interface.

```
public interface RegistryHandler {
// Deprecated Public Methods
#   public abstract Registry registryImpl(int port) throws java.rmi.RemoteException;
#   public abstract Registry registryStub(String host, int port) throws java.rmi.RemoteException,
        java.rmi.UnknownHostException;
}
```

The java.rmi.server Package

The java.rmi.server package defines the server-side classes and interfaces of RMI. Use
these classes to implement RMI services. Figure 17-6 shows the class hierarchy for this
package.

Developers usually only work with one class in this package: UnicastRemoteObject. This
class provides a mechanism for classes that implement the Remote interface to export
their service to the network. The remaining classes in this package provide support for
that operation, including the RMISocketFactory class, which allows you to change the type
of sockets that RMI services use. You could, for example, provide an implementation of
that class that uses SSL for its communications between client and server.

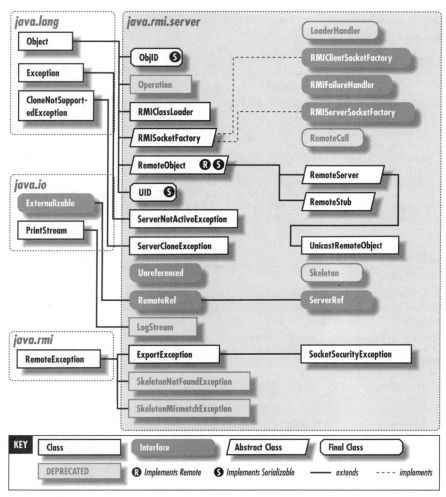

Figure 17-6: The java.rmi.server package

ExportException

java.rmi.server   *serializable checked*

This exception is thrown when a service cannot be exported; that is, the exportObject( )
method of the Activatable or UnicastRemoteObject class has failed.

```
public class ExportException extends java.rmi.RemoteException {
// Public Constructors
    public ExportException(String s);
    public ExportException(String s, Exception ex);
}
```

Hierarchy: Object→ Throwable(Serializable)→ Exception→ java.io.IOException→ java.rmi.RemoteException→ ExportException

Subclasses: SocketSecurityException

LoaderHandler Java 1.1; Deprecated in Java 1.2

java.rmi.server

This interface is deprecated in Java 2 and has no replacement. No public classes implement this interface.

```
public interface LoaderHandler {
// Public Constants
    public static final String packagePrefix;                              ="sun.rmi.server"
// Deprecated Public Methods
#   public abstract Object getSecurityContext(ClassLoader loader);
#   public abstract Class loadClass(String name) throws java.net.MalformedURLException, ClassNotFoundException;
#   public abstract Class loadClass(java.net.URL codebase, String name) throws java.net.MalformedURLException,
        ClassNotFoundException;
}
```

LogStream Java 1.1; Deprecated in Java 1.2

java.rmi.server

This class defines a logging mechanism; the mechanism is not specific to RMI. It is deprecated in Java 2. In a Jini environment, you can use the com.sun.jini.debug.Debug class to provide similar functionality.

```
public class LogStream extends java.io.PrintStream {
// No Constructor
// Public Constants
    public static final int BRIEF;                                         =10
    public static final int SILENT;                                        =0
    public static final int VERBOSE;                                       =20
// Deprecated Public Methods
#   public static java.io.PrintStream getDefaultStream();                  synchronized
#   public java.io.OutputStream getOutputStream();                         synchronized
#   public static LogStream log(String name);
#   public static int parseLevel(String s);
#   public static void setDefaultStream(java.io.PrintStream newDefault);   synchronized
#   public void setOutputStream(java.io.OutputStream out);                 synchronized
#   public String toString();                                             Overrides:Object
#   public void write(int b);                                           Overrides:PrintStream
#   public void write(byte[ ] b, int off, int len);                    Overrides:PrintStream
}
```

Hierarchy: Object→ java.io.OutputStream→ java.io.FilterOutputStream→ java.io.PrintStream→ LogStream

Returned By: LogStream.log()

ObjID Java 1.1

java.rmi.server *serializable*

Every object that is exported by RMI is given a unique object ID; that ID is encapsulated by this class. There are three special objects that have well-known IDs: the registry object, the activator object, and the distributed garbage collector object. All other objects will have an ID assigned to them; if the java.rmi.server.randomIDs property is true, then the ID will be based on a cryptographically strong random number.

Developers do not interact with this class.

```
public final class ObjID implements Serializable {
// Public Constructors
    public ObjID();
    public ObjID(int num);
// Public Constants
1.2 public static final int ACTIVATOR_ID;                                  =1
    public static final int DGC_ID;                                        =2
    public static final int REGISTRY_ID;                                   =0
// Public Class Methods
    public static ObjID read(java.io.ObjectInput in) throws java.io.IOException;
// Public Instance Methods
    public void write(java.io.ObjectOutput out) throws java.io.IOException;
// Public Methods Overriding Object
    public boolean equals(Object obj);
    public int hashCode();
    public String toString();
}
```

Hierarchy: Object→ ObjID(Serializable)

Passed To: java.rmi.dgc.DGC.{clean(), dirty()}

Returned By: ObjID.read()

Operation

java.rmi.server

This class is used in the skeleton of RMI to define which method should be invoked. It is deprecated, since in Java 2 there is no need for skeleton classes (though it can still be used for compatibility). Developers do not interact with this class directly.

```
public class Operation {
// Public Constructors
#   public Operation(String op);
// Deprecated Public Methods
#   public String getOperation();
#   public String toString();                                    Overrides:Object
}
```

Passed To: RemoteRef.newCall()

Returned By: Skeleton.getOperations()

RemoteCall

java.rmi.server

This interface is deprecated in Java 2; it needs no replacement. This interface was used only by certain methods of the RemoteRef class; developers never need to use this class.

```
public interface RemoteCall {
// Deprecated Public Methods
#   public abstract void done() throws java.io.IOException;
#   public abstract void executeCall() throws Exception;
#   public abstract java.io.ObjectInput getInputStream() throws java.io.IOException;
#   public abstract java.io.ObjectOutput getOutputStream() throws java.io.IOException;
```

public abstract java.io.ObjectOutput **getResultStream**(boolean *success*) throws java.io.IOException,
     java.io.StreamCorruptedException;
# public abstract void **releaseInputStream**() throws java.io.IOException;
# public abstract void **releaseOutputStream**() throws java.io.IOException;
}

Passed To: RemoteRef.{done(), invoke()}, Skeleton.dispatch()

Returned By: RemoteRef.newCall()

RemoteObject   Java 1.1

java.rmi.server   *serializable remote*

This class is the superclass for remote servers; its purpose is to provide common definitions of methods in the Object class. For the developer, the interesting implementation is
the equals() method, which returns true if the objects ultimately refer to the same server
object, even if one is local and one is remote.

public abstract class **RemoteObject** implements java.rmi.Remote, Serializable {
// *Protected Constructors*
     protected **RemoteObject**();
     protected **RemoteObject**(RemoteRef *newref*);
// *Public Class Methods*
1.2 public static java.rmi.Remote **toStub**(java.rmi.Remote *obj*) throws java.rmi.NoSuchObjectException;
// *Public Instance Methods*
1.2 public RemoteRef **getRef**();
// *Public Methods Overriding Object*
     public boolean **equals**(Object *obj*);
     public int **hashCode**();
     public String **toString**();
// *Protected Instance Fields*
     protected transient RemoteRef **ref**;
}

Hierarchy: Object→ RemoteObject(java.rmi.Remote, Serializable)

Subclasses: RemoteServer, RemoteStub

Passed To: RemoteRef.newCall()

RemoteRef   Java 1.1

java.rmi.server   *serializable*

Objects that implement remote references are used by the stubs (and skeletons) of RMI
to pass the data for a remote method invocation. Developers never use this interface
directly.

public interface **RemoteRef** extends java.io.Externalizable {
// *Public Constants*
     public static final String **packagePrefix**;   =*"sun.rmi.server"*
1.2 public static final long **serialVersionUID**;   =3632638527362204081
// *Public Instance Methods*
     public abstract String **getRefClass**(java.io.ObjectOutput *out*);
1.2 public abstract Object **invoke**(java.rmi.Remote *obj*, java.lang.reflect.Method *method*, Object[ ] *params*, long *opnum*)
         throws Exception;
     public abstract boolean **remoteEquals**(RemoteRef *obj*);
     public abstract int **remoteHashCode**();
     public abstract String **remoteToString**();

public abstract void **done**(RemoteCall *call*) throws java.rmi.RemoteException;
public abstract void **invoke**(RemoteCall *call*) throws Exception;
public abstract RemoteCall **newCall**(RemoteObject *obj*, Operation[ ] *op*, int *opnum*, long *hash*)
      throws java.rmi.RemoteException;
}

Hierarchy: (RemoteRef(java.io.Externalizable(Serializable)))

Implementations: ServerRef

Passed To: RemoteObject.RemoteObject(), RemoteRef.remoteEquals(),
RemoteServer.RemoteServer(), RemoteStub.{RemoteStub(), setRef()}

Returned By: RemoteObject.getRef()

Type Of: RemoteObject.ref

RemoteServer

Java 1.1

java.rmi.server   *serializable remote*

This is the superclass for remote server implementations, but it provides little value to
its subclasses. Developers can use the static getClientHost( ) method of this class from
within the implementation of a remote method to determine the host that the call is
coming from (there is, unfortunately, no further client identification provided).

The logging methods provided by this class are not marked as deprecated, but they
depend upon the deprecated LogStream class.

```
public abstract class RemoteServer extends RemoteObject {
// Protected Constructors
    protected RemoteServer();
    protected RemoteServer(RemoteRef ref);
// Public Class Methods
    public static String getClientHost() throws ServerNotActiveException;
    public static java.io.PrintStream getLog();
    public static void setLog(java.io.OutputStream out);
}
```

Hierarchy: Object→ RemoteObject(java.rmi.Remote, Serializable)→ RemoteServer

Subclasses: java.rmi.activation.Activatable, UnicastRemoteObject

RemoteStub

Java 1.1

java.rmi.server   *serializable remote*

This is the superclass for client stub implementations. Developers do not use this class
directly, except perhaps for type identification.

```
public abstract class RemoteStub extends RemoteObject {
// Protected Constructors
    protected RemoteStub();
    protected RemoteStub(RemoteRef ref);
// Deprecated Protected Methods
#   protected static void setRef(RemoteStub stub, RemoteRef ref);
}
```

Hierarchy: Object→ RemoteObject(java.rmi.Remote, Serializable)→ RemoteStub

Passed To: RemoteStub.setRef()

Returned By: ServerRef.exportObject(), UnicastRemoteObject.exportObject()

RMIClassLoader   Java 1.1

java.rmi.server

This class provides the mechanism by which clients and servers dynamically load code from each other: the class annotation (which is the value of the java.rmi.server.codebase property) is retrieved, and that URL is passed to the loadClass( ) method along with the name of the class that needs to be loaded. This class then uses an internal class loader to load the bytes from the URL and define the class.

Developers normally do not need to use this class directly; the class loading for RMI is transparent when the arguments are marshalled and unmarshalled. However, this class does provide a cheap and easy interface into the ClassLoader class.

```
public class RMIClassLoader {
// No Constructor
// Public Class Methods
1.2 public static String getClassAnnotation(Class cl);
    public static Class loadClass(java.net.URL codebase, String name) throws java.net.MalformedURLException,
        ClassNotFoundException;
1.2 public static Class loadClass(String codebase, String name) throws java.net.MalformedURLException,
        ClassNotFoundException;
// Deprecated Public Methods
#   public static Object getSecurityContext(ClassLoader loader);
#   public static Class loadClass(String name) throws java.net.MalformedURLException, ClassNotFoundException;
}
```

RMIClientSocketFactory   Java 1.2

java.rmi.server

An object that implements this interface is used to provide the sockets that are used for communication between client and server. The term "client" in the class name refers to the type of socket that this factory creates (a Socket object as opposed to a ServerSocket object); both clients and servers must create this type of socket. Normally, you would use a subclass of the RMISocketFactory class to provide this interface.

The default client socket factory attempts to create a socket as follows:

- It attempts to create a standard socket (e.g., by calling new Socket(host, port)).

- If that fails, it attempts to create an HTTP connection to the given host and port.

- If that fails, it attempts to call a cgi-bin script on the server; this cgi-bin script (if installed) will post the request to the server. The URL in this case is *http://hostname/java-rmi.cgi*.

```
public interface RMIClientSocketFactory {
// Public Instance Methods
    public abstract java.net.Socket createSocket(String host, int port) throws java.io.IOException;
}
```

Implementations: RMISocketFactory

Passed To: java.rmi.activation.Activatable.{Activatable(), exportObject()},
java.rmi.registry.LocateRegistry.{createRegistry(), getRegistry()}, UnicastRemoteObject.{exportObject(),
UnicastRemoteObject()}

RMIFailureHandler

java.rmi.server

An object that implements this interface is installed into the RMISocketFactory class via the setFailureHandler( ) method of that class. If such an object is installed, the failure( ) method will be called whenever the socket factory is unable to create a ServerSocket object. The failure( ) method should return a boolean value that indicates whether the RMI system should attempt to recreate the server socket.

By default, no such object is installed, and if a server socket is not able to be created, the RMI system will sleep for one second and try again to create the server socket.

```
public interface RMIFailureHandler {
// Public Instance Methods
    public abstract boolean failure(Exception ex);
}
```

Passed To: RMISocketFactory.setFailureHandler( )

Returned By: RMISocketFactory.getFailureHandler( )

RMIServerSocketFactory

java.rmi.server

An object that implements this interface provides the server sockets that are used to listen for RMI connections. Normally, you would use a subclass of the RMISocketFactory class to provide this interface.

```
public interface RMIServerSocketFactory {
// Public Instance Methods
    public abstract java.net.ServerSocket createServerSocket(int port) throws java.io.IOException;
}
```

Implementations: RMISocketFactory

Passed To: java.rmi.activation.Activatable.{Activatable( ), exportObject( )},
java.rmi.registry.LocateRegistry.createRegistry( ), UnicastRemoteObject.{exportObject( ),
UnicastRemoteObject( )}

RMISocketFactory

java.rmi.server

An RMISocketFactory is used to create RMI sockets for all remote or activatable objects that were not created with an explicit client or server socket factory. You can create a concrete subclass of this class and install it (with the setSocketFactory( ) method) so that your subclass is used to create all these sockets; otherwise, a default socket factory (the one that is returned from the getDefaultSocketFactory( ) method) is used. To install a socket factory, your code must be granted the runtime permission setFactory.

```
public abstract class RMISocketFactory implements RMIClientSocketFactory, RMIServerSocketFactory {
// Public Constructors
    public RMISocketFactory();
// Public Class Methods
1.2 public static RMISocketFactory getDefaultSocketFactory();                              synchronized
    public static RMIFailureHandler getFailureHandler();                                  synchronized
    public static RMISocketFactory getSocketFactory();                                    synchronized
    public static void setFailureHandler(RMIFailureHandler fh);                           synchronized
    public static void setSocketFactory(RMISocketFactory fac) throws java.io.IOException;  synchronized
// Methods Implementing RMIClientSocketFactory
```

```
    public abstract java.net.Socket createSocket(String host, int port) throws java.io.IOException;
// Methods Implementing RMIServerSocketFactory
    public abstract java.net.ServerSocket createServerSocket(int port) throws java.io.IOException;
}
```

Hierarchy: Object→ RMISocketFactory(RMIClientSocketFactory, RMIServerSocketFactory)

Passed To: RMISocketFactory.setSocketFactory()

Returned By: RMISocketFactory.{getDefaultSocketFactory(), getSocketFactory()}

ServerCloneException   Java 1.1

java.rmi.server   *serializable checked*

This exception is thrown if an attempt to clone a UnicastServerObject fails, which means that the cloned object was not able to be exported.

```
public class ServerCloneException extends CloneNotSupportedException {
// Public Constructors
    public ServerCloneException(String s);
    public ServerCloneException(String s, Exception ex);
// Public Methods Overriding Throwable
    public String getMessage();
1.2 public void printStackTrace();
1.2 public void printStackTrace(java.io.PrintStream ps);
1.2 public void printStackTrace(java.io.PrintWriter pw);
// Public Instance Fields
    public Exception detail;
}
```

Hierarchy: Object→ Throwable(Serializable)→ Exception→ CloneNotSupportedException→ ServerCloneException

ServerNotActiveException   Java 1.1

java.rmi.server   *serializable checked*

This exception is thrown by the RemoteServer.getClientHost( ) method if that method is called outside of the context of a remote method invocation.

```
public class ServerNotActiveException extends Exception {
// Public Constructors
    public ServerNotActiveException();
    public ServerNotActiveException(String s);
}
```

Hierarchy: Object→ Throwable(Serializable)→ Exception→ ServerNotActiveException

Thrown By: RemoteServer.getClientHost(), ServerRef.getClientHost()

ServerRef   Java 1.1

java.rmi.server   *serializable*

This is the interface that all server-side remote objects must implement. Developers do not use this class directly.

```
public interface ServerRef extends RemoteRef {
// Public Constants
1.2 public static final long serialVersionUID;                    =-4557750989390278438
// Public Instance Methods
```

```
    public abstract RemoteStub exportObject(java.rmi.Remote obj, Object data) throws java.rmi.RemoteException;
    public abstract String getClientHost() throws ServerNotActiveException;
}
```

Hierarchy: (ServerRef(RemoteRef(java.io.Externalizable(Serializable))))

Skeleton
Java 1.1; Deprecated in Java 1.2

java.rmi.server

This is the interface used by skeleton classes in the Java 1.1 RMI protocol. This interface is deprecated in Java 2, which does not use skeleton classes. However, by default, *rmic* still produces stubs and skeletons for use with 1.1-based clients. Developers never use this interface.

```
public interface Skeleton {
// Deprecated Public Methods
#   public abstract void dispatch(java.rmi.Remote obj, RemoteCall theCall, int opnum, long hash) throws Exception;
#   public abstract Operation[ ] getOperations();
}
```

SkeletonMismatchException
Java 1.1; Deprecated in Java 1.2

java.rmi.server
serializable checked

This exception is thrown when a method invocation dispatched through the server's skeleton class cannot find the appropriate method. This indicates that the method signatures have changed or that the stub and skeleton were generated with different versions of *rmic*.

```
public class SkeletonMismatchException extends java.rmi.RemoteException {
// Public Constructors
#   public SkeletonMismatchException(String s);
}
```

Hierarchy: Object→ Throwable(Serializable)→ Exception→ java.io.IOException→ java.rmi.RemoteException→ SkeletonMismatchException

SkeletonNotFoundException
Java 1.1; Deprecated in Java 1.2

java.rmi.server
serializable checked

This exception is thrown when a skeleton class cannot be found when exporting a remote object.

```
public class SkeletonNotFoundException extends java.rmi.RemoteException {
// Public Constructors
    public SkeletonNotFoundException(String s);
    public SkeletonNotFoundException(String s, Exception ex);
}
```

Hierarchy: Object→ Throwable(Serializable)→ Exception→ java.io.IOException→ java.rmi.RemoteException→ SkeletonNotFoundException

SocketSecurityException
Java 1.1

java.rmi.server
serializable checked

This exception is thrown when you attempt to export a server and the server is unable to create the server socket it needs to listen for requests.

```
public class SocketSecurityException extends ExportException {
// Public Constructors
    public SocketSecurityException(String s);
    public SocketSecurityException(String s, Exception ex);
}
```

Hierarchy: Object→ Throwable(Serializable)→ Exception→ java.io.IOException→
java.rmi.RemoteException→ ExportException→ SocketSecurityException

UID   Java 1.1

java.rmi.server   *serializable*

This class creates an ID that is unique for the host on which it was generated. The ID is
not unique between different VMs running simultaneously on the same host. If a
machine runs only a single VM, this ID will be unique even if the VM (or machine) fails
and restarts unless the clock is set backwards while the VM is not running.

```
public final class UID implements Serializable {
// Public Constructors
    public UID();
    public UID(short num);
// Public Class Methods
    public static UID read(java.io.DataInput in) throws java.io.IOException;
// Public Instance Methods
    public void write(java.io.DataOutput out) throws java.io.IOException;
// Public Methods Overriding Object
    public boolean equals(Object obj);
    public int hashCode();
    public String toString();
}
```

Hierarchy: Object→ UID(Serializable)

Returned By: UID.read()

UnicastRemoteObject   Java 1.1

java.rmi.server   *serializable remote*

This is the superclass for most (nonactivatable) remote services. A remote service is created by implementing a Remote interface and by either subclassing this class or by using
the static exportObject( ) method of this class. Those two techniques are identical; the
constructors of this class simply call the exportObject( ) method for you.

```
public class UnicastRemoteObject extends RemoteServer {
// Protected Constructors
    protected UnicastRemoteObject() throws java.rmi.RemoteException;
1.2 protected UnicastRemoteObject(int port) throws java.rmi.RemoteException;
1.2 protected UnicastRemoteObject(int port, RMIClientSocketFactory csf, RMIServerSocketFactory ssf)
        throws java.rmi.RemoteException;
// Public Class Methods
    public static RemoteStub exportObject(java.rmi.Remote obj) throws java.rmi.RemoteException;
1.2 public static java.rmi.Remote exportObject(java.rmi.Remote obj, int port) throws java.rmi.RemoteException;
1.2 public static java.rmi.Remote exportObject(java.rmi.Remote obj, int port, RMIClientSocketFactory csf,
                              RMIServerSocketFactory ssf) throws java.rmi.RemoteException;
1.2 public static boolean unexportObject(java.rmi.Remote obj, boolean force)
        throws java.rmi.NoSuchObjectException;
// Public Methods Overriding Object
```

```
    public Object clone() throws CloneNotSupportedException;
}
```

Hierarchy: Object→ RemoteObject(java.rmi.Remote, Serializable)→ RemoteServer→ UnicastRemoteObject

Subclasses: java.rmi.activation.ActivationGroup

Unreferenced   Java 1.1
java.rmi.server

If a service implements this interface, its unreferenced( ) method will be called when all client references to the object have been removed—either because the stub object on the client(s) have been garbage collected, or because the client(s) have failed to renew their lease to the service. This is a good time for activatable servers to invoke their inactive( ) method.

```
public interface Unreferenced {
// Public Instance Methods
    public abstract void unreferenced();
}
```

CHAPTER 18

Class, Method, and Field Index

The following index allows you to look up a class or interface and find what package it is defined in. It also allows you to look up a method or field and find what class it is defined in. Use it when you want to look up a class but don't know its package, or when you want to look up a method but don't know its class.

D

DAYS: TimeConstants
Debug: com.sun.jini.debug
debug(): InProgress
Debug.WriterFactory: com.sun.jini.debug
defaulted(): GetField
defaultReadObject(): ObjectInputStream
defaultWriteObject(): ObjectOutputStream
deletePersistentStore(): ReliableLog
denied: RenewResults
desc: Ticket
destroy(): DestroyAdmin, FileSystem
DestroyAdmin: com.sun.jini.admin
detail: ActivationException, LogException, RemoteException, ServerCloneException
DGC: java.rmi.dgc
DGC_ID: ObjID
dirty(): DGC
disableDelivery(): MailboxRegistration
discard(): DiscoveryManagement, LookupCache, LookupDiscovery, LookupDiscoveryManager, LookupDiscoveryRegistration, LookupLocatorDiscovery
discarded: RemoteDiscoveryEvent
discarded(): DiscoveryListener
discovered(): DiscoveryListener
DiscoveryAdmin: net.jini.lookup
DiscoveryEvent: net.jini.discovery
DiscoveryGroupManagement: net.jini.discovery
DiscoveryListener: net.jini.discovery
DiscoveryLocatorManagement: net.jini.discovery
DiscoveryManagement: net.jini.discovery
DiscoveryPermission: net.jini.discovery
discoveryPort: Constants
dispatch(): Skeleton
done(): RemoteCall, RemoteRef
doRenew(): AbstractLease, LandlordLease
drain(): ObjectOutputStream
dump(): FastList
DURATION: Lease

E

enableDelivery(): MailboxRegistration
enableReplaceObject(): ObjectOutputStream
enableResolveObject(): ObjectInputStream
enclosedBy(): NestableServerTransaction
ensureCurrent(): LeaseDurationPolicy, LeasePolicy
ensureDir(): FileSystem

Entry: net.jini.core.entry
EntryBean: net.jini.lookup.entry
EntryBeans: net.jini.lookup.entry
entrySet(): AbstractLeaseMap
equal(): LookupAttributes
equals(): AbstractEntry, AbstractLeaseMap, ActivationDesc, ActivationGroupDesc, ActivationGroupID, ActivationID, CommandEnvironment, DiscoveryPermission, IncomingMulticastAnnouncement, IncomingMulticastRequest, IncomingUnicastResponse, LandlordLease, LookupLocator, MarshalledObject, ObjID, RemoteObject, ServerTransaction, ServiceID, Ticket, UID, UUID, VMID, WeakKeyReference
ERROR: StatusType
error(): StreamPlugThread
eventID: EventRegistration, RemoteEvent
EventMailbox: net.jini.event
EventRegistration: net.jini.core.event
exceptionMap: LeaseMapException
executeCall(): RemoteCall
expiration: AbstractLease
ExpirationWarningEvent: net.jini.lease
ExportException: java.rmi.server
exportObject(): Activatable, ServerRef, UnicastRemoteObject
Externalizable: java.io

F

Factory: com.sun.jini.lease.landlord.LandlordLease
failure(): RMIFailureHandler
FastList: com.sun.jini.collection
FastList.Node: com.sun.jini.collection
FileSystem: com.sun.jini.system
finalize(): LogInputStream, LookupDiscovery
firstPending: TaskManager
floor: Location
flush(): ObjectOutput, ObjectOutputStream
followLink(): AddressBean, CommentBean, EntryBean, LocationBean, NameBean, ServiceInfoBean, StatusBean
forClass(): ObjectStreamClass
FOREVER: Lease
FROM_GROUP: LookupDiscoveryManager
FROM_LOCATOR: LookupDiscoveryManager

G

get(): AbstractLeaseMap, GetField, MarshalledObject, WeakTable

getActions(): DiscoveryPermission

getActivationDesc(): ActivationSystem

getActivationGroupDesc(): ActivationSystem

getAddress(): IncomingMulticastRequest

getAdmin(): Administrable

getAnnouncementAddress(): Constants

getAttributes(): JoinManager

getBeanClass(): EntryBeans

getBoolean(): MultiCommandLine, POSIXCommand-Line

getBuilding(): LocationBean

getClassAnnotation(): RMIClassLoader

getClassName(): ActivationDesc, ActivationGroupDesc

getClientHost(): RemoteServer, ServerRef

getCommandEnvironment(): ActivationGroupDesc

getCommandOptions(): CommandEnvironment

getCommandPath(): CommandEnvironment

getComment(): CommentBean

getCookie(): LeasedResource

getCountry(): AddressBean

getData(): ActivationDesc, ActivationGroupDesc

getDefaultSocketFactory(): RMISocketFactory

getDefaultStream(): LogStream

getDiscoveredLocators(): LookupLocatorDiscovery

getDiscoveryManager(): ClientLookupManager, Join-Manager

getDisplayName(): BasicServiceType, ServiceType

getDouble(): MultiCommandLine, POSIXCommandLine

getEntryClasses(): ServiceRegistrar

getEventRegistration(): LookupDiscoveryRegistration

getException(): LeaseRenewalEvent

getExceptions(): LookupUnmarshalException

getExpiration(): AbstractLease, Lease, Lease-dResource, LeaseRenewalEvent, LeaseRenewal-Manager

getFailureHandler(): RMISocketFactory

GetField: java.io.ObjectInputStream

getField(): ObjectStreamClass

getFields(): ObjectStreamClass

getFieldValues(): ServiceRegistrar

getFloor(): LocationBean

getFrom(): LookupDiscoveryManager

getGroupID(): ActivationDesc

getGroups(): DiscoveryGroupManagement, Incoming-MulticastAnnouncement, IncomingMulticastRe-quest, IncomingUnicastResponse, JoinManager, LookupDiscovery, LookupDiscoveryManager, LookupDiscoveryRegistration, ServiceRegistrar

getHost(): LookupLocator

getIcon(): BasicServiceType, ServiceType

getID(): Activatable, EventRegistration, RemoteEvent

getInputStream(): MultiCommandLine, POSIXCom-mandLine, RemoteCall

getInt(): MultiCommandLine, POSIXCommandLine

getJoinSet(): JoinManager

getLease(): EventRegistration, Expira-tionWarningEvent, LeaseRenewalEvent, LookupDis-coveryRegistration, MailboxRegistration, RenewalFailureEvent, ServiceRegistration

getLeaseRenewalManager(): ClientLookupManager, JoinManager

getLeastSignificantBits(): ServiceID, UUID

getListener(): MailboxRegistration

getLocality(): AddressBean

getLocation(): ActivationDesc, ActivationGroupDesc

getLocator(): IncomingMulticastAnnouncement, Ser-viceRegistrar

getLocators(): DiscoveryLocatorManagement, Join-Manager, LookupDiscoveryManager, LookupDis-coveryRegistration, LookupLocatorDiscovery

getLog(): RemoteServer

getLong(): MultiCommandLine, POSIXCommandLine

getLookupAttributes(): JoinAdmin

getLookupGroups(): JoinAdmin

getLookupLocators(): JoinAdmin

getLookupServices(): ClientLookupManager

getManufacturer(): ServiceInfoBean

getMemberGroups(): DiscoveryAdmin

getMessage(): ActivationException, LogException, LookupUnmarshalException, RemoteException, ServerCloneException, ThrowThis

getModel(): ServiceInfoBean

getMostSignificantBits(): ServiceID, UUID

getName(): NameBean, ObjectStreamClass, Object-StreamField, ServiceInfoBean, TxnConstants

getObjectStreamClass(): GetField

getOffset(): ObjectStreamField

getOperands(): MultiCommandLine, POSIXCommand-Line

getOperation(): Operation

getOperations(): Skeleton

getOrAdd(): WeakTable

getOrganization(): AddressBean

getOrganizationalUnit(): AddressBean

getOutputStream(): LogStream, MultiCommandLine, POSIXCommandLine, RemoteCall

getPending(): TaskManager
getPort(): IncomingMulticastRequest, LookupLocator
getPostalCode(): AddressBean
getPostEventServiceItem(): ServiceDiscoveryEvent
getPreEventServiceItem(): ServiceDiscoveryEvent
getPropertyName(): Debug
getPropertyOverrides(): ActivationGroupDesc
getRandomAccessFile(): MultiCommandLine, POSIX-CommandLine
getReader(): MultiCommandLine, POSIXCommandLine
getRef(): RemoteObject
getRefClass(): RemoteRef
getRegistrar(): IncomingUnicastResponse, LookupLocator
getRegistrars(): DiscoveryEvent, DiscoveryManagement, LookupDiscovery, LookupDiscoveryManager, LookupDiscoveryRegistration, LookupLocatorDiscovery, RemoteDiscoveryEvent
getRegistrationObject(): RemoteEvent
getRegistry(): LocateRegistry
getRenewalSetLease(): LeaseRenewalSet
getRequestAddress(): Constants
getRestartMode(): ActivationDesc
getResultStream(): RemoteCall
getRoom(): LocationBean
getSecurityContext(): LoaderHandler, RMIClassLoader
getSequenceNumber(): EventRegistration, RemoteEvent
getSerialFormat(): AbstractLease, Lease
getSerialNumber(): ServiceInfoBean
getSerialVersionUID(): ObjectStreamClass
getServiceID(): IncomingMulticastAnnouncement, ServiceEvent, ServiceRegistrar, ServiceRegistration
getServiceIDs(): IncomingMulticastRequest
getServiceItem(): ServiceEvent
getServiceTypes(): ServiceRegistrar
getSeverity(): StatusBean
getShortDescription(): BasicServiceType, ServiceType
getSocketFactory(): RMISocketFactory
getSource(): EventRegistration
getState(): ServerTransaction, TransactionManager
getStateOrProvince(): AddressBean
getStillMarshalledRegs(): LookupUnmarshalException
getStorageLocation(): StorageLocationAdmin
getStreet(): AddressBean
getString(): MultiCommandLine, POSIXCommandLine
getSystem(): ActivationGroup, ActivationGroupID
getThrowable(): RenewalFailureEvent

getTransition(): ServiceEvent
getType(): ObjectStreamField
getTypeCode(): ObjectStreamField
getTypeString(): ObjectStreamField
getUndiscoveredLocators(): LookupLocatorDiscovery
getUnicastPort(): DiscoveryAdmin
getUnmarshalledRegs(): LookupUnmarshalException
getValue(): Lease
getVendor(): ServiceInfoBean
getVersion(): ServiceInfoBean
getVMID(): Lease
getWriter(): Debug, MultiCommandLine, POSIXCommandLine
granted: RenewResults
groups: IncomingMulticastAnnouncement, IncomingMulticastRequest, IncomingUnicastResponse

H

handback: RemoteEvent
hashCode(): AbstractEntry, AbstractLeaseMap, ActivationDesc, ActivationGroupDesc, ActivationGroupID, ActivationID, CommandEnvironment, DiscoveryPermission, IncomingMulticastAnnouncement, IncomingMulticastRequest, IncomingUnicastResponse, LandlordLease, LookupLocator, MarshalledObject, ObjID, RemoteObject, ServerTransaction, ServiceID, UID, UUID, VMID, WeakKeyReference
head(): FastList
HelpOnlyException: com.sun.jini.system.CommandLine
host: LookupLocator
HOURS: TimeConstants

I

id: Created, ServerTransaction
implies(): DiscoveryPermission
inactive(): Activatable
inactiveGroup(): ActivationGroup, ActivationMonitor
inactiveObject(): ActivationGroup, ActivationMonitor
IncomingMulticastAnnouncement: net.jini.discovery
IncomingMulticastRequest: net.jini.discovery
IncomingUnicastRequest: net.jini.discovery
IncomingUnicastResponse: net.jini.discovery
indexFirstNull(): RemoteDiscoveryEvent
InProgress: com.sun.jini.thread
inProgress(): InProgress
insertRegistrars(): RemoteDiscoveryEvent
InternalSpaceException: net.jini.space

InvalidObjectException: java.io
invoke(): RemoteRef
isDiscarded(): RemoteDiscoveryEvent
isEmpty(): AbstractLeaseMap, WakeupManager
isNested(): NestableServerTransaction, ServerTransaction
isPrimitive(): ObjectStreamField
isUnique(): VMID
items: ServiceMatches

J

JavaSpace: net.jini.space
join(): ServerTransaction, TransactionManager
JoinAdmin: net.jini.admin
JoinManager: com.sun.jini.lookup, net.jini.lookup

K

keyGC(): KeyGCHandler
KeyGCHandler: com.sun.jini.collection.WeakTable
keySet(): AbstractLeaseMap

L

Landlord: com.sun.jini.lease.landlord
Landlord.RenewResults: com.sun.jini.lease.landlord
LandlordLease: com.sun.jini.lease.landlord
LandlordLease.Factory: com.sun.jini.lease.landlord
LandlordLeaseFactory: com.sun.jini.lease.landlord
LandlordLeaseMap: com.sun.jini.lease.landlord
lease: Created, EventRegistration
Lease: java.rmi.dgc, net.jini.core.lease
LeaseDeniedException: net.jini.core.lease
LeasedResource: com.sun.jini.lease.landlord
LeaseDurationPolicy: com.sun.jini.lease.landlord
LeaseException: net.jini.core.lease
leaseFor(): LeaseDurationPolicy, LeasePolicy
LeaseListener: com.sun.jini.lease, net.jini.lease
LeaseManager: com.sun.jini.lease.landlord
LeaseMap: net.jini.core.lease
LeaseMapException: net.jini.core.lease
LeasePolicy: com.sun.jini.lease.landlord
LeaseRenewalEvent: com.sun.jini.lease, net.jini.lease
LeaseRenewalManager: com.sun.jini.lease, net.jini.lease
LeaseRenewalService: net.jini.lease
LeaseRenewalSet: net.jini.lease
list(): Naming, Registry
loadClass(): LoaderHandler, RMIClassLoader

LoaderHandler: java.rmi.server
loadFactor: TaskManager
locality: Address
LocateRegistry: java.rmi.registry
Location: net.jini.lookup.entry
LocationBean: net.jini.lookup.entry
locator: IncomingMulticastAnnouncement
log(): LogStream
LogException: com.sun.jini.reliableLog
LogHandler: com.sun.jini.reliableLog
LogInputStream: com.sun.jini.reliableLog
LogOutputStream: com.sun.jini.reliableLog
logSize(): ReliableLog
LogStream: java.rmi.server
lookup(): ClientLookupManager, LookupCache, Naming, ObjectStreamClass, Registry, ServiceRegistrar
LookupAttributes: com.sun.jini.lookup.entry
LookupCache: net.jini.lookup
LookupDiscovery: net.jini.discovery
LookupDiscoveryManager: net.jini.discovery
LookupDiscoveryRegistration: net.jini.discovery
LookupDiscoveryService: net.jini.discovery
LookupLocator: net.jini.core.discovery
LookupLocatorDiscovery: com.sun.jini.discovery, net.jini.discovery
LookupUnmarshalException: net.jini.discovery

M

MailboxRegistration: net.jini.event
main(): StreamPlugThread
makeLink(): AddressBean, CommentBean, EntryBean, LocationBean, NameBean, ServiceInfoBean, StatusBean
makeNewDir(): FileSystem
manufacturer: ServiceInfo
map: AbstractLeaseMap
marshal(): OutgoingMulticastAnnouncement, OutgoingMulticastRequest, OutgoingUnicastRequest, OutgoingUnicastResponse
MarshalException: java.rmi
MarshalledObject: java.rmi
marshalledRegs: RemoteDiscoveryEvent
matches(): LookupAttributes
maxPacketSize: OutgoingMulticastAnnouncement, OutgoingMulticastRequest
maxThreads: TaskManager
mgr: ServerTransaction
minMaxPacketSize: OutgoingMulticastAnnouncement, OutgoingMulticastRequest

MINUTES: TimeConstants
model: ServiceInfo
modify(): LookupAttributes
modifyAttributes(): JoinManager, ServiceRegistration
modifyLookupAttributes(): JoinAdmin
MultiCommandLine: com.sun.jini.system

N

name: Name, ServiceInfo
Name: net.jini.lookup.entry
NameBean: net.jini.lookup.entry
Naming: java.rmi
needThread(): TaskManager
NestableServerTransaction: net.jini.core.transaction.server
NestableTransaction: net.jini.core.transaction
NestableTransaction.Created: net.jini.core.transaction
NestableTransactionManager: net.jini.core.transaction.server
nestedException: InternalSpaceException
nestedExceptions: UnusableEntryException
newCall(): RemoteRef
newInstance(): ActivationGroup, ActivationInstantiator
newLease(): Factory, LandlordLeaseFactory
newPermissionCollection(): DiscoveryPermission
newUUID(): UUIDFactory
next: Node
next(): Node
NO_FIELDS: ObjectStreamClass
NO_GROUPS: DiscoveryGroupManagement, LookupDiscovery
NO_WAIT: JavaSpace
Node: com.sun.jini.collection.FastList
NORMAL: StatusType
NoSuchObjectException: java.rmi
NotBoundException: java.rmi
NOTCHANGED: TransactionConstants
NOTICE: StatusType
notify(): JavaSpace, LeaseListener, RemoteEventListener, ServiceRegistrar
NotSerializableException: java.io

O

ObjectInput: java.io
ObjectInputStream: java.io
ObjectInputStream.GetField: java.io
ObjectInputValidation: java.io
ObjectOutput: java.io
ObjectOutputStream: java.io
ObjectOutputStream.PutField: java.io
ObjectStreamClass: java.io
ObjectStreamConstants: java.io
ObjectStreamException: java.io
ObjectStreamField: java.io
ObjID: java.rmi.server
Operation: java.rmi.server
organization: Address
organizationalUnit: Address
OutgoingMulticastAnnouncement: net.jini.discovery
OutgoingMulticastRequest: net.jini.discovery
OutgoingUnicastRequest: net.jini.discovery
OutgoingUnicastResponse: net.jini.discovery

P

packagePrefix: LoaderHandler, RemoteRef
parent: NestableServerTransaction
parseDouble(): CommandLine
parseInputStream(): CommandLine
parseInt(): CommandLine
parseLevel(): LogStream
parseLong(): CommandLine
parseOutputStream(): CommandLine
parseRandomAccessFile(): CommandLine
parseReader(): CommandLine
parseString(): CommandLine
parseWriter(): CommandLine
partialEntry: UnusableEntryException
plugTogether(): StreamPlugThread
port: IncomingMulticastRequest, LookupLocator
POSIXCommandLine: com.sun.jini.system
postalCode: Address
prepare(): TransactionParticipant
prepareAndCommit(): TransactionParticipant
PREPARED: TransactionConstants
prev(): Node
printStackTrace(): ActivationException, InternalSpaceException, RemoteException, ServerCloneException, ThrowThis
ProgrammingException: com.sun.jini.system.CommandLine

Class Index

LeaseDurationPolicy, LeasePolicy
RenewalFailureEvent: net.jini.lease
renewAll(): AbstractLeaseMap, Landlord, LandlordLeaseMap, LeaseMap
renewed(): LeaseManager
renewFor(): LeaseRenewalManager, LeaseRenewalSet
RenewResults: com.sun.jini.lease.landlord.Landlord
renewUntil(): LeaseRenewalManager
replaceObject(): ObjectOutputStream
reset(): ObjectOutputStream, RetryTask
resolveClass(): ObjectInputStream
resolveObject(): ObjectInputStream
RetryTask: com.sun.jini.thread
retryTime(): RetryTask
RMIClassLoader: java.rmi.server
RMIClientSocketFactory: java.rmi.server
RMIFailureHandler: java.rmi.server
RMISecurityException: java.rmi
RMISecurityManager: java.rmi
RMIServerSocketFactory: java.rmi.server
RMISocketFactory: java.rmi.server
room: Location
roTasks: TaskManager
run(): RetryTask, StreamPlugThread
runAfter(): RetryTask, Task

S

SC_BLOCK_DATA: ObjectStreamConstants
SC_EXTERNALIZABLE: ObjectStreamConstants
SC_SERIALIZABLE: ObjectStreamConstants
SC_WRITE_METHOD: ObjectStreamConstants
schedule(): WakeupManager
SECONDS: TimeConstants
seqNum: EventRegistration, RemoteEvent
serialFormat: AbstractLease
Serializable: java.io
SerializablePermission: java.io
serialNumber: ServiceInfo
serialVersionUID: RemoteRef, ServerRef
SERVER_VERSION: VersionConstants
ServerCloneException: java.rmi.server
ServerError: java.rmi
ServerException: java.rmi
ServerNotActiveException: java.rmi.server
ServerRef: java.rmi.server
ServerRuntimeException: java.rmi
ServerTransaction: net.jini.core.transaction.server
service: ServiceItem
serviceAdded(): ServiceDiscoveryListener

serviceChanged(): ServiceDiscoveryListener
ServiceControlled: net.jini.lookup.entry
ServiceDiscoveryEvent: net.jini.lookup
ServiceDiscoveryListener: net.jini.lookup
ServiceEvent: net.jini.core.lookup
ServiceID: net.jini.core.lookup
serviceID: IncomingMulticastAnnouncement, Ser-
viceEvent, ServiceItem, ServiceTemplate
ServiceIDListener: com.sun.jini.lookup,
net.jini.lookup
serviceIDNotify(): ServiceIDListener
serviceIDs: IncomingMulticastRequest
ServiceInfo: net.jini.lookup.entry
ServiceInfoBean: net.jini.lookup.entry
ServiceItem: net.jini.core.lookup
ServiceItemFilter: net.jini.lookup
ServiceMatches: net.jini.core.lookup
ServiceRegistrar: net.jini.core.lookup
ServiceRegistration: net.jini.core.lookup
serviceRemoved(): ServiceDiscoveryListener
ServiceTemplate: net.jini.core.lookup
ServiceType: net.jini.lookup.entry
serviceTypes: ServiceTemplate
setActivationDesc(): ActivationSystem
setActivationGroupDesc(): ActivationSystem
setAttributes(): JoinManager, ServiceRegistration
setBuilding(): LocationBean
setComment(): CommentBean
setCountry(): AddressBean
setDefaultStream(): LogStream
setExpiration(): LeasedResource, LeaseRenewalManager
setExpirationWarningListener(): LeaseRenewalSet
setFailureHandler(): RMISocketFactory
setFloor(): LocationBean
setGroups(): DiscoveryGroupManagement, JoinManager, LookupDiscovery, LookupDiscoveryManager,
LookupDiscoveryRegistration
setLocality(): AddressBean
setLocators(): DiscoveryLocatorManagement, Join-
Manager, LookupDiscoveryManager, LookupDiscoveryRegistration, LookupLocatorDiscovery
setLog(): RemoteServer
setLookupGroups(): JoinAdmin
setLookupLocators(): JoinAdmin
setManufacturer(): ServiceInfoBean
setMemberGroups(): DiscoveryAdmin
setModel(): ServiceInfoBean
setName(): NameBean, ServiceInfoBean
setOffset(): ObjectStreamField

setOrganization(): AddressBean
setOrganizationalUnit(): AddressBean
setOutputStream(): LogStream
setPostalCode(): AddressBean
setRef(): RemoteStub
setRenewalFailureListener(): LeaseRenewalSet
setRoom(): LocationBean
setSerialFormat(): AbstractLease, Lease
setSerialNumber(): ServiceInfoBean
setSeverity(): StatusBean
setSocketFactory(): RMISocketFactory
setStateOrProvince(): AddressBean
setStorageLocation(): StorageLocationAdmin
setStreet(): AddressBean
setSystem(): ActivationGroup
setUnicastPort(): DiscoveryAdmin
setVendor(): ServiceInfoBean
setVersion(): ServiceInfoBean
severity: Status
shutdown(): ActivationSystem
SILENT: LogStream
size(): AbstractLeaseMap
Skeleton: java.rmi.server
SkeletonMismatchException: java.rmi.server
SkeletonNotFoundException: java.rmi.server
skip(): LogInputStream, ObjectInput
skipBytes(): ObjectInputStream
snapshot(): JavaSpace, LogHandler, ReliableLog
snapshotSize(): ReliableLog
SocketSecurityException: java.rmi.server
source: EventRegistration, RemoteEvent
start(): InProgress
startTime(): RetryTask
stateOrProvince: Address
Status: net.jini.lookup.entry
StatusBean: net.jini.lookup.entry
StatusType: net.jini.lookup.entry
stop(): InProgress, WakeupManager
stopWhenEmpty(): WakeupManager
StorageLocationAdmin: com.sun.jini.admin
STREAM_MAGIC: ObjectStreamConstants
STREAM_VERSION: ObjectStreamConstants
StreamPlugThread: com.sun.jini.thread
street: Address
StubNotFoundException: java.rmi
SUBCLASS_IMPLEMENTATION_PERMISSION:
    ObjectStreamConstants
SUBSTITUTION_PERMISSION: ObjectStreamConstants
SYSTEM_PORT: ActivationSystem

T

tail(): FastList
take(): JavaSpace
takeIfExists(): JavaSpace
task: Ticket
Task: com.sun.jini.thread.TaskManager
TaskManager: com.sun.jini.thread
TaskManager.Task: com.sun.jini.thread
tasks: TaskManager
TC_ARRAY: ObjectStreamConstants
TC_BASE: ObjectStreamConstants
TC_BLOCKDATA: ObjectStreamConstants
TC_BLOCKDATALONG: ObjectStreamConstants
TC_CLASS: ObjectStreamConstants
TC_CLASSDESC: ObjectStreamConstants
TC_ENDBLOCKDATA: ObjectStreamConstants
TC_EXCEPTION: ObjectStreamConstants
TC_MAX: ObjectStreamConstants
TC_NULL: ObjectStreamConstants
TC_OBJECT: ObjectStreamConstants
TC_REFERENCE: ObjectStreamConstants
TC_RESET: ObjectStreamConstants
TC_STRING: ObjectStreamConstants
terminate(): ClientLookupManager, DiscoveryManagement, JoinManager, LookupCache, LookupDiscovery, LookupDiscoveryManager, LookupLocatorDiscovery, TaskManager
ThreadDesc: com.sun.jini.thread.WakeupManager
threads: TaskManager
throwRemoteException(): ThrowThis
ThrowThis: com.sun.jini.proxy
Ticket: com.sun.jini.thread.WakeupManager
TimeConstants: com.sun.jini.constants
timeout: TaskManager
TimeoutExpiredException: net.jini.core.transaction
toString(): AbstractEntry, Debug, LandlordLease, LogStream, LookupLocator, ObjectStreamClass, ObjectStreamField, ObjID, Operation, RemoteObject, ServiceID, ThreadDesc, Ticket, UID, UUID, VMID
toStub(): RemoteObject
totalMatches: ServiceMatches
transaction: Created
Transaction: net.jini.core.transaction
Transaction.Created: net.jini.core.transaction
TransactionConstants: net.jini.core.transaction.server
TransactionException: net.jini.core.transaction
TransactionFactory: net.jini.core.transaction
TransactionManager: net.jini.core.transaction.server

TransactionManager.Created: net.jini.core.transaction.server

TransactionParticipant: net.jini.core.transaction.server

transition: ServiceEvent

TRANSITION_MATCH_MATCH: ServiceRegistrar

TRANSITION_MATCH_NOMATCH: ServiceRegistrar

TRANSITION_NOMATCH_MATCH: ServiceRegistrar

tryOnce(): RetryTask

TxnConstants: com.sun.jini.constants

type: BasicServiceType

U

UID: java.rmi.server

unbind(): Naming, Registry

unblock(): InProgress

UnexpectedException: java.rmi

unexportObject(): Activatable, UnicastRemoteObject

UnicastRemoteObject: java.rmi.server

UnknownEventException: net.jini.core.event

UnknownGroupException: java.rmi.activation

UnknownHostException: java.rmi

UnknownLeaseException: net.jini.core.lease

UnknownObjectException: java.rmi.activation

UnknownTransactionException: net.jini.core.transaction

UnmarshalException: java.rmi

unmarshalRegistrars(): RemoteDiscoveryEvent

Unreferenced: java.rmi.server

unreferenced(): Unreferenced

unregister(): Activatable

unregisterGroup(): ActivationSystem

unregisterObject(): ActivationSystem

UnusableEntryException: net.jini.core.entry

unusableFields: UnusableEntryException

update(): ReliableLog

usage(): MultiCommandLine, POSIXCommandLine

useProtocolVersion(): ObjectOutputStream

userProg(): StreamPlugThread

UUID: com.sun.jini.proxy

UUIDFactory: com.sun.jini.proxy

V

validateObject(): ObjectInputValidation

values(): AbstractLeaseMap

vendor: ServiceInfo

VERBOSE: LogStream

version: ServiceInfo

VersionConstants: com.sun.jini.constants

VMID: java.rmi.dgc

VOTING: TransactionConstants

W

waiterNotify(): ReadersWriter

waitFor(): RetryTask

waitUntilQuiet(): InProgress

waitWhileBlocked(): InProgress

waitWhileStarted(): InProgress

WakeupManager: com.sun.jini.thread

WakeupManager.ThreadDesc: com.sun.jini.thread

WakeupManager.Ticket: com.sun.jini.thread

WARNING: StatusType

WeakKeyReference: com.sun.jini.collection

WeakTable: com.sun.jini.collection

WeakTable.KeyGCHandler: com.sun.jini.collection

when: Ticket

write(): JavaSpace, LogOutputStream, LogStream, ObjectOutput, ObjectOutputStream, ObjID, PutField, UID

writeBoolean(): ObjectOutputStream

writeByte(): ObjectOutputStream

writeBytes(): ObjectOutputStream, ServiceID, UUID

writeChar(): ObjectOutputStream

writeChars(): ObjectOutputStream

writeDouble(): ObjectOutputStream

writeExternal(): Externalizable

writeFields(): ObjectOutputStream

writeFloat(): ObjectOutputStream

writeInt(): ObjectOutputStream

writeLock(): ReadersWriter

writeLong(): ObjectOutputStream

writeObject(): ObjectOutput, ObjectOutputStream

writeObjectOverride(): ObjectOutputStream

writer(): WriterFactory

WriterFactory: com.sun.jini.debug.Debug

writerWait(): ReadersWriter

writeShort(): ObjectOutputStream

writeStreamHeader(): ObjectOutputStream

writeUnlock(): ReadersWriter

writeUpdate(): LogHandler

writeUTF(): ObjectOutputStream

Index

addLookupAttributes( ) (JoinAdmin),
120
Address attribute, 78
Address class, 316
AddressBean class, 317
Administrable interface, 118, 120, 292
    client, modifying to use, 122
    running the example, 124
administrable services, 118, 228
    implementation, 119
administration APIs, 117–127
administration interfaces, customizing,
    124–127
AlreadyBoundException, 336
announcement of lookup services
    interval for sending, 225
    multicast data packets, creating for,
        304
    multicast protocol, using, 295
    unmarshalling datagram packets,
        298
APIs
    administration APIs, 117–127
    client-side transaction APIs,
        145–147
    com.sun.jini packages, 227
    distributed events, handling of, 11
    EventMailbox API, 173
    JavaSpaces API, 156–159
    Jini
        classes, defining, 265–290
        version in use, 233
    LeaseRenewalService API, 172
    LookupDiscoveryService API, 170
    new services, Jini 1.1, 12
    servers, 7
    server-side transaction APIs,
        150–153
    services development and, 17
    template matching, 10
    web site information on, 18
applications
    as clients, 13
    communicating with hardware
        devices, 11
    notifying of changes in registered
        services, 277
    service interfaces, discovering and
        learning in Jini community,
        15

applyUpdate( ), 136, 140
    LogHandler class, 252
arguments (command-line) (see com-
    mand-line arguments)
asynchronous lookup, 277
atomic operations, 143
atomic writes (reliable logs), 250
attributes (services)
    changes, notifying lookup service
        of, 314
    client modification, preventing, 321
    defining, 80
    Entry interface and, 77–81
    join manager, propagating changes
        to lookup services, 246
    lookup service, registration with,
        316
    LookupAttributes class, 248
    notifying client of changes, 312
    specifying by, 10
    specifying in searches, 65

B

backend process (FrontEndSpace),
        extra command-line argu-
        ments for, 223
BadInvocationException, 255
BasicServiceType class, 247
batching events for delivery, 173
batching lease renewals into lease
        maps, 239, 273
beans, providing for lookup service
        entries, 316
billing client, implementation of,
        191–194
binary options (command-line
        arguments), specifying, 141
blocking, 130
block( ) (InProgress), 259
bug in renewFor( ) method, 239

C

cached values, marking as transient,
        37
callback methods, RMI appearing to
        servers as, 36

event mailbox service, 168, 173
    mercury implementation of,
        217–219
    (see also mercury)
EventMailbox interface, 173, 307
EventRegistration class, 104, 269
events, 102
    delivery in separate thread, 130
    IDs for, 103, 105
    JavaBeans specification, 102
    net.jini.core.event package,
        268–270
    sequence numbers, 141
        JavaSpaces service, handling of,
            158
        saving in reliable logs, 137
    service discovery events, 315
    UnknownEventException, 270
    (see also remote events)
example directory, 20
Exception class, 341
exceptions
    remote interfaces, 41
    RemoteException, 42, 339
    renew( ) method, handling, 70
    RMI, handling of, 35
    wrapper between RMI servers and
        proxies, 249
exceptions (LookupDiscovery)
    mercury, printing to file, 219
    norm, printing to file, 220
executable jar file, creating for Jini
        classes, 189
expiration of leases, 70, 236, 351
    time for, getting, 271
    time, setting for, 243
ExpirationWarningEvent class, 308
expireLeases( ), 93
Expirer class, 133
ExportException, 355
exportObject( ), 355
    Activatable class, 343
    UnicastRemoteObject class, 41, 364
Externalizable interface, 36, 326

F

factory class for landlord leases, 99
failure of lease renewal, 311
failure( ) (RMIFailureHandler), 361
FastList class, 129, 230
fiddler, 168, 212–215
    options, 213
    system properties supported by,
        213
FiddlerAdmin interface, 214
FileSystem class, 256
filtering service items, 312, 316
finalizer, running for stubs, 53
followLink( ) (EntryBean), 319
FrontEndSpace service, 12, 221
    backend process, extra command
        line arguments for, 223

G

garbage collecting
    distributed garbage collector (RMI),
        351
    outrigger, controlling, 224
    RMI stubs, 53, 338
    weak key references and, 232
    weak references and, 230
get( ) (MarshalledObject), 337
getAdmin( ) (Administrable), 118, 228,
        292
getClientHost( ) (RemoteServer), 359,
        362
getException( ) (LeaseRenewalEvent),
        309
getExpiration( )
    Lease interface, 271
    LeaseRenewalManager class, 309
GetField class, 329
getInstance( ) (ConvertService), 94
getLease( ), 89, 94
    ExpirationWarningEvent class, 308
    LeaseRenewalEvent class, 309
    LookupDiscoveryRegistration inter-
        face, 170, 301
    MailboxRegistration class, 307
    RenewalFailureEvent class, 311

interfaces, 46
  leasing, defining for, 10
  minimum for Jini community, 19
  obtaining from Jini Technology
      Starter Kit, 19
  between server and clients, defin-
      ing, 268
  service implementations, need to
      know, 15
  service interface, 7
  services, changing to use leasing,
      88
  specifying in search for service, 65
  transaction system, used by client,
      146
internal deployment use, SCSL rights,
    17
InternalSpaceException, 324
InvalidObjectException, 327
I/O exceptions (ConnectIOException),
    336
IOException class, RemoteException
    class vs., 339
IP addresses, multicast request and
    announcement protocol, 295
isDiscarded( ), 170
  RemoteDiscoveryEvent class, 305

J

jar files
  EventMailbox and MailboxRegistra-
      tion, not included in, 173
  executable, creating for Jini service
      classes, 189
  for fiddler code, 213
  FrontEndSpace and TransientSpace,
      code for, 222
  Jini Starter Kit components, corre-
      sponding to, 21
  lib directory, containing for Jini, 20
  mahalo code, containing, 215
  mercury code, containing, 218
  norm code, containing, 220
  reggie code, containing, 224

Java
  object serialization and dynamic
      class loading, use by Jini, 11
  packages important to Jini, 326–365
  prerequisites for Jini use, 15
  Remote Method Invocation (RMI)
      (see RMI)
  resource bundles, 247
  virtual machines (see virtual
      machines)
  weak references, 230
Java 2 Standard Edition platform
  downloading from web site, 18
  Jini, requirement for, 13
Java Development Kit (JDK), SCSL
    provisions for, 17
Java Technology Compatibility Kit
    (TCK), Jini TCK vs., 17
JavaBean classes
  finding for entry classes, 319
  lookup service entries, assigning to,
      316
JavaBeans, events specification, 102
javadoc API documentation, 20
java.io package, 326–334
java.policy files for Jini examples, 20
java.rmi package, 335–342
java.rmi.activation package, 342–351
java.rmi.dgc package, 351
java.rmi.registry package, 353
java.rmi.server package, 354–365
JavaSpace interface, 156–159, 324
JavaSpaces service, 155–167, 324
  downloading specification, inter-
      faces and classes, 19
  embedding in Jini services, 163–167
  Entry objects in, 267
  implementation, example of,
      159–163
  Jini, outrigger implementation of,
      221–224
  permissions for, 199
  transactions and, 150
JavaSpaces Specification, 12
JavaSpaces Technology Kit (JSTK), 19
  unzipping and installing in direc-
      tory, 21

timeout values (cont'd)
    norm, specifying for, 221
    outrigger, setting for, 223
    reggie, unicast discover protocol,
        225
TimeoutExpiredException, 282
timeouts, read operations in
        JavaSpace, 157
tools.jar file, class files for HTTP
        server, 24
tracing by property name and subsys-
        tem, 234
trackConversions( ), 106
transaction client, 144
transaction data, storing in reliable
        logs, 137
transaction ID, 152
Transaction interface, 146, 283, 287
    Created class, 283
transaction manager, 143
    finding, 145
    name, defining for, 216
    requests, types of, 152
transaction objects, 147, 279
TransactionConstants interface, 233,
        288
TransactionException, 284
TransactionFactory class, 146, 279,
        284, 287
TransactionManager interface, 146,
        279, 287–288
    Created class, 289
TransactionParticipant interface, 150,
        289
transactions, 11, 143–154
    basic steps in using, 147
    client-side transaction APIs,
        145–147
    JavaSpaces service, 163
    Jini, 279–285
    Jini transaction framework, 147–154
        guarantees to commit or abort
            transactions, 154
        nestable transactions, 149
        server-side transaction APIs,
            150–153
        two-phase commit protocol,
            147–149
    mahalo service for, 215–217

overview, 143–145
    parties to transactions, 144
    RMI and, 12
transient instance variables, 36
    (see also instance variables)
transient mode, running fiddler in, 213
TransientSpace service, 12, 221
transition data (ServiceEvent), 112
transporting code, 45
tryOnce( ) (RetryTask), 260
TTL (see time to live)
two-phase commit protocol, 147–149,
        280
    commit phase, 149
    prepare phase, 148
        leases, not expiring during, 145
    TimeoutExpiredException, 282
TxnConstants class, 233

U

UID class, 364
unblock( ) (InProgress), 259
UnexpectedException, 342
unicast discovery protocol, 9, 71, 234,
        293, 295
    DiscoveryLocatorManagement
        interface and, 297
    join manager, participation in, 245
    LookupDiscoveryManager, han-
        dling of, 300
    LookupDiscoveryManager, use of,
        72
    LookupLocatorDiscovery class, use
        of, 302
    net.jini.core.discovery package,
        support for, 265
    OutgoingUnicastRequest class, 304
    unmarshalling incoming requests,
        299
    unmarshalling incoming response,
        299
UnicastRemoteObject class, 41, 270,
        364
unique identifiers for hosts, 364
unique object IDs, 356

About the Authors

Scott Oaks is a Java Technologist at Sun Microsystems, where he has worked since 1987. While at Sun, he has specialized on many disparate technologies, from the SunOS kernel to network programming and RPCs to the X Window System to threading. Since early 1995, he has primarily focused on Java and bringing Java technology to end users; he writes a monthly column on Java solutions for *The Java Report*.

Around the Internet, Scott is best known as the author of olvwm, the OPEN LOOK window manager. He is also the author of *Java Threads* and *Java Security* (O'Reilly & Associates). Scott holds a Bachelor of Science degree in mathematics and computer science from the University of Denver, and a Master of Science degree in computer science from Brown University. Prior to joining Sun, he worked in the research division of Bear, Stearns.

In his other life, Scott enjoys music (he plays flute and piccolo with community groups in New York), cooking, theater, and traveling with his husband, James.

Henry Wong is a Senior Architect at Sun Microsystems, where he has worked since 1989. Originally hired as a consultant to help customers with special device drivers, kernel modifications, and DOS interoperability products, Henry has also worked on Solaris ports, performance tuning projects, and multithreaded design and implementations for benchmarks and demos. Since early 1995, Henry has been involved in developing Java prototypes, and supporting customers who are using Java.

Prior to joining Sun, Henry earned a Bachelor of Engineering degree in chemical engineering from The Cooper Union in 1987. He joined a small software company in 1986, working on SCSI device drivers, image and audio data compression, and graphics tools used for a medical information system.

When not in front of a computer, Henry is an instrument-rated private pilot, who also likes to dabble in archery, cooking, and traveling to different places with his wife, Nini.

Colophon

Our look is the result of reader comments, our own experimentation, and feedback from distribution channels. Distinctive covers complement our distinctive approach to technical topics, breathing personality and life into potentially dry subjects.

The animal appearing on the cover of *Jini in a Nutshell* is a lar gibbon (Hylobates lar). Of the nine species of gibbon, the lar is the smallest. Gibbons inhabit the tropical rain forests of southern Asia, specifically Thailand, Malaysia, and Indonesia.

Gibbons range in color from brown to black. The lar gibbon is characteristically marked with white hands, feet, and face rings. Color is not specific to gender; males or females can show either color, but their white markings are always present. A male and female typically join in a monogamous relationship that consists of the mated pair and their offspring. The mated pair tends to stay together in the same territory and continue to reproduce as the mature offspring leave the group.

Lar gibbons possess a unique swinging posture that is employed to reach fruit within the branches of their territory. They are extremely picky eaters, consuming only ripe fruit and new leaves and buds. Lar gibbons occupy the upper canopy of the rain forest. They rarely, if ever, descend to the forest floor.

Colleen Gorman was the production editor and proofreader for *Jini in a Nutshell*, Maureen Dempsey, Mary Anne Weeks Mayo, and Jane Ellin provided quality control, and Nancy Kotary and Jane Ellin copyedited the book. Emily Quill and Ann Schirmer provided production assistance. Lenny Muellner provided SGML support. Ellen Troutman-Zaig wrote the index.

Edie Freedman designed the cover of this book, using an original illustration created by Lorrie LeJeune. Kathleen Wilson produced the cover layout with Quark XPress 3.3 using Adobe's ITC Garamond font. Whenever possible, our books use RepKover™, a durable and flexible lay-flat binding. If the page count exceeds RepKover's limit, perfect binding is used.

The interior layouts were designed by Edie Freedman and Nancy Priest, with modifications by Alicia Cech, and implemented in gtroff by Lenny Muellner. Interior fonts are Adobe ITC Garamond and Adobe ITC Franklin Gothic. The illustrations that appear in the book were produced by Robert Romano and Rhon Porter using Macromedia FreeHand 8 and Adobe Photoshop 5. This colophon was written by Maureen Dempsey.